P9-BZQ-079

Analyzing Computer System Performance with Perl::PDQ

Neil J. Gunther

Analyzing Computer System Performance with Perl::PDQ

With 176 Figures and 59 Tables

Neil J. Gunther
Performance Dynamics Company
4061 East Castro Valley Blvd.
Suite 110, Castro Valley
California 94552
USA
http://www.perfdynamics.com/

Library of Congress Control Number: 2004113307

ACM Computing Classification (1998): C.0, C.2.4, C.4, D.2.5, D.2.8, D.4.8, K.6.2

ISBN 3-540-20865-8 Springer Berlin Heidelberg New York

Springer is a part of Springer Science+Business Media

springeronline.com

Printed in Germany

Cover design: KünkelLopka, Heidelberg
Production: LE-TeX Jelonek, Schmidt & Vöckler GbR, Leipzig
Typesetting: By the author
Printed on acid-free paper 45/3142/YL - 5 4 3 2 1 0

Common sense is the pitfall of performance analysis

Preface

Motivation

This book arose out of an attempt to meet two key objectives. The first was to communicate the theory and practice of performance analysis to those who need it most, viz. IT professionals, system administrators, software developers, and performance test engineers. Many of the currently available books on computer performance analysis fall into one of three distinct camps:

1. Books that discuss tuning the performance of a particular platform, e.g., Linux, Solaris, Windows. These books explain how you can turn individual software "knobs" with the hope that this will tune your platform.
2. Books that emphasize formal queueing theory under the rubric of performance modeling. These books are written by mathematicians for mathematicians and therefore are burdened with too much Greek for the average IT professional to suffer through.
3. Books that employ queueing theory without the Greek but the performance models are unrealistic because they are essentially academic toys.

Each of these categories has pedagogic merit, but the focus tends to be on detailed particulars that are not easily generalized to a different context. These days, IT professionals are required to be versed in more than one platform or technology. It seemed to me that the best way to approach the performance analysis of such a panoply is to adopt a *system* perspective. The system view also provides an economy of thought. Understanding gained on one system can often be applied to another. Successful performance analysis on one platform often translates successfully to another, with little extra effort. Expressed in today's vernacular—*learn once, apply often.*

Second, I wanted to present system performance principles in the context of a software tool, *Pretty Damn Quick*© (PDQ), that can be applied quickly to address performance issues as they arise in today's hectic business environment. In order to meet the pressures of ever-shortening time horizons, performance analysis has to be done in *zero time*. Project managers cannot and will not allow their schedules to be stretched by what they perceive as inflationary performance analysis. A performance analysis tool based on a scripting language helps to meet these severe time constraints by avoiding the need to wrestle with compilers and debuggers.

Why Perl?

Defending the choice of a programming language is always a losing proposition, but in a recent poll on `slashdot.org`, Perl (Practical Extraction and Reporting Language,) was ranked third after Bourne shell and Ruby in terms of ease of use for accomplishing a defined set of tasks with a scripting language. Python, Tcl, and Awk, came in fifth, seventh, and eighth respectively, while Java (interpreted but not a scripting language) came in last. Neither *Mathematica*nor PHP were polled. On a more serious note, John Ousterhout (father of Tcl), has written an essay (`home.pacbell.net/ouster/scripting.html`) on the general virtues of scripting languages for prototyping. Where he says *prototyping*, I would substitute the word *modeling*.

I chose Perl because it fitted the requirement of a rapid prototyping language for computer performance analysis. The original implementation of PDQ was in C (and still is as far as the library functions are concerned). To paraphrase a leading UNIX™ developer, one of the disadvantages of the C language is that you can spend a lot of time in the debugger when you stab yourself with a misreferenced pointer. Perl has a C-like syntax but is much more forgiving at runtime. Moreover, Perl has arguably become the most ubiquitous of the newer-generation scripting languages, including MacPerl on MacOS (prior to MacOS X). One reason for Perl's ubiquity is that it is designed for extracting text and data from files. Why not for extracting performance data? It therefore seemed like a good choice to offer a Perl version of PDQ as an enhancement to the existing toolset of system administrators. By a happy coincidence, several students, who were also system administrators, began asking me if PDQ could be made available in Perl. So, here it is. Bonne programmation!

How should PDQ be used? In my view, the proper analysis of computer performance data requires a conceptual framework within which the information hidden in those data can be revealed. That is the role of PDQ. It provides a framework of expectations in which to assess data. If you do performance analysis without such a framework (as is all too common), how can you know when you are wrong? When your conclusion does not reconcile with the data, you must stop and find where the inconsistency lies. It is much easier to detect inconsistencies when you have certain expectations. Setting some expectations (even wrong ones) is far better than not setting any.

I sometimes liken the role of PDQ to that of a subway map. A subway map has two key properties. It is an *abstract* representation of the real situation in that the distances between train stations are not in geographical proportion, and it is *simple* because it is uncluttered by unimportant real-world physical details. The natural urge is to create a PDQ "map" adorned with an abundance of physical detail because that would seem to constitute a more faithful representation of the computer system being analyzed. In spite of this urge, you should strive instead to make your PDQ models as simple and abstract as a subway map. Adding complexity does not guarantee accuracy. Unfortunately, there is no simple recipe for constructing PDQ maps. Einstein reputedly said that things should be as simple as possible, but no simpler. That should certainly be the goal for applying PDQ, but like drawing any good map there are aspects that remain more in the realm of art than science. Those aspects are best demonstrated by example, and that is the purpose of Part II of this book.

Book Structure

Very simply, this book falls into two parts, so that the typical rats-nest diagram of chapter dependencies is rendered unnecessary.

Part I explains the fundamental metrics used in computer performance analysis. Chapter 1 discusses the zeroth metric, time, that is common to all performance analysis. This chapter is recommended reading for those new to computer performance analysis but may be skipped in a first reading by those more familiar performance analysis concepts. The queueing concepts encoded in PDQ tool are presented in Chaps. 2, 3, and 5, so these chapters may also be read sequentially.

For those familiar with UNIX platforms, a good place to start might be Chap. 4 where the connection between queues (buffers) and the *load average* metric is dissected at the kernel level. Linux provides the particular context because the source code is publicly available to be dissected—on the Web, no less! The generalization to other operating systems should be obvious. Similarly, another starting point for those with a UNIX orientation could be Appendix B *A Short History of Buffers* (pun intended) which summarizes the historical interplay between queueing theory and computer performance analysis, commencing with the ancestors of UNIX viz. CTSS and Multics.

Irrespective of the order you choose to read them, none of the chapters in Part I requires a knowledge of formal probability theory or stochastic methods. Thus, we avoid the torrent of Greek that otherwise makes very powerful queueing concepts incomprehensible to those readers who would actually benefit from them most. Any performance analysis terminology that is unfamiliar can most likely be found in the Glossary (Appendix A).

Part II covers a wide variety of examples demonstrating how to apply PDQ. These include the performance analysis of multicomputer architectures in Chap. 7, analyzing benchmark results in Chap. 8, client/server scalability in Chap. 9, and Web-based applications in Chap. 10. These chapters can be read in any order. Dependencies on other chapters are cross-referenced in the text.

Chapter 6 (Pretty Damn Quick (PDQ)—A Slow Introduction) contains the PDQ *driver's manual* and, because it is a reference manual, can be read independently of the other chapters. It also contains many examples that were otherwise postponed from Chaps. 2–5.

Appendix F contains the steps for installing Perl PDQ together with a complete list of the Perl programs used in this book. The more elementary of these programs are specially identified for those unfamiliar with writing Perl scripts.

Classroom Usage

This book grew out of class material presented at both academic institutions and corporate training facilities. In that sense, the material is pitched at the graduate or mature student level and could be covered in one or two semesters.

Each chapter has a set of exercises at the end. These exercises are intended to amplify key points raised in the chapter, but instructors could also complement them with questions of their own. I anticipate compiling more exercises and making them available on my Web site (`www.perfdynamics.com`). Solutions to selected exercises can be found in Appendix H.

> Key points that should be retained by both students and practitioners are contained in a box like this one.

Prerequisites and Limitations

This is a book about performance analysis, not performance tuning. The world is already full of books explaining how to tune this or that application on this or that platform. Whereas performance tuning is about particulars, the power of performance analysis comes from discerning general principals. General principals are often best detected at the system level. The payoff is that a generalizable analysis technique learned once will find application in solving a wide variety of future performance problems.

Good analysis requires clarity of thought, and clear thinking benefits from the structure of formalism. The formalism used throughout this book is queueing theory or what might be more accurately termed *queueing theory lite*. By that I mean the elements of queueing theory are presented in a minimalist style without the need for penetrating many of the complexities of mathematical queueing theory, but without loss of correctness. That said, a knowledge of mathematics at the level of high-school algebra is assumed throughout the text (it is hard to imagine doing any kind of meaningful performance analysis without it), and those readers exposed to introductory probability and calculus will find most of the concepts transparent.

Queueing theory algorithms are encoded into PDQ. This frees the performance analyst to focus on the application of queueing concepts to the problem at hand. Inevitably, there is a price for this freedom. The algorithms contain certain assumptions that facilitate the solution of queueing models. One of these is the *Poisson* assumption. In probability theory, the Poisson distribution is associated with events which are statistically *random* (like the clicks of a Geiger counter). PDQ assumes that arrivals into a queue and departures from the service center are random. How well this assumption holds up against behavior of a real computer system will impact the accuracy of your analysis.

In many cases, it holds up well enough that the assumption does not need to be scrutinized. More often, the accuracy of your measurements is the more important issue. All measurements have errors. Do you know the magnitude of the errors in your performance data? See Sect. D.7 in Appendix D. In those cases where there is doubt about the Poisson assumption, Sect. D.8 of Appendix D provides a test together with a Perl script to analyze your data for randomness. One such case is packet queueing.

Internet packets, for example, are known to seriously violate the Poisson assumption [See Park and Willinger 2000]. So PDQ cannot be expected to give accurate performance predictions in that case, but as long as the performance analysis is conducted at the transaction or connection level (as we do in Chap. 10), PDQ is applicable. For packet level analysis, alternative performance tools such simulators (see e.g., NS-2 http://www.isi.edu/nsnam/ns/) are a better choice. One has to take care, however, not to be lulled into a false sense of security with simulators. A simulation is assumed to be more accurate because it allows you to construct a faithful representation of the real computer system by accounting for every component—sometimes including the proverbial kitchen sink. The unstated fallacy is that complexity equals completeness. An example of the unfortunate consequences that can ensure from ignoring this point is noted in Sect. 1.7.

Even in the era of simulation tools, you still need an independent framework to validate the results. PDQ can fulfill that role. Otherwise, your simulation stands in danger of being just another pseudo-random number generator. That PDQ can act like an independent framework in which to assess your data (be it from measurement or simulation) is perhaps its most important role. In that sense, the very act of modeling can be viewed as an organizing principle in its own right. *A fortiori*, the insights gained by merely initiating the construction of a PDQ model may be more important than the results it produces.

Acknowledgments

Firstly, I would like to thank the alumni of my computer performance analysis classes, including *Practical Performance Methods* given at Stanford University (1997–2001), UCLA Extension Course 819.328 *Scalable Server Performance and Capacity Planning*, the many training classes given at major corporations, and the current series *Guerrilla Capacity Planning* sponsored by Performance Dynamics. Much of their feedback has found its way into this book. My Stanford classes replaced those originally given by Ed Lazowska, Ken Sevcik, and John Zahorjan. I finally attended their 1993 Stanford class, several years after reading their classic text [Lazowska et al. 1984]. Their approach inspired mine.

Peter Harding deserves all the credit for porting my C implementation of PDQ to Perl. Several people said they would do it (including myself), but only Peter delivered.

Ken Christensen, Robert Lane, David Latterner, and Pedro Vazquez reviewed the entire manuscript and made many excellent suggestions that improved the final content. Jim Brady and Steve Jenkin commented on Appendix C and Chap. 4, respectively. Ken Christensen also kindly provided me with a copy of Erlang's first paper. An anonymous reviewer helped tidy up some of the queue-theoretic discussion in Chaps. 2 and 3. Myron Hlynka and Peter Taylor put my mind at rest concerning the recent controversial claim that Jackson's 50-year-old theorem (Chap. 3) was invalid.

Giordano Beretta rendered his expert scientific knowledge of image processing as well as a monumental number of hours of computer labor to improve the quality of the illustrations. His artistic flair reveals itself in Fig. 2.1. Andrew Trevorrow deserves a lot of thanks, not only for porting and maintaining the OzTeX implementation of LaTeX 2_ε on MacOS, but for being very responsive to email questions. The choice of OzTeX was key to being able to produce camera-ready copy in less than a year. Mirko Fluher kindly provided remote access to his Linux system in Melbourne, Australia.

It is a genuine pleasure to acknowledge the cooperation and patience of my editor Ralf Gerstner, as well as the excellent technical support of Frank Holzwarth and Jacqueline Lenz at Springer-Verlag in Heidelberg. Tracey Wilbourn meticulously copyedited the penultimate manuscript and Michael Reinfarth of LE-TeX GbR in Leipzig handled the final production of the book.

Aline and Topin Dawson provided support and balance during the otherwise intense solitary hours spent composing this book. My father tolerated several postponed trans-Pacific visits during the course of this project. Only someone 95 years young has that kind of patience.

I would also like to take this opportunity to thank the many diligent readers who contributed to the errata for *Practical Performance Analyst* [Gunther 2000a]. In alphabetical order they are: M. Allen, A. Bondi, D. Chan, K. Christensen, A. Cockcroft, L. Dantzler, V. Davis, M. Earp, W.A. Gunther, I.S. Hobbs, P. Kraus, R. Lane, T. Lange, P. Lauterbach, C. Millsap,

D. Molero, J. A. Nolazco-Flores, W. Pelz and students, H. Schwetman, P. Sinclair, D. Tran, B. Vestermark, and Y. Yan. I trust the errata for this book will be much shorter.

And finally to you, dear reader, thank you for purchasing this book and reading this far. Don't stop now!

Warranty Disclaimer

No warranties are made, express or implied, that the information in this book and the associated computer programs are error free, or are consistent with any particular standard of merchantability, or that they will meet your requirements for any particular application. They should not be relied upon for solving a problem the incorrect solution of which could result in injury to a person or loss of property. The author disclaims all liability for direct or consequential damages resulting from the use of this book.

Palomares Hills, California N.J.G.
July, 2004

Contents

Part II Practice of System Performance Analysis

Part III Appendices

Part I

Theory of System Performance Analysis

1

Time—The Zeroth Performance Metric

1.1 Introduction

Time is the basis of all computer performance management (Fig. 1.1). It is so fundamental that it could be called the zeroth-order performance metric. In the context of computer performance analysis, time manifests itself in a multitude of metrics like service time, response time, round-trip time, memory latency, and mean time to failure, to name just a few. In view of this variety, it would seem fitting to open a book on performance analysis with a review of these various performance metrics. Surprisingly, there seems to be no precedent for such a discussion in any of the readily available textbooks on computer performance analysis. It is about time someone provided a brief discourse about time, and that is what we offer in this chapter.

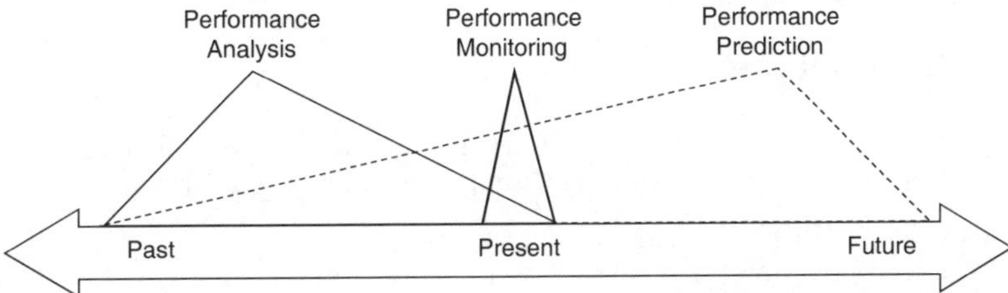

Fig. 1.1. Three aspects of performance management depicted according to the timespan they cover. Performance monitoring (*black*) is narrow and suffers mostly from systematic errors. Performance analysis (*dark gray*) introduces slightly more error because it derives new quantities from historical data. Performance prediction amplifies both these error sources and others into future projections

This chapter covers a wide range of concepts about time and related metrics. The reader should be aware that not all the definitions are treated in equal depth. The four major topics covered in this chapter are types of clocks and timescales, response time measurement, metrics for assessing computer reliability, and the performance impact of metastable lifetimes on both computer chips and computer systems.

We begin by reviewing definitions of time. Since time is actually quite a subtle concept, we start out with some basic dictionary definitions, and then move on to refine these simple definitions to meet the more stringent requirements of computer system performance analysis. This leads us into considerations about time and its measurement with clocks, both physical and virtual. This is especially important to understand in the context of synchronizing distributed computer systems. We close the section on time with a brief discussion of computing time scales. An understanding of the shear breadth of computing time scales is fundamental to the way we do performance analysis and modeling.

The second major topic we cover is the variety of response time metrics and their corresponding measurement distributions. Rather than elaborate on the various statistical distributions used to model response characteristics, we refer the reader to the statistical tools and documentation readily available in commonly used spreadsheet software packages. The exponential distribution is seen to play a pivotal role in modeling response times.

The next major topic covers metrics used to assess uptime, availability, and related formal concepts in reliability models. These metrics are very important in the analysis of large-scale commercial computing systems. A key metric is the mean time between failures, which takes us into our final topic, the metastability of computer components and systems [see also Gunther 2000a, Part III]. This is another area that is often overlooked in most books on computer performance analysis. Metastability can have a significant impact on computer system performance.

1.2 What Is Time?

One place to start refining our various notions of time is a dictionary. The online Merriam-Webster dictionary (`http://www.m-w.com/`) states:

> Main Entry: **time**
> Pronunciation: ‘tIm
> Function: *noun*
> Etymology: Middle English, from Old English *tIma*; akin to Old Norse *tImi* time, Old English tId – see TIDE
> **1a:** the measured or measurable period during which an action, process, or condition exists or continues : DURATION **1b:** a nonspatial continuum that is measured in terms of events which succeed one another from past through present to future.
> **2:** the point or period when something occurs : OCCASION ...
> **4a:** an historical period ...
> **8a:** a moment, hour, day, or year as indicated by a clock or calendar.
> **8b:** any of various systems (as sidereal or solar) of reckoning time.

9a: one of a series of recurring instances or repeated actions.

Performance analysts need more precise definitions than these. We begin by reviewing notions about physical time and its measurement using physical clocks. Later, we shall extend the definitions of physical time and physical clocks to include logical time and logical clocks.

1.2.1 Physical Time

The concept of time is fundamental, but it is also elusive. Much of the modern era in physics has been preoccupied with rethinking our concepts of time, most notably through Einstein's theories of relativity. One of the most significant outcomes of that relativistic view is the intimate relationship between space and time. At extremely short distances, say the size of an electron (about 10^{-15} m), space and time become an inseparable four-dimensional continuum. At extremely large distances, say the size of the universe (about 10^{+26} m), the expansion (and possibly eventual collapse) of the universe may be responsible for the apparent direction of time [Gold 1967, Hawking 1988]. But these fundamental properties of physical time lie well outside those that are needed to analyze the operation of computer systems, so we shall not pursue them any further.

In computer performance analysis we are more concerned with the measurement of timescales related to various computational operations. In this context, Mills [1992] provides the following definitions. The time of an event is an abstraction that determines the ordering of events in a given temporal frame of reference or time-scale. A physical clock is a stable oscillator, or frequency generator, together with a counter that records the number of cycles since being initialized at a given time. The value of the counter at any time t is called its *epoch* and is recorded as the time stamp $T(t)$ of that epoch. In general, epochs are not continuous and depend on the precision of the counter.

1.2.2 Synchronization and Causality

Humans make plans on the basis of time. The key concept of time that permits such planning is the notion of global time. Humans reckon global time from loosely synchronized physical clocks such as wrist watches. To synchronize clocks means to match them in both frequency and time. In order to synchronize physical clocks, there must be some common frame of reference for comparing both time and frequency.

Among the possible frames of reference for synchronizing clocks are the human heartbeat, the pendulum, and astronomical oscillators such as the sun, the moon, other planets, and even more exotic cosmological objects, such as pulsars. Unfortunately, the frequencies of these oscillators are relatively unstable and are not always precisely known. Instead, the ultimate reference oscillator has been chosen by international agreement to be a synthesis of multiple observations of certain atomic transitions of hydrogen, cesium, and rubidium. Local clocks used in computer systems and networks tend to use crystal oscillators. Some of the more important (and not completely solved) issues arise in computing environments where clocks need to be distributed. There, one must take into account the range of latencies incurred by both remote computation and remote communication.

1.2.3 Discrete and Continuous Time

A common distinction that arises in performance analysis and performance modeling is that between *discrete* and *continuous* time. The difference can be thought of using the following simple analogy. Consider a conventional clock that has a seconds hand. On some clocks the seconds hand sweeps around the face, while on others it jumps between each seconds mark. The first case is a form of continuous time, the latter is closer to discrete time. In the latter case, events can only occur when the hand is on a mark not in between. Throughout most of this book we shall assume that clocks run continuously rather than by discrete *ticks*. See e.g., Appendix C.

Discrete time approaches continuous time as the tick intervals become infinitesimally small. In a discrete time picture, moments in time are regarded as distinct steps and any event can only occur at each time step. Further discussion about discrete time and its importance for stochastic processes, queueing theory, and simulation can be found respectively in such texts as Kleinrock [1976], Bloch et al. [1998].

1.2.4 Time Scales

Current digital microprocessors and memories operate at nanosecond cycle times although, at the time of writing, microprocessors are rapidly entering the subnanosecond regime. A nanosecond is a period of time so short that it is well outside our everyday experience, and that makes it impossibly small to comprehend. For the computer performance analyst, however, it is important to be equipped with a concept of relative timescales.

A nanosecond (10^{-9} s), or one billionth of a second, is an incomprehensibly small amount of time that can be related to something incomprehensibly fast—the speed of light. Light is capable of travelling roughly eight times around the earth's equator in one second or about a third of a gigameter per second (2.997×10^8 m/s, to be exact). On a more human scale, a nanosecond is the time it takes a light beam to travel the length of your forearm—approximately one foot. This is a useful mnemonic because it accounts for why computer system buses that operate at 1 GB/s transfer rates are restricted to about one foot in length.

Example 1.1. Some contemporary shared-memory multiprocessors support memory buses capable of peak transfer rates of about 1 GB/s. What are the engineering constraints imposed on a designer?

Current chip carrier pinouts limit data paths to about 128 bits or 16 bytes in width. To support a bus with bandwidth of 1 GB/s, the bus clock frequency needs to be

$$\frac{1024 \text{ MB}}{16 \text{ B}} = 64 \text{ MHz},$$

or 64 mega cycles per second. Since a typical bus may be only two thirds efficient, the designer would be wiser to use a 100-MHz bus clock which corresponds to a bus-cycle time of 10×10^{-9} seconds per cycle or a 10 ns cycle time. Therefore, all devices that interface to the bus must settle in less than 10 ns.

About 60% of this 10 ns is required to drive voltage levels and to allow clock skew. That only leaves about 4 nanoseconds to set the appropriate voltage levels on the bus. It takes about 2 ns to propagate an electric signal on a bus that is fully loaded capacitively with various devices (e.g., processor caches, memory modules, I/O buses). That means that the maximum bus length should be

$$\frac{4 \text{ ns}}{2 \text{ ns/ft}} = 2 \text{ ft}.$$

But it takes two phases to set the voltage levels (half in one direction, and the other half on reflection). Therefore, the maximum advisable length is about one foot. □

It is also important for the performance analyst to have some feel for the order-of-magnitude differences in timescales that operate inside a digital computer. Table 1.1 is intended to capture some of these tremendous differences by rating the various computer access times in terms of a nanosecond that has been inflated to equal one second. The processor is taken to be an Intel Pentium 4 with a clock frequency of 3.2 GHz which has a subnanosecond instruction cycle time.

On this inflated scale we see that it takes about 15 min for a main memory access, about 4 months for a disk access, almost 32 years for a simple database transaction, and hundreds of years for a tape access.

An important consequence arises out of this huge range of timescales. We do not need to take them all in to account when predicting the performance of a computer system. Only those changes that occur on a timescale similar to the quantity we are trying to predict will have the most impact on its value. All other (i.e., faster) changes in the system can usually be ignored. They are more likely to be part of the *background noise* rather than the main theme.

Example 1.2. In modeling the performance of a database system where the response time is measured in seconds, it would be counterproductive to include all the times for execution of every CPU instruction. □

Table 1.1. Nominal computer access times scaled up to human proportions such that one nanosecond is scaled up to one second. The *upper portion* of the table relates CPU and memory speeds, while the *lower portion* refers to storage technologies with progressively longer latencies

Computer	Conventional		Scaled	
subsystem	time	unit	time	unit
CPU cycle	0.31	ns	0.31	s
L1 cache	0.31	ns	0.31	s
L2 cache	1.25	ns	1.25	s
Memory bus	2.00	ns	2.00	s
DRAM chip	60.00	ns	1.00	min
Disk seek	3.50	ms	1.35	month
NFS3 read	32.00	ms	1.01	year
RDBMS update	0.50	s	15.85	year
Tape access	5.00	s	1.59	century

Another way to think about this is from the standpoint of steady-state conditions. When the measured value of a performance metric does not change appreciably over the duration of the measurement interval, it is said to be at its steady-state value. Using Example 1.2, as long as any changes occurring in a computer subsystem have reached steady state on the timescale of interest, the subsystem can either be ignored or aggregated with other subsystems in a performance model. Similarly, the average service demand might be used to represent the CPU time rather than evaluating it separately within an explicit CPU model. In the time between the arrival of each transaction, it can safely be assumed that the CPU has reached steady state.

1.3 What Is a Clock?

In this section we review the concept of a clock, both physical and logical, as it pertains to measuring time in a distributed computing environment. We shall see that certain common notions have to be refined and that there are profound implications for performance analysis measurements.

1.3.1 Physical Clocks

As defined earlier, a physical clock is a combination of a stable oscillator and a counter. The value of the counter at time t gives the epoch at time stamp $T(t)$. A local computer clock can be constructed in hardware from some kind of oscillator or a stabilized phase-locked loop that consists of two main components:

1. a controlled oscillator
2. a phase detector

A more detailed discussion of these technicalities can be found in Mills [1992].

The stability of this physical clock is a measure of how well a clock maintains a constant frequency. Its accuracy refers to how well its frequency and time compare to defined standards. Its precision refers to how accurately these quantities can be maintained within a particular time-keeping system. In the context of performance measurement in distributed computer environments, clock stability can be more significant than clock synchronization [Dietz et al. 1995].

The clock *offset* is the time difference between two clocks. If we denote this offset by the symbol Ω, then the clock *skew* is the change in clock offset (or frequency difference) with respect to continuous time, and can be written as the derivative $\mathrm{d}\Omega/\mathrm{d}t$. The clock *drift* is the time variation in the skew or the second derivative of the offset with respect to time $\mathrm{d}^2\Omega/\mathrm{d}t^2$.

1.3.2 Distributed Physical Clocks

The preceding discussion of physical clocks implicitly assumes the clocks were local. By analogy with the concept of a local clock, a system of distributed clocks can be regarded as a set of coupled oscillators, each comprising two main components:

1. a software update algorithm (that functions as a phase detector)
2. a local clock (that functions as a controlled oscillator)

This is the basis of network time protocol (NTP) discussed in Mills [1992].

Clock synchronization requires long periods with multiple comparisons in order to maintain accurate timekeeping. The accuracy achieved is directly related to the time taken to achieve it. Other distributed clock synchronization protocols include DTS (Digital Time Service), TSP (Time Stamp Protocol), and DCE (Distributed Computing Environment) Time Service.

1.3.3 Distributed Processing

A distributed system is comprised of a collection of processes that are typically separated spatially. Processes coordinate with one another, via the exchange of messages, to complete a computational task. Three types of actions can be taken by a process:

1. compute (intraprocess)
2. send a message (interprocess)
3. receive a message (interprocess)

These actions can be taken asynchronously, i.e., a process that has sent a message is not required to wait for acknowledgment to complete. Computation generates a set of distributed events. To make progress toward a common goal, it is necessary to know the causal relationship between events, e.g., process B cannot compute before the results of process A are available to it.

This requirement amounts to a form of causality in which A must precede B. Causality can be regarded as a (binary) precedence relation.

1.3.4 Binary Precedence

We can define the binary relation (denoted by $\rightarrow$) such that $A \rightarrow B$ means event A "happened before" event B [Lamport 1978] or A "precedes" B in time. Such a relation is *transitive* in that, if $A \rightarrow B$ and $B \rightarrow C$, then $A \rightarrow C$. It is also assumed to be *irreflexive* in that an event preceding itself, $A \rightarrow A$, has no meaning in this context. Also, two events are defined to be *concurrent* if $A \not\rightarrow B$ and $B \not\rightarrow A$. These requirements define a partial ordering on the set of all events $\{e_i\}$.

Only a partial ordering of events is possible at this level since it may not be possible, in general, to say which of A and B occurred first. Lamport [1978] showed how total ordering could be achieved from this partial ordering. We need to establish a total ordering of events for the purposes of synchronization, especially in the case where there is a requirement for consistency of shared data, as there is in any multiprocessor computer system. To maintain data consistency, requests must be granted in the order in which they were issued.

1.3.5 Logical Clocks

Although physical time can be maintained to accuracies of a few tens of milliseconds using protocols such as NTP [Mills 1992], this is not adequate for capturing process precedence in distributed systems, which can occur on microsecond timescales. However, in a distributed computation, both progress toward a common goal and the interprocess communication synchrony can be accommodated using logical clocks. A logical clock can be implemented with

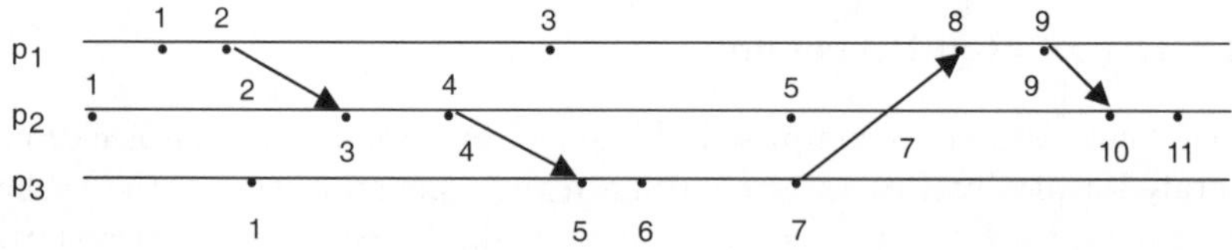

Fig. 1.2. Procedure for local and global clock synchronization (adapted from Raynal and Singhal [1996])

simple counters. There is no inherent or physical timing mechanism. Let the logical clock $C(e)$ be the time stamp (i.e., some positive integer) of the event e. The logical clock function $C(\cdot)$ is a mapping of e to an element $C(e)$ in the time domain T. A logical clock satisfies the (weak) consistency condition:

$$e_1 \rightarrow e_2 \Rightarrow C(e_1) < C(e_2) .$$

In order for such a clock to *tick* consistently, it must come equipped with some rules for consistently updating logical time. The following procedures provide an example of the updating that must go on at both the local and a global levels.

1. Local clock:
   - Prior to executing an event (send, rcv, intraprocess), a process p_i must increment its local counter such that:
   - $C_i = C_i + 1$.
2. Global clock:
   - Each message carries the local clock value C_i of the sender process at send time.
   - The recipient process p_j evaluates its counter as $C_j = \text{MAX}(C_i, C_j)$.
   - The recipient process updates its local clock according to local procedure 1: $C_j = C_j + 1$.
   - The recipient process then delivers the message.

Example 1.3. Referring to Fig. 1.2, each process has its own time line. Events occurring within each process are shown as dots. Messages between events are shown as arrows. Using the above rules, the second event of process p_1 (the second dot in Fig. 1.2) gets its time stamp from updating its local clock i.e., $2(= 1 + 1)$. Similarly, the third event of process p_1 updates the local clock to generate a time stamp of $3(= 2 + 1)$.

The second event of process p_1, however, requires sending a message to process p_2. The receipt of this message from p_1 generates the second event for process p_2. Using the above rules, process p_1 updates its clock from 1 to 2, prior to sending the message, then p_1 sends that value along with its message. Prior to receiving the message from p_1, process p_2 would have computed its local time to be $2(= 1+1)$. Instead, it calculates the $\text{MAX}(2, 2)$, which in this case produces the same result. Next, according to procedure 2, p_2 must now update its own local clock to be $3(= 2 + 1)$ and finally deliver the message.

Later, p_1 receives a message from event 7 of process p_3. Process p_3 sends the message with its local time included. Process p_1 then computes its local time. Prior to receiving the message from p_3, p_1 would have computed its local time as $4(= 3+1)$. Instead, it now computes its local time to be $max(4, 7)+1 = 8$.

Also, note the weak consistency between event 3 of process p_1 and the third event of process p_2. The third event of process p_2 computes its local time stamp as 4. Hence, $C1(e3) < C2(e3)$, but event 3 of p_1 occurred after event 3 of p_2. □

This still only provides a partial ordering since an ambiguity remains. Two or more events belonging to different processes can have the same time stamp. Such a circumstance appears in Fig. 1.2. The second dot of process p2 and the third dot of process p1 have the same time stamp, 3. Such ambiguities can be eliminated by using the process ID (or pid) since these are monotonically increasing numbers. In this way, we can achieve a total ordering of events in a distributed system.

Meeting the strong consistency condition:

$$e_1 \to e_2 \Leftrightarrow C(e_1) < C(e_2) ,$$

requires a generalization from vector to *tensor* clocks [Raynal and Singhal 1996], whereby the local and global times are permanently stored and not merged as they are in the scalar clock paradigm just described. This generalization is used to ensure so-called "liveness" properties in distributed algorithms, i.e., requests are time-stamped and serviced according to the total order on these time stamps. This is essential for MIMD (multiple instructions multiple data) multiprocessor architectures that employ some form of read–modify–write operation in which asynchronous processes communicate by applying read, write, and read–modify–write operations to a shared memory.

A read-modify-write operation atomically reads a value v from a memory location, writes back $f(v)$, where f is a predefined function, and returns v to the caller. Nearly all modern processor architectures support some form of read-modify-write for interprocess synchronization. Common read-modify-write instructions include:

- Test-and-Set
- Fetch-and-Add
- Compare-and-Swap
- Load-linked/Store-conditional

Other applications that require total ordering of events include distributed tracing and debugging, distributed database checkpointing, maintaining consistency in replicated databases, and deadlock avoidance and detection.

1.3.6 Clock Ticks

Every computer system has a fundamental interval of time defined by the hardware clock. This hardware clock has a constant ticking rate, which is used to synchronize everything on the system. To make this interval known to the system, the clock sends an interrupt to the UNIX™ kernel on every clock *tick*. The actual interval between these ticks depends on the type of platform. Most UNIX systems have the CPU tick interval set to 10 ms of wall-clock time.

The specific tick interval is contained in a constant called `HZ` defined in a system-specific header file called `param.h`. For example, the C code:

```
#define HZ     100
```

in the header file means that 1 s of wall-clock time is divided into 100 ticks. Alternatively, a clock interrupt occurs once every 100th of a second or 1 tick = 1 s / 100 = 10 ms. The constant labeled `HZ` should be read as *frequency number*, and not as the SI unit of frequency *cycles per second*. The latter actually has the symbol Hz. We shall revisit this convention in Chap. 4.

Generic performance analysis tools are resident on all the major computer operating systems. For example, some variants of the UNIXoperating system have System Activity Reporter (SAR) [Peek et al. 1997, Musumeci and Loukides 2002]. Other UNIX variants and the Linux operating system [Bovet and Cesati 2001] has `procinfo`, `vmstat`. The Microsoft Windows 2000® operating system has a System Monitor [Friedman and Pentakalos 2002]. IBM Multiple Virtual Storage (MVS®, now z/OS®) has Resource Measurement Facility (RMF), and System Management Facility (SMF) [Samson 1997]. See Appendix D for more details about performance tools.

Unfortunately, these generic performance tools do not possess the timing resolution required for measuring high-frequency *events* accurately. Moreover, tracing events at high frequency usually incurs high resource overhead in terms of compute and I/O cycles.

The more efficient tradeoff that is usually adopted is to *sample* the counters that reside in the local operating system at a prescribed interval. Most performance management tools work this way. A potentially serious drawback to sampling (even at 100 times per second) is that the samples may be taken on a clock edge. This can introduce errors as large as 20% or more in CPU usage data, for example (see Sect. D.7). More recently, platform vendors have started to introduce hardware-resident counters to gather event-triggered process data at much higher clock resolution than is available from the operating system alone [see, e.g., Cockcroft and Pettit 1998, Chap. 15, p. 420 ff.].

But sampling performance data across multiple operating system instances on different servers (such as would appear in a typical distributed business enterprise) introduces new difficulties when it comes to accurately determining system-level performance metrics such as end-to-end response times. How do you know that the clocks on each server are correctly synchronized and that data samples are correctly ordered? Distributed timing protocols such as NTP (Sect. 1.3.2) can help to resolve the correct ordering of sampled performance data.

1.3.7 Virtual Clocks

For the sake of completeness we point out that virtual time should not be confused with the discussion of logical time in Sect. 1.3.5. Virtual time is a term that arises in the context of distributed discrete-event simulations and an algorithm known as "Time Warp" that permits some of the above notions of precedence (i.e., causality) to be violated under certain circumstances.

Under Time Warp, processes are permitted to proceed as rapidly as possible by advancing clocks without concern for possible violations of causality. This approach introduces the possibility of an erroneous simulation occurring. In that case, previous computations are erased by rolling back the computation to a known error-free state. The simulation then proceeds forward using the error-free data until the next error is detected. Virtual time in the Time Warp protocol is simply the counterpart of the physical time presented by the environment. Distributed simulations lie outside the scope of this book.

1.4 Representations of Time

As we noted in Sects. 1.2.1 and 1.3.1, the use of time stamps is essential for any kind of computer performance analysis. There are, it turns out, many possible representations of time for that purpose.

On UNIX and Linux systems, there are different commands and C procedures for invoking time stamps. The simplest and most obvious of these is the `date` command which produces the recognizable calendar-based time stamp, e.g., `Thu Oct 23 08:02:07 2003` at the shell. Internally, however, this date is stored as a 32-bit unsigned integer. In the case of the preceding timestamp, that integer is `1066860127`.

However, the integer representation of the time stamp varies across different computing platforms. For example, the current time of writing is represented by the number `3149683906` on a PowerPC MacOS computer. This discrepancy is not an error, but it does raise questions about how this 32-bit integer is generated and what it means. Several variants of the UNIX operating systems already store certain time intervals as 64-bit integers, and this trend will continue as 64-bit architectures become more ubiquitous. Currently, Perl5 does not handle 64-bit integers.

1.4.1 In the Beginning

In Sects. 1.2.1 and 1.3.1 we defined the term *epoch*. Different computing platforms and different timing functions keep time encoded in terms of different starting epochs. Table 1.2 summarizes some of those functions available in the Perl 5 environment. These timing functions match many of those in the C library. Coordinated Universal Time (UTC) is the recent standardized replacement for Greenwich Mean Time (GMT). The reason the acronym UTC does not match either the English phrase or the French phrase, *Temps Universel Coordonné*, has to do with an attempt at international political correctness whereby the *average* over both phrases was taken.

So, the 32-bit unsigned integer mentioned earlier encodes the number of seconds since the starting epoch defined on that particular platform. For example, MacOS[1] encodes the number of seconds since January 1, 1904, while UNIX encodes the number of seconds since January 1, 1970.

[1] The MacOS® epoch turned 100 years old on January 1, 2004.

Table 1.2. Perl time functions

`time()`	Returns the value of time in seconds since 00:00:00 UTC, January 1, 1970.
`times()`	Gives process times in terms of the CPU time (not calendar time) broken out as user (or application) time and system (or kernel) time.
`strftime()`	Is a POSIX routine to format date and time.
`gettimeofday()`	Returns the time expressed in seconds and microseconds since midnight (00:00) UTC, January 1, 1970. The resolution is never worse than 100 HZ, which is equal to 10 ms.
`strftime()`	Is a POSIX routine to format date and time.
`localtime()`	Representing the number of seconds since midnight January 1, 1900. The same as the `ctime()` or *calendar time* function in the C library.
`gettimeofday()`	Returns the time is expressed in seconds and microseconds since midnight (00:00) UTC, January 1, 1970. The resolution is never worse than 100 HZ, which is equal to 10 ms.

1.4.2 Making a Date With Perl

All time elements are numeric and stored in a data structure called `tm`

```
struct tm {
  int     tm_sec;          /* seconds */
  int     tm_min;          /* minutes */
  int     tm_hour;         /* hours */
  int     tm_mday;         /* day of the month */
  int     tm_mon;          /* month */
  int     tm_year;         /* year since 1900 */
  int     tm_wday;         /* day of the week */
  int     tm_yday;         /* day in the year */
  int     tm_isdst;        /* daylight saving time */
};
```

and defined in the UNIX header file `<time.h>`. The field `tm_year` is the number of years since 1900. The calendar year 2003 is therefore represented as `tm_year = 103`. The corresponding Perl array is:

```
($sec,
$min,
$hour,
$mday,
$mon,
$year,
$wday,
$yday,
$isdst)
```

These values and the differences in the results returned by the functions in Table 1.2 can be seen most easily by running the following Perl script on your favorite platform:

```
#! /bin/perl
# timely.pl

use Time::Local;
($sec,$min,$hrs,$mdy,$mon,$Dyr,$wdy,$ydy,$DST) = localtime(time);

print "\n======  Representations of Time ======\n";
print "The fields in struct tm: \n";
print "struct tm {\n";
print "\ttm_sec $sec\n";
print "\ttm_min $min\n";
print "\ttm_hrs $hrs\n";
print "\ttm_mdy $mdy\n";
print "\ttm_mon $mon\n";
print "\ttm_Dyr $Dyr (years since 1900)\n";
print "\ttm_wdy $wdy\n";
print "\ttm_ydy $ydy\n";
print "}\n";

print "\n";
print "Equivalent of UNIX ctime() formatting: \n";
$now = localtime;
print "$now\n";
print "\n";
print "Equivalent GMT time: \n";
$now = gmtime;
print "$now\n";
print "\n";
print "Integer representation from timelocal(): \n";
$uint = timelocal($sec,$min,$hrs,$mdy,$mon,$Dyr);
printf( "%u or %e Seconds since 1/1/1900\n", $uint, $uint);
```

The output on a Linux system looks like this:

```
======  Representations of Time ======
The fields in struct tm:
struct tm {
    tm_sec 32
    tm_min 44
    tm_hrs 10
    tm_mdy 6
    tm_mon 9
    tm_Dyr 103 (years since 1900)
    tm_wdy 1
    tm_ydy 278
}
```

```
Equivalent of UNIX ctime() formatting:
Mon Oct  6 10:44:32 2003

Equivalent GMT time:
Mon Oct  6 17:44:32 2003

Integer representation from timelocal():
3148281872 or 3.148282e+09 Seconds since 1/1/1900
```

The function `timelocal()` shows the integer corresponding to the time stamp in `localtime()`.

1.4.3 High-Resolution Timing

Clearly, functions like `localtime()` in Table 1.2 can only produce time stamps with an accuracy that is no better than one second. You can, however, get up to six decimal digits of precision (i.e., microseconds) with a Perlmodule called *HiRes*. The following Perlscript presents a simple example of how more accurate elapsed times can be measured using the `HiRes` module:

```
#! /usr/bin/perl
# timrez.pl

use Time::HiRes;

  $t_start = [Time::HiRes::gettimeofday];

  # Do some work ...
  system("ls");

  $t_end = [Time::HiRes::gettimeofday];
  $elaps = Time::HiRes::tv_interval ($t_start, $t_end);
  $msecs = int($elapsed*1000);

print "\nElapsed time is $elaps seconds\n";
```

Note that the amount of work (listing the files in a local directory) is relatively small and therefore takes less than one second to complete. The resulting output:

```
Elapsed time is 0.01276 seconds
```

demonstrates that it took about 12.8 ms in fact. Since the HiRes module is not a Perlbuilt-in, you must download it from the Comprehensive Perl Archive Network (CPAN) `search.cpan.org/` and install it using the directions in the Appendix F. In addition to high resolution timing, Perlalso offers the *Benchmark* module to perform a more sophisticated analysis of timing results.

1.4.4 Benchmark Timers

The *Benchmark* module is a Perlbuilt-in, so its functions are accessible by default for measuring elapsed times. The following simple example shows how `Benchmark` objects are created and differenced to produce the elapsed time:

```
#! /usr/bin/perl
# bench1.pl

use Time::Local;
use Benchmark;
$t_start = new Benchmark;

# The routine that is measured
print "Benchmark started.\n";
open(OUT, ">dev/null");
for ($i = 0; $i < int(1e+7); $i++) {
    print OUT ".";
}

$t_end = new Benchmark;
$td = timediff($t_end, $t_start);
print "\nWorkload time:",timestr($td),"\n";
```

The output looks like this:

```
Benchmark started.
Workload time:41 wallclock secs (40.16 usr +  0.40 sys = 40.56 CPU)
```

The `Benchmark` module is also capable of performing much more sophisticated kinds of timing analyses, such as the following pairwise comparisons:

```
#! /usr/bin/perl
# bench2.pl

use Time::Local;
use Benchmark qw(cmpthese); # explicit import required

# The routine that is measured
print "Benchmark started.\n";
cmpthese( -4, {
    alpha_task => "++\$i",
    beta_task => "\$i *= 2",
    gamma_task => "\$i <<= 2",
    delta_task => "\$i **= 2",
    }
);

# Benchmark the benchmark code ...
print "==============\n";
```

```
print "CPU time for Benchmark module to execute:\n";
my ($user, $system, $cuser, $csystem) = times();
printf("%4.2f (usr) %4.2f (sys)\n", $user, $system);
printf("%4.2f (usr) %4.2f (sys)\n", $cuser, $csystem);
print "===============\n";
```

On a 500-MHz Pentium III processor, the output looks like this:

```
Benchmark started.
Benchmark: running alpha_task, beta_task, delta_task, gamma_task for
at least 4 CPU seconds...
alpha_task:  4 wallclock secs ( 4.01 usr +  0.00 sys =  4.01 CPU) @
3940537.31/s (n=15789733)
 beta_task:  4 wallclock secs ( 4.29 usr +  0.00 sys =  4.29 CPU) @
 1094158.32/s (n=4699410)
delta_task:  4 wallclock secs ( 4.06 usr +  0.00 sys =  4.06 CPU) @
861472.88/s (n=3494134)
gamma_task:  3 wallclock secs ( 4.11 usr +  0.00 sys =  4.11 CPU) @
2414453.00/s (n=9913744)
                Rate delta_task  beta_task gamma_task alpha_task
delta_task  861473/s         --       -21%       -64%       -78%
beta_task  1094158/s        27%         --       -55%       -72%
gamma_task 2414453/s       180%       121%         --       -39%
alpha_task 3940537/s       357%       260%        63%         --
===============
CPU time for Benchmark module to execute:
111.17 (usr) 0.15 (sys)
0.00 (usr) 0.00 (sys)
===============
```

The table of timing results is sorted from slowest to fastest, and shows the percentage speed difference between each pair of tests.

This is all very convenient, but beware the overhead! Notice that the each task executed for 4 cpu-seconds but post-processing the results caused the script to take more than 2 min of wall-clock time to complete.

It is also important to be aware that certain `Benchmark` functions must be explicitly imported into your scripts in order to become activated. One of these is the `cmpthese()` function. Notice also that the second argument in `cmpthese()` is a Perlhash reference. See `search.cpan.org/~jhi/perl-5.8.1/lib/Benchmark.pm`, which updates the description of the `Benchmark` module in Wall et al. [2003].

1.4.5 Crossing Time Zones

Finally, it is worth noting that Perloffers a very convenient way of allowing you to time stamp remote UNIX servers from a single location. There are two essential steps:

1. Select the time zone using the parameter file in `/usr/share/zoneinfo/`.

2. Set the time zone using the POSIX **tzset()** function.

As a very simple example of how this capability works, imagine there are three servers: one in Melbourne, Australia; another in Paris, France and the other in San Francisco, California. If you are in Melbourne and you want to compare a server located there with the one located in San Francisco, the following Perl script will give the correct timestamp for each server:

```
#! /usr/bin/perl
# timetz.pl

use Time::Local;
use POSIX qw(tzset);

my @dayofweek = (qw(Sunday Monday Tuesday Wednesday Thursday Friday
    Saturday));
my @monthnames = (qw(Jan Feb Mar Apr May Jun Jul Aug Sep Oct Nov Dec));
my ($sec, $min, $hour, $mday, $mon, $year, $wday, $yday);

%zone = (Melbourne => 0, Paris => 1, SanFrancisco => 2);
$zonelocal = $zone{Melbourne};
$zoneremote = $zone{SanFrancisco};

# Get the local time first ...
$now = localtime();

# Set the remote time zone ...
if ($zoneremote == $zone{Melbourne}) {
        $ENV{TZ} = ':/usr/share/zoneinfo/Australia/Melbourne';
        $rplace = "Melbourne";
}
if ($zoneremote == $zone{Paris}) {
        $ENV{TZ} = ':/usr/share/zoneinfo/Europe/Paris';
        $rplace = "Paris";
}
if ($zoneremote == $zone{SanFrancisco}) {
        $ENV{TZ} = ':/usr/share/zoneinfo/US/Pacific';
        $rplace = "San Francisco";
}
tzset();

# Get the remote time
($sec, $min, $hour, $mday, $mon, $year, $wday, $yday) = localtime();
$year += 1900;

if ($zonelocal == $zone{Melbourne}) {
        $lplace = "Melbourne";
}
if ($zonelocal == $zone{Paris}) {
```

```
        $lplace = "Paris";
}
if ($zonelocal == $zone{SanFrancisco}) {
        $lplace = "San Francisco";
}

print "Local   position: $lplace\n";
print "Local   time is $now\n";
print "Remote  position: $rplace\n";
print "Remote  time is $hour:$min:$sec\n";
print "Remote  date is $dayofweek[$wday], $monthnames[$mon] $mday,
    $year\n";
```

The output is:

```
Local server in Melbourne
Local time is Fri Oct 24 08:06:32 2003
Remote  server in San Francisco
Remote  time is 15:6:32
Remote  date is Thursday, Oct 23, 2003
```

In other words, you do not have to run separate Perlscripts on each server to get the correct local and remote time stamps. Using `tzset()` could be a useful device for triggering data collection from several remote servers located in different geographical regions. Of course, it will not account for any drift or skew between the clocks (Sect. 1.3.1) on different servers.

The context for the discussion in this section has been data collection and performance monitoring. In Chap. 6 we look at how some of these same functions can be applied in the context of performance modeling with PerlPDQ.

1.5 Time Distributions

In this section we review two probability distributions commonly used in the performance characterization of computer systems: the exponential and gamma distributions. Rather than getting bogged down in too many mathematical details, it is suggested that readers familiarize themselves with these statistical functions available in both commercial software such as Microsoft Excel, Mathematica, and the statistical package called S^+ (`www.insightful.com`), and public domain packages such R (`www.r-project.org`) and the CPAN statistics archive `search.cpan.org`.

Most of the queueing models discussed throughout this book, assume that characteristics such as the times between arrivals (interarrival times) and the periods of time to service a request (service times), are distributed according to an exponential distribution. An exponential distribution is the signature of random processes in action.

However, the assumption that the distribution of interarrival and service times is exponential, is often applied more for mathematical simplicity rather empirical accuracy. As we shall see in Chaps. 2 and 3, the exponential distribution also has special mathematical properties that facilitate the prediction of computer system performance when represented as a system of queues (see Appendix C). Although the exponential distribution is an approximation, it is often a good one because, although most computer system processes are not random, they often act as though they are.

The end-to-end response times or round-trip response time (RTT) is the time is takes a request to traverse all of the necessary service components in a computer system; including servers and network segments. Since the end-to-end response time is the accumulation of these component times, it typically belongs to a distribution that is more general than the simple exponential distribution (see Fig. 5.9 in Chap. 5). The gamma distribution is one example of a more general distribution that can be used to fit end-to-end response time measurements.

1.5.1 Gamma Distribution

The gamma distribution is a continuous statistical function [Orwant et al. 1999]. The Perl module `GammaDistribution.pm` is available from CPAN. It is also available in other tools such as Excel. The gamma *density* function $f(t)$ is defined as:

$$f(t, \alpha, \beta) = \frac{t^{\alpha-1}}{\beta^{\alpha}\, \Gamma(\alpha)}\, \mathrm{e}^{-t/\beta}\,, \tag{1.1}$$

where the gamma function:

$$\Gamma(\alpha) = \int_0^{\infty} t^{\alpha-1}\, \mathrm{e}^{-t}\, \mathrm{d}t \tag{1.2}$$

is a generalization of the factorial function $a! = a \times (a-1) \times \ldots \times 2 \times 1$ by virtue of $\Gamma(a+1) = a!$.

The gamma *distribution* function $F(t)$ is the integral of (1.1). The two parameters α and β determine the shape and scale of the distribution, respectively. The mean and variance of the gamma distribution are respectively $\alpha\beta$ and $\alpha\beta^2$. Certain values of the parameters α and β relate the gamma distribution to other well-known distributions in probability theory and statistics [Allen 1990, Trivedi 2000].

1.5.2 Exponential Distribution

Under certain conditions, the general gamma distribution reduces to the special case of an exponential distribution. In particular, if $\alpha = 1$, the gamma distribution (1.1) becomes equivalent to the exponential distribution:

$$f(t, \lambda) = \lambda \, e^{-\lambda t} , \tag{1.3}$$

with mean $= 1/\lambda$ and variance $= 1/\lambda^2$. The corresponding exponential distribution function is given by:

$$F(t, \lambda) = 1 - e^{-\lambda t} , \tag{1.4}$$

where the gamma distribution parameter β has been replaced by $\lambda = 1/\beta$. The exponential density function $f(t)$ and its distribution function $F(t)$ are plotted together in Fig. 1.3 for the parameter value $\lambda = \beta = 1$.

As noted in Sect. 1.5, the exponential distribution is often used in computer performance analysis to characterize interarrival times and service times.

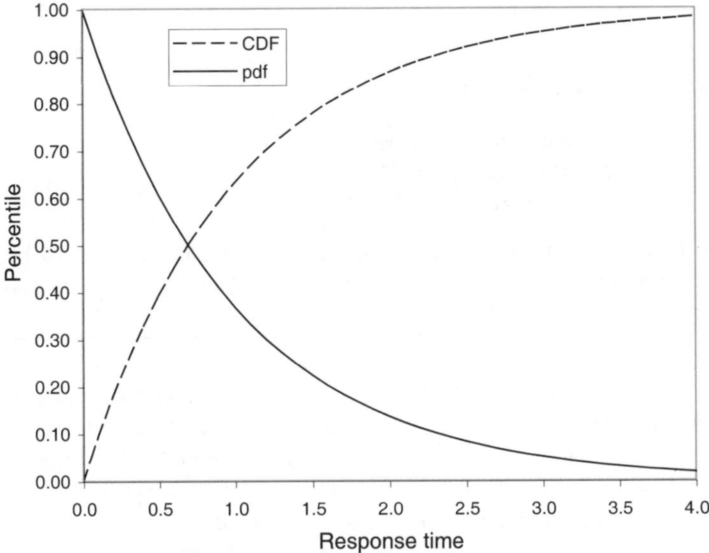

Fig. 1.3. Exponential density (*curve*) and distribution (*bars*) functions

By tabulating values of the exponential distribution in Table 1.3, we note that since the mean time (e.g., the mean service time S) has the value $S = 1$ in Fig. 1.3, the 80th percentile (0.7981) is about 1.6 times the magnitude of S, the 90th percentile (0.8997) is about $2.3S$, and the 95th percentile (0.9502) is $3S$. Assuming the measured distribution of times actually conforms to the exponential distribution, we can state the following rule of thumb.

Table 1.3. Exponential service time distribution

Service time (s)	Density function	Distribution function
1.5	0.2231	0.7769
1.6	0.2019	0.7981
1.7	0.1827	0.8173
...	...	...
2.1	0.1225	0.8775
2.2	0.1108	0.8892
2.3	0.1003	0.8997
2.4	0.0907	0.9093
...	...	...
2.9	0.0550	0.9450
3.0	0.0498	0.9502

If the mean service time is S, then:

1. 80th percentile occurs at $S_{80} \approx 5S/3$
2. 90th percentile occurs at $S_{90} \approx 7S/3$
3. 95th percentile occurs at $S_{95} \approx 9S/3$

Since the distribution of arrival rates and service times is assumed to be exponentially distributed in PDQ (Chap. 6), this rule of thumb can also be applied to those attributes in PDQ models.

In Sect. 1.5 it was pointed out that measurements of end-to-end response times on real computer systems require a more general distribution than the exponential distribution. Based on Sect. 1.5.1, an obvious candidate is the gamma probability distribution. In the remainder of this section, we show to apply the gamma distribution to performance measurements from a network-based computer system. We shall investigate client/server systems in more detail in Chap. 9.

1.5.3 Poisson Distribution

The Poisson distribution is used to represent discrete events occuring randomly in continuous time t. Example events are radioactive decay and the number of incoming telephone calls during some period $t = T$.

Consider the period T to be broken into a large number of intervals N. If events occur at a constant rate λ, the probability that there are exactly n events in a period T is given by the product of the probability that there is one even in each of n intervals of width T/N, times the probability that there are no events in the remaining $N - n$ intervals:

$$\Pr(n \text{ events}) = \lim_{N\to\infty} \left(\frac{\lambda T}{N}\right)^n \times \frac{N!}{n!(N-n)!}\left(1-\frac{\lambda T}{N}\right)^{N-n} \tag{1.5}$$

The combinatorial factor accounts for the possible arrangements of intervals with events among intervals with none. More formally, the probability density function (PDF) is:

$$f(n,t) = \mathrm{e}^{-\lambda t}\frac{(\lambda t)^n}{n!}\,,\ n = 1, 2, \ldots \tag{1.6}$$

Strictly speaking, (1.6) is called the discrete probability mass function (PMF) when the random variable is discrete. It follows from (1.6) that the probability that there are no events at all during the period T is:

$$f(0,t) = \mathrm{e}^{-\lambda t}\,. \tag{1.7}$$

In other words, the distribution of time intervals is exponential. This is the basis for the important connection between the Poisson and the exponential distributions.

> If the number of events are Poisson distributed then the time intervals between the events are exponentially distributed. Hence, if arrivals into a queue are generated by a Poisson process, the interarrival times will be exponentially distributed. We make particular use of this result in Chap. 2.

The cumulative distribution function (CDF) is:

$$F(n,t) = \sum_{k=0}^{n} f(k,t)\,. \tag{1.8}$$

In the limit that the sum becomes infinite, the discrete terms approach the continuous function $\mathrm{e}^{\lambda t}$ and (1.8) becomes:

$$\sum_{k=0}^{\infty} f(k,t) = \mathrm{e}^{-\lambda t}\mathrm{e}^{\lambda t} = 1\,. \tag{1.9}$$

The mean and variance of a Poisson distribution are identical:

$$E(n) = \lambda t\ ,\ Var(n) = \lambda t\,. \tag{1.10}$$

1.5.4 Server Response Time Distribution

Consider an application running on a server that is connected by a local network to its clients. Performance data is collected from both the server-side and the network. Table 1.4 summarizes the performance statistics based on

Table 1.4. Summary of server-side statistics

Statistic	Value
Sample mean (s)	0.82
Sample standard deviation (s)	1.95
Gamma mean μ	0.82
Gamma variance σ^2	3.81
Calculated α parameter	0.18
Calculated β parameter	4.62

measurements from the server-side and fitting the scale and shape parameters of the gamma distribution to those data.
From these measured data, combined with the sample mean and variance for those data, the gamma function parameters can be calculated from the following equations:

$$\alpha = \frac{\mu^2}{\sigma^2} \, , \beta = \frac{\mu}{\alpha} \, . \tag{1.11}$$

The fitted response time functions for the side-server statistics are shown in Fig. 1.4(a). The response time density function exhibits a very sharp peak near the origin together with a long tail extending to the right along the time axis. The predicted 80th, 90th, and 95th percentile response times are shown in Table 1.5. From the third column we see that 80% of the requests take 1.0 s or less, 90% take less than 2.5 s, and 95% take less than 4.3 s.

Table 1.5. Predicted server-side percentiles

Response Time (s)	Density Function	Distribution Function
1.0	0.1182	0.7981
2.5	0.0403	0.9007
4.3	0.0175	0.9488

1.5.5 Network Response Time Distribution

A similar set of data from measurements of network response times is summarized in Table 1.6. The fitted response time distributions are shown in Fig. 1.4(b).

The corresponding 80th, 90th, and 95th percentile response times for the network measurements are shown in Table 1.7. We see from Fig. 1.4 that the average response time of the network is approximately twice as long as it is for the server. On the other hand, the spread, as measured by the variance,

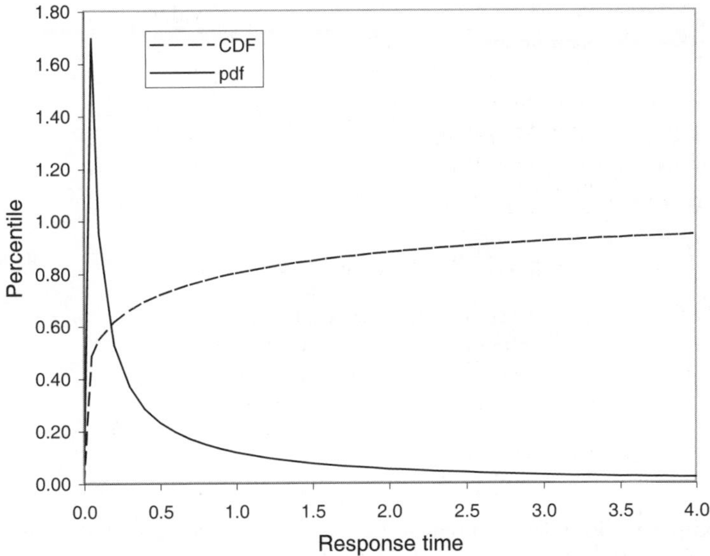

(a) Server response functions based on the gamma probability distribution statistics in Table 1.4

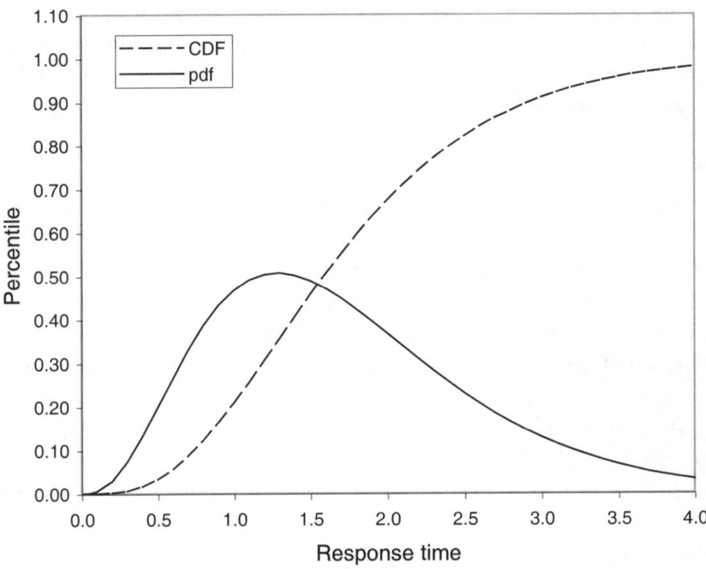

(b) Network response functions based on the gamma probability distribution statistics in Table 1.6

Fig. 1.4. Fitted response time distributions for (a) the server and (b) the local network measurements. The predicted response time percentiles are summarized in Tables 1.5 and 1.7, respectively

Table 1.6. Summary of network statistics

Statistic	Value
Sample mean (s)	1.74
Sample standard deviation (s)	0.89
Gamma mean μ	1.74
Gamma variance σ^2	0.80
Estimated α parameter	3.76
Estimated β parameter	0.46

Table 1.7. Predicted network percentiles

Response time (s)	Density function	Distribution function
2.4	0.2538	0.7959
3.0	0.1285	0.9076
3.4	0.0764	0.9479

is approximately four times greater for the server because of its longer tail (Fig. 1.4(a)) of the fitted gamma distribution.

When server and network response time data are availabe as separate measurements (like Sects. 1.5.4 and 1.5.5) but one wants to predict the combined response time for both systems operating together then, technically speaking, the two gamma distributions have to be *convolved* [Allen 1990, Verma 1992] to get the correct estimate. However, in practice, a gamma distribution often provides a sufficiently good fit for measurements of the combined system (see Fig. 5.9 in Chap. 5). Brownlee and Ziedins [2002] discuss the successful application of the gamma function to response time measurements of Internet domain name servers (DNS).

1.6 Timing Chains and Bottlenecks

Distributed computer systems (such as the client/server architectures discussed in Chap. 9) comprise logical processes mapped onto a number of physical computing resources. A request, such as a database transaction, typically requires the use of a sequence of these logical processes. The logical processing is accommodated by a succession of software components. The time taken at each stage to process the transaction adds up to the response time observed by the user who initiated the transaction. Users are often concerned with so-called *end-to-end response time.* The process with the longest processing time is the time-sink and therefore the key determinant of the response time. It is therefore given a special name—*bottleneck.*

The view of the user is not so different from that of the computer performance analyst in that both of them desire to associate the length of the response time with time-sinks. Both the user and the analyst would like to know how much time is spent in each stage of processing the database transaction during its "flight" through the system software. On average, the sum of the times spent in each processing stage should equal the measured end-to-end response time within some allowed tolerance.

Fig. 1.5. Response time represented as links in a timing chain

Another way to think about the role of time-sinks or bottlenecks is to view each processing stage as a link in a chain of processing events. Each link corresponds to a processing stage. Borrowing a term well-known to auto mechanics, we call the chain in Fig. 1.5 a *timing chain*. The number of links in the chain corresponds to the number of *instrumented* processing stages, i.e., processing stages that can be measured with probes. This is usually best achieved by including the probes within the application code. In order for the end-to-end response time to be the sum of the time spent in each stage, the measurements must be sequential and the probe points must be contiguous. There cannot be any missing links! (See Exercise 1.2.)

Figure 1.5 shows one possible timing chain arrangement. There are only three links in the chain because only gross system instrumentation is available. In other words, there are only contiguous probes in the client application, the start and end of network services, and the database server.

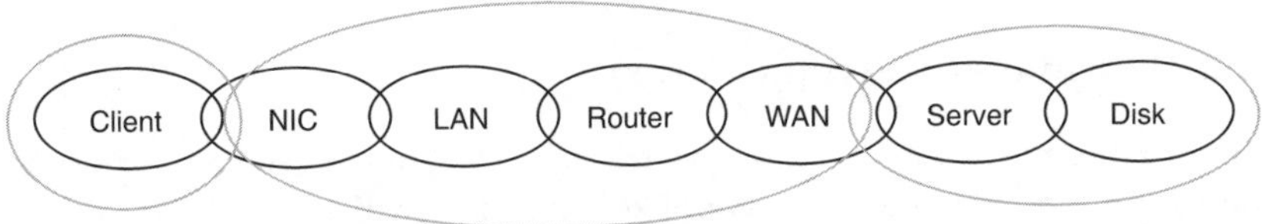

Fig. 1.6. Further decomposition of the timing chain in Fig. 1.5

Suppose the bottleneck is now found to be present somewhere in the network. It would useful if the network services link in the timing chain of Fig. 1.5 could be further decomposed with finer resolution to determine more precisely which network service was responsible for the bottleneck. Such a decomposed timing chain is shown in Fig. 1.6. In this case, there are probes corresponding to seven links instead of just three. Once again, there cannot be any missing links. The network services link in Fig. 1.5 has been expanded to become four links:

1. NIC card

2. LAN networking
3. Router
4. WAN networking

while the server link in Fig. 1.5 has been expanded to become two links:

1. Server platform (CPU, O/S, etc.)
2. Server disks

Finer resolution of process times requires additional instrumentation probes; this is not always available, but it is always a worthy goal.

1.6.1 Bottlenecks and Queues

We shall further formalize this timing chain concept in terms of the queue residence times in Chap. 2. Each link in the timing chain can be replaced by a queueing center. The flight of each transaction comprises units of work consuming resources at a series of queueing centers that represent the various processing stages: applications processing, communications, database processing, and so on.

Since there can be many transactions being processed simultaneously at each stage, there is the possibility of contention among the transactions at each queueing center. The processing time at each stage is then given by the sum of the time the transaction has to *wait* to obtain the necessary processing resources plus the time it actually takes to get processed when it finally can access the resource. Clearly, the more heavily loaded the system, the longer the queues will tend to be, and therefore the longer the time spent waiting at each stage. The end-to-end response time then is the sum of each of these processing times; it is formally known as the *residence time.*

1.6.2 Distributed Instrumentation

A significant problem remains, however, for distributed server performance monitoring. Performance data sampled across many distributed servers is not only incomplete in the sense of Sect. 1.3.6, but it has no universal format and no universal storage format. At best, any such comprehensive solutions are proprietary to a specific platform or a specific tool vendor. Some of these issues have already been addressed and *standardized* solutions do exist. Among them are:

- Application Quality Resource Management (AQRM): Download the specifications from `www.opengroup.org/aquarium`.
- Application Management Information Base (APPLMIB): An application management schema that can be read by SNMP agents. See `www.ietf.org/html.charters/OLD/applmib-charter.html`. This is a descendent of network management protocols reaching up into the application management level.

- Application Response Measurement (ARM): Download the specifications-from `www.opengroup.org/management/arm.htm`.
- Simple network management protocol (SNMP): See `www.ietf.org/html.charters/snmpv3-charter.html`
- Universal measurement architecture (UMA): Download this specification from `www.opengroup.org/products/publications/catalog/c427.htm`.

For a more detailed comparison of the performance management capabilities these standards see Gunther [2000a, Chap. 4] and Appendix D.

1.6.3 Disk Timing Chains

A file I/O operation under the UNIX operating system can be represented as a timing chain [Vahalia 1996] with queues. It is important to understand the limitations of what the UNIX kernel can actually measure and what gets reported (sometimes erroneously) in certain UNIX I/O performance tools such as `iostat`. The I/O operation begins with the user program issuing a request

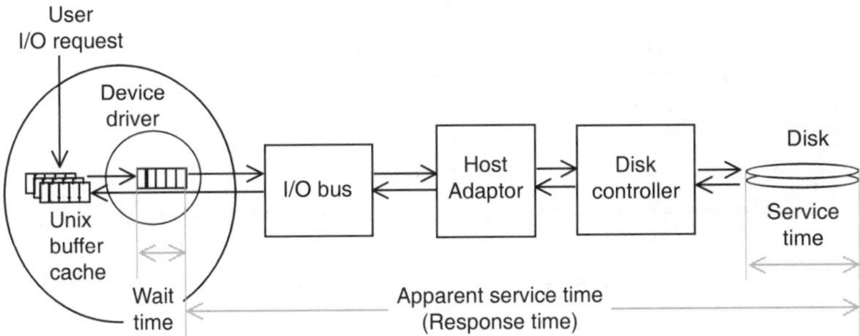

Fig. 1.7. Timing path of a file I/O command

to read or write data. Since this I/O involves the file system, it first gets queued in the UNIX buffer cache. The request is then sent to the UNIX device driver (Fig. 1.7), where it is further queued until the driver can obtain an uncontended path to the disk controllers. After the I/O operation has been serviced at the disk (the data is read or written), it returns an interrupt to the device driver, thus starting the service of the next I/O operation.

The UNIX device driver only keeps counts of I/O completions. The wait count in UNIX tools like `iostat` is the number of I/O requests in the driver queue [Cockcroft and Pettit 1998]. Once the I/O has been issued (i.e., once it has left the driver queue) it is considered to be in service. But this is not the service time at the disk. To reach the platter, it must traverse the I/O bus down to the target disk. Consequently, the so-called service time can be highly variable. This is really a reflection of the fact that it is a response time, and not a service time. Since the time to traverse each of these subsystems (or timing chain links) lies outside the UNIX kernel, it cannot account for each of them separately. Hence, the total time is a response time and not a service time.

1.6.4 Life and Times of an NFS Operation

As an example of a timing chain that has been resolved at the microsecond level, using sophisticated measurement probes [Nelson and Cheng 1991], we follow the chain of processing events in the network file system (NFS) read operation like that shown in Fig. 1.8 Although this data is more than a decade old, the magnitudes have not changed too significantly. Total end-to-end response time was measured at 47.2 ms. These measurements exclude client processing and Ethernet contention. The detailed timing breakdown of the timing chain consists of the following processing steps:

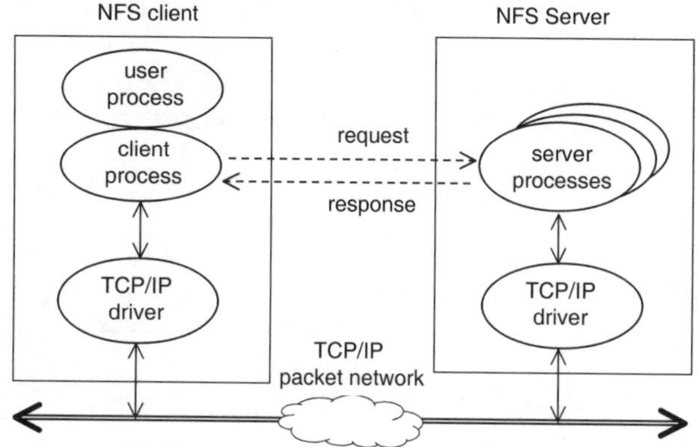

Fig. 1.8. Processing an NFS operation

- Ethernet transmission time 0.16 ms from:
  - Inbound to the server from the client-side
  - Best case assumes no ethernet contention
  - Single UDP datagram containing the NFS ReadOp RPC call
  - 100 B includes: RPC, UDP, and IP headers, file handle and offset, userid (see Glossary in Appendix A)
  - Assumes no network contention
- Packet processing time 3.5 ms each way, comprising:
  - Disassembly of the NFS ReadOp request
  - IP, UDP, RPC and NFS
  - DMA transfer time
- File processing time 1.5 ms each way, comprising:
  - All file system processing

  - Messages between Ethernet controller, file, and disk
  - Two request–reply pairs (four total) for NFS disk read
- I/O driver time 0.370 ms each way:
  - Kernel, elevator queueing, disk device bus commands
- Random disk access of 8 KB; 29.5 ms, comprising:
  - Disk device select and transfer
  - Disk command decode and processing
  - Average seek time (17.5 ms)
  - Average rotational latency (7.5 ms)
  - 8 KB data transfer (16 sectors on the same track)
  - Device cleanup and handshake (0.260 ms)
- Server-side Ethernet Transmission time of 6.8 ms, comprising:
  - 6 IP packets
  - RPC reply is one datagram but many IP packets
  - 8 KB data + IP, UDP, RPC header (500 B)
  - 5 full packets (1,512 B) + 6 partial packets

It should be clear that disk accesses constitute the primary bottleneck, followed by remote procedure call (RPC) processing and the transmission of data back to the requesting client. The disk is the primary bottleneck, taking approximately 30 ms to retrieve 8 KB of data. Since the RPC mechanism involves memory-to-memory copying, it is a major contributor to the 7 ms at the secondary bottleneck.

The cautious reader should note that Redundant Arrays of Inexpensive Disks (RAID), and Storage Area Networks (SAN) usually do not offer the possibility of resolving timing chains in this way. For the most part, they remain proprietary black boxes.

1.7 Failing Big Time

Achievable performance can be constrained significantly by poor reliability or lack of stability in a computer system. The importance of this, often ignored, aspect of performance analysis is captured in the time-honored adage, "*High performance, high reliability, low cost; pick two!*" On the other hand, those who do recognize its importance have created a hybrid metric called *performability* to reflect the intimate relationship between performance and reliability.

History is littered with examples demonstrating the sometimes tragic consequences of ignoring reliability issues; some can be found on the Internet newsgroup `comp.risks` or the Web digest at `http://catless.ncl.ac.uk/Risks`. One of the most public and tragic examples of miscalculating reliability was the loss of NASA space shuttle *Challenger* (STS-51-L) and its crew on January 28, 1986 [Gunther 2000a]. Sadly, history repeated itself on February 1, 2003 with loss of the *Columbia* space shuttle (STS-107) and its crew, apparently because of the same kind of poor risk-management practices [Gunther

2002b] that were identified 17 years earlier during the Challenger investigation (see, e.g., `www.ralentz.com/old/space/feynman-report.html`).

1.7.1 Hardware Availability

The concept of *availability* is closely related to reliability, but, since it is a little easier to grasp, we discuss it first. The availability metric is now in widespread use as a way to assess the reliability of commercial computers. The average availability of a computer system can be calculated from the measured `uptime` command as reported by UNIX administration tools. (See Chap. 4. A queueing model that incorporates the notions of availability, breakdown and, repair is discussed in Chaps. 3 and 6.)

The availability A can be defined simply in terms of the time the system is up during some observation period T. We denote the total time the system is up as T_{up} and the total time it is down for repair as T_{down}. Then

$$A = \frac{T_{\mathrm{up}}}{T} = \frac{T_{up}}{T_{\mathrm{up}} + T_{\mathrm{down}}} . \tag{1.12}$$

From this definition, it is clear that the availability metric lies in the range $0 \leq A \leq 1$.

Example 1.4. Suppose a computer system has a measured up time of 41.25 days and was down for 10 h. What is the average availability? Since 41.25 days is 990 h, we can use 1.12 to write:

$$A = \frac{990}{990 + 10} = 0.99 . \tag{1.13}$$

In other words, the system is available 99.0% of the time □

This availability appears satisfactory, but, as we shall see shortly, there are two shortcomings in using an availability metric alone. The first shortcoming has to do with 99.0% availability not being a sufficient measure for most production operations. The second shortcoming arises from the multiplicity of up and down times that satisfy the same availability criterion.

1.7.2 Tyranny of the Nines

To satisfy real-world computer availability requirements with regard to the first shortcoming, we need to introduce more digits after the decimal point in the availability metric A. A commonly stated requirement for commercial computing systems is 99.99% availability over the course of a 7 (day) by 24 (hour) operating year. How much downtime does that correspond to?

Example 1.5. A useful yardstick from Table 1.1 is 1 yr $= 32 \times 10^6$ s.
(a) 99.9% available means $32 \times 10^6 \times 10^{-3} = 32,000$ s or 9 h per year downtime.
(b) 99.99% available means $32 \times 10^6 \times 10^{-4} = 3,200$ s or approximately 1 h of downtime per year.
(c) 99.9999% means $32 \times 10^6 \times 10^{-6}$ s or 32 s of downtime per year. □

> An availability of $99.X\% \equiv 10^{-(2+X)}$ occurrences. Noting that $2+X$ is also the number of *nines* in the availability number, we arrive at the mnemonic: $99.99\ldots9\% = 10^{-(\text{number of 9's})}$ occurrences per year.

Achieving and maintaining these levels of availability in a cost-effective manner leads some computer manufacturers to refer to this constraint as *The tyranny of the nines.*

1.7.3 Hardware Reliability

The second shortcoming stems from the multiplicity of T_{up} and T_{down} times that satisfy the same availability criterion expressed as the ratio in (1.12).

Example 1.6. Each pair of up and down times in Table 1.8 correspond to 99% availability. The last entry might strike the astute reader as unrealistic, but, as we shall see in Sect. 1.8.1, such timescales can arise in the context of the reliability of very large scale integration (VLSI) computer chips. □

Table 1.8. Identical availability ratios

T_{up}	T_{down}	Unit
990	10	h
99	1	h
99	1	s

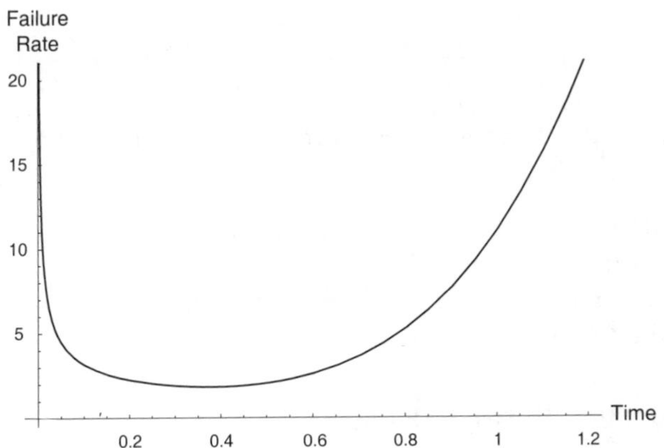

Fig. 1.9. Classic *bathtub* shape of the failure rate $h(t)$

The instantaneous failure rate $h(t)$ (also known as the *hazard* rate [Trivedi 2000]) is generally determined by direct measurement. A typical failure curve is shown in Fig. 1.9. Initially, failures arise from inherent defects in the system, e.g., by virtue of poor design, or the manufacturing process itself. Corrections to these processes eventually reduce the failure rate. After this *wear-in* period, the failure rate becomes relatively constant during the *working life* of the system. Ultimately, however, the failure rate begins to increase as hardware components reach their *end of life* and wear out. These three phases produce the classic *bathtub* shape of the failure function. Notice that $h(t)$ is not necessarily symmetric about the *working life* period. By defining the *cumulative failure rate*,

$$H(t) = \int_0^t h(s)\,\mathrm{d}s, \tag{1.14}$$

the reliability $R(t)$ can be written as

$$R(t) = \mathrm{e}^{-H(t)} . \tag{1.15}$$

The reliability corresponding to Fig. 1.9 is shown in Fig. 1.10. The reliability is

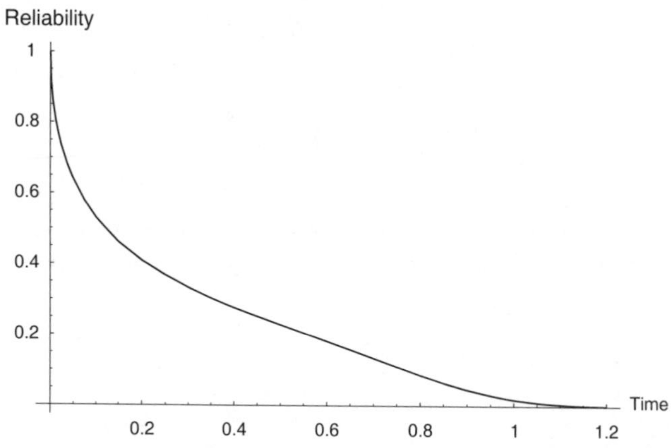

Fig. 1.10. Reliability function $R(t)$ corresponding to Fig. 1.9

the probability that the system has remained *up* until time t given that it was already up at time $t = 0$. The ambiguity that can arise in the availability ratio (1.12) can be removed by using a different measure, the *mean time between failures* or MTBF.

1.7.4 Mean Time Between Failures

Conveniently, the MTBF can be defined in terms of reliability $R(t)$:

$$\mathrm{MTBF} = \int_0^\infty R(t)\,\mathrm{d}t\ . \tag{1.16}$$

Various reliability models can be constructed for (1.16) by an appropriate choice of $h(t)$. Some of the best known reliability models are based on the exponential, and the Weibull distributions, which we briefly summarize here.

Exponential distribution. This is a one-parameter reliability model where the instantaneous failure rate,

$$h(t) = \lambda\ , \tag{1.17}$$

is constant. Then, $H(t) = \lambda t$, and (1.15) becomes the exponential reliability function:

$$R(t) = \mathrm{e}^{-\lambda t}\ . \tag{1.18}$$

Substituting this into (1.16) produces:

$$MTBF = \frac{1}{\lambda}\ . \tag{1.19}$$

In other words, the MTBF is just the inverse of the failure rate. The main feature of exponential models is that they represent system failures that are statistically independent or random in time, which is also known as the "ageless" property.

Weibull distribution. This is an alternative model specified by two parameters. The instantaneous failure rate is:

$$h(t) = \lambda\,\alpha t^{\alpha-1}\ . \tag{1.20}$$

Parameter values of $\alpha \neq 1$ represent various degrees of aging or fatiguing. When $\alpha = 1$, the Weibull distribution reduces to the exponential failure function given by (1.17). The additive Weibull model,

$$h(t) = \lambda\,\alpha t^{\alpha-1} + \gamma\,\beta t^{\beta-1}\ , \tag{1.21}$$

with parameter set $\alpha = 5$, $\beta = 1/2$, $\gamma = 2$, and $\lambda = 2$ was used to produce Figs. 1.9 and 1.10.

Now, we are in a position to express the previously defined availability A in terms of the mean time between failures (MTBF) and mean time to repair (MTTR) of a failed hardware system. The MTTR includes response time, time to isolate the fault, time to apply the fix, and time to verify that the fix works. Then:

$$A = \frac{MTBF}{MTBF + MTTR}\ . \tag{1.22}$$

In Chap. 2, these notions of breakdown and repair times are revisited within the context of a queueing system known as the repairman model.

1.7.5 Distributed Hardware

So far, we have only considered the availability of a single component. The component might represent a complete computer or just a computer subsystem. In a distributed computer system there are dependencies and redundancies that impact the availability of the aggregate system. In the simplest cases the components are configured in a chain or in series. Alternatively, redundant components can be configured in a parallel arrangement. The assessment of series and parallel availability differs significantly.

1.7.6 Components in Series

If there are k components in series that are statistically independent of each other, then the joint availability can be calculated from

$$A_{\text{series}} = A_1 \times A_2 \times \ldots \times A_k , \tag{1.23}$$

where each A_k is calculated from (1.22), depending on the available data.

Example 1.7. Consider a database transaction system involving a client workstation, a fileserver, a gateway, and the database server itself. Assume the database server and the fileserver are both 99.99% available while the workstation and the gateway respectively are only 99.1% and 99.7% available. The joint availability is given by:

$$A_{\text{series}} = (0.9999)^2 \times (0.9910) \times (0.9970) = 98.78\%.$$

The important point is that the joint availability can never be greater than the availability of the *weakest link* in the chain of components. □

1.7.7 Components in Parallel

The availability of a system comprising k redundant components is expressed most simply in terms of the complement $U_k = (1 - A_k)$ of the availability for each component. The availability of components connected in parallel that are otherwise independent of each other can be written as:

$$A_{\text{para}} = 1 - (U_1 \times U_2 \times \ldots \times U_k) . \tag{1.24}$$

U_k is called the *unavailability*.

Example 1.8. Consider a two-node database server each of which only has 99.1% availability. The *joint* availability, however, is given by:

$$A_{\text{para}} = 1 - (1 - 0.991)^2$$

or 99.99%. □

In reality, computer system configurations are composed of complex networks that involve combinations of series and parallel networks. In that case assessing availability (if it can be calculated at all) requires more complicated techniques [Xie 1991] than those briefly presented here.

1.7.8 Software Reliability

Because software and hardware have very different failure modes, modeling the reliability of software tends to be more difficult than it is for hardware. Faults in software do not arise from "fatigue" in software processes but rather from the execution path containing a defect or "bug." This is quantified in a measure called the *mean time between defects* (MTBD).

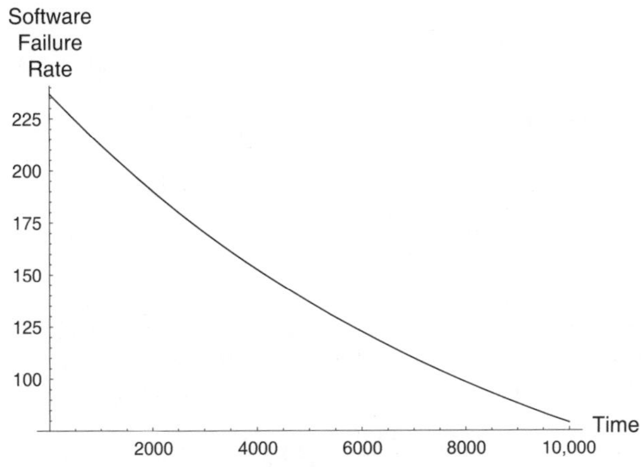

Fig. 1.11. Software failure model

There is always a finite set of unresolved bugs present in software. But that finite number need not be a decreasing quantity. Bugs can be removed and in the removal process new bugs or side-effects can be introduced unintentionally. They will cause failures that can only be detected in the future. Consequently, the failure rate will tend to fall very slowly over time (Fig. 1.11).

In a widely used model, the number of bugs $B(t)$ reported at time t is given by:

$$B(t) = \beta_0 \left(1 - \mathrm{e}^{-\lambda t/\beta_0}\right) , \tag{1.25}$$

where β_0 is the initial number of defects (Fig. 1.12). The corresponding MTBD,

$$\mathrm{MTBD} = \frac{1}{\lambda} \, \mathrm{e}^{\lambda t/\beta_0} , \tag{1.26}$$

also increases with time, in contrast to the constant time of the exponential model in (1.19).

1.8 Metastable Lifetimes

Related to predictions about reliability and mean time to failure is the concept of metastability and metastable lifetimes. In physics and chemistry, a

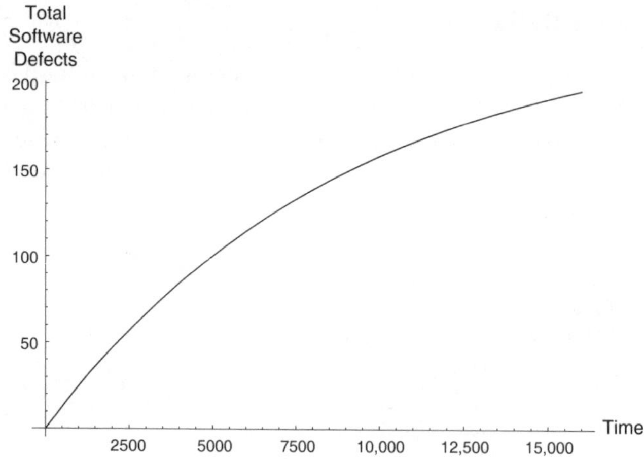

Fig. 1.12. Cumulative reported software bugs

metastable state is an excited energy state with a temporary lifetime that is shorter than the lowest energy, stable state (or *ground* state). There are two identifiable forms of metastable behavior in computer systems:

1. *Microscopic metastability.* This form of metastable behavior occurs in VLSI chips (e.g., synchronizers and arbiters). It can lead to total failure at the system level.
2. *Macroscopic metastability.* This form of metastable behavior occurs in computer systems and computer networks.

We briefly review both forms of metastability. A more detailed discussion of metastability and its deeper consequences for computer performance can be found in Gunther [2000a, Part III].

1.8.1 Microscopic Metastability

All computer systems hardware requires clocking synchronization of some kind to handle interrupts, to perform bus arbitration, to initiate memory refreshes and so on. In general, any computer system that comprises several subsystems each running with different clock generators, requires synchronizers to enable communication between the various subsystems. These synchronizers are usually built upon more elementary devices called flip-flops. The output of the digital synchronizer, shown in Fig. 1.13, simply toggles between a 1 or 0 depending on whether a 1 or 0 appears on the asynchronous input relative to the other input signal, usually a periodic system clock. The synchronized state occurs when the input signal edges rise or fall simultaneously. In more detail, this requires that the edges of the input signals arrive during the required setup and hold windows specified by the tolerances of the synchronizer. From

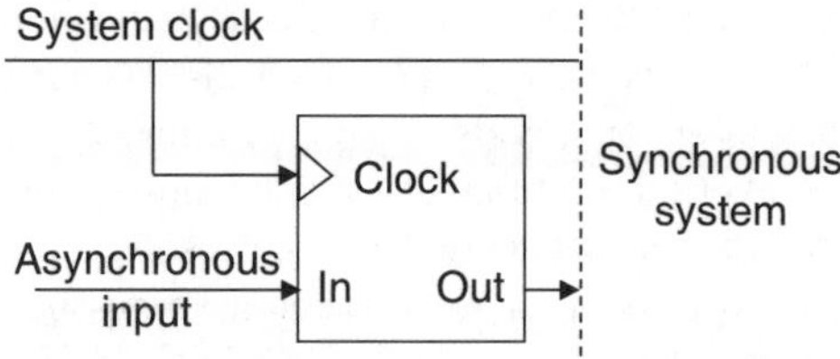

Fig. 1.13. A simple synchronizer circuit

a digital point of view, if the signals fail to meet the transition window in a given clock cycle, they should meet it in the next cycle. There is, however, a third possibility.

When the setup and hold criteria are not met, the synchronizer can go into a third state: a metastable state with the output pin midway between a 1 and 0 (in terms of voltage level). To make matters worse, the length of time the synchronizer might stay in this *undecided* state before resolving to a legitimate 1 or 0 has no limit or bound. All that can be said is the likelihood of a synchronizer output pin staying in a metastable state diminishes exponentially with time according to (1.3). Only after an infinite time would the probability be zero.

In addition, the metastable output can ramify to the inputs of other devices. The gross physical consequences of such microscopic metastability include intermittent memory corruption and other inexplicable system crashes. The intermittency of these effects makes diagnosis extremely difficult. This problem was considered significant enough within the electronics industry that it made the cover of the July 1988 issue of *Electronic Design*. At that time, some people thought there was a way around this problem. It has finally been accepted by engineers that microscopic metastability must be accommodated in a circuit design, since it cannot be totally eliminated.

Accommodating metastability usually takes the form of imposing a sufficient delay to allow any metastable condition to decay into a known state before being propagated. A required delay can be determined if the MTBF can be calculated. We can use the reliability equations derived earlier to calculate that MTBF. Experimental measurements have revealed that the setup window w for the input signal is a function of three parameters: T_0 and τ, which are specific to the type of synchronizer technology being used, and the resolution time $t_{\mathrm{r}} = t_{\mathrm{c}} - t_{\mathrm{s}}$ which is a function of the clock period t_c and the setup time t_{s} [Kleeman and Cantoni 1987]. The width of the window is given by:

$$w = T_0 \, \mathrm{e}^{-\, t_{\mathrm{r}}/\tau} \, . \tag{1.27}$$

If the asynchronous input signal occurs within w, the output of the synchronizer remains metastable for a period greater than the resolution time t_{r}. Equation (1.27) is essentially a restatement that the smaller the timing window, the longer the output will take to resolve (as expressed by t_{r}). A small setup window occurs when the clock edge and asynchronous input occur very close together in time. Conversely, (1.27) also tells us that the resolution time gets exponentially smaller for a wider setup window.

Letting α be the average number of asynchronous input events, the probability that the synchronizer settles within the resolution period t_r (i.e., does not fail) is given by $\exp(-\alpha w)$. If we further assume that the asynchronous events are statistically independent, we can write the reliability R for k input events as:

$$R(t) = [\exp(-\alpha w)]^k \equiv \exp(-\alpha w k) \; . \tag{1.28}$$

Equation (1.16) previously defined the relationship between the mean failure rate and the reliability. Since (1.28) is independent of time, (1.16) takes the simpler form $R = \exp(-\lambda)$. Transposing this expression, we can write the mean failure rate as $\lambda = -\ln R$. Note that λ is also a constant in this case. But the number of input events k is dependent on the clock frequency $f_c = 1/t_c$ and substituting this frequency for k in (1.28) gives the mean failure rate:

$$\lambda = -\ln R \equiv \alpha w f_c \; . \tag{1.29}$$

Taking (1.29) together with the definition for w in (1.27) provides the complete expression for the failure rate:

$$\lambda = \alpha f_c T_0 \, e^{-t_r/\tau} \; . \tag{1.30}$$

The mean failure rate gets exponentially smaller with increasing resolution time. Because we have already assumed an exponential distribution for the inter-arrival time of asynchronous events, the MTBF, according to (1.19), is given by the inverse of the failure rate in equation (1.30). That is:

$$\text{MTBF} \equiv \frac{1}{\lambda} = \frac{e^{-t_r/\tau}}{\alpha f_c T_0} \; . \tag{1.31}$$

Example 1.9. Some typical synchronizer parameter values are $T_0 = 0.40$ s and $\tau = 1.5$ ns. For a 10-MHz system clock the setup time is $t_s = 20$ ns, and hence $t_s < (100 - 20)$ ns or about 80 ns. If the asynchronous input changes at a mean frequency of $\alpha = 100,000$ times per second then the MTBF according to (1.31) is:

$$\text{MTBF} = 3.63 \times 10^{11} \text{ s.}$$

Since we already established that there are 32 × 106 s in a year, this MTBF corresponds to more than 100 centuries! Of course, if 20,000 of these synchronizer chips are sold per year, then at least one device could be expected to fail each year.

Increasing the clock speed can shorten the MTBF disastrously. Suppose the previous system is upgraded to use a 16 MHz clock but the synchronizer components remain in place. What is the new MTBF? Repeating the same calculation procedure gives:

$$\text{MTBF} = 3.1\,\text{s}.$$

It is noteworthy that the MTBF is now much smaller than the MTTR. If it only took an hour to repair the failure (optimistic for such an insidious problem) by replacing the synchronizer with a faster technology, the average availability would become

$$A = 0.086\%\,.$$

This is a numerical definition of "Dead in the water!" The only good news here is that the upgraded computer system would probably never make it beyond any kind of system bootup test without a complete redesign. □

1.8.2 Macroscopic Metastability

The failure of important communication networks over the last decade has become all too familiar. The entire AT&T phone system was brought to its knees in 1990 by a software bug that escaped the quality assurance process. A similar problem occurred in an AT&T frame-relay network on April 14, 1998 that shut down automated bank teller machines and other business activities. These are examples of sudden but hard failures that were publicly attributed to "programming" errors.

1.8.3 Metastability in Networks

It is less obvious that a computer network can become degraded very suddenly even though the average traffic load on the network remains constant. This sudden congestion manifests itself as a spontaneous collapse in performance, seen as an orders-of-magnitude drop in packets/second delivered or a concomitant increase in packet routing delay. Such effects have been seen on the Internet since 1986 and led to the implementation of the *slow start* congestion avoidance algorithm for TCP/IP. The same algorithm that was intended to avoid high packet latency became responsible for slowing down the HTTP 1.0 Web protocol.

Clearly, it is important to understand the dynamics of this kind of performance collapse so as to choose avoidance strategies that are less sensitive to future changes on the Internet. How can we picture the sudden onset of this kind of performance collapse?

The network can be represented as a circuit of queues (Chap 3), where the queues represent individual network devices such as routers and bridges. The state of this system is reflected in the queue lengths at these devices. Packets arrive into a router, possibly enqueue, receive service, and finally depart to the next routing stage. These simultaneous arrivals and departures cause the queue length to fluctuate about some average value. The average queue length determines other performance metrics, e.g., response time and throughput. These metrics can be calculated most easily if the network is in *steady state* with the average queue lengths remaining stable over long periods of time.

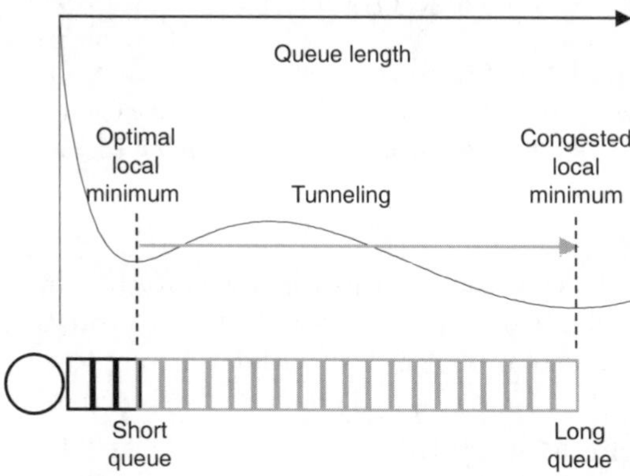

Fig. 1.14. Quantum-like tunneling model of network (router) congestion. The local minimum that corresponds to congestion (*right*) is also the global minimum of the system. Therefore, it will be a long time before the system revisits the optimal minimum (*left*) and the average queue become short again

Under certain conditions, such as that shown in Fig. 1.14, certain queues can fluctuate about more than one stable average length, i.e., a relatively *short* stable average, and a relatively *long* stable average. A long queue means that it will take a long time before a request is serviced, on average. More importantly, the presence of two stable queue lengths implies that the network may fluctuate dynamically between these two extremes. It turns out that this transition between stable queue lengths can occur very suddenly in real networks as well as other computer systems [Gunther 2000a, Part III].

Since the queue lengths are a measure of such important macroscopic performance metrics as response time, it would be very useful to have both a *qualitative* and a *quantitative* understanding of the dynamics of these large fluctuations or large transients. In conventional modeling approaches, large transients are difficult to calculate.

Given that there are two stable queue lengths, it follows that there must be an intermediate or *metastable* state between them—the maximum separating the two stable minima in Fig. 1.14. This metastability is analogous to the microscopic metastability of synchronizers and arbiters discussed in Sect. 1.8.1. A well-known example of such macroscopic metastability is *thrashing* in virtual memory computers. The performance question we would like to address is, for a given load on the computer system, what is the mean time to thrashing?

Example 1.10. Suppose the likelihood of a computer's performance degrading or even failing is exceedingly small, say 0.0001%, and the average request rate for computational processing is ten requests per second. The meantime to reach the critical state of failure or severe degradation can be crudely estimated using (1.30) and (1.31).

Since the parameters are constants, the failure rate is given by the probability of failure multiplied by the access rate:

$$\lambda = 10 \times 10^{-6} ,$$

and the mean time between failures is then given by

$$MTBF = \frac{1}{\lambda} = 10^5 \text{ s},$$

which is about 28 h, or slightly longer than a day! □

1.8.4 Quantumlike Phase Transitions

The author recognized that the problem of estimating the mean transition time is analogous to calculating the decay rate of an atom in quantum mechanics [Gunther 1989]; it is a kind of one-dimensional *phase transition* like that in Fig. 1.14 and known as *quantum tunneling* [See Gunther 2000a,b]. Clearly, a computer or a network, even though it is stochastic, cannot exhibit quantum behavior in the strict sense of that term. For one thing, all the probabilities are real-valued, not complex numbers. However, the formalism of quantum mechanics can be applied if the wave functions are "rotated" in the complex plane. Then, quantum mechanics becomes identical to the stochastic processes described by statistical mechanics [Albert and Barabasi 2002]. This insight is also reflected in the animated logo for `www.perfdynamics.com`. Quantum like phase transition phenomena have since been used to explain the dynamics operating within telephone networks [Gunther 1990], packet-radio networks [Gunther and Shaw 1990], as well as more socially-oriented networks, including everything from stock market crashes [Sornette 2002] to Hollywood blockbusters [DeVany and Walls 1996].

A significant virtue of the tunneling method is that it enables fast numerical computation versus doing very long simulations. It could therefore be used in a predictive way to *shape the network* locally so as to ensure optimal performance without the risk of global performance collapse. Such schemes have been considered for admission control in ATM networks.

Related approaches for estimating mean transition times have included catastrophe theory [Nelson 1984], and large deviations theory [Schwartz and Weiss 1995]. A readable account of the application of large deviations concepts to real communications networks can be found in Walrand and Varaiya [1996].

1.9 Review

In this chapter we reviewed some of the concepts of time that appear in the context of computer system performance analysis. A primary motivation for writing this chapter is the difficulty in finding a discussion of such disparate concepts in one place.

We examined the more common notion of physical time and contrasted it with the less familiar concept of logical time together with the corresponding requirements for implementing both physical and logical clocks. From these concepts we saw the importance of having rules for synchronization to maintain the order of events in distributed computer systems.

Next, we reviewed some of the features of response time, a key system-level performance metric. We saw how there can be significant variation in real measurement data of response times, and that this variation often can be fitted to a gamma probability distribution. In many cases, the gamma distribution simplifies to the exponential distribution. This is the distribution that is assumed in solving most of the queueing circuit models in this book.

Finally, we considered measures of computer reliability and metastability. The exponential distribution also plays an important role there. Metastability can have a significant impact on computer system performance.

Exercises

1.1. Time zones. What is the current time in Timbuktu? Use the Perl `tzset` function to confirm your answer.

1.2. Timing chains. For the timing chain in Fig. 1.6, each "link" has the following maximal data rates:

Client CPU	500 TPS
NIC card	2400 pkt/s
LAN network	1050 pkt/s
Router	7000 pkt/s
WAN network	800 pkt/s
Server CPU	120 TPS
Server Disk	52.25 IO/s

Where is the bottleneck for a transaction workload that generates 20 pkt/s and 1 disk I/O?

1.3. Time representations. (**a**) Using the fields: `$sec`, `$min`, `$hour`, `$mday`, `$mon`, `$year`, `$wday`, `$yday`, `$isdst`, as arguments to the Perl function `timelocal`, find the integer value of your birth date.
(**b**) Check its correctness by converting the integer to the number of years since the zeroth epoch on your platform.

1.4. Availability. The MTBF of a computer system is 720 h, or approximately 1 month of continuous operation. The MTTR is 3 h. (**a**) Using (1.22), what is the availability of this system?
(**b**) How much downtime does this represent over the course of a year?

2

Getting the Jump on Queueing

2.1 Introduction

Think about the times you have had to wait in line because other people wanted the same thing you did, and you get that sinking feeling so often associated with the phenomenon of queueing, the bane of modernity. You queue while commuting to work, while boarding an aircraft, at a grocery store, at the post office, the doctor's office or connecting to a Web site (TCP listen queue).

In this chapter, you will learn how to characterize the phenomenon of queueing from a more technical standpoint, one that is useful for analyzing the performance of computer systems. What makes queueing concepts valuable for the performance analyst is the ability to estimate important performance metrics, for example, response time and throughput, based on measurable queue attributes such as server utilization.

Unfortunately, what makes queueing concepts difficult for many performance analysts is that queues involve random (or stochastic) behavior that makes their application unintuitive—especially when expressed in terms of the usual mathematics found in most textbooks on queueing theory. Consequently, a large class of people who should be using queueing concepts are excluded by its impenetrability.

The purpose of this chapter in particular, and this book in general, is to remove that impediment. You should think of the queueing concepts presented here as a kind of *lingua franca* for performance analysis. After reading this chapter, you will have a clearer understanding of terms like *throughput*, *residence time*, and *utilization* and the relationships between them.

In this chapter we focus on single queues where a customer or request only visits one queueing center and then departs (also known as *open* queues) or returns to the same queue (also known as *closed* queues). In the next chapter, we consider requests that are serviced by many queues because multiple queues are required to analyze the performance of real computer systems.

Many of the more mathematical aspects of probability theory will be deliberately suppressed through the use of averages. This means that higher moments, such as the variance, cannot be calculated directly, but we can apply some percentile rules of thumb. After reading this chapter you should have a stronger intuitive understanding of the basic performance metrics and how they are interrelated through the characterization of queues.

The general idea is to jump-start you into some of the most powerful results in queueing theory without invoking much more than high-school algebra. In Chap. 3 we extend these basics concepts to systems of queues for analyzing real computer systems. To help you locate a queueing formula in the future, the *Compendium* in Appendix E provides a summary with cross-references to all the formulas presented here and in the next chapter. We commence with some definitions.

2.2 What Is a Queue?

Like the notion of time discussed in Chap. 1, we begin by checking the dictionary definition. Merriam-Webster online `www.m-w.com/` states:

> Main Entry: **queue**
> Pronunciation: 'kyü
> Function: *noun*
> Etymology: French, literally, tail, from Latin *cauda, coda*
> **2 :** a waiting line especially of persons or vehicles.
> **3 a :** a sequence of messages or jobs held in auxiliary storage awaiting transmission or processing. **b :** a data structure that consists of a list of records such that records are added at one end and removed from the other.

Perhaps more significantly for this book, a queue is the natural paradigm for representing a *buffer*. For the moment, we assume the the queue has unlimited waiting room.

Understanding and predicting the availability of telephone lines led to one of the earliest applications of formal queueing theory [Erlang 1917]. Given that a telephone system is comprised of a complex switching network, it may surprise you to know that queueing theory was not robustly applied to the performance analysis of computer systems until almost 40 years ago [Scherr 1967, Moore 1971, Buzen 1971]. The reason for this historical lag is discussed in Appendix B.

2.3 The Grocery Store—Checking It Out

Consider a familiar occurrence of queueing: a trip to the grocery store or supermarket. Having obtained all the items on your grocery list, you head for the checkout stands. There, you find lines of customers waiting to be served: the queues (Fig. 2.1). You survey those queues to find the shortest line. Or, perhaps you also glance at the size of the loads in each shopping cart ahead of you. You continue to strategize briefly over which queue you *think* will deplete the fastest until, finally, you give up thinking about it and just join one. Having joined the line you think is likely to have the best performance,

Fig. 2.1. A typical grocery store checkout. A customer with a loaded shopping cart arrives at the left only to enqueue with customers already waiting (some of whom are getting impatient), while an already served customer happily departs the store

you are shocked to see that the customer currently having their groceries rung up needs a price check on that item. Your waiting time now goes through the roof. When this happens to me, I prefer to think of a queue as a line of customers waiting to be *severed*!

2.3.1 Queueing Analysis View

Now, here is the grocery store scenario in queueing parlance. The checkout aisles are the queues, and the cashier is the service center or server. Using our schematic symbols, the situation at the grocery store can be represented more abstractly by Fig. 2.2. In a large grocery store there are perhaps ten or more

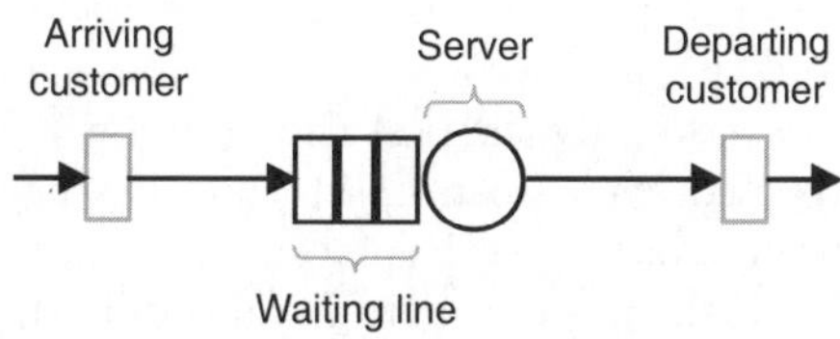

Fig. 2.2. Grocery checkout represented as queueing center

checkouts. This battery of checkouts form parallel centers or parallel queues shown schematically in Fig. 2.3.

You, the customer in the grocery store, are a request token in the queue belonging to the checkout aisle you have selected. As each customer ahead of you reaches the cashier, a certain amount of time is required to ring up and bag their groceries. This is called the service time. Full shopping carts take longer to service than ones with fewer items. That is why you checked all the carts ahead before finally joining your checkout line. The combined waiting time and service time is called the residence time (denoted R). Many grocery

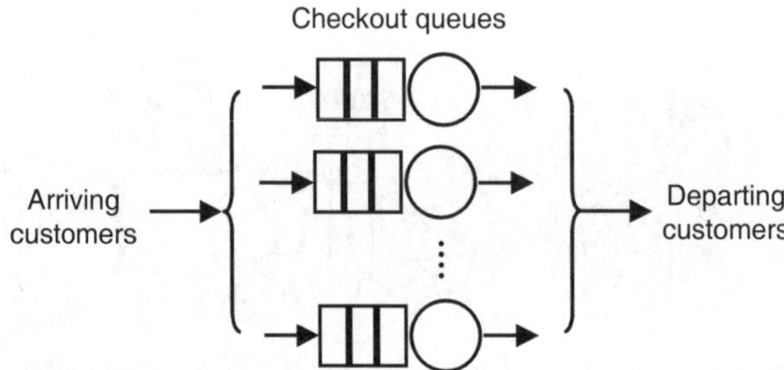

Fig. 2.3. Grocery store checkouts represented as parallel queues

stores provide an express lane for customers with fewer than ten purchase items. Such customers are treated as a special class. With one express lane, there are two customer classes defined by their respective service times (i.e., the number items in their grocery carts). Other stores further distinguish customers based on whether or not they will pay by credit card or cash. This corresponds to three customer classes, and so on.

2.3.2 Perceptions and Deceptions

If you had fewer than ten items but the express line happened to be unusually long you might decide to join one of the shorter lines at a regular checkout. Even if the service times are longer, your closer proximity to the cashier may lead to a shorter residence time. In taking this risk you have also created a multiclass queue.

Notice that the word risk was used. You cannot be certain that your guess about which line to join was really the best choice and will lead to the shortest residence time. Unexpected events can upset your strategy. The customer in service discovers an item is damaged. Replacement means an assistant has to physically locate the shelf the item came from and bring the replacement item back to the checkout stand. In the meantime service is halted and frustration sets in. The automated teller machine goes offline or a customer decides to write a check as payment. Whatever the cause, the residence time appears to be unpredictable.

A more subtle level of uncertainty involves your assumption about constant service times. It was an unfounded assumption because every customer ahead of you in the queue had a different number of items (most greater than ten presumably), so the actual service times will vary considerably. With all this uncertainty, it is surprising we ever endure grocery shopping at all!

2.3.3 The Post Office—Snail Mail

By way of contrast, a different example of everyday queueing occurs in the post office—a recognized time waster. A rather obvious difference between

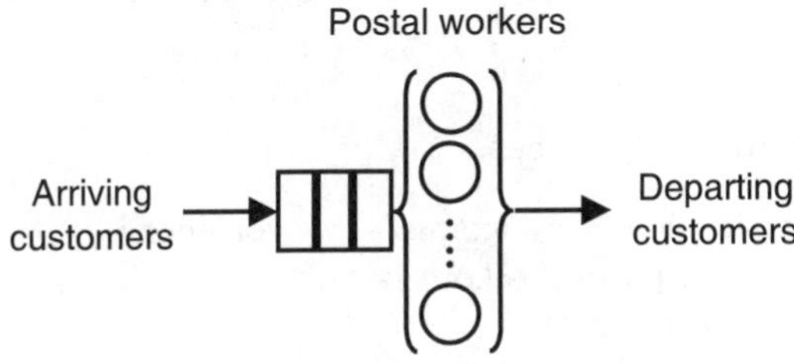

Fig. 2.4. Post office represented as multiserver queueing center

the post office and the grocery store is the existence of just one queue with multiple servers viz, postal clerks (2.4). Is this the reason it seems to take forever in the post office? Would it be more efficient if the post office used parallel queues like the grocery store? We shall address these questions in Sect. 2.10.2.

2.4 Fundamental Metric Relationships

To further formalize the characteristics of queues for the purpose of computer performance analysis, we introduce some simple mathematical relationships based solely on measurable performance quantities. The sophisticated name used to describe this approach is operational analysis, and the formalism was developed primarily by Denning and Buzen [1978]. Several textbooks on computer performance analysis [see, e.g., Lazowska et al. 1984] base their queueing methods on this operational approach. We adopt many of the same notational conventions. The rest of this chapter presents these observational or opera-

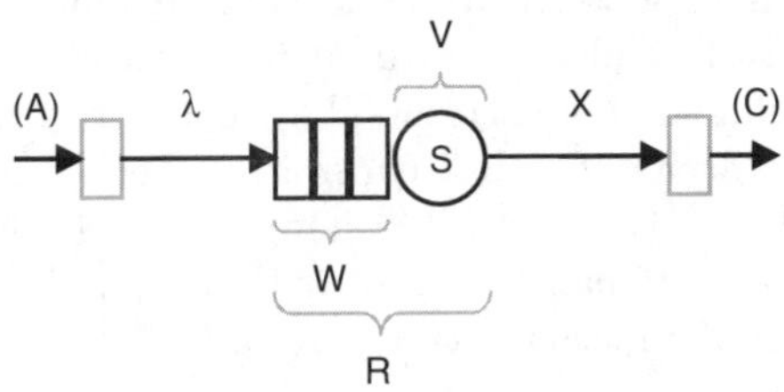

Fig. 2.5. Components of a queueing center

tional laws and only requires a knowledge of intermediate algebra. These observational laws are the key to understanding the major results of queueing theory and their practical application to computer performance analysis. After reading this chapter, you should have a good grasp of the essentials of queueing theory without having been consumed by the imponderable mathematics of probability that usually accompanies expositions on formal queueing theory.

2.4.1 Performance Measures

Returning to our grocery store example, we consider how to characterize the performance a grocery store checkout in terms of the fundamental measurable quantities listed in Table 2.1.

Table 2.1. Measurable performance quantities

T	Total observation time or measurement period
K	Total number of queueing nodes k in the system
A	Count of arrivals into system during measurement period T
A_k	Count of arrivals into queue k during measurement period T
C	Count of global system completions during the period T
C_k	Count of completions that departed the queue k during T
V_k	Count of repeated visits to the server k during T
B_k	Total time server k was busy during measurement period T

In this chapter we mostly discuss single queues, i.e., a single waiting line feeding one or more servers. In Chap. 3 we discuss the representation of computer systems by more than one queueing center or *node* in the terminology of PDQ (Chap. 6). It will be convenient to have a way to enumerate which queue we are talking about. For this purpose we introduce a k-subscript notation for each queueing parameter. In this chapter, $K = 1$, but for a queueing network with $K > 1$ queues the subscript k has the range of values $1 \leq k \leq K$. Properties that refer to the entire queueing system will generally have the k-subscript suppressed. When it is obvious that we are discussing a single queue, we will also tend to drop the k-subscript to keep equations uncluttered.

Counts, such as A_k and C_k, are used by a variety of generic UNIX performance tools. Different k's correspond to counters belonging to different device drivers, e.g., drivers for disk controllers (Sect. 1.6.3) and network interface cards (Sect. 1.6.4). Figure 2.6 shows the packet counts produced by the Solaris® `netstat` command. The busy time B_k is the aggregate of all the busy periods during the measurement period T. A busy period occurs when the server is not idle.

Example 2.1. To make the performance characterization concrete, suppose we stand near the checkout counter for a period of $T = 30$ minutes and use a

```
Name Mtu  Net/Dest  Address   Ipkts    Ierrs Opkts   Oerrs Collis Q
lo0  8232 loopback  localhost 77814    0     77814   0     0      0
hme0 1500 server1   server1   10658566 3     4832511 0     279257 0
```

Fig. 2.6. Output of Solaris `netstat -i` command showing packet counts

stopwatch to measure the time it takes for the cashier to ring up the groceries of 10 customers. The measured busy periods (in minutes) are noted down as: 1.23, 2.01, 3.11, 1.02, 1.54, 2.69, 3.41, 2.87, 2.22, 2.83. As an expedient, we can assign these values to a Perl array variable called `@busyData` and compute a set of performance measures programatically. □

Since we have collected the busy period measurements for 10 customers, there must have been $C = 10$ completions, and therefore at least $A = 10$ arrivals, during the $T = 30$ min measurement period. This gives us enough data to calculate the arrival rate and throughput.

2.4.2 Arrival Rate

In keeping with queueing theory notation, we denote the system arrival rate by λ. Based on Fig. 2.5 it is defined as:

$$\lambda = \frac{A}{T}, \tag{2.1}$$

where A denotes the arrival count in Table 2.1. If we measured the checkout for a relatively short period T, we would expect the number of customers completing service to be different from the number of customers that arrived at the checkout during the same period.

We could have a situation where $C = 10$ customers complete in $T = 30$ min but $A = 18$ customers have arrived in that same period. However, if we assume that the number of customers arriving at the checkout does not cause the queue to grow in an unbounded way (see the stability condition (2.27)), and we measure the checkout for a sufficiently long period of time, it is legitimate to expect that the number of customers completing service C will be very close to the number of customers A that arrived at the checkout during that same period. In other words, $A = C$ as $T \to \infty$. Dividing both A and C by the measurement period T to produce (2.1) and (2.4) respectively, we can define this *steady state* condition:

$$\lambda = X\,, \tag{2.2}$$

as a matching of the *input* and *output* rates. Equation (2.2) is referred to as the *Flow Balance* assumption [Lazowska et al. 1984]. We have suppressed the subscripts because it is completely generalizable to the system level.

We want the difference $(\lambda - X)$ to be small. In practice this criterion is usually satisfied by choosing the measurement period T to be one to two orders of magnitude longer than the average busy period, as it is in Example 2.1. Using those measurements together with the steady state assumption (2.2), the Perl program in Example 2.2 calculates a numerical value for the arrival rate.

Example 2.2.

```
#! /usr/bin/perl
# arrivals.pl

# Array of measured busy periods (min)
@busyData = (1.23, 2.01, 3.11, 1.02, 1.54, 2.69, 3.41, 2.87,
    2.22, 2.83);

$T_period = 30;                      # Measurement period (min)
$A_count = @busyData;                # Steady-state assumption
$A_rate = $A_count / $T_period; # Arrival rate

printf("Arrival count      (A): %6d \n", $A_count);
printf("Arrival rate (lambda): %6.2f Cust/min\n", $A_rate);

# Output ...
# Arrival count      (A):     10
# Arrival rate (lambda):   0.33 Cust/min
```

□

The inverse of the arrival rate $1/\lambda_k$ is called the *interarrival* period.

In the context of intrinsic computer performance measurement tools the parameters A_k and C_k correspond to internal *counters*, usually implemented as memory locations or registry objects in the operating system. The reported *rates* λ_k and X_k, such as kB/s or pkts/s, are calculated from those counters by the resident performance tools using the relations (2.3) and (2.1). For example, Fig. 2.6 shows paging I/O rates reported by the Solaris `vmstat` command.

```
procs  memory            page                 disk          faults          cpu
r b w swap  free re mf pi p fr de sr s0 s1 s2 s3  in  sy  cs us sy id
0 0 0 11456 4120 1  41 19 1  3  0  2  0  4  0  0  48 112 130  4 14 82
0 0 1 10132 4280 0   4 44 0  0  0  0  0 23  0  0 211 230 144  3 35 62
0 0 1 10132 4616 0   0 20 0  0  0  0  0 19  0  0 150 172 146  3 33 64
0 0 1 10132 5292 0   0  9 0  0  0  0  0 21  0  0 165 105 130  1 21 78
```

Fig. 2.7. Output of Solaris `vmstat` command showing paging I/O rates

In passing, we note that UNIX is really an experiment that escaped from "the lab" some 30 years ago and has been mutating ever since. It was never intended that the simple counters, originally implemented by developers to gauge the performance impact of changing the kernel code [Saltzer and Gintell 1970], would still be used today by a vast array of commercial and noncommercial performance management tools. A similar comment can be made about other operating systems. Moreover, the operating system is only one source of performance data, and a very limited one in the context of modern distributed applications. It is curious then that attempts to standardize on a broader collection framework with multiple data sources (Appendix D) have not been widely publicized by vendors or demanded by customers.

2.4.3 System Throughput

Referring to Fig. 2.5, the system throughput (no subscripts):

$$X = \frac{C}{T}, \tag{2.3}$$

is defined as the total number of requests that completed service during the measurement period. Using the measurements in Example 2.1 we write a simple Perl program (Example 2.3) to calculate a numerical value for the system throughput at the grocery store checkout.

Example 2.3.

```
#! /usr/bin/perl
# thruput1.pl

# Array of measured busy periods (min)
@busyData = (1.23, 2.01, 3.11, 1.02, 1.54, 2.69, 3.41, 2.87,
    2.22, 2.83);

$T_period = 30;                     # Measurement period (min)
$C_count = @busyData;               # Completion count
$X =  $C_count / $T_period;         # System throughput
printf("Completion count  (C): %6d \n", $C_count);
printf("System throughput (X): %6.2f Cust/min\n", $X);
printf("Normalized throughput: %6d Cust every %4.2f min\n", 1, 1/$X);

# Output ...
# Completion count  (C):     10
# System throughput (X):   0.33 Cust/min
# Normalized throughput:      1 Cust every 3.00 min
```

□

The throughput is 0.33 customers per minute or, expressed a little more intuitively, 1 customer completes every 3 min.

2.4.4 Nodal Throughput

Whereas the system throughput in (2.3) can be thought of as a *global* view of throughput, each queueing node can also have its own *local* throughput:

$$X_k = C_k/T\,. \tag{2.4}$$

In the case where there is only one queue, the nodal throughput (2.4) is identical to (2.3). The system throughput (and other system parameters) have no subscript.

2.4.5 Relative Throughput

As noted in Chap. 1, real computer system is generally comprised of a number of subsystems such as processors, disks, various types of memories that operate on different time scales. We could measure the completions at each component subsystem (*local* completions), and we could also measure the throughput of the entire computer system (*global* completions). In general, we would get different results because the completions are measured in different units. The number of local disk operations, for example, is likely to be more than the number of global database transactions because each completed transaction invokes multiple reads and writes.

These local and global measures can be related via the so-called *forced flow law* which states that the number of local completions and global completions must be proportional:

$$C_k \propto C\,. \tag{2.5}$$

in steady-state. The constant of proportionality is the number of local operations executed during T or the *visit count* V_k. Hence,

$$C_k = V_k C\,. \tag{2.6}$$

If a single database transaction requires 3 disk operations, then there must be $V_{\text{disk}} = C_k/C = 3$ visits to the disk per transaciton. If we divide both sides of this proportionality by T and substitute (2.4) we find:

$$X_k = V_k X\,, \tag{2.7}$$

which is called the *relative throughput*. The forced flow law requires that the throughputs (or flows) must also be in relative proportion in steady-state. The visit count is not always an integer.

Example 2.4. A database server pulls 20,108 tmpC in a TPC-C benchmark. Each transaction induces approximately 6 IO/s at a disk. How many disks should be configured for the benchmark?

$$\frac{20,108 \text{ tpmC}}{60 \text{ s}} = 335.13 \text{ TPS}.$$

By the forced flow law (2.7):

$$V_{disk} = \frac{6 \text{ IO/s}}{335.13 \text{ TPS}} = 0.018 = \frac{1}{55.56} \text{ IO per transaction} .$$

Therefore, each TPC-C transaction requires at least 56 physical disks. □

We shall make use of the concept of relative throughput in Chap. 3.

2.4.6 Service Time

The service time is the time spent per customer at the actual cash register of the checkout at the grocery store. More formally, the average service time at a particular queueing node k

$$S_k = \frac{B_k}{C_k} , \tag{2.8}$$

is the busy time B_k per customer.

Example 2.5.

```
#! /usr/bin/perl
# servtime.pl

# Array of measured busy periods (min)
@busyData = (1.23, 2.01, 3.11, 1.02, 1.54, 2.69, 3.41, 2.87,
    2.22, 2.83);

# Compute the aggregate busy time
foreach $busy (@busyData) {
    $B_server += $busy;
}

$C_server = @busyData;                 # Completions
$S_time = $B_server / $C_server;      # Service time (min)
printf("Number of completions (C): %6d \n", $C_server);
printf("Aggregate busy time   (B): %6.2f min\n", $B_server);
printf("Mean Service time     (S): %6.2f min\n", $S_time);

# Output ...
# Number of completions (C):     10
# Aggregate busy time   (B):  22.93 min
# Mean Service time     (S):   2.29 min
```

□

Equation (2.8) can be read as *the busy time per customer.* Since S_k has the units of time (min in Example 2.5), the corresponding rate $\mu = 1/S_k$ is formed from the inverse of (2.8) and is called the *service rate.* It provides an alternative way to characterize a server. In general, we prefer to use the service time throughout this book.

2.4.7 Service Demand

Implicit in the definition of (2.8) is the notion that the customer, or request, only requires one visit to the server. When multiple visits are required (e.g., when a customer forgets to purchase an item at the grocery store in Sect. 2.3), we generalize the definition of service time to:

$$D_k = V_k S_k \,, \tag{2.9}$$

where V_k is the average number of visits to queueing center. D_k is called the *service demand.* We shall consider the precise definition of V_k in Chap. 3. In subsequent expressions for derived performance metrics such as residence time and queue length, the reader should keep in mind that they can be expressed in terms of the service demand D_k. For clarity, however, we shall replace D_k by S_k without loss of generality.

2.4.8 Utilization

Following queueing theory convention, the utilization is denoted by ρ. The utilization of the server at queueing node k is the fraction of time that the server is busy during the measurement period T. More formally:

$$\rho_k = \frac{B_k}{T} \,. \tag{2.10}$$

Since the busy time cannot exceed the measurement period ($B_k \leq T$), it follows that the utilization is bounded in the range:

$$0 \leq \rho_k \leq 1 \,. \tag{2.11}$$

Since ρ_k in (2.10) is a ratio of two times, it has no formal units (it is *dimensionless*) and is therefore often expressed as a percentage.

Applying (2.10) to the data in Example 2.1 the utilization of the checkout cashier is calculated in Example 2.3.

Example 2.6.

```
#! /usr/bin/perl
# utiliz1.pl

# Array of measured busy periods (min)
@busyData = (1.23, 2.01, 3.11, 1.02, 1.54, 2.69, 3.41, 2.87,
    2.22, 2.83);

# Compute the aggregate busy time
foreach $busy (@busyData) {
    $B_server += $busy;
}
```

```
$T_period = 30;                    # Measurement period (min)
$rho = $B_server / $T_period;      # Utilization
printf("Busy time   (B): %6.2f min\n", $B_server);
printf("Utilization (U): %6.2f or %4.2f%%\n", $rho, 100 * $rho);

# Output ...
# Busy time   (B):  22.93 min
# Utilization (U):   0.76 or 76.43%
```

□

As Example 2.3 demonstrates, it is preferable to use the decimal representation of ρ during the calculation and convert to percentages at the end. In Sect. 2.5, we shall see that the server utilization can also be defined in terms of another fundamental relationship called *Little's law.*

2.4.9 Residence Time

The average *residence time* R_k is the total time spent at the queueing center. It is the total time you spend getting through the checkout in the case of the grocery store. It is the sum of the average time spent waiting in line W_k together with the average service time S_k once you get to the cashier (Fig. 2.5). More formally:

$$R_k = W_k + S_k \ . \tag{2.12}$$

Similarly, the time you spend at the dentist is the time you spend in the *waiting room* plus the time you spend in the *chair.*

In contrast to the residence time, the average *response time*:

$$R = \sum_k^K R_k \ , \tag{2.13}$$

is the sum of the average residence times (2.12) at each of k queueing centers in a system of queues (see Chap 3). This is also referred to as the *end-to-end* response time. When $k = 1$, the response time and the residence time are identical. We shall these terms interchangeably when the meaning is clear from the context.

Although (2.12) provides a fundamental definition of residence time, very often both the residence time and the waiting time need to be calculated. In other words, if we do not know W_k, we cannot determine R_k. We need expressions for the residence time that do not involve W_k directly, and that is what we consider in the following sections.

2.5 Little's Law Means a Lot

Sometimes even seasoned performance analysts fail to appreciate just how powerful averages can be for understanding the otherwise very complicated dynamics of queues. One of the most powerful application of averages is contained in a simple mathematical relation known as Little's law. Little's law appears in many guises throughout the literature on performance analysis of both computer systems and manufacturing systems.

In queueing theory notation, Little's law:

$$Q_k = \lambda \, R_k \,, \tag{2.14}$$

states that the average queue length Q is equal to the average arrival rate λ into the queueing center defined by (2.1) multiplied by the time spent at the queueing center, i.e., the average residence time R defined by (2.12). Applying the definitions of the utilization (2.10) and arrival rate (2.1), we can also write:

$$\rho_k = \frac{C_k}{T} \times \frac{B_k}{C_k} = \lambda \, S_k \,. \tag{2.15}$$

This is a special case of (2.14) where the waiting time prior to receiving service is not included.

2.5.1 A Little Intuition

Equation (2.14) can be appreciated intuitively with the aid of the following example. It is the "rush hour" commute and you are stuck in traffic at the entrance to a toll way. At this time of day it takes 15 min to get past the toll booths and onto the freeway. While waiting, you start counting cars arriving at the toll-way entrance during a 5 min interval. You see 25 new cars in 5 min. How many cars are waiting with you at the toll entrance? Little's law tells us how to estimate that number.

We know the arrival rate λ is 25 new cars in a 5 min period, and we know that it takes 15 min to get through the toll entrance, which is our residence time R. Applying (2.14) produces:

$$\frac{25 \text{ new cars}}{5 \text{ min}} \times 15 \text{ min} = 75 \text{ cars} \,. \tag{2.16}$$

Here, $Q = 25$ cars refers to the total number of cars enqueued at the toll entrance. It is an average value because there may actually be more or fewer cars, statistically speaking. If a sufficient number of measurements are repeated, however, they should converge to the value predicted by Little's law.

Seen in this way, Little's law may not appear all that remarkable. But remember that queues, like a toll-way entrance or the line at the grocery checkout, are subject to significant fluctuations over short intervals of time. The exact number of cars or customers enqueued at any instant cannot be known ahead of time, it can only be expressed as a probability estimate. Even in the presence of fluctuations, however, an essential feature of queueing can be expressed in terms of the average quantities in Little's law. This result is actually more general than queueing theory and J. D. Little [1961] (see `www.`

informs.org/Prizes/whoisLittle.html) has his name attached to (2.14) because he was the first to prove it mathematically in a way that included the complexity of fluctuations. In Sect. 2.5.2 we present a simpler graphical proof.

As a reminder of complexity involved in queueing, Fig. 2.8 shows the number of customers in a single queueing center as a function of time. The height of each bar corresponds to the number of resident customers at each time step. The time series in Fig.2.8 looks erratic. That is because it is erratic!

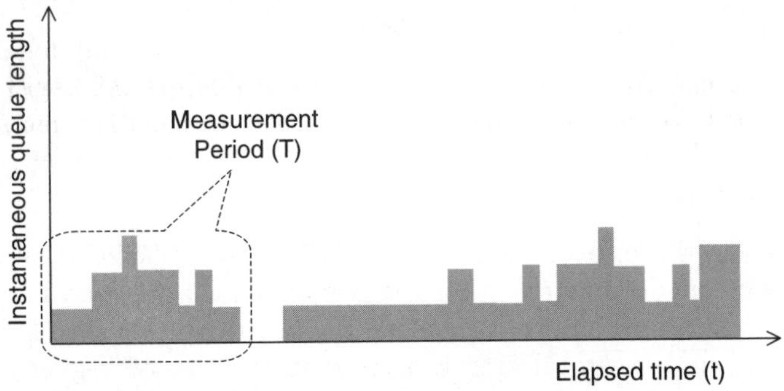

Fig. 2.8. The instantaneous value of the queue length or the number of customers in the system as a function of time t. These values are reported in performance monitoring tools like the UNIX load average (discussed in Chap. 4)

It is *stochastic*. Arrivals and departures at the queueing center are stochastic processes that are represented by probability distributions. As promised in Sect. 2.1, our goal throughout this book is to understand and apply the results of queueing theory without getting too deeply into the mathematics of stochastic processes. A fundamental relationship that helps to make this possible is Little's law.

2.5.2 A Visual Proof

In this section we examine more closely what happens in the queueing process to see how the average quantities in Little's law can be extracted from the otherwise erratic behavior of queues. In Fig. 2.9, we have plotted a section of Fig.2.8 in such a way as show both arriving customers (the upper curve) and departing customers (the lower curve) at each time step during some measurement period T. The area contained in the shaded region between the two curves corresponds to the total number of customer-seconds elapsed during the measurement period T. It is defined by end points where the number of arrivals equals the number of departures. The reason for this assumption is to ensure that customers are not spontaneously created or removed from the

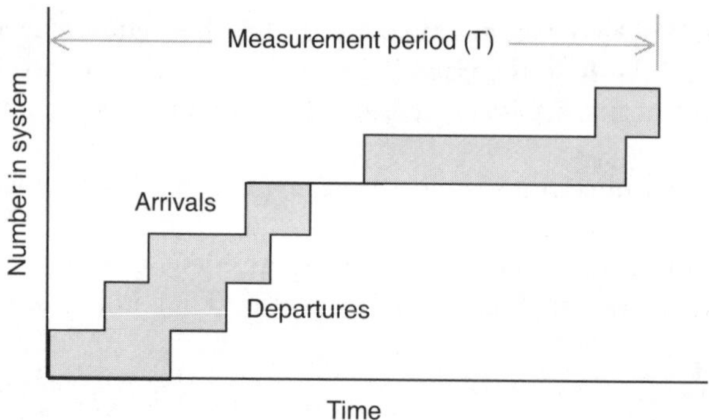

Fig. 2.9. The number of arrivals (*upper edge*) and departures (*lower edge*) per time step. The *shaded region* is the number of customers remaining in the system per time step

system during the measurement period. The system is said to be *work conserving.* We now demonstrate that the size of shaded area can be calculated in two different ways, and that equating the two results leads to Little's law.

First, we find the total area contained in the shaded region of Fig. 2.9 by summing the six *horizontal* subrectangles marked out in Fig. 2.10. The numerical values are summarized in Table 2.2 with the corresponding column totals presented on the last line. Each rectangle has either unit height (corresponding to one arrival) or zero height (corresponding to no arrivals). Recalling the definition for the measured number of arrivals, A in Table 2.1, we see that the total height corresponds to the cumulative number of arrivals during the measurement period. Since there are 6 non-zero steps, $A = 6$ total arrivals during T.

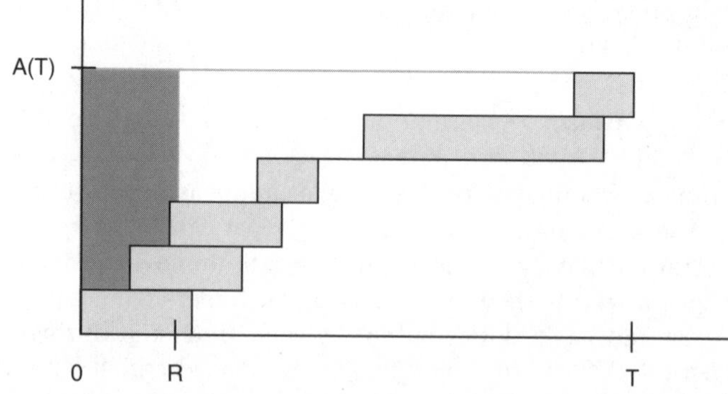

Fig. 2.10. Shaded area of Fig. 2.9 arranged into 6 horizontal rectangles. The large uniform rectangle (*left*) of dimension $A \times R$ represents the equivalent aggregated area

The numbers in the right column of Table 2.2 are the individual rectangle areas, and their sum gives the area of the shaded region:

$$area = sum\ of\ rectangular\ areas = 11 \text{ units}. \qquad (2.17)$$

The height of each rectangle is 1 unit. The width of each horizontal rectangle (the left column of Table 2.2) represents the actual time each arrival spends in the system. The area can also be calculated as the sum of these widths

Table 2.2. Data for horizontal rectangles. The last row shows the totals for each column. Note that the segment with no rectangle (*center*) does not contribute since there is no new arrival in that step

Rectangle	Width	Height	Area
1	2.00	1	2.00
2	2.00	1	2.00
3	2.00	1	2.00
4	1.00	1	1.00
5	3.00	1	3.00
6	1.00	1	1.00
	11.00	6	11.00

multiplied by their common height:

$$area = common\ height \times total\ width = (1 \times 11.00) = 11.00 \text{ units}. \qquad (2.18)$$

The average residence time R is the average time that arrivals spend in the system. Therefore R corresponds to the average rectangular width in Fig. 2.10. Equivalently, R is the total width divided by the number of rectangles. Multiplying and dividing (2.18) by the six horizontal rectangles produces:

$$area = (6 \times height) \times \frac{total\ width}{6} = A \times R. \qquad (2.19)$$

In this last step of our analysis of the horizontal rectangles in Fig. 2.10, we see that the shaded area corresponds to the total number of arrivals during T multiplied by their average residence time.

Turning now to Fig. 2.11, we calculate the shaded area of Fig. 2.9 by summing the eleven *vertical* rectangles. The results are summarized in Table 2.3. The sum of the rectangle widths, by definition, must equal the length of the measurement period $T = 8$. The width of each rectangle corresponds to a time interval where there was no change in either the number of arrivals or departures. The height of each vertical rectangle corresponds to the number of customers in the system during that time interval. If the intervals were infinitesimally small, the height of each vertical rectangle would correspond to the *instantaneous* number of customers in the system or the instantaneous queue length. The time-averaged number of customers in the system Q is given

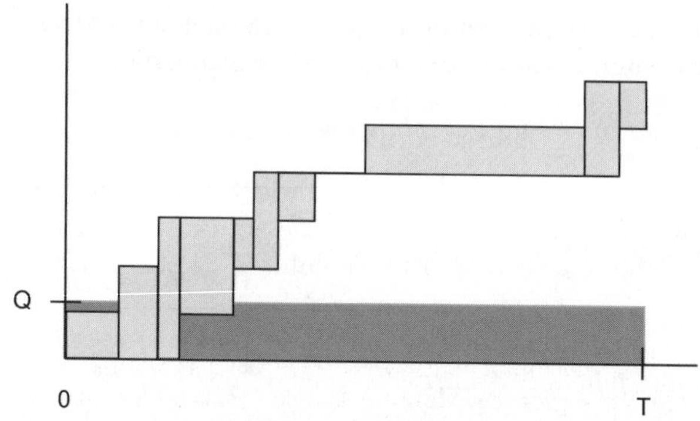

Fig. 2.11. Shaded area of Fig. 2.9 arranged into 11 vertical rectangles. The shaded region shows the equivalent area aggregated into a uniform rectangle of dimension $Q \times T$

by the sum of all the vertical rectangle areas divided by the total measurement period T:

$$Q = \frac{sum\ of\ vertical\ areas}{T} . \tag{2.20}$$

In Fig. 2.11, Q is shown as a large uniform rectangle at the bottom of the figure. It is the average number of customers in the system during the measurement period T.

Table 2.3. Data for vertical rectangles. The last row shows the totals for each column, Here, the 8th rectangle width is part of the total measurement period even though it has zero height

Rectangle	Width	Height	Area
1	1.00	1	1.00
2	1.00	2	2.00
3	0.25	3	0.75
4	1.00	2	2.00
5	0.25	1	0.25
6	0.50	2	1.00
7	0.50	1	0.50
8	0.50	0	0.00
9	2.00	1	2.00
10	0.50	2	1.00
11	0.50	1	0.50
	8.00	16	11.00

To arrive at Little's law, we need to relate the shaded area in Fig. 2.9 to the average number of customers Q in the system. Multiplying and dividing the area in Fig. 2.11 by the measurement period T produces:

$$area = \frac{sum\ of\ vertical\ areas}{T} \times T = Q \times T. \tag{2.21}$$

where we substituted (2.20) for Q. From this analysis of the vertical rectangles we find that the shaded area corresponds to the average number of customers in the system multiplied by the measurement period.

Finally, bringing all these areal relationships together we establish Little's result. From (2.19) we know that the area can be expressed as $AR = 11$ units. We also know from (2.1), that the measured arrivals is related to the arrival rate by $A = \lambda T$ so (2.19) can be rewritten as:

$$area\ (horizontal) = 11 = (\lambda T)R. \tag{2.22}$$

From (2.21) we know that the area can also be expressed as:

$$area\ (vertical) = 11 = QT. \tag{2.23}$$

Since the areas are identical, we can combine (2.22) and (2.23) into a single equation:

$$QT = (\lambda T)R, \tag{2.24}$$

which, after canceling the factors of T, reduces to (2.14), as promised.

This visual proof brings out another important point. So far, we have not been very clear about what we meant by the term *average*. Little's law refers to the average number of customers in the queueing system (under the assumption that it is work conserving). But averaged over what?

In the above example $Q = \lambda R = 0.75 \times 1.8333 = 1.375$ customers. Could we not have estimated the same number using the data in Table 2.3? The total of the Width column is the period $T = 8$, and the total of the Height column is $N = 16$, the aggregate number of customers in the system during T. Therefore, we might expect that N/T should give us the correct average for Q. But $N/T = 16/8 = 2$. Alternatively, if we average N over the number of vertical rectangles V, we get $N/V = 16/11 = 1.455$. Why are all these averages different?

The average N/V is simply an *arithmetic* average of the rectangle heights, not a *time-based* average. Since $N > V$, the ratio N/V overestimates the value of Q. The average formed by N/T on the other hand, assumes the sample intervals (widths) are uniform when, in fact, they are not. Each rectangle needs to be weighted by its width to give the correct proportion of time that a customer spends in the system relative to T. The timebase is correct but the customer population is not weighted correctly so N/T incorrectly estimates Q. From this we see the importance of the term *time-weighted average*. We return to this concept in Chap. 4.

2.5.3 Little's Microscopic Law

As we did in the case of deriving Little's law, let us assume a computer system can be treated as a black box with measurement duration sufficient to justify the assumption that the number of arrivals into the system equals the number of completions departing from it. The utilization of a server, defined in (2.10), is the average fraction of time the server is busy. We can rewrite ρ as:

$$\rho = \frac{C}{T} \times \frac{B}{C}. \tag{2.25}$$

On substituting (2.4) and (2.8) into (2.25) it becomes:

$$\rho = X\,S = \lambda\,S. \tag{2.26}$$

It is *microscopic* version of Little's law, also known as the *utilization law*. Since ρ is related to the service time at the center, we can also interpret it as the *mean number of customers in service* at the center.

Example 2.7. Consider a disk that is servicing 50 I/O per second from an application. Using the available performance monitoring tools, the average I/O service time is determined to be 10 ms. The utilization law given by 2.26 tells us that the disk must be $50 \times 0.010 = 51\%$ busy. Notice that the concept of queue length did not enter this calculation. □

Because a server cannot be more than 100% utilized, we have $\rho \leq 1$, and from (2.26) it follows that:

$$\lambda < S^{-1} \tag{2.27}$$

in order that the queue not grow in an unbounded way.

2.5.4 Little's Macroscopic Law

By an analogous argument, we can determine the mean number of resident customers in the system. Let

- τ be the total residence time summed over all completions
- R be the mean residence time per completion τ/C
- X be the mean system throughput

The queue length (or the total number of requests in the system) can now be expressed as:

$$Q = \frac{\tau}{T} = \frac{C}{T} \times \frac{\tau}{C}, \tag{2.28}$$

from which it follows that:

$$Q = XR = \lambda R. \tag{2.29}$$

Equation (2.29) is the *macroscopic* version of Little's law, which can be written either in terms of the throughput X or λ as a consequence of the steady-state assumption in (2.2).

By analogy with (2.26), Q is a measure of system occupancy: the mean number of customers in the system. Since we could rewrite (2.29) as

$$Q = \lambda(W + S), \tag{2.30}$$

it is clear that the difference between (2.26) and (2.29) is that the latter includes the waiting time W.

Example 2.8. Consider the previous example of disk servicing 50 I/O per second and include buffering that might be present at the disk controller or in the device driver. Suppose the average number of buffered requests is 5. What is the average time spent at the disk? Rearranging (2.29) we find that $R = 5/50 = 100$ ms. Subtracting out the known service time of 10 ms, we see that an I/O request spends 90 ms in the buffer. □

2.6 Unlimited Request (Open) Queues

Up to this point, we have just been establishing an appropriate set of relationships between directly measurable quantities pertaining to a single queue. These relationships are expressed purely in terms of the average values of measurable quantities. Keeping in mind that queues actually behave according to random or stochastic processes, the degree of simplification afforded by the use of averages is quite remarkable. We now employ these observational laws to characterize some of the most common queueing configurations that arise in computer system performance analysis.

2.6.1 Single Server Queue

Figure 2.2 assumes that the number of customers arriving from outside the checkout queue is not limited. In other words, there is an infinite pool of customers outside the grocery store. Some fraction of this pool is arriving into the checkout queue at a rate λ. For this reason, the queues we discuss in this section are termed *open* queues.

It is possible that some many customers might arrive at the checkout that the queue could become infinitely long. To avoid this situation, we assume that the stability condition (2.27) holds.

Denoting the service *rate* by $\mu = S^{-1}$, (2.27) can also be written as $\lambda < \mu$. This condition says that the arrival rate must be less than the service rate in order that the waiting line at an open queue not become infinitely long.

In Sect. 2.8) we discuss the case where the number of customers is limited to some finite value (like a buffer).

2.6.2 Measured Service Demand

In cases where the the service time and the number of visits are difficult to measure, Little's law (2.26) can be rearranged as:

$$D_k = \frac{\rho_k}{X} \,, \tag{2.31}$$

to calculate the service demand (2.9) rather than the service time.

As noted in Sect. 2.4.2, only measurements that have been sampled over a reasonable period of time should be used to evaluate the performance parameters ρ_k, A, and D_k. A reasonable period T means *many multiples* of the longest busy period.

2.6.3 Queueing Delays

As you approach a checkout in the grocery store (Sect. 2.3), your expected time to get through it, i.e., your residence time (Sect. 2.4.9), consists of two components:

1. The expected time for all those ahead of you to complete their service, i.e., a queueing component.
2. Your expected service time once you get to the cashier, i.e., a service component.

Since the average service time S is assumed to be the same for every customer and the average queue length is Q, the expected time for you to reach the cashier is QS. These two components of your residence time can be summarized as:

$$R = QS + S \,. \tag{2.32}$$

We have dropped the k-subscripts for convenience here. If you were the only customer arriving at the checkout, then $Q = 0$ (no queueing) and your residence time would be precisely S. Otherwise, you have to join the end of the line and wait.

Using Little's macroscopic law (2.14) to replace Q in (2.32) by λR gives:

$$R = (\lambda R)\, S + S \,. \tag{2.33}$$

Solving for R we find:

$$R = \frac{S}{1 - \lambda S} \,, \tag{2.34}$$

and a further substitution of Little's microscopic law (2.15) into the denominator of (2.34) results in:

$$R = \frac{S}{1 - \rho} . \tag{2.35}$$

The following rules of thumb for the dispersion of M/M/1 residence times:

$$\mathsf{R} = 1\mathsf{S} \text{ at } \rho = 0\,,$$
$$\mathsf{R} = 2\mathsf{S} \text{ at } \rho = 1/2\,,$$
$$\mathsf{R} = 4\mathsf{S} \text{ at } \rho = 3/4\,,$$

follow from (2.35) and are also visually evident in Fig.2.12.

Equation (2.35) enables the average *residence time* to be determined, even if the arrival rate is not known. The measured utilization at the server can be used instead. The residence time characteristic for a single server queueing

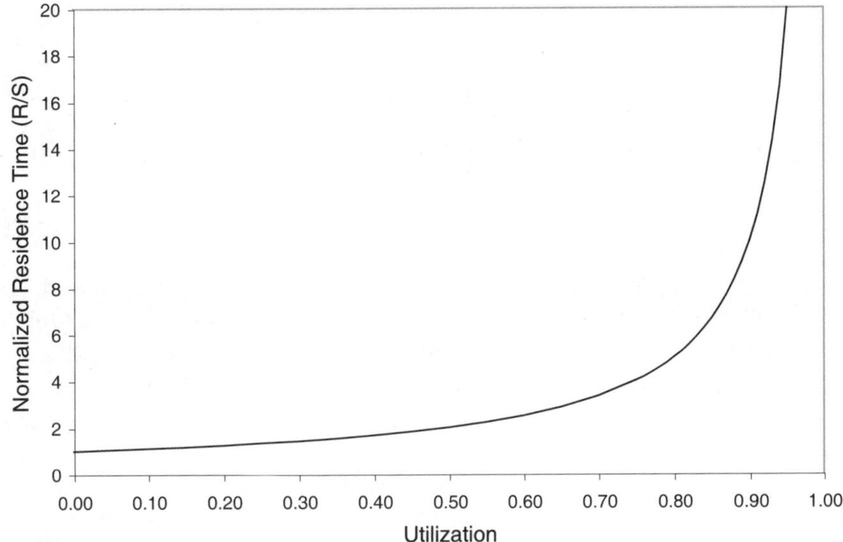

Fig. 2.12. Typical response time characteristic for a single server queueing center. For convenience, the response time R has been normalized to the service time S so that $R/S = 1$ at zero server utilization

center is plotted in Fig. 2.12 as a function of the server utilization. To make the curve more generic, the response time R has been scaled by the service time S to produce the normalized queueing delay R/S. Since the utilization ρ is bounded (2.11), it follows that R is essentially equivalent to the service time when $\rho \simeq 0$, while it rapidly approaches an infinite value as $\rho \to 1$. This happens because the queue length becomes unbounded when the stability condition (2.27) is not satisfied, i.e., when $\rho = 1$.

We can also interpret (2.35) as an inflated service time. The inflation factor is $(1-\rho)$ for a single server. Since ρ can be interpreted as the fraction of time the server is busy (during T), the quantity $(1-\rho)$ can be interpreted as the fraction of time the server is available. If the server is available, then $R = S$ because there is no queueing.

Multiplying both sides of (2.35) by λ produces:

$$Q = \frac{\rho}{1-\rho}, \tag{2.36}$$

which is the average queue length expressed as a function of the server utilization. It is also equivalent to the mean number of requests in the system—a single waiting line and a single server in this case.

If, instead of being in a grocery store, you were on the phone waiting for customer support to answer, you might consider your waiting time to be far more critical than your residence time. From (2.32) we see that your expected *waiting time* W as you join the queue (Fig. 2.5) is given by:

$$W = QS\,. \tag{2.37}$$

Multiplying both sides of (2.36) by S produces:

$$W = \frac{\rho S}{1-\rho}, \tag{2.38}$$

which is the waiting time counterpart of (2.35) expressed in terms of the server utilization. The average length of the waiting line L can be determined by writing Little's law (2.14) as $L = \lambda W$ and appling it to (2.38) to give:

$$L = \frac{\rho^2}{1-\rho}\,. \tag{2.39}$$

Equation (2.39) can be verified by noting that

$$L = Q - \rho\,, \tag{2.40}$$

which states that the waiting line length is equal to the queue length *minus* the average number of customers in service. Substituting (2.36) into (2.40) and simplifying also establishes (2.39).

> A cautionary note is in order. It may seem contradictory that the waiting time W in (2.37) is expreseed in terms of the total queue length Q rather than the length of the waiting line L. You may be thinking (2.37) should be written as $W = LS$, but that is incorrect. By definition, the waiting *line* length L EXCLUDES the customer currently in service, but the waiting *time* W must INCLUDE the time for the customer currently in service. Hence, $W = QS$ and therefore $W \neq LS$.

It is noteworthy that these results for the average queueing delays at a single server queue are identical to those that would be obtained using the more mathematical methods of probability theory and stochastic analysis [See e.g., Kleinrock 1976, Allen 1990].

Example 2.9. Measurements of a network gateway reveal that packets arrive on average at 125 packets per second (pps) and the gateway takes about 2 ms to forward them on.

Performance metric	Symbol	Value	Unit
Service time	S	2.00	ms
Server utilization	ρ	25.00	percent
Number of pkts in gateway	Q	0.33	pkts
Mean waiting time	W	0.66	ms
Mean response time	R	2.66	ms

Using this information, the performance characteristics can be tabulated using the results of Sect. 2.6.3. □

The utilization can be thought of as reflecting the request load on the server. Under a light load ($\rho < 0.50$), the response time is close to the average service time. As the load is increased above 50%, however, the response time increases slowly at first and then very dramatically under heavy loads ($\rho \gg 0.50$). The reader might care to compare this definition of *load* based on utilization with the definition of the UNIX *load average* discussed in Chap. 4.

Example 2.10. This example uses a Perl program to calculate various delays for the grocery store data in Example 2.1.

```
#! /usr/bin/perl
# residence.pl

# Array of measured busy periods (min)
@busyData = (1.23, 2.01, 3.11, 1.02, 1.54, 2.69, 3.41, 2.87,
2.22, 2.83);

# Compute the aggregate busy time
foreach $busy (@busyData) {
    $B_server += $busy;
}
$T_period = 30;                    # Measurement period (min)
$C_server = @busyData;             # Completions
$S_time = $B_server / $C_server; # Service time (min)
$rho = $B_server / $T_period;      # Utilization
$R_time = $S_time / (1 - $rho);  # Service time (min)
$Q_length = $rho / (1 - $rho);   # Queue length
$W_time = $Q_length * $S_time;   # Waiting time (min)
printf("Service time    (S): %6.2f min\n", $S_time);
printf("Utilization   (rho): %6.2f     \n", $rho);
printf("Residence time (R): %6.2f min\n", $R_time);
```

```
printf("Queue length   (Q): %6.2f \n", $Q_length);
printf("Waiting time   (W): %6.2f min\n", $W_time);

# Output ...
# Service time    (S):   2.29 min
# Utilization   (rho):   0.76
# Residence time (R):   9.73 min
# Queue length    (Q):   3.24
# Waiting time    (W):   7.44 min
```

□

By virtue of (2.35) the nonlinear curve in Fig. 2.12 is a *hyperbola.* When lightly loaded, the queueing center operates near the *foot* of the hyperbola, while under heavy loading the delay climbs quickly up in the *leg* of the curve. As the load approaches 100% busy, the response time becomes infinite. To avoid such unbounded queue growth, we assume the condition $\rho < 1$ holds.

The average response time R in (2.35) is the mean of a very large set of response times that are exponentially distributed (Sect. 1.5.2), so the following rules of thumb apply:

1. 80th percentile occurs at $R_{80} \simeq 5R/3$
2. 90th percentile occurs at $R_{90} \simeq 7R/3$
3. 95th percentile occurs at $R_{95} \simeq 9R/3$

These rules of thumb can be used to compute the corresponding percentile curves of the response time distribution shown in Fig. 2.13. We observe from Fig. 2.12 that at $\rho = 0.50$ the queueing delay causes the response time to become *twice* the service time, while at $\rho = 0.75$ the delay has increased to *four* service times. Once again, this reflects the hyperbolic nature of the response time characteristic.

Example 2.11. Let the service time $S = 1$ s, and let the interarrival time be 2 s. What is the mean response time and the mean queue length? From (2.15), the utilization can be evaluated as:

$$\rho = \lambda S.$$

Since $\lambda^{-1} = 2$, it follows that $\lambda = 0.5$ / s. Substituting these values produces:

$$\rho = 0.5 \times 1.0 = 0.5,$$

from which we conclude that the server is 50% busy. The mean response time is:

$$R = \frac{S}{1 - \rho} = 2.0\,\text{s},$$

and

$$Q = \frac{\rho}{1 - \rho} = 1.0$$

is the mean number of requests in the system. □

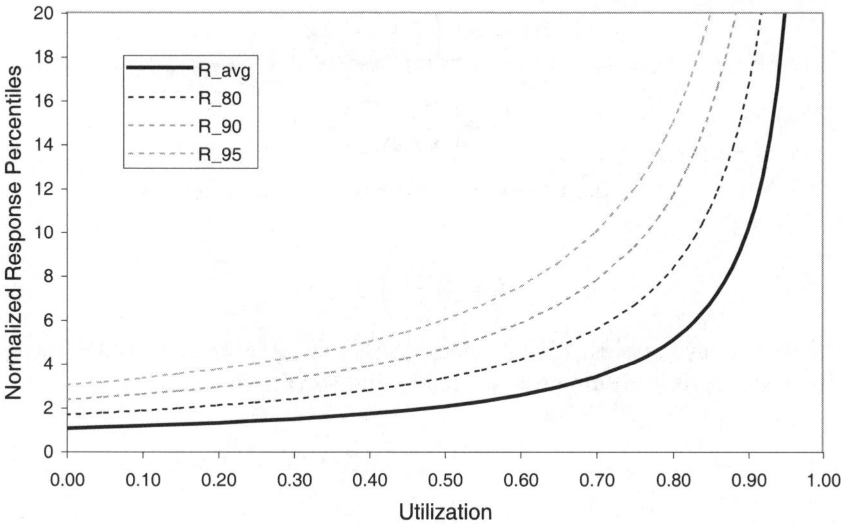

Fig. 2.13. Percentiles for exponential response times

Let us summarize our analysis of queues so far. We have established a set of parameters such as arrival rate λ and service time S that can be used to characterize a uniserver queue. These parameters are related to one another through relationships such as Little's law. In general, these relationships are called *observational laws* in the performance literature. Applying these observational laws, we developed an equation for calculating the mean response time of a uniserver queue without resorting to any of the usual sophisticated stochastic analyses found in most performance textbooks. The corresponding Perl PDQ model for the single-server open queue is presented in Chap. 6, Sect. 6.7.2.

With these concepts in place for a single queue, we now have a good foundation upon which to analyze more sophisticated queues. Consider what happens when another queueing center is made available to handle arrivals. Such a *twin queue* configuration is logically equivalent to opening another checkout line in the grocery store.

2.6.4 Twin Queueing Center

Figure 2.14 shows the flow of identical customers into a twin queueing center, where each queue has its own server and each server has the same average service time S. The original stream of arrivals having rate λ is split into two equal substreams each with intensity $\lambda/2$. Equation (2.33) can be rewritten as:

Fig. 2.14. Twin ($q = 2$) parallel queueing centers

$$R = \left(\frac{\lambda}{2}R\right) S + S\,, \tag{2.41}$$

where we have applied Little's macroscopic law $Q = \lambda R/2$ to the substream. Rearranging in the same way as before and solving for R, we find:

$$R = \frac{S}{1 - \frac{1}{2}\lambda S}\,, \tag{2.42}$$

The only difference between (2.42) and (2.34) is the factor of a half appearing with the utilization in the denominator. Emphasizing the utilization at a single queueing center with the notation $\rho_1 = \lambda S$, we can rewrite (2.42) as:

$$R = \frac{S}{1 - \frac{1}{2}\rho_1}. \tag{2.43}$$

The residence time at the twin center is shorter than that for the single center in Sect. 2.6.1 because the server in the twin center is only half as busy as the single center due to the splitting of arrivals into two equal streams.

2.6.5 Parallel Queues

We can generalize the twin queueing center to q parallel queueing centers depicted in Fig. 2.15. The q-parallel center response time becomes:

$$R = \frac{S}{1 - \frac{1}{q}\lambda S}. \tag{2.44}$$

Clearly, $\rho_1 = \lambda S$ becomes smaller as q increases, and so therefore does R. In fact, as $q \to \infty$, it follows that $R \to S$ because every arrival tends to get its own server in Fig. 2.29, and there is no queueing. We shall make use of this utilization scaling in Sect. 7.4.2.

Another way to write (2.44) is to define the *offered load* or *traffic intensity* as:

$$q\rho = \lambda S\,, \tag{2.45}$$

for a q-parallel center. Equation (2.44) can then be written as:

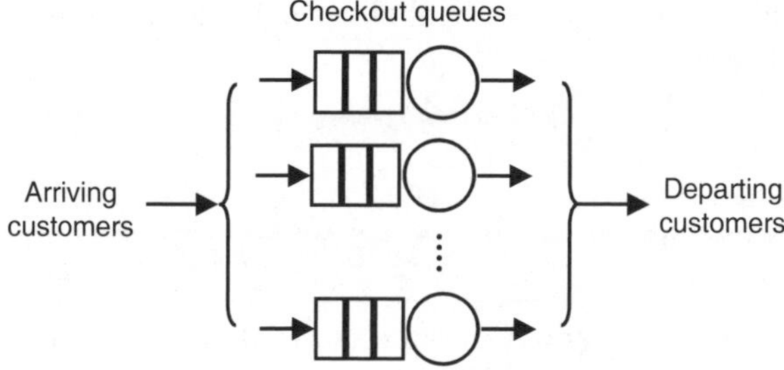

Fig. 2.15. q parallel queues

$$R = \frac{S}{1 - \rho} \, . \tag{2.46}$$

which is identical in form to single server queue (2.35), with the proviso that the utilization is defined by (2.45) so that the stability condition $\rho < 1$ is still satisfied.

Example 2.12. Many Internet service providers (ISP) employ a terminal-style interface, called *chat rows*, to field technical support questions from their subscribers. For example, callers may assign themselves randomly to one of ten such chat rows and then wait until they are prompted by a technician to explain their problem. Once the caller has selected a chat row, they cannot defect to another row. Each chat row is serviced by a technician, and all discussions are carried on via their respective keyboards.

Measurements show that callers connect at an average rate of three per minute. Each caller waits an average of three minutes before being addressed and then two minute chatting with the technician before signing off. Subscribers have complained about the average waiting time of three minutes. Consequently, the ISP would like to know how many more technicians should be added to reduce the waiting time to an average of one minute. The chat rows can be modeled as ten parallel queues.

The mean arrival rate is $\lambda = 3$ calls per minute (cpm). The mean service time is $S = 2$ min, so the utilization is $\rho = 3 \times 2 = 6$ or 600%. Using the definition $\rho = \lambda S/q$ with $q = 10$, the load on each chat server is $\rho = 0.60$. The response time can be calculated from (2.44) as:

$$R = \frac{2}{1 - 0.60} = 5 \, \text{min}.$$

The mean waiting time is therefore:

$$W = 5 - 2 = 3 \text{ min},$$

which is what the subscribers are complaining about. The existing situation is summarized in the following table.

Performance Metric	Symbol	Value	Unit
Number of technicians	q	10	N/A
Mean throughput	X	3	pps
Service time	S	2	ms
Utilization	ρ	60	percent
Mean response time	R	5	min
Mean waiting time	W	3	min

The first three lines show input parameters while the lower part of the table shows model outputs.

Performance Metric	Symbol	Value	Unit
Number of technicians	q	18	N/A
Mean throughput	X	3	pps
Service time	S	2	ms
Utilization	ρ	33	percent
Mean response time	R	3	min
Mean waiting time	W	1	min

By trial and error choices for q, we find that adding another 8 technicians (for a total of 18) will bring the waiting time down to the required 1 m. The results are summarized in the above table. □

When we present shorthand notations for queues in Sect. 2.9.2, we shall see that there is no special notation for parallel queues. The reason should be clear. Equation (2.46) states that a q-parallel center is mathematically equivalent to q single queues each serving one qth the workload.

2.6.6 Dual Server Queue—Heuristic Analysis

Suppose we add an identical server to the common queue as shown in Fig. 2.16. Nothing else is changed. This is the service configuration one typically finds for bank tellers, post office clerks (Sect. 2.3.3), call centers (see Sect. 2.7.1) and multiprocessor CPUs. (see Chap. 7).

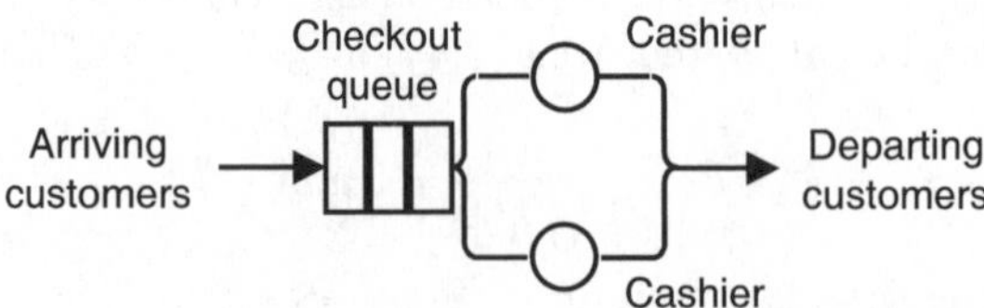

Fig. 2.16. A dual ($m = 2$) server queue

With two servers available to service customers, we can reasonably assume that the average residence time will be reduced. The question is, by how much? Naively, you might expect that the residence time would be halved because the server capacity has been doubled. Unfortunately, the queueing behavior is more complex than that by virtue of how the waiting line forms.

Since the dual server has twice the uniserver capacity, it can support twice the traffic intensity. Using the definition (2.45) we can write the general traffic intensity as:

$$m\rho = \lambda S\,, \tag{2.47}$$

where the factor of m here represents the number of fixed-capacity servers rather than the number of queues. Only during those periods when all m servers are busy, will the waiting line grow, but (2.47) guarantees stability $\rho < 1$. As you will see in Sect. 2.7.1, the qeueing behavior in the m-server case is very subtle and unintuitive. Therefore, we set the stage for those developments by presenting a heuristic analysis of queueing at a dual server.

Low Load Case

Consider firstly the case where the arrival rate is low. In this low traffic limit as $\rho \to 0$ there will be no queueing, so every arriving customer can expect to find one or the other server available. This situation mimics the twin queues of Sect. 2.6.4 but without the queues (in this low traffic limit). Therefore, we assume that the dual server residence time can be approximated by the twin queue residence time (2.42) with low traffic:

$$R_{\text{low}} \approx \frac{S}{1 - (\frac{\lambda}{2})S}\,. \tag{2.48}$$

Using (2.47) to replace $\lambda S/2$ with ρ, (2.48) becomes:

$$R_{\text{low}} \approx \frac{S}{1-\rho}\,. \tag{2.49}$$

If $\rho = 0$ exactly then there are no customers in service and an average customer arriving would incur an expected service time S. Of course, as the load increases ($\rho >> 0$) two queues will begin to form and (2.49) will diverge from the correct behavior because there is only a single waiting line, not two, at the dual server in Fig. 2.16.

High Load Case

Next, we consider the other extreme where the arrival rate is high. In that limit the traffic intensity $2\rho \to 2$, which means both servers will be very busy ($\rho \to 1$) and the waiting line will tend to be very long. This situation mimics a single large waiting line but with a server that is twice as fast as the uniserver queue discussed in Sect. 2.6.1 because there is twice the server capacity and that makes it is possible to have two customers being serviced simultaneously.

We assume that the dual server residence time can be approximated by the uniserver residence time (2.35):

$$R_{high} \approx \frac{S/2}{1 - \lambda(\frac{S}{2})} , \tag{2.50}$$

but with S replaced by $S/2$ to represent a server that is operating twice as fast. Using (2.47) to replace $\lambda S/2$ with ρ, (2.50) becomes:

$$R_{high} \approx \frac{S}{2(1-\rho)} . \tag{2.51}$$

Since (2.51) is only an approximation, it will also diverge from the correct behavior as the load decreases ($\rho << 1$). We need to find a representation of the response time that contains both of these extreme queueing behaviors as well as the correct intermediate behavior.

Intermediate Case

The only distinction between the approximations (2.49) and (2.51) is a factor of $\frac{1}{2}$. This suggests that we write a generalized response time function:

$$R_\phi = \frac{S\phi(\rho)}{1-\rho} . \tag{2.52}$$

where the numerator corresponds to a load-dependent pseudo-server which has a variable mean service time $S\phi(0) = S$ at low loads and $S\phi(1) = S/2$ at high loads. Various forms of a *load-dependent servers* are also presented in Chaps. 6 and 10. The function $\phi(\rho)$ therefore needs to satisfy the conditions:

$$\phi(\rho) = \begin{cases} 1 \text{ as } \rho \rightarrow \epsilon, \\ \\ \frac{1}{2} \text{ as } \rho \rightarrow 1 - \epsilon. \end{cases} \tag{2.53}$$

where ϵ is a vanishingly small quantity. A simple function of the server utilization ρ which meets these requirements is:

$$\phi(\rho) = \frac{1}{1+\rho} . \tag{2.54}$$

To check that (2.54) produces the correct limiting behavior in (2.52) at low loads, we replace ρ by ϵ:

$$R_\phi = \frac{S}{1-\epsilon}\left(\frac{1}{1+\epsilon}\right) = \frac{S}{1-\epsilon^2} = S , \tag{2.55}$$

where terms that are $O(\epsilon^2)$ can be disregarded. The average residence time becomes the average service time, as expected. Similarly, at high loads:

$$R_\phi = \frac{S}{1-(1-\epsilon)} \left(\frac{1}{1+(1-\epsilon)} \right) = \frac{S}{1-(1-\epsilon)^2} = \frac{S}{2\epsilon} , \tag{2.56}$$

which corresponds to a large number (ϵ^{-1}) of enqueued customers, each requiring an average service time of $S/2$. Equation (2.56) supports our earlier assumption that a dual server acts like a double-speed uniserver at high loads.

The complete expression for intermediate dual server residence times is:

$$R_\phi = \frac{S}{1-\rho} \left(\frac{1}{1+\rho} \right) , \tag{2.57}$$

which simplifies to:

$$R = \frac{S}{1-\rho^2} , \tag{2.58}$$

the subscript ϕ now being redundant. As we shall confirm in Sect. 2.7.5, the formula in (2.58) gives the average residence time at a dual server queue for *all* loads $\rho < 1$, so our guess for $\phi(\rho)$ in (2.54) is justified.

> The performance advantage of the dual server queue can be understood intuitively as follows. It is a single waiting line feeding a pseudo-server which acts like a twin queue center at low loads but progressively becomes a double-speed uniserver at high loads.

The queue length can be obtained from Little's law $Q = \lambda R$ applied to (2.58):

$$Q = \frac{\lambda S}{1-\rho^2} = \frac{2\rho}{1-\rho^2} . \tag{2.59}$$

where we have used (2.47) with $m = 2$. The waiting line length is:

$$L = Q - 2\rho = \frac{2\rho^3}{1-\rho^2} , \tag{2.60}$$

and the corresponding waiting time is given by:

$$W = \frac{L}{\lambda} = \frac{\rho^2 S}{1-\rho^2} , \tag{2.61}$$

by virtue of Little's law $L = \lambda W$. The same heuristic reasoning can be applied to develop an approximate formula for the multiserver response time.

2.7 Multiserver Queue

If we generalize (2.54) as:

$$\phi(m, \rho) = \frac{1-\rho}{1-\rho^m} = \frac{\rho^{m-1}}{1+\rho+\rho^2+\ \dots\ +\rho^{m-1}} , \tag{2.62}$$

for m servers, the corresponding residence time (2.52) becomes:

$$R_\phi = \frac{S}{1-\rho^m}, \tag{2.63}$$

where $\rho = \lambda S/m$. Unlike (2.58), however, (2.63) is only an approximation to the exact result which we present in Sect. 2.7.1. Nonetheless, (2.63) is very useful for fast manual calculations.

Table 2.4. Comparison of approximate and exact (*italics*) normalized multiprocessor response times (R/S) as a function of server utilization ρ and the number of servers m

	ρ									
m	0.3333		0.5000		0.6666		0.7500		0.9000	
1	1.4999	*1.4999*	2.0000	*2.0000*	2.9994	*2.9994*	4.0000	*4.0000*	10.000	*10.0000*
2	1.1250	*1.1250*	1.3333	*1.3333*	1.7997	*1.7997*	2.2857	*2.2857*	5.2632	*5.2632*
3	1.0384	*1.0454*	1.1429	*1.1579*	1.4209	*1.4443*	1.7297	*1.7570*	3.6900	*3.7235*
4	1.0125	*1.0194*	1.0667	*1.0870*	1.2460	*1.2837*	1.4629	*1.5094*	2.9078	*2.9694*
5	1.0041	*1.0091*	1.0323	*1.0521*	1.1516	*1.1959*	1.3111	*1.3694*	2.4419	*2.5250*
6	1.0014	*1.0045*	1.0159	*1.0330*	1.0962	*1.1423*	1.2165	*1.2811*	2.1342	*2.2335*
7	1.0005	*1.0023*	1.0079	*1.0218*	1.0621	*1.1071*	1.1540	*1.2212*	1.9168	*2.0285*
8	1.0002	*1.0012*	1.0039	*1.0148*	1.0406	*1.0828*	1.1113	*1.1785*	1.7558	*1.8769*
16	1.0000	*1.0000*	1.0000	*1.0011*	1.0015	*1.0173*	1.0101	*1.0511*	1.2274	*1.3696*
32	1.0000	*1.0000*	1.0000	*1.0000*	1.0000	*1.0020*	1.0001	*1.0104*	1.0356	*1.1432*
64	1.0000	*1.0000*	1.0000	*1.0000*	1.0000	*1.0001*	1.0000	*1.0011*	1.0012	*1.0485*

The normalized response times R/S predicted by (2.63) are shown in the left hand columns of Table 2.4. Right hand columns (italics) show the *exact* R/S values derived in Sect. 2.7.2. The selected set of utilizations and server configurations corresponds to those found in many current commercial multiprocessors (cf. Chap. 7). A subset of four m values are plotted in Fig. 2.17.

The uppermost curve corresponds to the single server case shown previously in Fig. 2.12. As the number of servers is increased in the sequence $m = 1, 4, 16, 64$, we see that the general trend is to push the knee of the curve toward the lower right corner of the plot .

How accuate is the approximate expression (2.63) for estimating multiserver residence times? To answer that question, we need to compare it with the *exact* formula for multiserver residence times. That involves something called the *Erlang C function.*

2.7.1 Erlang's C Formula

The *exact* multiserver residence time can be calculated using the formula:

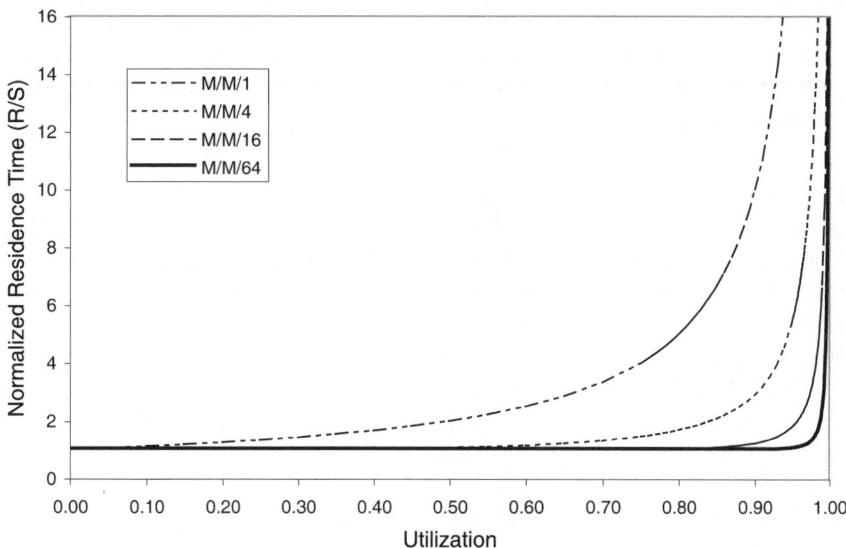

Fig. 2.17. Normalized response times (R/S) for multiple servers $m = 1, 4, 16, 64$. The *upper curve* corresponds to the single server case

$$R = \frac{C(m,\rho)S}{m(1-\rho)} + S\,, \tag{2.64}$$

where the first term is the expected waiting time W. The corresponding queue length (number of customers in the queueing center, including the ones in service) is given by Little's law $Q = \lambda R$:

$$Q = \frac{\rho C(m,\rho)}{m(1-\rho)} + m\rho\,. \tag{2.65}$$

$C(m,\rho)$ is the probability that all the servers are busy and therefore customers arriving with traffic intensity (2.47) will have to wait for service. This probability is defined by the rather complicated function:

$$C(m,\rho) = \frac{\frac{(m\rho)^m}{m!}}{(1-\rho)\sum_{n=0}^{m-1}\frac{(m\rho)^n}{n!} + \frac{(m\rho)^m}{m!}}\,, \tag{2.66}$$

which is known as *Erlang's C function.* Notice that if $m = 1$ then $C(1,\rho) = \rho$ (the probability that the single server is busy) so (2.64) reduces to the residence time (2.35) for a uniserver queue, and similarly the queue length (2.65) reduces to (2.36).

Historically, this is where it all started. A. K. Erlang [1917] developed this pioneering application of queueing theory to telephone systems. The m servers represent telephone trunk lines accepting calls measured in *Erlang* units. The number of Erlangs cannot exceed the number of servers. As noted in Appendix B, it was another 50 years before queueing theory was applied to electronic computer performance analysis.

Erlang's influence lives on today. Equation (2.64) can be used to analyze the response time characteristics of a customer support call center. A number of assumptions must be made in that case. One assumption is that the a waiting caller does not leave the queue (defect), another is that the pool of callers is infinite. In practice this usually means that the number of callers is at least 10 times greater than the number of servers.

Ericsson, the Swedish cell phone company, developed a functional programming language called *Erlang* (`www.erlang.org/about.html`) for building more reliable telecommunication systems.

2.7.2 Accuracy of the Heuristic Formula

As noted previously, (2.63) is only an approximation for multiserver response time (2.64) but it is clearly more suitable for manual calculations. Another approach is to find efficient algorithms to compute (2.64) exactly, and we take up that idea in Sect. 2.7.4. With the Erlang C function defined, we can now compare the relative accuracy of (2.63) and (2.64).

Table 2.4 contains the *exact* response times shown in italics. Note that both the approximate and exact response times are identical for queueing centers with one and two server. Deviations occur only for $m > 2$.

Overall, the approximate expression in (2.63) tends to *underestimate* the exact response time (2.64). The relative errors are plotted in Fig. 2.18 for the same range of server configurations (horizontal axis) as appear in Tables 2.4 and server utilizations $\rho \geq 0.50$ (vertical axis).

The largest errors appear as the dark band toward the top of the figure. The maximum error of 15% occurs in the neighborhood of $m = 64$ and $\rho = 0.98$. This error falls rapidly to about 5% for $\rho > 0.98$. For moderate loads with server utilization in the range $0.50 < \rho < 0.65$, the relative varies from about 2.5% at $m = 8$ (gray region on the left side of Fig. 2.18) to about 0.5% at $m = 16$ (white region).

Figure 2.18 can be used to visually determine whether or not you need to resort to the exact formula (2.64) for multiserver response times. If the load is very high (say, $rho > 0.90$) and the number of servers is large (say, $m > 20$), then the approximate response time formula (2.63) will have about 10% error. The question becomes, can you live with that error? On the other hand, any m-way configuration running a load ρ that puts you in the white region of Fig. 2.18 has relatively small error and using (2.63) is expeditious.

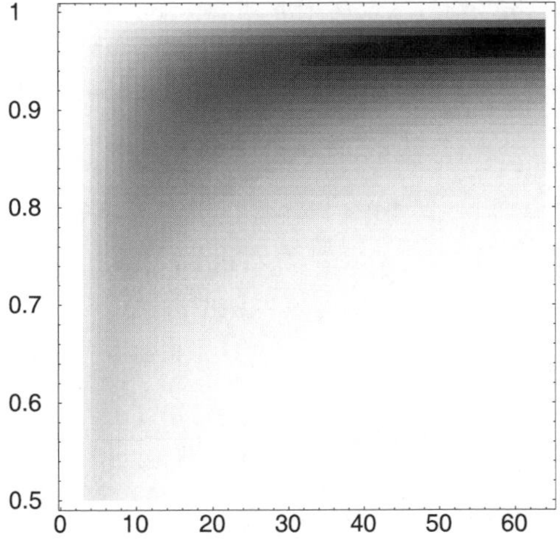

Fig. 2.18. Relative error for the approximate solution in (2.63) plotted as a function of server capacity m and load ρ. Server configurations span $1 \leq m \leq 64$ processors (*horizontal axis*) for utilizations in the range $0.5 \leq \rho \leq 1.0$ (*vertical axis*). The largest errors (about 10–15%) occur in the *black band* at *top right*. The least errors (*white*) occur in narrow strips at the *left*, *top*, and the large quadrant at *lower right*, as well as for all $\rho < 0.5$ (not shown)

2.7.3 Erlang's B Formula

Whereas the Erlang C function pertains to an multiserver queueing system, the Erlang B function,

$$B(m, \rho) = \frac{\frac{(m\rho)^m}{m!}}{\sum_{n=0}^{m} \frac{(m\rho)^n}{n!}} , \tag{2.67}$$

gives the probability that all the servers are busy and that customers (or calls) are dropped completely rather than being queued up. This is what happens when you try to make a phone call and all the circuits are busy; you hang up and try again later. In other words, there is no queueing. Formally, $B(m, \rho)$ is the probability that the call is dropped or *lost*. Equation (2.67) can be rewritten as:

$$B(m, \rho) = \frac{\mathrm{e}^{-m\rho} \frac{(m\rho)^m}{m!}}{\mathrm{e}^{-m\rho} \sum_{n=0}^{m} \frac{(m\rho)^n}{n!}} \equiv \frac{\mathrm{PDF}}{\mathrm{CDF}} , \tag{2.68}$$

to make explicit that it is the ratio of the discrete probability density function (PDF or more strictly the PMF) to the cumulative distribution function (CDF) of a Poisson distribution (Sect. 1.5.3) with mean equal to the traffic intensity $m\rho$. The complement of $B(m, \rho)$:

$$\Re(m, \rho) = \frac{\sum_{n=0}^{m-1} \frac{(m\rho)^m}{m!}}{\sum_{n=0}^{m} \frac{(m\rho)^n}{n!}} \equiv 1 - \frac{\mathrm{PDF}}{\mathrm{CDF}} , \tag{2.69}$$

is called the *Poisson ratio* where the difference in the upper limits of the summations should be carefully noted. We can use (2.69) to simplify the notation for both Erlang's B function (2.67):

$$B(m, \rho) = 1 - \mathfrak{R}(m, \rho) \,, \tag{2.70}$$

and Erlang's C function (2.66):

$$C(m, \rho) = \frac{1 - \mathfrak{R}(m, \rho)}{1 - \rho \mathfrak{R}(m, \rho)} \,, \tag{2.71}$$

from which it also follows that:

$$C(m, \rho) = \frac{B(m, \rho)}{1 - \rho \left[1 - B(m, \rho)\right]} \,. \tag{2.72}$$

Equation (2.72) forms the basis of the iterative algorithms for solving multi-server queues presented in Sect. 2.7.4.

Extending this approach enables us to see why the residence time in (2.63) is only an appoximation for $m > 2$. Both of the Erlang functions are probabilities that can be expressed in terms of the Poisson ratio (2.69). The denominator of the pseudo-server function $\phi(m, \rho)$ in (2.62) is a finite *geometric* series. The first two terms of the series were guessed in (2.54). This suggests that we form a corresponding geometric ratio:

$$G(m, \rho) = \frac{\rho^{m-1}}{\sum_{n=0}^{m-1} \rho^n} \equiv \frac{\text{PDF}}{\text{CDF}} \,, \tag{2.73}$$

which is bounded by $0 \leq G \leq 1$. Equation (2.73) bears some similarity to the Erlang's B function (2.67). The relationship between (2.73) and the $\phi(m, \rho)$ function is given by:

$$\phi(m, \rho) = \rho^{1-m} \, G(m, \rho) \,. \tag{2.74}$$

The Erlang functions are associated with the Poisson distribution whereas the approximate function $\phi(m, \rho)$ is associated with the geometric distribution.

2.7.4 Erlang Algorithms in Perl

As Allen [1990] noted, some people regard manual calculation of the Erlang formulae (2.67) or (2.66) as an unnatural act! Consequently, considerable industry has been devoted to finding efficient algorithms for the computation of these functions. Jagerman [1974] found that $B(m, \rho)$ can be computed recursively as:

$$B(m, \rho) = \frac{\rho B(m-1, \rho)}{1 + \rho B(m-1, \rho)} \,, \tag{2.75}$$

which can be applied to calculate $C(m, \rho)$ using (2.72). The following Perl code `erlang.pl` employs the relations to calculate the normalized residence time for an $M/M/m$ queue:

```
#! /usr/bin/perl
# erlang.pl

## Input parameters
$servers = 8;
$erlangs = 4;

if($erlangs > $servers) {
    print "Error: Erlangs exceeds servers\n";
    exit;
}

$rho     = $erlangs / $servers;
$erlangB = $erlangs / (1 + $erlangs);
for ($m  = 2; $m <= $servers; $m++) {
    $eb  = $erlangB;
    $erlangB = $eb * $erlangs / ($m + ($eb * $erlangs));
}

$erlangC  = $erlangB / (1 - $rho + ($rho * $erlangB));
$normdwtE = $erlangC / ($servers * (1 - $rho));
$normdrtE = 1 + $normdwtE;                # Exact
$normdrtA = 1 / (1 - $rho**$servers);    # Approx

## Output results
printf("%2d-server Queue\n", $servers);
printf("--------------------------------\n");
printf("Offered load     (Erlangs): %8.4f\n", $erlangs);
printf("Server utilization  (rho): %8.4f\n", $rho);
printf("Erlang B       (Loss prob): %8.4f\n", $erlangB);
printf("Erlang C    (Waiting prob): %8.4f\n", $erlangC);
printf("Normalized    Waiting Time: %8.4f\n", $normdwtE);
printf("Normalized   Response Time: %8.4f\n", $normdrtE);
printf("Approximate Response Time: %8.4f\n", $normdrtA);
```

More recently, the widespread availability of symbolic computation tools like *Mathematica* (Wolfram Research, USA) enable the modern performance analyst to avoid "unnatural acts" by typing in a complicated formula, such as (2.66), using conventional mathematical notation.

Let us use *Mathematica* to check the results produced by the iterative algorithms in `erlang.pl` for the case where $m = 8$ and $\rho = 0.5$. Equation (2.67) is expressed verbatim in *Mathematica* as a function called *EB* which takes two parameters m and ρ as its arguments:

$$In[1] := \ \mathrm{EB}[\mathrm{m}\_, \rho\_] := \frac{\frac{(\mathrm{m}\rho)^{\mathrm{m}}}{\mathrm{m}!}}{\sum_{\mathrm{k}=0}^{\mathrm{m}} \frac{(\mathrm{m}\rho)^{\mathrm{k}}}{\mathrm{k}!}} \ .$$

The *Mathematica* function *EB* is then called by simply entering its name with the specific values, $m = 8$ and $\rho = 0.5$ at $In[2]$. The corresponding output $Out[2]$ gives the numerical result:

$$In[2] := \ \mathtt{EB}[8, 0.5]$$
$$Out[2] = \ 0.0304201$$

The corresponding output of `erlang.pl` is:

```
1  8-server Queue
2 --------------------------------
3 Offered load      (Erlangs):   4.0000
4 Server utilization  (rho):   0.5000
5 Erlang B        (Loss prob):   0.0304
6 Erlang C    (Waiting prob):   0.0590
7 Normalized   Waiting Time:   0.0148
8 Normalized  Response Time:   1.0148
9 Approximate Response Time:   1.0039
```

Comparing line 5 (the Erlang *B* function) with the corresponding *Mathematica* value, we see that they agrees to four decimal places. Similarly, the *Mathematica* expression for (2.66) is a function labeled *EC*:

$$In[1] := \mathtt{EC}[\mathtt{m\_}, \rho\_] := \frac{\frac{(\mathtt{m}\rho)^{\mathtt{m}}}{\mathtt{m}!}}{(1-\rho)\sum_{\mathtt{k}=0}^{\mathtt{m}-1}\frac{(\mathtt{m}\rho)^{\mathtt{k}}}{\mathtt{k}!} + \frac{(\mathtt{m}\rho)^{\mathtt{m}}}{\mathtt{m}!}},$$

Applying *EC* with the particular arguments, $m = 8$ and $\rho = 0.5$, produces the following numerical output:

$$In[2] := \ \mathtt{EC}[8, 0.5]$$
$$Out[2] = 0.059044$$

We see that line 6 (the Erlang *C* function) is also in agreement with the *Mathematica* calculation to four decimal places.

2.7.5 Dual Server Queue—Exact Analysis

We are now in a position to reexamine the dual server queue discussed in Sect. 2.6.6 using the the Erlang *B* and *C* functions. For $m = 2$ the Poisson ratio

$$\mathfrak{R}(2, \rho) = \frac{1 + 2\rho}{1 + 2\rho + 2\rho^2}, \tag{2.76}$$

gives the corresponding Erlang B function (2.67)

$$B(2,\rho) = \frac{2\rho^2}{1 + 2\rho + 2\rho^2} . \tag{2.77}$$

The Erlang C function (2.66) is simply

$$C(2,\rho) = \frac{2\rho^2}{1+\rho} . \tag{2.78}$$

The reader will note the equivalence between the respective denominators in (2.78) and (2.54), the pseudo-server function $\phi(\rho)$ defined in Sect. 2.6.6. It is the numerator, however, that disguishes them. $C(2,\rho)$ is a probability function defined over the range $0 \leq C(2,\rho) \leq 1$, while $\phi(\rho)$ is a decreasing function of ρ defined in the range $1 \leq \phi(\rho) \leq \frac{1}{2}$. The dual server waiting time can be expressed in terms of the Erlang C function (2.78):

$$W = \frac{C(2,\rho)\, S}{2(1-\rho)} = \left(\frac{\rho^2}{1-\rho^2} \right) S . \tag{2.79}$$

From the definition of residence time (2.12) it follows that:

$$R = W + S = \frac{S}{1-\rho^2} , \tag{2.80}$$

in agreement with our heuristic derivation of (2.58) in Sect. 2.6.6. The average queue length is given by Little's macroscopic law (2.14):

$$Q = \lambda\, R = \frac{2\rho}{1-\rho^2} , \tag{2.81}$$

and the average length of the waiting line is:

$$L = Q - 2\rho = \frac{2\rho^3}{1-\rho^2} , \tag{2.82}$$

which can also be obtained from Little's law $L = \lambda W$.

These formulae are straightforward enough to manually check the results produced by `erlang.pl` in Sect. 2.7.4. For arithmetic convenience, we choose the values `$servers` $= 2$ and `$erlangs` $= 1$ for the variables so that the server utilization is $\rho = \frac{1}{2}$. The program output is:

```
 2-server Queue
---------------------------------
Offered load     (Erlangs):   1.0000
Server utilization  (rho):    0.5000
Erlang B        (Loss prob):  0.2000
Erlang C     (Waiting prob):  0.3333
Normalized     Waiting Time:  0.3333
Normalized    Response Time:  1.3333
Approximate Response Time:    1.3333
```

Manually, we begin by calculating the Erlang B function (line 5):

$$B(2, \frac{1}{2}) = \frac{1/2}{5/2} = \frac{1}{5}, \tag{2.83}$$

and substituting this result into (2.72) to evaluate the Erlang C function :

$$C(2, \frac{1}{2}) = \frac{1/2}{3/2} = \frac{1}{3}. \tag{2.84}$$

which should be compared with line 6. Substituting $C(2, \frac{1}{2})$ into (2.79) gives the normalized waiting time (line 7):

$$W = \frac{1/4}{3/4} = \frac{1}{3}, \tag{2.85}$$

and the corresponding normalized residence time (2.80) is:

$$R = 1 + 1/3 = 1\frac{1}{3}. \tag{2.86}$$

which should be compared with line 8. Clearly, the manual calculations confirm the script output.

2.8 Limited Request (Closed) Queues

Another type of feedback occurs in queueing centers where the total number of customers is finite and fixed. In contrast to the open queueing centers discussed in Sect. 2.6, which have a potentially infinite source of customers, these centers are known as *closed* centers.

2.8.1 Closed Queueing Center

The constraint on the number of customers is tantamount to a form of negative feedback or self regulation. The finite population of N customers is either preparing to join the queue (this is sometimes called the "thinking" state with think-time denoted by Z) or they are already at a queueing center, either enqueued or being serviced. Fig. 2.19 illustrates a closed queueing center. The feedback property is easily understood as follows. If, during some period, all N customers are at the service center, then there cannot be any new arrivals at the service center. The system is maximally busy. In such circumstances the response time will be at its worst. In general, as the service center gets busy, the rate at which it gets busier is reduced, thus lowering any further congestion at the service center.

As a consequence of this feedback, performance metrics, such as average throughput and average response time, now become functions of the customer population state, respectively $X = X(n)$ and $R = R(n)$, where $n = 1, 2, ..., N$. We shall see in Chap. 3 that this kind of self-regulating queueing center is very important for modeling certain aspects of computer system performance.

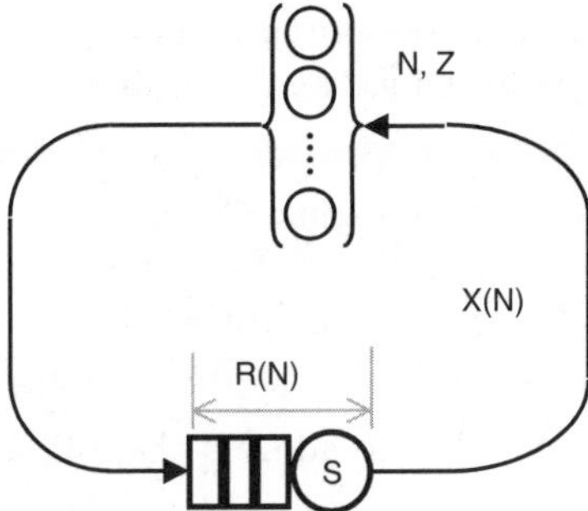

Fig. 2.19. A closed queueing center containing a finite population of N customers each with an infinite center think-time Z

2.8.2 Interactive Response Time Law

Just as we found formal expressions for the response times in open queueing centers, we would like to do the same for the feedback center. Assuming the simplest case of a uniserver ($m = 1$) center in Fig. 2.19, we can express the throughput of the system as follows:

$$X(N) = \frac{N - Q}{Z} . \tag{2.87}$$

This equation simply states that the throughput is a function of arrivals at the center, which occurs at a rate equal to the inverse of the think-time moderated by the number of outstanding requests already in the system $(N - Q)$. Just as for the restaurant example, we assume that there cannot be more than one request outstanding. Using Little's law $Q = XR$ yet again, we can rewrite (2.87) as:

$$Z\,X(N) = N - XR . \tag{2.88}$$

Since we have X on both sides of this equation, we collect those terms. The result is an expression of the throughput.

$$X(N) = \frac{N}{R + Z} . \tag{2.89}$$

A final rearrangement of terms produces the response time for a closed uniserver center:

$$R = \frac{N}{X(N)} - Z, \tag{2.90}$$

which is sometimes referred to as the *Interactive Response Time law* [Lazowska et al. 1984, Jain 1990]. We note in passing that the throughput in (2.87) is a performance measure that is an *output* of solving the model. This is in contrast to all the previous queueing centers we have studied. There, the throughput was assumed equivalent to the arrival rate and was provided as an input performance measure (typically via the utilization ρ) to solve the model.

Example 2.13. A UNIX timeshare computer system used by software developers is monitored for performance and reveals the following measurement data:

- average number of active user logins: $N = 230$
- average time between compilations: $Z = 300$ s
- average CPU utilization: $\rho_{\text{cpu}} = 48\%$ busy
- average CPU service demand: $D_{\text{cpu}} = 0.63$ s/compile

The system administrator wishes to address the following performance questions:

1. What is the CPU throughput for this development workload?
2. What is the average compilation time?

Applying Little's microscopic law, given by (2.26), to the CPU,

$$X = \rho_{\text{cpu}}/D_{\text{cpu}} = 0.48/0.63 = 0.7636 \text{ compiles/s}.$$

Applying (2.90), the system administrator discovers

$$R = 300 = 1.21 \text{ s}$$

for the average compilation time. □

2.8.3 Repairman Algorithm in Perl

Generalizing the above equations to a multiserver center complicates the exact solution. The following Perl code is provided to aid in solving the general repairman problem.

```
#! /usr/bin/perl
# repair.pl

if ($#ARGV != 4) {
   printf "Usage: repair m S N Z\n";
   exit(1);
}
$m = $ARGV[0];
$S = $ARGV[1];
$N = $ARGV[2];
$Z = $ARGV[3];
$p = $p0 = 1;
$L = 0;

for ($k = 1; $k <= $N; $k++) {
   $p *= ($N - $k + 1) * $S / $Z;
   if ($k <= $m) {
      $p /= $k;
   } else {
```

```
        $p /= $m;
    }
    $p0 += $p;
    if ($k > $m) {
        $L += $p * ($k - $m);
    }
}

$p0  = 1.0 / $p0;
$L  *= $p0;
$W   = $L * ($S + $Z) / ($N - $L);
$R   = $W + $S;
$X   = $N / ($R + $Z);
$U   = $X * $S;
$rho = $U / $m;
$Q   = $X * $R;

printf("\n");
printf("  M/M/%ld/%ld/%ld Repair Model\n", $m, $N, $N);
printf("  ----------------------------\n");
printf("  Machine pop:       %4d\n", $N);
printf("  MT to failure:     %9.4f\n", $Z);
printf("  Service time:      %9.4f\n", $S);
printf("  Breakage rate:     %9.4f\n", 1 / $Z);
printf("  Service rate:      %9.4f\n", 1 / $S);
printf("  Utilization:       %9.4f\n", $U);
printf("  Per Server:        %9.4f\n", $rho);
printf("  \n");
printf("  No. in system:     %9.4f\n", $Q);
printf("  No in service:     %9.4f\n", $U);
printf("  No.  enqueued:     %9.4f\n", $Q - $U);
printf("  Waiting time:      %9.4f\n", $R - $S);
printf("  Throughput:        %9.4f\n", $X);
printf("  Response time:     %9.4f\n", $R);
printf("  Normalized RT:     %9.4f\n", $R / $S);
printf("  \n");
```

Example 2.14. Suppose the UNIX computer in Example 2.13 is being considered for upgrading to a two-way multiprocessor system because another 200 programmers have just been hired due the company winning a new development contract. What will be the impact on the current system with 430 programmers?

Using the `repair.pl` program we find $\rho_{\text{cpu}} = 88\%$, and $R = 5.009$ s. The CPU becomes saturated, and compilations can be expected to take five times longer.

Consider an upgrade to a two-way multiprocessor. As Allen [1990] has pointed out, processor interference effects require that service time be inflated to reflect CPU cycles lost to overhead. In Chap. 7 we shall see that a reasonable choice for such processor interference is around 3% of each CPU. Therefore, we set $S = 0.66$ s and run `repair.pl` again. CPU utilization falls to 47%, and $R = 0.8465$ s, which is better than the current compilation time. □

As we shall see in Chap. 3, a closed queueing center is the simplest example of what is often termed a *queueing network* in that it involves a flow of customers through more than one kind of center: the queueing center and an infinite server (i.e., no queueing). Since the term *network* has more in common with electrical networks than with communication networks, we prefer to use the term queueing *circuit* to avoid such confusion.

2.8.4 Response Time Characteristic

The interactive response time law (2.90) has the general characteristic shown in Fig. 2.20. It is a *convex* function. In fact, note that it has a *hockey stick* shape compared with that for an open-queue response time characteristic. Note that the load (horizontal axis) in Fig. 2.20 is defined here in terms of the number of active users N, and not the utilization ρ as in Fig. 2.12.

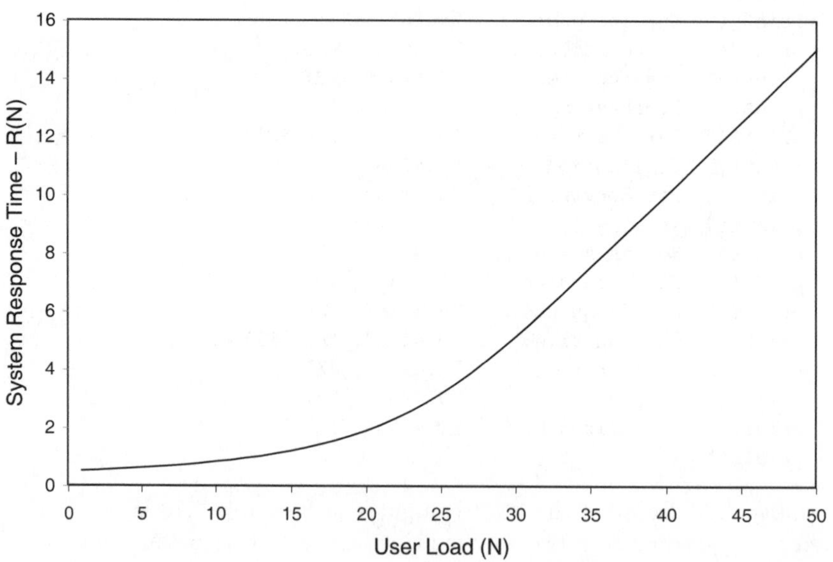

Fig. 2.20. Convex response time characteristic of a finite request queue

The terms convex and concave have particular mathematical definitions. Essentially, a convex function is bowl ⌣ shaped, which means its gradient appears to rotate in an anti-clockwise direction as we move from left to right along the response time curve. An important consequence is that a *knee* develops in the curve and that knee is associated with the optimal load point (see Chap. 5).

Conversely, a *concave* function is bump ⌒ shaped. Therefore, the gradient appears to rotate in a clockwise direction for a concave function. These mathematical definitions are in contradistinction to the same terms applied to the shape of lenses (which may be more familiar to you). A convex lens ⌒ is bow shaped, while a concave lens ⌣ caves in, not out! In Sect. 2.8.5 you will see that the throughput characteristic for a closed queue (Fig. 2.19) is a concave function.

2.8.5 Throughput Characteristic

The corresponding interactive throughput (2.89) has the general characteristic shown in Fig. 2.21. As defined in Sect. 2.8.4, the throughput characteristic for a closed queue (Fig. 2.19) with a finite number of customers is a *concave* function.

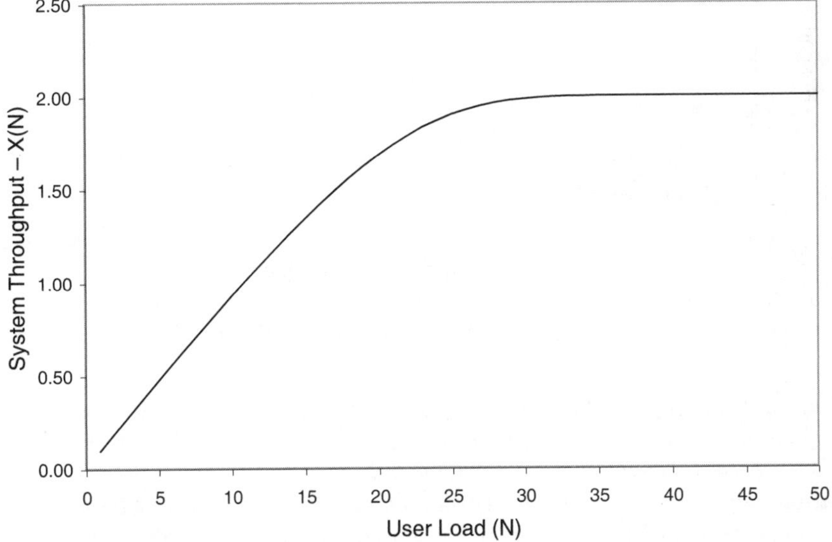

Fig. 2.21. Concave throughput characteristic of a finite request queue

> Figures 2.20 and 2.21 are fundamental performance signatures that you should study carefully and learn to recognize instantly. They occur very frequently, particularly in benchmarking measurements because the number of active requests is limited to the number of active workload generators. Throughput or response time data from such load-limited systems that do not conform to these signatures should be treated with immediate suspicion; the data is *bound* to be wrong!

Although we did not show it earlier, the corresponding throughput characteristic for an *open* queue simply tracks the server utilization ρ. This follows immediately from Little's law (2.15) with λ replaced by X. Therefore, instead of having a rounded knee like that shown in Fig. 2.21, the throughput is a straight line segment rising up to a sharp knee where the server becomes 100% busy, $\rho = 1$.

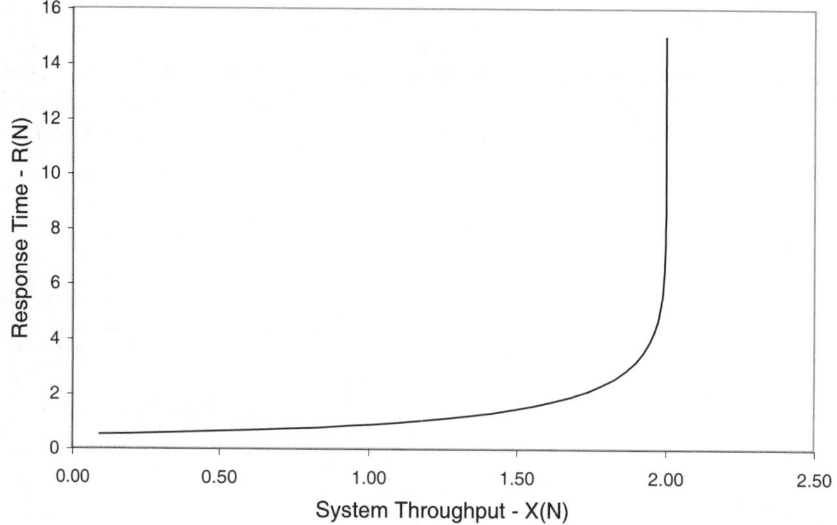

Fig. 2.22. Combined throughput-delay (X-R) curve

Some authors [e.g., Splaine and Jaskiel 2001, p. 241] combine the throughput and response time data together in the same X versus R plot (Fig. 2.22). These *throughput-delay* plots also have a convex shape. This type of representation may be compact but it also can be misleading because it resembles the response time in Fig. 2.17 for an *unlimited* request queue. This can act as a visual miscue. Moreover, it is not very useful from the standpoint of assessing performance bounds and optimal loads—topics we discuss in Chap. 5.

2.8.6 Finite Response Times

Unlike the open queueing centers we discussed previously, the finite population in closed queueing centers means that there is a worst-case response time rather than an infinite response time at 100% utilization. Denoting this maximum in the normalized response time as $R_{\max} = R/S$, we see that the worst-case ($Z = 0$) response time is given by:

$$R_{\max} = \frac{N}{m} . \tag{2.91}$$

This result can be easily understood in the following way. For a closed queueing center we have the *Response Time Law* given by (2.90). Normalizing by the service time S produces:

$$\frac{R}{S} = \frac{N}{XS} - \frac{Z}{S} . \tag{2.92}$$

Noting that $\rho = XS$, from Little's law (2.15), we can rewrite (2.92) as:

$$\frac{R}{S} = \frac{N}{\rho} - \frac{Z}{S} . \tag{2.93}$$

Substituting ρm into (2.93) produces:

$$\frac{R}{S} = \frac{N}{\rho m} - \frac{Z}{S} , \tag{2.94}$$

which is the corresponding response time law for a closed multiserver center. Setting the think-time to $Z = 0$ and $\rho = 1$ corresponds to the worst-case response time $R_{\max}$ of (2.91).

$$\frac{R}{S} = \frac{N}{m} . \tag{2.95}$$

Some example results generated using the `repair.pl` code in Sect. 2.8.3 are collected in Table 2.5.

Table 2.5. Finite response time limit for $N = 64$

	m			
Z	1	4	8	16
1.0000	63.0000	15.0000	7.0000	3.0000
0.1000	63.9000	15.9000	7.9000	3.9000
0.0100	63.9900	15.9900	7.9900	3.9900
0.0010	63.9990	15.9990	7.9990	3.9990
0.0001	63.9999	15.9999	7.9999	3.9999

For the repairmen system with $m > 1$, $R_{\max}$ increases with N. For a fixed number of m servers and small N, the repairmen system, with its feedback property, has better response times than the open center. Increasing the number of servers m in an open center produces a better response up to moderate loads. Under conditions of heavy traffic, the queue length in the open center grows rapidly, whereas a closed center terminates at $R_{\max}$.

2.8.7 Approximating a Closed Queues

If we allow the size of the finite population N in a finite request queueing center to grow indefinitely, it will begin to approach an infinite source of requests, and its characteristics should therefore approach those of an open queueing center. Since the latter queue is generally easier to apply, it could be useful to know under what circumstances we can replace closed queueing centers by open centers. The following rule of thumb is useful:

> An open queueing model is a reasonably accurate approximation to a closed queueing model if N is at least ten times larger than the number of requests Q_{w} waiting for service, i.e., $N \geq 10 \times Q_{\text{w}}$.

We can use our previous equations for an multiserver queue to render this rule of thumb into a quantitative criterion. We want to calculate an upper bound on the load beyond which the open approximation is not valid.

The rule of thumb states that $Q_{\text{w}} \leq N/10$. This condition may be observed on a real computer system, e.g., the run-queue load average in a UNIX system (Chap. 4). The number of requests waiting in line is $Q_{\text{w}} = Q - \rho$, i.e., the difference between the number of requests in the system and the number of requests in service. For an multiserver queue, the number of requests in the system is given by (2.65). The number of requests in service is $m\rho$. Hence, an approximation to the number of requests waiting in line is:

$$Q_{\text{w}} \simeq \frac{m\rho}{1-\rho^m} - m\rho \,. \tag{2.96}$$

We want to determine the value of ρ that satisfies the condition $Q_{\text{w}} \leq 0.10N$. This can be accomplished more easily by first rearranging (2.96) so that it reads:

$$Q_{\text{w}} - Q_{\text{w}}\,\rho^m - m\,\rho^{m+1} = 0 \,, \tag{2.97}$$

which can be solved using any root-finder program such as that available in *Mathematica* and similar tools.

For the repairman queue with a finite population of $N = 10$, the rule of thumb tells us the bound on the number of requests waiting in line is $Q_{\text{w}} \leq 1$. The corresponding bound on the server load will differ depending how many servers are available. We can determine that load by solving (2.97).

Example 2.15. Consider the simplest case of an uniserver queue which we render (2.97) in the following *Mathematica* program:

```
In[1] := (* Solve for the utilizations *)
         Nsys = 22.5;
         m = 1;
         Qw = N[Nsys/10];
         busy = Solve[Qw - Qwρ^m - mρ^(1+m) == 0, ρ];
         TableForm[busy]
Out[1] =
          ρ → -3.
          ρ → 0.75
```

The first set of results labeled *Out*[1], show that the server load ρ has *two* possible values: $\rho = -3.0$ and $\rho = 0.75$. This follows from the fact that $m = 1$ and therefore $m + 1 = 2$, corresponding to a second degree equation. Hence, there are two solutions but we are only interested in the one with a positive value viz, $\rho = 0.75$.

```
In[2] := (* Solve for the queue lengths *)
         β = Select[ρ /. busy, Positive];
         β = First[β];
         Q = Qw + mβ;
         {Qw, Q, β}
Out[2] = {2.25, 3., 0.75}
```

The list of results labeled *Out*[2] summarizes the values for queue lengths Q_{w}, Q, and ρ, respectively. We see that the total queue length is $Q = 3.0$, as expected for an $M/M/1$ queue with the server running at 75% busy. □

In the next example, we examine how things change when we add another server while keeping the number of finite requests the same.

Example 2.16. For a dual-server queue with Nsys = 22.5 we find:

```
In[3] := Nsys = 22.5;
         m = 2;
         ...
Out[3] =
         ρ → −0.947707 − 0.749737 I
         ρ → −0.947707 + 0.749737 I
         ρ → 0.770414
Out[4] = {2.25, 3.79083, 0.770414}
```

Since $m + 1 = 3$, we now have three possible roots, of which two are complex numbers and one is positive-valued. Moreover, the waiting line is kept at the same length but there are more requests in service, making Q larger. We note also that the two servers are busier. □

Finally, we add two more servers in the next example.

Example 2.17. For an $M/M/4$ queue we find:

```
In[5] := Nsys = 22.5;
         m = 4;
         Qw = N[Nsys/10];
         busy = Solve[Qw − Qwρ^m − mρ^(1+m) == 0, ρ];
         TableForm[busy]
```

$Out[5] =$

$\rho \rightarrow -0.858095 - 0.498703\,\mathtt{I}$
$\rho \rightarrow -0.858095 + 0.498703\,\mathtt{I}$
$\rho \rightarrow 0.176156 - 0.825562\,\mathtt{I}$
$\rho \rightarrow 0.176156 + 0.825562\,\mathtt{I}$
$\rho \rightarrow 0.801377$

$Out[6] = \{2.25, 5.45551, 0.801377\}$

Since $m + 1 = 5$, we now have five possible roots, of which four are complex numbers (denoted by the I term above) and one is positive-valued. The four servers are now running at about 80% busy. □

It will be useful to prepare the way for the client/server model discussed in Chap. 9 by verifying that the open queue approximation can be applied to that problem. We shall see that although there are a finite number of requesters in that system (closed circuit), we can model it as an open queueing circuit. We use (2.97) to examine the assumption.

Example 2.18. The baseline client/server architecture has $N = 100$ client terminals or benchmark drivers.

$In[7] :=$ `Nsys = 100;`
`m = 1;`
`...`

$Out[7] =$

$\rho \rightarrow -10.9161$
$\rho \rightarrow 0.91608$

$Out[8] = \{10., 10.9161, 0.91608\}$

This shows that an open queueing circuit approximation is justified as long as the queue length on any PDQ node does not exceed $Q = 10.92$ with the server no more than $\rho = 0.92$ busy. □

As we shall see in the baseline client/server model, all PDQ queueing nodes are less than 15% busy.

Example 2.19. The production client/server environment must support $N = 1,500$ users.

$In[9] :=$ `Nsys = 1500;`
`m = 1;`
`...`

$Out[9] =$

$\rho \rightarrow -150.993$
$\rho \rightarrow 0.993421$

$Out[10] = \{150., 150.993, 0.993421\}$

An open queueing model is justified as long as the total queue length is such that $Q < 151$ with the server load at $\rho < 0.99$. □

In the production client/server model, all PDQ queueing nodes are less than 85% busy. Indeed, we shall see that these conditions are fulfilled, and therefore an open PDQ circuit is a valid approximation for that situation.

2.9 Shorthand for Queues

We now introduce some general terminology and schematic symbols that are common currency among queueing theorists and will also be used throughout the remainder of this book.

2.9.1 Queue Schematics

As described in the preceding section, a queueing center comprises a server and a collection of requests that arrive, queue for service, and then depart. This is depicted schematically in Fig. 2.23. Throughout this book, we simplify Fig. 2.23 further by dropping any explicit depiction of arrivals and departures, resulting in Fig. 2.24. When we use the word queue we shall mean the complete center comprising the waiting requests and the server or service center. Hence, the term queue length shall mean the number of waiting requests and the one already in service. We follow Lazowska et al. [1984] in the use of this terminology.

Fig. 2.23. Schematic representation of a customer or request arriving (from the left) into a line of customers waiting to be served. A customer that has received service is shown departing the server to the right

Fig. 2.24. The symbolic representation of a FIFO queueing server used throughout this book

Requests appear as tokens in Fig. 2.24, which are shown as boxes when enqueued. It is important to keep in mind that these schematic representations should not be taken too literally. They are static representations of a dynamic situation in which the queue size is fluctuating in some random way as requests arrive, are serviced, and depart from the center.

A queue can also be thought of as behaving like a linked list where items are added at one end, and removed at the other. In the context of Perl, a queue is like an *array* variable [Schwartz and Phoenix 2001]. If `@que` is such a variable, then arrivals in Fig. 2.24 correspond to `unshift(@que)` and departures to `pop(@que)`. In fact, these routines could form the basis of a queueing simulator.

Most queueing servers, like that in Fig. 2.24, service requests in first-in-first-out (FIFO) or first-come-first-served (FCFS) order. Another possible service discipline, which occurs in computer memory stacks, for example, is called last-in-first-out (LIFO) or last-come-first-served (LCFS) order. The LIFO queue shown in Fig. 2.25 can be thought of quite literally stacking up requests like a dish dispenser in a cafeteria.

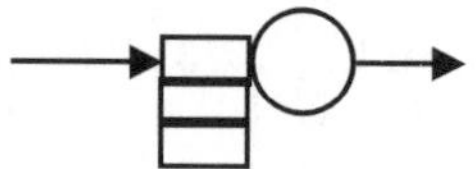

Fig. 2.25. Last-in-first-out (LIFO) queueing discipline

For the Perl queue `@que`, LIFO arrivals would correspond to `push(@que)` and departures to `pop(@que)`.

2.9.2 Kendall Notation

A commonly used shorthand notation for queues is due to Kendall [1951]. A queueing center (the waiting line together with the server) is classified according to a generic descriptor:

$$P_{\mathrm{a}}/P_{\mathrm{s}}/m/B/N/Q\,,$$

whose form resembles UNIX directory notation but does not refer to a tree structure. The first symbol refers to the distribution of interarrival time periods, the second to the distribution of service periods, and so on. A complete description appears in Table 2.6. The Kendall descriptor $M/G/4/50/2000/\mathrm{LIFO}$, for example, represents a queueing center with the following characteristics:

- The period P_a between successive arrivals into the queueing center is exponentially distributed or Markovian [Bloch et al. 1998]. See Sect. 2.11.2.
- The period P_s required to service each request is distributed in some general way. At least the mean and the standard deviation are usually known. See Sects. 2.11.9 and 2.11.10.
- The queue is serviced by $m = 4$ servers.

Table 2.6. Kendall queueing notation

Symbol	Meaning
P_A	Type of probability distribution that represents the periods between **arrivals** into the queueing center (e.g., deterministic (D), memoryless (M) or exponential, general (G))
P_S	Type of probability distribution that represents the periods required to **service** each request in the queueing center (e.g., M, D, G)
m	Number of servers at the queueing center
B	Buffer size or maximum length of the waiting line
N	Allowed population size, which may be either limited (finite) or unlimited (∞)
D	Type of service scheduling discipline (e.g., FIFO, LIFO)

- The queueing center can only buffer $B = 50$ requests comprised of 4 in service at each of the servers and 46 enqueued. Once the buffer is full, any additional requests overflow the system and are lost until the queue shrinks.
- The source of requests contains capacity for $N = 2,000$ requests.
- The scheduling discipline D is last-in-first-out.

A more typical example of a queueing center that arises in computer systems has the formal Kendall descriptor: $M/M/m/\infty/\infty/\text{FIFO}$. This symbol denotes an m-server queueing center with Markovian arrivals and exponentially distributed service times. The waiting line has unlimited buffering, the source of requests is infinite, and the service policy is FIFO. By convention, if either of B or N are unconstrained (i.e., infinite) and the queueing discipline is FIFO, those parts of the descriptor are suppressed and the reduced notation becomes simply $M/M/m$. In other words, it is the Kendall descriptor for the multiserver queue discussed in Sects. 2.7 and 2.7.1.

An $M/M/m$ queueing center can be used to make a very simple representation of a multiprocessor computer where the servers represent CPUs and the queue represents the process run-queue. More sophisticated models of multiprocessors can be constructed using an $M/M/m//N$ queue, and we consider that application in Chaps. 4 and 7.

There is no Kendall notation for parallel queues because they are mathematically equivalent to a set of $M/M/1$ queues. We could use $q(M/M/1)$ but this is not conventional Kendall notation.

2.10 Comparative Performance

We introduced queueing concepts for analyzing the performance of a grocery store in Sect. 2.3, and the post office in Sect. 2.3.3. We are now in a position to apply those queueing representations to dispassionately address the earlier question about the relative merits of those service architectures. Expanding the question slightly, and employing the Kendall shorthand for queues (Sect. 2.9.2), we shall compare:

1. Boarding an aircraft represented by a highly efficient $M/M/1$ queue.
2. The post office represented by an $M/M/m$ queue with m-servers.
3. The grocery store represented by a set of q parallel queues.

To make the comparison fare, we suppose that the number of service resources is equivalent, i.e., $q = m$, and therefore that the single-file $M/M/1$ queue has a server that is m times faster than the servers at the $M/M/m$ queue.

This type of performance comparison appears in different guises, sometimes even confounding performance experts. For example, a system architect might be confronted by such a comparison when choosing between a multiprocessor or a cluster platform to deploy an application (Chap. 7).

To keep the analysis simple, let us choose $q = m = 2$ (as we did in Sect. 2.6.6) and therefore the uniprocessor should have a service rate that is *twice* that of the other configurations. The performance metric of interest here is the response time R. Recasting the original question, we now have:

1. An $M/M/1$ queue (Fig. 2.24) with response time defined by (2.35) to represent aircraft boarding.
2. An $M/M/2$ queue (Fig. 2.14) with 2 servers and response time defined by (2.63) to represent the post office.
3. A multiqueue (Fig. 2.16) comprising $q = 2$ queues and response time defined by (Fig. 2.44) to represent the grocery store.

Figure 2.26 shows the result of using the respective equations to calculate the response times for these three queues.

2.10.1 Multiserver Versus Uniserver

At light loads ($\rho \ll 1$) there is little queueing, so the service time dominates the contribution to the response time in both cases. The service time at the uniserver is shorter by a factor of two, relative to the dual server (Fig. 2.27), so the uniserver also has the shorter response time. This performance advantage is diminished under heavy loads, however, since queueing begins to dominate the response time characteristic. Hence, these two curves become indistinguishable as they approach saturation ($\rho \to 1$). We already saw this effect in Sect. 2.6.6.

2.10.2 Multiqueue Versus Multiserver

The relative response time of the multiqueue is denoted by $2(M/M/1)$ in (Fig. 2.27). As before, under light loads ($\rho \ll 1$) there is very little queueing and the performance is determined by the respective service times. Both the dual queue and the dual server have servers that operate at the same rate

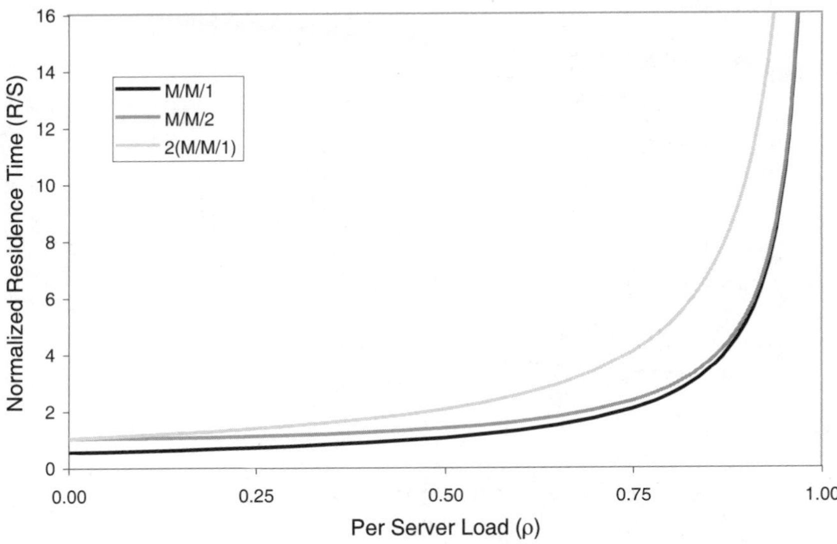

Fig. 2.26. Comparison of normalized response times R/S determined by three kinds of queueing delays: uniserver $M/M/1$, multiserver $M/M/2$, and multiqueue $2(M/M/2)$

(under our earlier assumption) so the response times are essentially identical because both service times are equal.

Under heavy loads the response time is dominated by the waiting time. Customers arriving at the dual queue $2(M/M/1)$, however, suffer a distinct disadvantage compared to those in the dual-server $M/M/2$ queue. Refering to Fig. 2.44, we see that a customer must decide which of the two queues to join. We assume there is a 50-50 chance of joining one or other of the two queues. Once they join a queue they are essentially waiting in an $M/M/1$ queue, but with a server that is twice as slow as the fast $M/M/1$ uniserver representing aircraft boarding. Obviously, they are worse off than if they were being serviced by the fast uniserver.

Customers waiting in the $M/M/2$ queue have twice the capacity servicing the single line. Even though the server operates at the same rate as a server in the dual queue, the customer at the head of the waiting line gets the next available server. Recall that we are looking at this from the standpoint of average service times. In reality, individual service times will deviate about the average time. Consider the case when the customer ahead of you has a significantly larger service time than the average. If you are waiting in one of the dual server queues, you must wait for that customer to complete before you can get served. Alternatively, if you are waiting in the dual server queue,

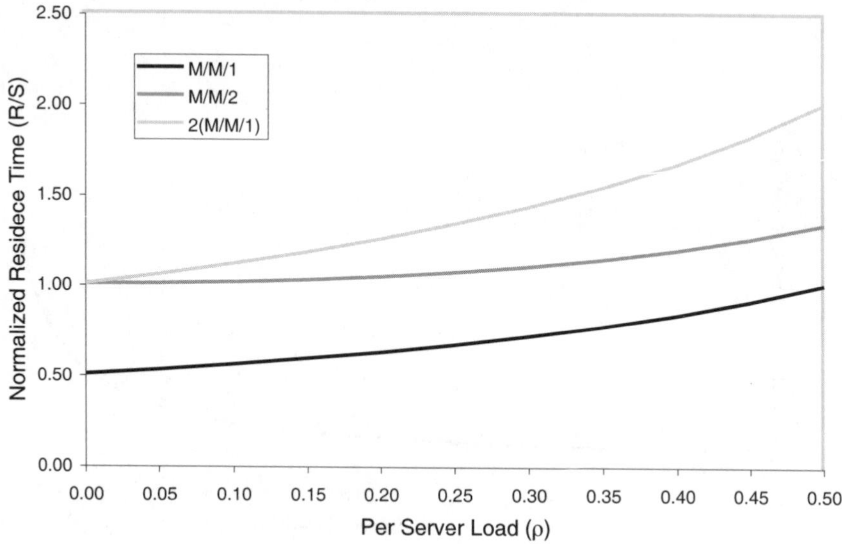

Fig. 2.27. Comparison of response times under light traffic shows that the multiserver and the multiqueue are initially less distinguishable than the uniserver (cf. Fig. 2.28)

you will be served as soon as the other server becomes available. Hence, the dual server outperforms the dual queue at moderate to heavy loads. This conclusion is also consistent with Sect. 2.6.6.

2.10.3 The Envelope Please!

Under the assumptions in this analysis, the best performance belongs to aircraft boarding while the the worst performer is the grocery store. Expressed in computer architecture terms, the worst performer is a cluster! As if to add insult to injury, the best performer is the fastest available uniprocessor. This is the same conclusion reached by Gene Amdahl [1967] in Sect. 8.3.2.

Unfortunately, acquiring the fastest uniprocessor is not always an option because it may be too expensive (as it used to be for mainframes). A more viable economic solution is to use a multiserver queue. This another the reason for the popularity of *symmetric multiprocessor* computers, discussed in Chap. 7. If a multiserver is generally to be preferred over the multiqueue, why does the post office seem to have so much worse performance than the grocery store? Remembering that it is easy to get perceptions confused with facts, here is a plausible explanation. The average service time in either place is very similar. In the grocery store, each customer generally has more items than a typical customer in the post office. However, the post office employees tend

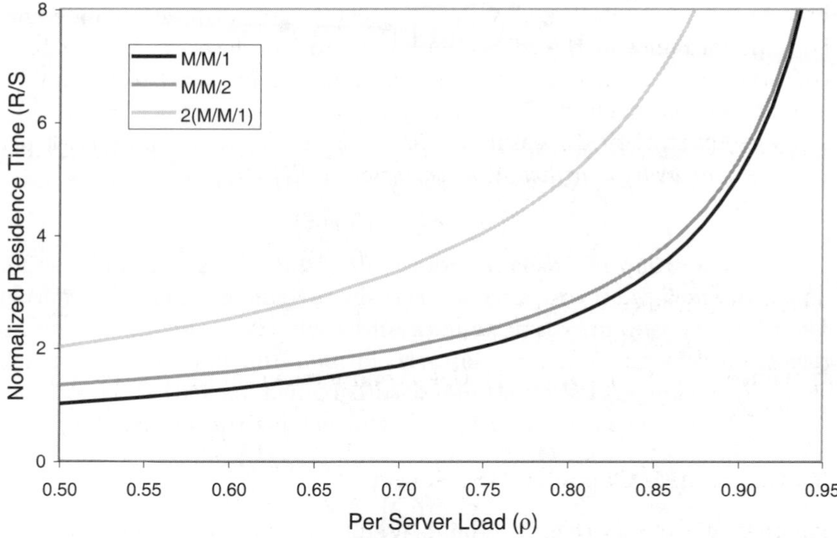

Fig. 2.28. Comparison of response times in the heavy traffic region where the multiserver and the uniserver become indistinguishable

to go through more tedious motions per item (including sometimes leaving their station for mysterious reasons). Assuming approximately similar service times, the post office usually only has three stations open simultaneously while the grocery store can incrementally open up to around ten checkouts. The grocery store has more capacity under heavy traffic. If the grocery store were restricted to opening only three checkouts, then standing in line at the post office might seem like a pleasure!

2.11 Generalized Servers

In our discussion so far, we have assumed that both arrivals and departures occur during intervals that are distributed exponentially in time, i.e., interactions with the queueing center follow a Poisson or memoryless process (Appendix C). This assumption, although important because of its widespread applicability for computer performance analysis, is not always valid.

For example, the service time distribution for accessing a local area network can depend on packet size and the existing traffic on the network. There may be significant correlations between data that has just been packetized and the remaining data that is yet to be packetized. Such correlations can induce a high degree of variance in the measured service periods. At dowstream network devices, measurements of Internet traffic indicate that packet arrivals are not always Poisson but arise from a self-similar or fractal-type process (see, e.g., Park and Willinger [2000]). Provided we are only considering performance at the connection or transaction level we will not have be concerned about self-similarity, but we should be prepared to accommodate significan variance effects in our analysis.

A useful statistical measure of dispersion about the mean service period $E(S)$ is the *squared coefficient of variation* or SCOV:

$$C_{\mathrm{S}}^2 = \frac{\sigma_{\mathrm{S}}^2}{S^2} \equiv \frac{Var(S)}{E^2(S)}\,, \tag{2.98}$$

where the variance:

$$Var(S) = E(S^2) - E^2(S)\,, \tag{2.99}$$

is defined as in terms of $E(S^2)$, the second moment of the service time distribution.

2.11.1 Infinite Capacity (IS) Server

Another type of service center that is useful for computer performance models is represented in Fig. 2.29. Here a request is serviced immediately, without having to wait in a queue at all. In queueing parlance, this is tantamount to having a server available, no matter how many requests there may be to service. For this reason it is sometimes called an *infinite capacity service center*, which is commonly abbreviated to *infinite server* or simply IS.

The most common application of an IS is in a closed queueing system where there is a finite number of requests and the service time at the IS corresponds to a delay period. Since the IS has historically represented users at their terminals [Scherr 1967], this delay is called the *think time.* If the number

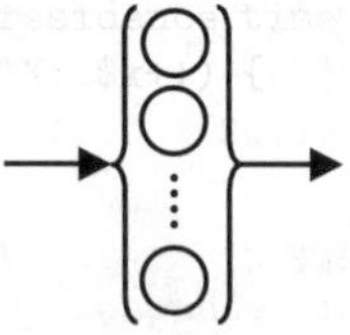

Fig. 2.29. A delay center or infinite server with no queues

of servers is finite then a queue will form when all the available servers are occupied. Such a multiserver queueing center is depicted in Fig. 2.30.

With these schematic conventions in place, we can now proceed to characterize queueing servers in more detail. Because queues exhibit different performance characteristics depending on the nature of the arrival and service processes, it is useful to employ a compact notation to denote which processes are being assumed. To analyze a queueing center we need to specify the following characteristics:

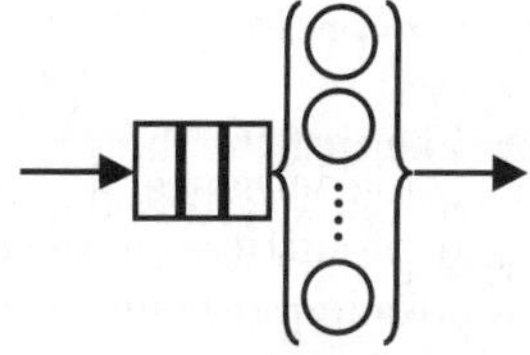

Fig. 2.30. A single queue with multiple servers

- the probability distribution of the periods between arrivals into the queueing center
- the probability distribution of the service periods for each request in the queueing center
- number of servers at the queueing center
- buffer size or storage capacity at the queueing center
- the total number of requests that can be present at the queueing center
- the type of service policy

Some of the more common time distributions used to model arrival or service periods are presented briefly in the following sections.

2.11.2 Exponential (M) Server

For an exponential server the service time follows the exponential distribution discussed in Chap. 1. The exponential distribution is a *continuous* function.

For the arrivals process it means that the period between the last arrival and the next is completely independent of the previous arrival period. Similarly, for service periods. Since the periods are not correlated in time, the corresponding processes are sometimes said to be *memoryless* or *Markovian* (See Appendix C). The *number* of arrivals in any period follow a *Poisson* distribution. Consequently, arrivals that are completely random belong to a Poisson process. The mean and the standard deviation of the service times are identical for the exponential distribution or equivalently:

$$E(S) = S \; , \; Var(S) = S^2 \; . \tag{2.100}$$

and therefore it has unit coefficient of variation (2.98):

$$C_S = 1 \, . \tag{2.101}$$

The exponential density function with mean $S = 1$ in Fig. 1.3, demonstrates that most periods are short compared with the average whereas only a few periods tend to be longer than the average or $90\% < 2.3S$, $63\% < S$. Since computer systems often exhibit completely random behavior, the exponential distribution is surprisingly ubiquitous in queueing models.

2.11.3 Deterministic (D) Server

The current service period is identical to the previous service period, therefore all periods are constant with no statistical variation between them. The expected service time is therefore:

$$E(S) = const.$$

So, the mean service time is equal to all the service periods, and the SCOV (2.98) is zero. In contrast to the $M/M/1$ residence time (2.35), the $M/D/1$ residence time is:

$$R = \frac{\rho S}{2(1-\rho)} + S\,. \tag{2.102}$$

The difference is that the waiting time is halved. Applying Little's law $Q = \lambda R$ to (2.102), we can write the $M/D/1$ queue length in terms of the $M/M/1$ queue length as:

$$Q_{\mathrm{M/D/1}} = \left(\frac{\rho}{1-\rho}\right)\left(1 - \frac{1}{2}\rho\right) \equiv Q_{\mathrm{M/M/1}}\left(1 - \frac{1}{2}\rho\right)\,. \tag{2.103}$$

If the interarrival periods are also deterministic (D), the queue becomes $D/D/1$, and there is actually no queueing at all until $\rho = 1$. A simple example of this phenomenon is a manufacturing conveyor belt that feeds boxes into a shrink-wrapping station. All the boxes are spaced out evenly so their arrival at the shrink-wrapper is deterministic (the first D), and the shrink-wrap process takes the same deterministic time (the second D) for each box. Boxes can never pile up unless the spacing becomes boxes becomes zero ($\rho = 1$).

2.11.4 Uniform (U) Server

In a uniform server the service period is bounded by some finite interval. If If the service time has a continuous distribution and is uniformly distributed on the interval from a to b, the mean and variance of the service time are:

$$E(S) = \frac{a+b}{2}\,,\; Var(S) = \frac{(b-a)^2}{12}\,. \tag{2.104}$$

The queueing characteristic lies between that of the deterministic and exponential distributions.

2.11.5 Erlang-k (E_k) Server

The Erlang-k server is sometimes employed as an artifact for generalizing the continuous exponential distribution while maintaining mathematical tractability. The service center is represented by series of k delay *stages* (Fig. 2.31), each having service periods which are exponentially distributed

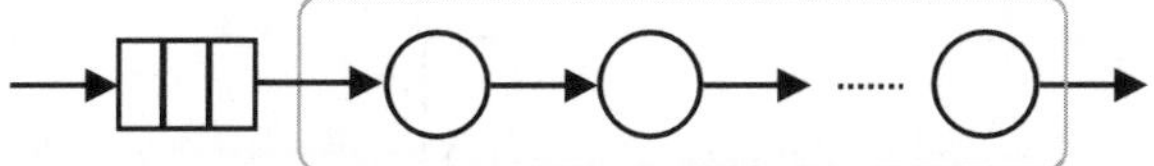

Fig. 2.31. Erlang server with k stages

with the same average S. There is no queueing at any of the internal stages because the next request cannot start service until the previous request has completed all k stages. The service time distribution for such a service center is said to be *Erlang-k*.

$$E(S) = S \ , \ Var(S) = \frac{S^2}{k} \ . \tag{2.105}$$

The coefficient of variation (2.98) is therefore:

$$C_S = \frac{1}{\sqrt{k}} \ . \tag{2.106}$$

Mathematically, the Erlang-k distribution is a special case of the gamma distribution discussed in Chap. 1.

2.11.6 Hypoexponential (*Hypo–k*) Server

A variant of the staged server like the Erlang-k server, but with each service stage having a different mean service period. The hypoexponential distribution has less variability than the exponential distribution, hence its name.

Hypoexponential distribution $C_S < 1$. Most periods are close to the average, $C = \frac{1}{2}$ implies $90\% < 2.0S$, only $57\% < S$.

2.11.7 Hyperexponential (H_k) Server

This is another variant on a staged server which is in some sense the *dual* of the Erlang-k model. A hyperexponential distribution has more variability than the exponential distribution.

It can be represented by a number exponential servers different mean service times arranged in parallel. The simplest model has two parallel stages in the service center (Fig. 2.32). Suppose the upper stage has mean exponential service time S_1 and the lower stage has exponential service time S_2. A customer entering the service center chooses the upper stage with probability α_1 or the lower stage with probability α_2, where $\alpha_1 + \alpha_2 = 1$. After being serviced the selected stage, the customer exists the service center. The next customer is not permitted to enter the service center until the original customer has completed service. The expected service time in the service center is:

$$E(S) = \alpha_1 S_1 + \alpha_2 S_2 \, . \tag{2.107}$$

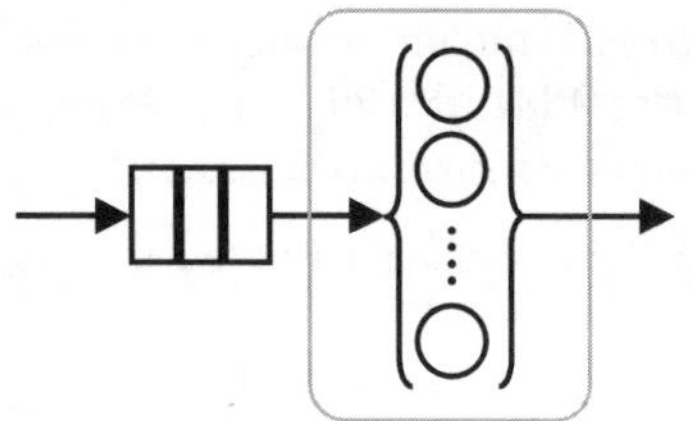

Fig. 2.32. Hyperexponential server

and the variance is:

$$Var(S) = 2\alpha_1 S_1 + 2\alpha_2 S_2 - (\alpha_1 S_1 + \alpha_2 S_2)^2 \,. \tag{2.108}$$

The SCOV for the Hyperexponential distribution $C_S > 1$, so most periods are further from mean than for the exponential distribution. For example $C = 2.0$ implies 90% $< 2.8S$, and 69% $< S$.

2.11.8 Coxian (*Cox–k*) Server

The Coxian distribution is another type of staged server (Fig. 2.33) with staged exponentially distributed service times S_i for i = 1,2, ..., k stages, and probability

$$A_i = \prod_{i=0}^{k-1} a_i \,, \tag{2.109}$$

of advancing to the ith server and branching probability b_i of exiting after the ith server. The next request cannot enter the service center until the current request has either completed all stages or exited after the ith stage. Consequently, there is no queueing inside the composite service center.

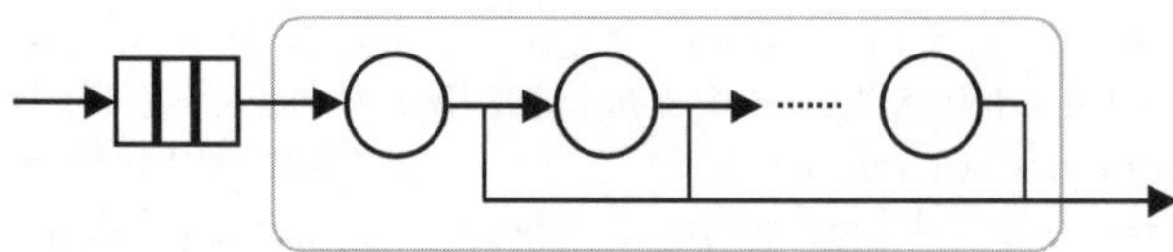

Fig. 2.33. Coxian server

The expected service time in the service center is:

$$E(S) = \sum_{i=1}^{k} A_i b_i \left(\prod_{j=1}^{i} S_j \right) \tag{2.110}$$

and the variance is:

$$Var(S) = E(S^2) - E^2(S) \tag{2.111}$$

where $E(S^2)$ is given by:

$$E(S^2) = \sum_{i=1}^{k} A_i b_i \left[\left(\prod_{j=1}^{i} S_j^2 \right) + \left(\prod_{j=1}^{i} S_j \right)^2 \right] \tag{2.112}$$

2.11.9 General (G) Server

The period for a general server is not characterized by any single probability distribution because the corresponding process is completely arbitrary. A typical example is a process that generates a bimodal distribution of time periods. For example, in a token ring network there is one distribution for the time to pass a token between nodes and another distribution that describes the period for which a token is held by a node on the network.

Properties of these service time distributions are listed in Table 2.6. In the case of network packetization one might prefer to model the service time distribution as an $M/G/1$ queueing center. In another situation one might want to model best-case performance using constant service time, i.e., an $M/D/1$ queueing center. How are these different queueing types related to our previous discussion? PDQ assumes that all queueing centers are Markovian, but residual service times can be incorporated using the techniques of Lazowska et al. [1984].

Table 2.7. Properties of some generalized service time distributions arranged in order of decreasing squared coefficient of variation. Details regarding the distributions are presented in the referenced sections

$M/G/1$ type	C_S^2	Service pattern	Reference
$M/H_k/1$	> 1	Clustered	Sect. 2.11.7
$M/M/1$	1	Randomized	Sect. 2.11.2
$M/U/1$	1/3	Regular ($a = 0$, $b = 1$)	Sect. 2.11.4
$M/E_k/1$	$1/k$	Peaked	Sect. 2.11.5
$M/D/1$	0	Constant	Sect. 2.11.3

In addition to the distributions of time periods just described, different scheduling policies can be used to determine the order in which requests are serviced. Some of the more common policies include:

- First-In-First-Out (FIFO). FIFO is more common in computer hardware parlance while first-come-first-served (FCFS) is the typical queue-theoretic term. Requests are serviced from the head of the queue. This is the most common type of service and the one you most commonly experience in everyday life.

- Last-In-First-Out (LIFO). LIFO corresponds the order in which dishes are taken from a stack of washed plates in a cafeteria. Last-come-first-served (LCFS) is the more typical queue-theoretic terminology.
- Round Robin (RR). Time at a resource (e.g., a CPU) is allocated in a small, fixed amount called a quantum. Requests circulate, in order, via the queue until their total service time is satisfied.
- Processor sharing (PS). Processor sharing is a simple analytic approximation to RR where the time quantum becomes tiny compared to the mean service time. Each of N waiting requests receives $1/N$ of the server's capacity. For example, 20 tasks would see only 5 MIPS of a 100 MIPS processor when they received service. The benefit is that they all see 5 MIPS.
- Priority. Some customers may receive special preference and preempt the service of those already waiting in the queue. Interrupt priority levels in a computer system are an expression of this kind of service discipline.

2.11.10 Pollaczek–Khintchine Formula

Until now we have assumed that a newly arriving customer sees not only those customers already enqueued but also the customer in service and that this customer requires their full service time complement. It would seem more realistic to assume that some fraction of the service time still remains. This quantity is called the *residual service time.*

Using our earlier explicit notation $E(S) \equiv S$ for the expectation or average of the distribution of service periods (the first moment) and writing $E(S^2)$ for the second moment, the mean residual service time κ is defined by:

$$\kappa = \frac{E(S^2)}{2E(S)} . \tag{2.113}$$

With the residual service time included, the average waiting time now comprises two terms.

$$W = LE(S) + \kappa\rho \tag{2.114}$$

The first term is the time due to L customers in the waiting line, each with an average service time requirement of $E(S)$. The second term is the residual service time due to the customer currently in service. Since we are dealing with a single service center, the probability that the server is busy is ρ.

Like the derivation of (2.32) for the uniserver response time in Sect. 2.6.3, (2.114) is the average waiting time seen by an arriving customer. Applying Little's law $L = \lambda W$ to the first term in (2.114) produces:

$$E(W) = \lambda W E(S) + \rho \frac{E(S^2)}{2E(S)} , \tag{2.115}$$

and solving for W yields:

$$E(W)_{\mathrm{PK}} = \frac{\lambda E(S^2)}{2(1-\rho)}\,, \tag{2.116}$$

This is also known as the *Pollaczek–Khintchine* (or simply P–K) equation for the average waiting time at an $M/G/1$ queue. The corresponding expression for the average residence time:

$$E(R)_{\mathrm{PK}} = E(S) + \frac{\lambda E(S^2)}{2(1-\rho)} \tag{2.117}$$

follows from the general definition $R = S + W$ applied to (2.116).

Equation (2.117) can be written more transparently in terms of the SCOV (2.98) of the service time distribution:

$$R_{\mathrm{PK}} = S + \frac{\rho S}{2(1-\rho)}\,(1 + C_{\mathrm{S}}^2)\,. \tag{2.118}$$

where we have now dropped the explicit notation for the first and second moments. Employing the Kendall notation in Table 2.6 we note that (2.118) for $M/G/1$ reduces to the mean response time for an $M/D/1$ queue (2.102) when $C_{\mathrm{S}}^2 = 0$ and to the $M/M/1$ case when $C_{\mathrm{S}}^2 = 1$. Other generalized server queues are summarized in Table 2.7. Applying Little's law $Q = \lambda R$ to (2.118) yields:

$$Q_{\mathrm{PK}} = \rho + \frac{\rho^2}{2(1-\rho)}\,(1 + C_{\mathrm{S}}^2)\,. \tag{2.119}$$

A useful alternative arrangement is:

$$Q_{\mathrm{PK}} = \frac{\rho}{1-\rho} + \frac{\rho^2}{2(1-\rho)}\,(C_{\mathrm{S}}^2 - 1)\,. \tag{2.120}$$

which can be written symbolically as:

$$Q_{\mathrm{PK}} \equiv Q_{\mathrm{M/M/1}} + \frac{\rho^2}{2(1-\rho)}\,(C_{\mathrm{S}}^2 - 1)\,, \tag{2.121}$$

which can be compared with (2.103).

The important point to note when using (2.117) is that you must have measurements of the mean service period as well as the standard deviation or variance of the service periods.

2.11.11 Polling Systems

So far, in this chapter we have considered queues comprised of single waiting lines feeding one or more servers. Most of Sect. 2.7 is devoted to a detailed analysis of the performance gains due multiserver queues. This line of thought would justifiably lead you to the conclusion that having multiple waiting lines

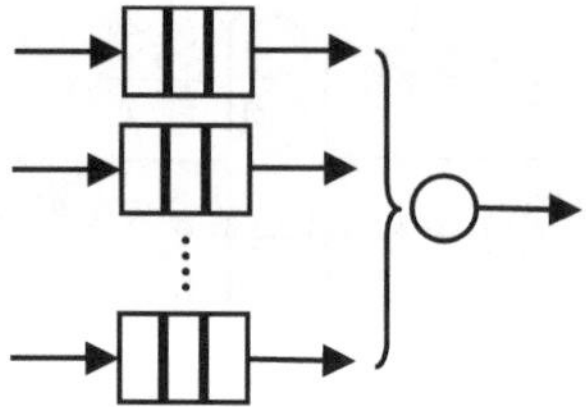

Fig. 2.34. Single server that polls incoming requests from multiple waiting lines

feeding a single server is a configuration that could not possibly offer any useful performance advantages.

In general this is true, but there are exceptions. The notion of keeping different track of different types of work by keeping them in different buffers (waiting rooms) arises in many computer and communication architectures, e.g., packet multiplexing in Internet routers [Keshav 1998, Gunther et al. 2003], and multiple priority queues in the UNIX sheduler [Vahalia 1996]. These are queueing configurations are known as *polling systems* 2.34.

A polling system contains a single server and $N > 1$ waiting lines with infinite capacity, indexed by $i = 1, 2, \ldots, N$. Customers arrive to waiting line n in accordance with a Poisson process having arrival rate λ_i, with $\lambda_i = \lambda_j$ in a *symmetric* system. The server visits each waiting line in cyclic (round robin) order, viz. 1, 2, ..., N, 1, 2, ... Without loss of generality, we can assume that the server is initially at queue $n = 1$.

If all waiting customers are serviced when the center is polled it is called an *exhaustive* system. Otherwise, in a *non-exhaustive* system, just one customer is serviced if the center is not empty when it is polled. Total arrival rate is:

$$\lambda = \sum_{i=1}^{N} \lambda_i \tag{2.122}$$

Total utilization:

$$\rho = \sum_{i=1}^{N} \rho_i \tag{2.123}$$

where the utilization $\rho_i = \lambda_i E(S)$. The average waiting time for a symmetric, non-exhaustive system is given by:

$$W_{\text{polling}} = \frac{1}{1 - g_i} \left[\frac{\lambda E(S^2)}{2(1-\rho)} + \frac{\Theta}{2(1-\rho)} \left(1 + \frac{\rho}{N} \right) \right] , \tag{2.124}$$

where Θ is the polling delay per waiting line and

$$g_i = \frac{\lambda_i \Theta}{1 - \rho} \tag{2.125}$$

is the average number of customers served per cycle at the ith waiting line. The stability condition is $g_i < 1$.

As the polling delay becomes very small $\Theta \to 0$, (2.124) reduces to the P–K equation (2.116). Another interesting special case is a token ring network (Fig. 2.35) where the second term in (2.124) respresents the latency of the network.

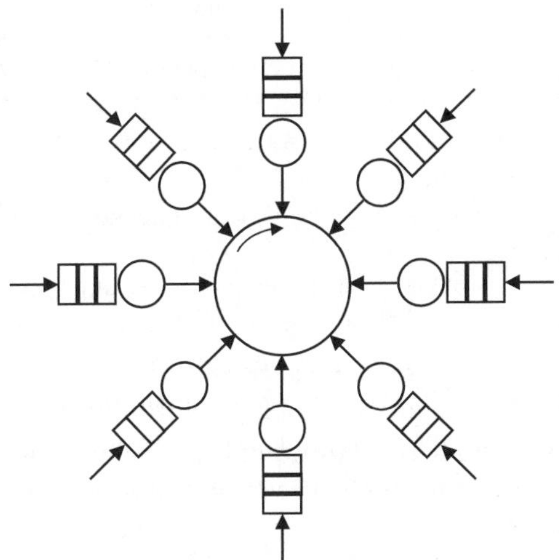

Fig. 2.35. Token ring network treated as a polling system

2.12 Review

We have covered a lot of ground in this chapter. For future reference and to help you locate a particular queueing formula, see the *compendium* provided in Appendix E. Cross-references to the corresponding explanatory text are also provided there.

Apart from the trivial exceptions of parallel queues and closed queues, our discussion has centered on single queues where a customer or request only visits one queueing center and then departs (in the case of open queues) or returns to the same queue (in the case of closed queues). In Chap. 3 we consider the interaction of many queues because systems of queues are required to analyze the performance of computer systems.

Many of the more mathematical aspects of probability theory were deliberately suppressed through the use of averages. This means that higher moments, such as the variance, cannot be calculated directly, but we can apply the percentile rules of thumb discussed in Chap 1.

At the very least, you should now have a stronger intuitive understanding of queues such that you can now make considerable headway with more erudite queueing texts such as [Allen 1990, Kleinrock 1976, Lazowska et al. 1984], and [Trivedi 2000].

Exercises

2.1. The *Pay-And-Pay* grocery store chain is considering ways to improve the performance of the waiting lines at their checkout stands. A heavily trafficed checkout stand is monitored for 120 min. In that period, 60 customers have their groceries rung up, and depart from the store. The checker was observed to be busy 75% of the time.
(**a**) What is the number of arrivals at that checkout line? Give reasons to support your conclusion.
(**b**) What is the average arrival rate into that waiting line?
(**c**) What is the average throughput at that checkout stand?
(**d**) What is the average service time per customer?
(**e**) What are the units of the service time metric in this problem?

2.2. The manager at *Pay-And-Pay* would like to know what will happen to a customer's residence time at the checkout stand in Exercise 2.1 if she adds another cashier to the end of the waiting line. In other words, if she creates a single waiting line feeding two servers. There are actually two plausible scenarios:
(**a**) Added capacity case. Assume that the *total* utilization with both checkers is 75%.
(**b**) Scaled traffic case. Assume that the utilization of each checker is 75%.
What important point about these two cases would you emphasize to the grocery store manager?

2.3. An image file takes 1 min to scan (on average). A computer system needs to be able to scan 75,000 files per month.
(**a**) How busy will the server be?
(**b**) What is the average waiting time at the scanner?
(**c**) How many scanning servers would be required to meet a service level objective of better than 1.3 min per image file?

2.4. Is there an *Erlang A* function? Explain your answer.

2.5. Apply Little's law to show that the comparison of response times in Fig. 2.26 is also reflected in the respective queue lengths.

2.6. What happens to Fig. 2.26 when the queue lengths or response times are plotted against arrival rate λ rather than utilization ρ.

2.7. Measurements of a UNIXdatabase server that supports 100 active users show that the average user response time is 1.5 s per transaction. The average CPU service time per transaction is found to be 300 ms, at 25% CPU time spent in the UNIXkernel and 50% in user space. What is the average think-time per transaction?

2.8. A server supports 70 active clients. You use a stopwatch to record and calculate the average time between the submission of transactions. You find it to be around 30 s. The paging disk has a measured service demand of 250 ms at 50% disk-busy. What is the average transaction response time?

2.9. An application server receives transactions at the rate of 8 transactions per second. If each transaction takes an average of 0.7 s to complete, how many transactions (on average) are simultaneously in the server?

2.10. A hotel bartender knows that, on average, 18 customers arrive per hour at the bar. Typically, there are 6 customers sitting at the bar. What is the average time each customer resides at the bar?

3

Queueing Systems for Computer Systems

3.1 Introduction

In Chap. 2 the analysis of queueing performance only involved a single queueing center. Even when more than one queueing center was available, the customer only visited one of them. Such single queueing centers can only be used successfully to represent a single device or elements of a computer system, e.g., a disk device. If the performance analyst is required to assess the interaction of various devices in the complete computer system, the analysis methods presented in Chap. 2 are not sufficient, in general.

In general, we need to develop ways for analyzing systems of queues in order to represent the performance attributes of real computer systems. This follows from the fact that execution of a computational workload usually involves more than one subsystem, e.g., CPU, memory, and I/O subsystems. In queueing parlance, this corresponds to a customer visiting more than one queueing center and possibly visiting each center more than once, e.g., the request spends some time at the CPU followed by some memory references, followed by additional CPU cycles, then some I/O, and so on.

Since several queues are involved in the execution of the workload, it is no longer clear how to apply the equations we developed in Chap. 2. Historically, this was also part of the reason that it took about 50 years to apply queueing concepts to computer systems (Appendix B). We could resort to solving the necessary system of queues by simulation techniques. This approach takes time to program (either in a simulation language or with a graphical interface) and will also take considerable real time to find and verify the steady-state solutions.

There is another technique that allows us to generalize from the concepts presented in Chap. 2 to solve systems of queues. It is based on a number of well-tested assumptions about the behavior of queues. It is known as *Mean Value Analysis* or MVA. We present that algorithm in this chapter. Once understood, however, you will not need to revisit it because it is embedded in PDQ.

In this chapter you will learn how to extend the characterization of single queueing centers to include a flow of customers or requests through a sytem of queues. This is necessary to analyze real computer systems because real computers involve more than one subsystem, e.g., CPU, memory, and I/O subsystems.s

We commence with a discussion of how flows of requests can be merged into a single queue as well as how they can split into multiple flows once they have been serviced. We then discuss both series and parallel circuits of queues that can be both open and closed. This also includes possibility of flows feeding back into the tail of a queue. The next topic is queueing circuits where more than one workload is serviced. This is necessary because many computer systems, especially application servers, run more than one task at a time. We then summarize all these aspects as a set of rules for applying queueing circuits in performance analysis.

Finally, we show how queueing circuits can be applied to some classic computer systems, e.g., time-share systems, fair-share systems, time-share systems with priority scheduling, and threaded servers.

3.2 Types of Circuits

In this and subsequent chapters we shall refer to a collection of queues that represent a computer system as a *circuit* of queues. In the formal queueing literature a system of queues is often referred to as a queueing *network*. In part, this terminology is historical legacy from a time before queueing models were widely applied to data networks. We prefer to emphasize the commonality with other engineering terminology such as *control theory* or signal processing [See e.g., Oppenheim et al. 1983]. These common attributes can be summarized as follows:

- circuits involve *flows* (e.g., electrons or requests)
- circuits have defined *inputs* and *outputs*
- circuits can be combined in *series* and *parallel* or both (see Sects. 3.4.1 and 3.4.5)
- circuits can be partitioned into *subcircuits* (or subroutines) (see Sect. 3.5.2)
- subcircuits can be *shorted out* to provide simplified solution techniques (discussed in Sect. 6.7.11 of Chap. 6)
- circuits can involve *feedback* which imposes a *closed* loop (see Sects. 3.4.3 and 3.5)

Clearly, the words *network* and *circuit* are interchangeable.

The most convenient way to begin classifying queueing circuits is to first determine if the circuit is *open* or *closed* or *mixed*. Just like the simplest *open* queues in Chap. 2 (e.g., $M/M/1$), circuits of open queues have arrivals that come from an external source, receive service at a succession of queueing centers like those shown in Fig. 3.1, and then depart from the queueing circuit

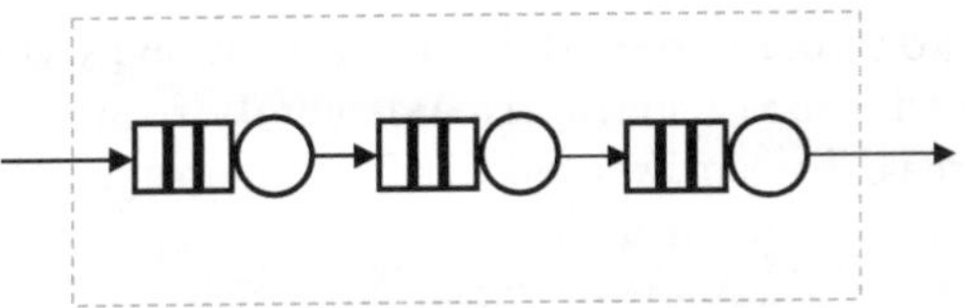

Fig. 3.1. A very simple open queueing circuit. The system is defined by the *dotted box*. Customers arrive come from outside the system, receive successive service at each of the queues in the circuit, and depart the system

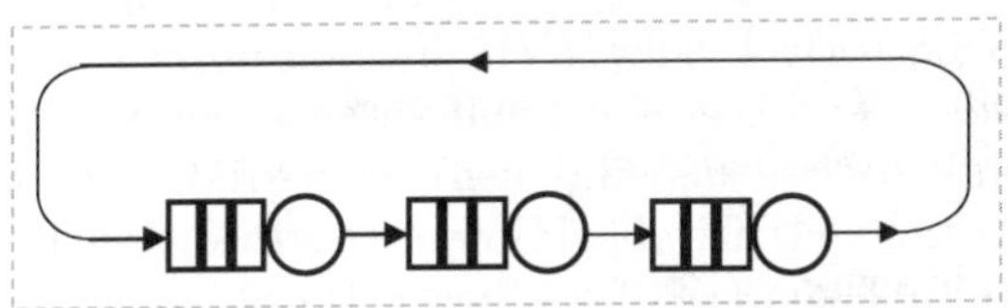

Fig. 3.2. A very simple closed queueing circuit. No customers arrive from outside the system (*dotted box*), so there is always a finite number of them in circulation

forever, never to return. Like their single queue counterparts, such open circuits of queues are usually parameterized by the rate λ of incoming requests. We consider more detailed examples of open circuit queues in Sect. 3.4.

A *closed* queueing circuit, like that shown in Fig. 3.2, has a *finite* number of requests that are constantly circulating within the circuit bounded by the dashed box. Since no new requests can arrive from or depart to the outside, the

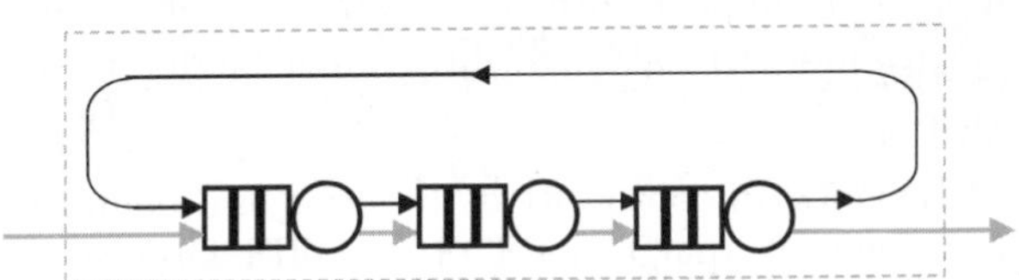

Fig. 3.3. A mixed open (grey arrows) and closed (back arrows) queueing circuit

total number of requests N remains constant and can be used a parameter to characterize the closed queueing circuit. More detailed examples are presented in Sect. 3.5.

It is also possible to have a combination of both types of circuits: some requests flowing into the circuit from outside and then departing, along with other requests that flow back into the same circuit, such as the one shown in Fig. 3.3.

Example 3.1. A common example where a mixed-class circuit might be used to represent a computer system is a time-share computer (Sect. 3.9.1) in which the interactive (closed) flow of requests is mixed with HTTP Get (open) requests from the Internet. Such a mixed circuit is solved by first calculating the effect of the open workload on the queueing resources separately and then calculating the performance of the closed workload in the presence of the diminished resources. □

We shall return to the interaction mixed workloads in Sect 3.7. For the moment, we limit ourselves to single-class workloads.

3.3 Poisson Properties

As we discussed in Sect. 2.11.2, Poisson processes are important for analyzing queueing effects because the interarrival times for requests are exponentially distributed in time while the number of arrivals in any interval is Poisson distributed. In this sense, a Poisson process is synonymous with completely randomized events.

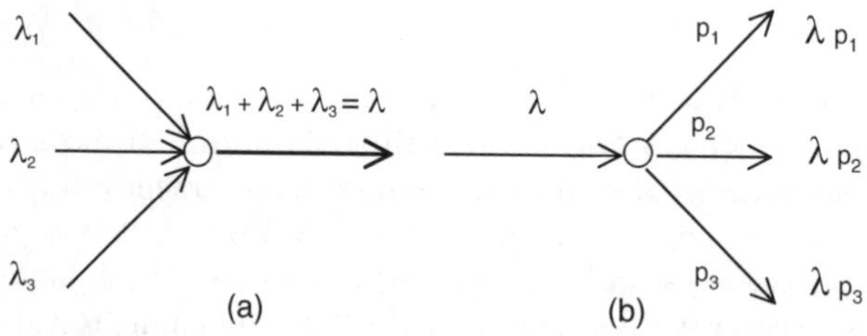

Fig. 3.4. Poisson streams showing (**a**) the merging of three arrival streams into one stream of intensity $\lambda = \lambda_1 + \lambda_2 + \lambda_3$, and (**b**) the branching of a single stream into three departure streams each selected with independent (Bernoulli) probabilities p_1, p_2, p_3 such that $p_1 + p_2 + p_3 = 1$

The interarrival process that generates this characteristic is often referred to as a *Poisson stream*; PDQ has a program variable called `streams` to enumerate different work flows. See Sect. 6.5.1 for a more detailed discussion. This Poisson property ensures the *memoryless*-ness of the arrivals (See Appendix C). This, in turn, leads to the so-called PASTA property we shall present in Sect. 3.3.3. The time to the next arrival is in no way correlated to the interval that belonged to the previous arrival. Furthermore, it allows us to handle *merging* and *branching* Poisson streams of requests in a simple way.

3.3.1 Poisson Merging

When several Poisson streams arrive at the same point (e.g., the same queue) they can be combined additively such that they can be treated as single stream having intensity equal to the sum of the independent streams. This is shown schematically in Fig. 3.4a.

This merging of Poisson streams follows from the properties of the *moment generating function* (MGF) for a Poisson random variable X:

$$G_X(\theta) = E(e^{\theta X}) = e^{\lambda t \ (\exp(\theta)-1)}, \tag{3.1}$$

where $E(\cdot)$ is the expectation or statistical mean. The MGF has the property that if X and Y are two independent random variables then:

$$G_{X+Y}(\theta) = G_X(\theta) \ G_Y(\theta). \tag{3.2}$$

For two Poisson random variables:

$$e^{\lambda_1 t \ (\exp(\theta)-1)} e^{\lambda_2 t \ (\exp(\theta)-1)} = e^{(\lambda_1+\lambda_2) \ t \ (\exp(\theta)-1)}, \tag{3.3}$$

In other words, the merging (superposition) of two Poisson streams produces a single Poisson stream with intensity equal to the sum of their intensities. This follows from the fact that the product of exponentials is equal to the exponential sum of the exponents in the MGF. The same conclusion can be extended to three streams (as in Fig. 3.4) or more.

3.3.2 Poisson Branching

The complement of merging Poisson streams is splitting or branching of a single stream into several independent Poisson streams. Figure 3.4b depicts the branching of a single stream into three departure streams each selected with independent Bernoulli probabilities p_1, p_2, p_3 such that the sum $p_1 + p_2 + p_3 = 1$.

> Poisson branching and merging is fundamental to routing the flow of requests in a queueing system. We have already seen it implicitly in Chap. 2 for parallel queues (Sect. 2.6.5) where arrivals split uniformly into separate streams for each queue, and for multiserver queues (Sect. 2.7) where requests are serviced from the waiting line by splitting them uniformly (i.e., with equal probability) into each server. In this chapter, we consider Poisson streams that flow between different queueing centers (e.g., CPU, disk, LAN) in a circuit representation of a computer system.

The formal proofs of these theorems for Poisson splitting (decomposition) and merging (superposition) can be found in more mathematical texts such as [Allen 1990] and [Trivedi 2000].

3.3.3 Poisson Pasta

Think back to the grocery store example in Sect. 2.3. One of the considerations you might have in choosing which line to join is the estimated amount of time remaining for the customer currently having their groceries rung up. This estimate would be very pertinent if they were the only customer ahead of you. It is the least amount of time you have to wait before you can begin your own service.

But how do things appear to a grocery shopper who is casually watching all the checkout lines without having joined any? We called this the *residual* service time given by (2.113) in Sect. 2.11.10, and it was the basis for the Pollaczek–Khintchine formula (2.118).

Technically, these two time estimates—the one belonging to the arriving customer and the other to external grocery shopper—can be shown to be different, in general. If, however, the arrivals are of the Poisson type we have been describing here, the time estimates will be equivalent. This important Poisson property is called the *PASTA* property: *Poisson Arrivals See Time Averages.*

All of the above Poisson properties have been stated without formal proof. The interested reader is encouraged to see the proofs in more mathematical books on queueing theory [Kleinrock 1976, Allen 1990, Trivedi 2000].

Certain kinds of Internet traffic produce arrivals that are highly correlated over extensive periods of time: from milliseconds to minutes. These time-based correlations seriously violate the above Poisson properties, and other techniques have to be applied to analyze such *non-Poisson* characteristics. An excellent account of the history of this problem (see also Appendix B) and some of the techniques that have been developed over the last decade to deal with it can be found in Park and Willinger [2000].

3.4 Open-Circuit Queues

Unlike the single queues we examined in Chap. 2, there is no equivalent of Kendall notation for circuits of queues. However, queueing circuits can be thought of as having many properties in common with electrical circuits, and some of those concepts and notations can be applied. The flow of requests in Fig. 3.1, for example, is analogous to electrical current flow.

Although requests are *discrete* entities (just like electrons), if there is a reasonable number of them being serviced in the queueing circuit such that time can be regarded as *continuous*, the analogy with *direct electrical current* is very apt. And just like an electric circuit (or the availability of components discussed in Sect. 1.7.5 of Chap. 1), the flow of requests between queues can coupled in *series* or in *parallel* or a combination of both.

In Sect. 3.9.4, we shall apply a form of circuit decomposition to threads scheduling. This is the queueing circuit analog of *Thevenin's theorem* for electrical circuits [Jain 1990, Sect. 36.2], which allows us to treat subcircuits separately by *shorting* them out from the entire circuit. But first, we consider different types of series queueing circuits in more detail.

3.4.1 Series Circuits

The most common type of series queueing circuit is one that involves *feedforward* queues (Fig. 3.5), where serviced requests flow out of the queueing center and into the tail of the queue at the next center.

Alternatively, the flow out of one queueing center can split into multiple flows (according to the rules of Sect. 3.3) that enqueue simultaneously at different queueing centers. An important example of this kind of splitting produces queues with *feedback* flows. A special case of feedback queueing occurs when there are no flows to and from the outside; it corresponds to a *closed* circuit (Sect. 3.5). We now examine each of these circuits in turn, starting with simple feedforward queues.

3.4.2 Feedforward Circuits

A series circuit comprising feedforward queues is also known as *tandem* queueing arrangement. Consider a series circuit in Fig. 3.5 consisting of three queue-

Fig. 3.5. A three-stage tandem circuit of queues

ing centers, each with service demands of $D_1 = 1$ s, $D_2 = 2$ s, and $D_3 = 3$ s, respectively and receiving arrivals at a rate of 0.10 requests/s. By virtue of the Poisson arrival properties discussed earlier, together with the assumption that the service periods are exponentially distributed, we can treat this tandem circuit of queues as a separable network of three independent $M/M/1$ queues. To establish the correctness of this approach, we calculate the utilization, response time and queue-length for each queueing center. The results are tabulated in Table 3.1. The input parameters for the open circuit appear in the upper half of the table and the outputs appear in the lower half.

In particular, Little's law tells us that the sum of the individual queue lengths should be equal to the total number of requests in the system as given by $\lambda(R_1 + R_2 + R_3)$. Indeed, we see from the entries (in bold) in Table 3.1 that this is true. The associated PDQ model in Perl is presented in Chap. 6, Sect. 6.7.6.

Because of the properties of Poisson streams, this result can be generalized to the case where the queueing centers are $M/M/m$ rather than $M/M/1$. In other words, a series circuit of $M/M/m$ multiserver queues is also separable. This is Jackson's theorem, which we shall examine more closely in Sect. 3.4.4.

Table 3.1. Tandem queueing circuit

Metric	Queue stage			Total
	1	2	3	
Arrival rate	0.10	0.10	0.10	
Service demand	1.00	2.00	3.00	
Utilization	0.10	0.20	0.30	
Response time	1.11	2.50	4.29	7.90
Queue length	0.11	0.25	0.43	**0.79**
Little's law				**0.79**

3.4.3 Feedback Circuits

So far, we have discussed queueing centers where a request arrives at random from an external source, queues for service, receives service, and then departs the center, never to return. Clearly, there are cases where a request that has already received service returns for further service:

- a customer forgets to purchase an item and must return to the store
- children form a line to repeat sliding in a playground
- packets must be retransmitted on a communication network

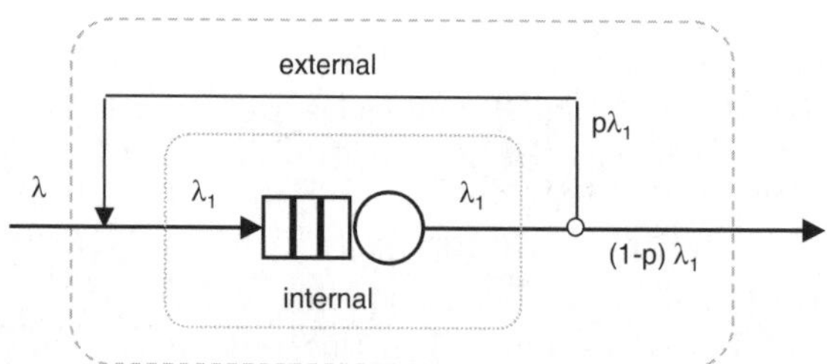

Fig. 3.6. An open queue where some portion of departing requests are feedback into the tail of the queue

This effect is called *feedback*, and Fig.3.6 shows how it is represented as a queueing diagram. External arrivals occur at a rate λ. Requests that have already received service either depart from the system or return to the tail of the queue with branching probability p. They therefore return with a (smaller) rate $p\lambda_1$, which combines with new arrivals, such that *effective* arrival rate into the queue is:

$$\lambda_1 = \lambda + p\lambda_1 \,. \tag{3.4}$$

This equation can be solved for λ_1 as:

$$\lambda_1 = \frac{\lambda}{1-p} \,. \tag{3.5}$$

The utilization of the server, as defined by (2.15), is

$$\rho = \lambda_1 S \; , \tag{3.6}$$

due to the *internal* arrival rate λ_1. The feedback flow would appear to present difficulties because we do not know how to represent the effects of the queue receiving inputs from both an *external* source and an *internal* source. Fortunately, we can demonstrate that such problems are illusory.

First, we define the mean number of visits to the server:

$$V_{\text{srv}} = \frac{C_{\text{srv}}}{C_{\text{sys}}} \; , \tag{3.7}$$

where C_{srv} is the number of completions at the *server* and C_{sys} is the number of completions measured at the *system* level where, in fact, there may be more the one queueing center. Applying the definition of throughput found in (2.3), (3.7) can be rewritten as:

$$\begin{aligned} V_{\text{srv}} &= \frac{C_{\text{srv}}/T}{C_{\text{sys}}/T} \; , \\ &= \frac{\lambda_{\text{srv}}}{\lambda} \; , \\ &= \frac{\lambda_1}{(1-p)\lambda_1} \; , \end{aligned} \tag{3.8}$$

where we have used the fact that $\lambda \equiv (1-p)\ \lambda_1$ in Fig 3.6. Hence, the mean number of visits to the server can be expressed in terms of the branching probability p such that:

$$V_{srv} = \frac{1}{(1-p)} \; . \tag{3.9}$$

The more return visits a request makes to the server, the greater is the accumulated service time, which is just the *service demand* $D = V_{\text{srv}} S$ defined by (2.9) in Chap. 2. Viewed externally, the total time spent in the system is therefore:

$$R = \frac{D}{(1-\lambda D)} \; , \tag{3.10}$$

which is the same as the response time for an $M/M/1$ queue.

Viewed internally, the *response time per visit* R_{v} can be expressed in terms of the local arrival rate λ_1 as:

$$R_{\text{v}} = \frac{S}{1-\lambda_1 S} \; . \tag{3.11}$$

The relationship between the system response time and the per-visit response time is simply:

$$R = V R_{\text{v}} \; . \tag{3.12}$$

Feedback is specified in terms of the number of visits V, which acts like a *scale factor* on the service time, not the queue length. To see this, consider Fig. 3.7 and recall that the queue length Q appears in the definition of response time according to (2.32). The per-visit response time of (3.12) is scaled by V and gives rise to the following steps:

$$\begin{aligned} R_{\mathrm{v}} &= V\,(S + SQ)\;, \\ &= VS + VSQ \text{ (by the distributive law)}\;, \\ &= D + DQ \text{ (by the definition } D = VS)\;, \\ &= D\,(1 + Q)\;. \end{aligned}$$

Clearly, the service time S is *dilated* by V to become the service demand D, while the number of requests in the queue remains unaffected.

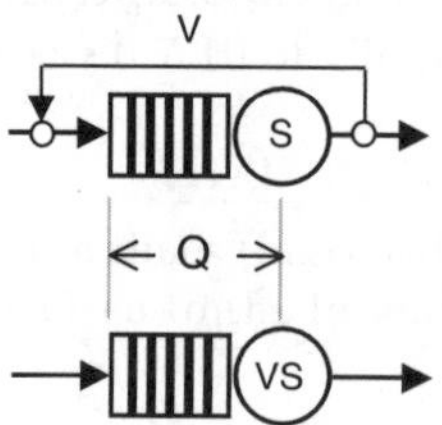

Fig. 3.7. Invariance of queue length under feedback dilatations

> Feedback is a time-dilatation transformation with scale parameter V, the mean number of visits to the server. The queue length Q is *invariant* under the scaling symmetry in (3.12). This invariance is depicted in Fig. 3.7 and is at the core of Jackson's theorem in Sect. 3.4.4.

Example 3.2. Command messages arrive into a satellite telemetry channel at a rate of one every 2 s and they take 0.75 s to process. Thirty percent of the transmission attempts are unsuccessful, and those messages must be enqueued for retransmission. Calculate the response time in the transmission channel as seen from the *internal* box in Fig 3.6. The internal arrival rate is

$$\lambda_1 = \frac{\lambda}{(1-p)} = 0.715\;.$$

From (3.9) the average number of visits per message is

$$V = \frac{1}{1-p} = 1.429\;.$$

The corresponding utilization is $\rho = \lambda_1 S = 0.536$. From (2.38) in Chap. 2 the time spent waiting in the queue is

$$W = \frac{\rho S}{1 - \rho} = 0.866 \text{ s} ,$$

and the *response time per visit* in the channel is: $R_v = W + S = 1.616$ ms. The total response time is the product $R = VR_v$:

$$R = 1.429 \times 1.616 = 2.310 \text{ s}.$$

In other words, the total response time is given by the response time per visit scaled up by the average number of visits due to retransmission feedback. □

In the next example, we repeat the response time calculation for the transmission channel as seen from the *external* box in Fig 3.6.

Example 3.3. The external arrival rate is $\lambda = 0.50$ messages/s. The service demand is $D = VS = 1.429 \times 0.75 = 1.072$ s. Then, from (3.10) the external response time is

$$R = \frac{1.072}{0.464} = 2.310 \text{ s} ,$$

which confirms that the both the *internal* and the *external* views are identical. This is the basis of Jackson's theorem, which we present in the Sect 3.4.4. □

These examples show that feedback can be accommodated in the tools like PDQ via (3.10) by relating branching probabilities and mean visits to the service demand. The interested reader can find the corresponding PDQ model in Sect. 6.7.7 of Chap. 6.

In passing, we note that all of the formulae in Chap. 2 that were previously expressed in terms of the service time S can be rewritten in terms of the service demand D. From a practical standpoint, the number of visits is often an easily measured quantity in computer systems.

3.4.4 Jackson's Theorem

So far, in this chapter we have considered both feedforward and feedback open queueing circuits. An example of a queueing circuit where both these effects are present is shown in Fig. 3.8a. Since multiple streams may join a queue because of feedback, the arrivals are correlated with previous service periods and therefore violate the Poisson properties of Sect. 3.3. Allen [1990] noted that the arrivals are actually a special case of a hyperexponential distribution H_2, which we discussed in Sect. 2.11.7. How does this complication affect our ability to analyze general queueing circuits and, in particular, how does it impact the use of PDQ?

> In a surprising result (totally unrelated to computer performance analysis) Jackson [1957] showed that although the arrivals into the queue are not Poisson-type, each queueing center still behaves statistically as though they it were an $M/M/1$ queue subjected to Poisson arrivals.

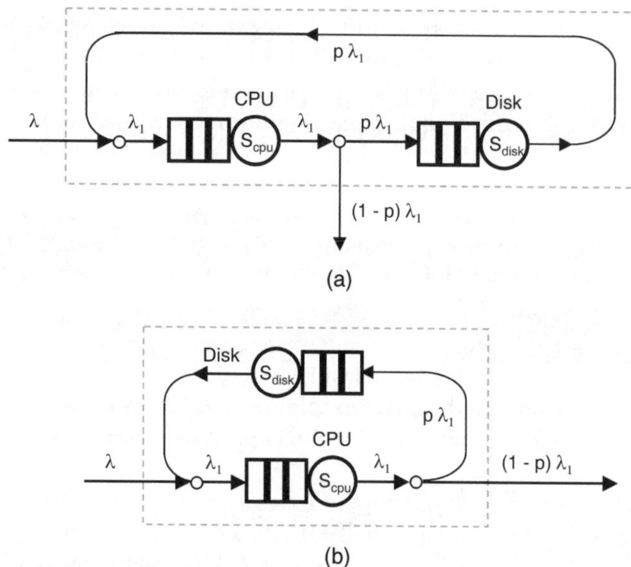

Fig. 3.8. A simple Jackson-type queueing circuit in (**a**) with its topologically equivalent circuit in (**b**)

We pause to reflect on the fact that this was the first major advance in queueing theory (Appendix B) since Erlang's pioneering work in 1917. Why? Because Erlang's results were for a single queue, whereas Jackson showed for the first time (albeit 40 years later) that it was possible to solve circuits of queues with rather complicated non-Poisson flows. As we noted in the Introduction, it is critical for the analysis of computer systems that systems of queues can be solved. Jackson's theorem demonstrates that that is indeed possible.

To understand this result more clearly, consider the simple circuit in Fig. 3.8a. External requests arrive at a rate λ. After executing on the CPU they may either depart the queueing circuit altogether or continue with branching probability p to perform some disk I/O operations. After completing I/O service the request feeds back into the CPU run-queue. This Jacksonian circuit can be rearranged topologically into the equivalent circuit shown in Fig. 3.8b. The stream of requests returning with rate $p\lambda_1$ combines with new arrivals coming from outside the circuit at rate λ to give an *effective* arrival rate into the CPU queue that is identical to (3.4).

The utilization at the CPU and disk can be written respectively as

$$\rho_{\text{cpu}} = \lambda_1 S_{\text{cpu}} = \frac{\lambda}{1-p} S_{\text{cpu}} , \tag{3.13}$$

and

$$\rho_{\text{disk}} = p\, \lambda_1 S_{\text{disk}} = \frac{\lambda\, p}{1-p} S_{\text{disk}} . \tag{3.14}$$

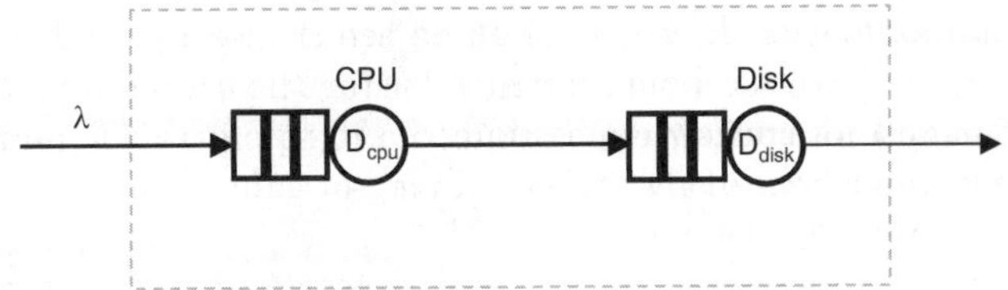

Fig. 3.9. Equivalent tandem circuit for Fig. 3.8 without feedback

Recalling that the service demand is $D = VS$, (3.13) can be rewritten as

$$\rho_{\text{cpu}} = \lambda D_{\text{cpu}} \ , \tag{3.15}$$

and (3.14) can be rewritten as

$$\rho_{\text{disk}} = \lambda D_{\text{disk}} \ . \tag{3.16}$$

By analogy with (3.10), the system response time of the tandem circuit the sum of the response times expressed in terms of (3.15) and (3.16):

$$R = \frac{D_{\text{cpu}}}{1 - \lambda D_{\text{cpu}}} + \frac{D_{\text{disk}}}{1 - \lambda D_{\text{disk}}} \ , \tag{3.17}$$

which is the same as the system response time for the simple tandem circuit without feedback in Fig. 3.9. This symmetry between the service demand and the service time weighted by the visit frequency is at the heart of Jackson's theorem. It allows us to fold all the complications of feedback and non-Poisson arrivals into the service demands of a series of $M/M/1$ queues. Next, we apply these insights based on Jackson's theorem to a more complex queueing circuits involving parallel queues in series.

3.4.5 Parallel Queues in Series

We consider a queueing circuit model of a passport application office that involves both series and parallel queues like that shown in Fig. 3.10. Upon entering the passport office you must register at *window 1* to validate your application. On average, this takes 20 s. From there, you have a 30% chance of being directed to *window 2* to fill out the application form and present your birth certificate which takes 10 min (on average). If you are among the 70% of applicants who do not have a suitable photograph, you will be directed to *window 3* to get one and that usually takes 5 min. After that, there is a 10% chance you will have to return to *window 2* or you may simply present the completed application for payment at *window 4* to receive your passport after 1 min.

As the arrows in Fig. 3.10 depict, this is an example of a parallel queueing circuit (*window 2* and *window 3*) in series with the queues associated with *window 1* and *window 4*. In addition, there are cross-coupled flows between the parallel queues. We solve this circuit by using the *branching ratios* shown in Fig. 3.10. These branching ratios simply correspond to the percentage of the departing traffic headed for the next queues.

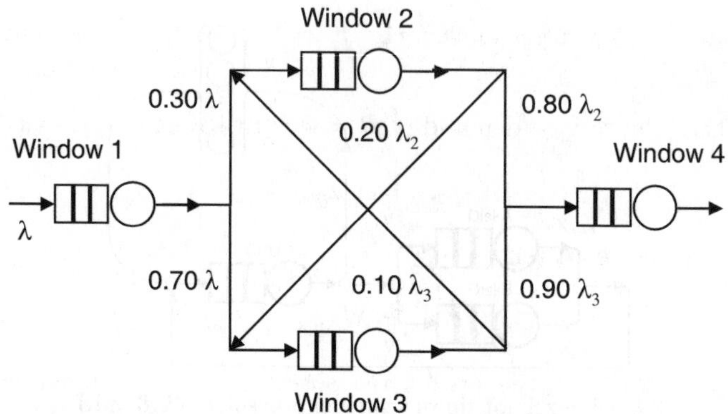

Fig. 3.10. Open queueing circuit model of a passport application office

To solve this rather complex problem, we first calculate the utilizations using Littles law given by (2.26) in Chap. 2, with X replaced by λ, the arrival rate into the passport office. The service times are expressed in seconds. The corresponding utilizations are:

$$\begin{aligned}\rho_1 &= 20\,\lambda\,,\\ \rho_2 &= 600\,\lambda_2\,,\\ \rho_3 &= 300\,\lambda_3\,,\\ \rho_4 &= 60\,\lambda_4\,.\end{aligned}$$

To evaluate ρ_2 and ρ_3, we need to determine λ_2 and λ_3. We use the Poisson merging rules in Sect. 3.3 to define those rates as:

$$\lambda_2 = 0.3\,\lambda + 0.1\,\lambda_3\,, \tag{3.18}$$

$$\lambda_3 = 0.7\,\lambda + 0.2\,\lambda_2\,. \tag{3.19}$$

This pair of simultaneous equations reflects the cross-coupling in the traffic flows. They can be solved with a little tedious algebra, setting up a spreadsheet or writing a Perl program like `passcalc.pl` below. To expedite the solution, it helps to first substitute (3.19) into (3.18) and rearrange terms to produce:

$$\begin{aligned}\lambda_2 &= 0.3\,\lambda + (0.1)(0.7)\,\lambda + (0.1)(0.2)\,\lambda_2\\ &= \frac{\lambda\,[0.3 + (0.1)(0.7)]}{1 - (0.1)(0.2)}\,.\end{aligned} \tag{3.20}$$

Equation (3.20) becomes the Perl variable `$L2` in `passcalc.pl`, and it can be substituted into (3.19) to solve for λ_3 or the Perl variable `$L3` in `passcalc.pl`.

Once λ_2 and λ_3 are known, we can use (2.36) from Chap. 2 to calculate the queue lengths at each of the passport office windows:

$$Q_k = \frac{\rho_k}{1 - \rho_k}, \; k = 1, 2, 3, 4.$$

Applying Little's law once again, we can calculate the average amount of time you can expect to spend in the passport office:

$$R = \frac{Q_1 + Q_2 + Q_3 + Q_4}{\lambda} .$$

These equations have been encoded in the following Perl script:

```
#! /usr/bin/perl
# passcalc.pl

$appsPerHour =  15;
$lambda = $appsPerHour / 3600;

#### Branching ratios
$p12 = 0.30;
$p13 = 0.70;
$p23 = 0.20;
$p32 = 0.10;
printf(" Arrival: %10.4f per Hr.\n", $appsPerHour);
printf(" lambda : %10.4f per Sec.\n", $lambda);
printf("----------------------------\n");

$L2 = $lambda * ($p12 + ($p32 * $p13)) / (1 - ($p32 * $p23));
$L3 = ($p13 * $lambda) + ($p23 * $L2);
printf(" lambda1: %10.4f * lambda\n", 1.0);
printf(" lambda2: %10.4f * lambda\n", $L2 / $lambda);
printf(" lambda3: %10.4f * lambda\n", $L3 / $lambda);
printf(" lambda4: %10.4f * lambda\n", 1.0);
printf("----------------------------\n");

$rho1 = $lambda * 20;
$rho2 = $L2 * 600;
$rho3 = $L3 * 300;
$rho4 = $lambda * 60;
printf("Uwindow1: %10.4f * lambda\n", $rho1 / $lambda);
printf("Uwindow2: %10.4f * lambda\n", $rho2 / $lambda);
printf("Uwindow3: %10.4f * lambda\n", $rho3 / $lambda);
printf("Uwindow4: %10.4f * lambda\n", $rho4 / $lambda);
printf("----------------------------\n");
$Q1 = $rho1 / (1 - $rho1);
$Q2 = $rho2 / (1 - $rho2);
```

```
$Q3 = $rho3 / (1 - $rho3);
$Q4 = $rho4 / (1 - $rho4);

printf("Qwindow1: %10.4f\n", $Q1);
printf("Qwindow2: %10.4f\n", $Q2);
printf("Qwindow3: %10.4f\n", $Q3);
printf("Qwindow4: %10.4f\n", $Q4);
printf("----------------------------\n");
$R = ($Q1 + $Q2 + $Q3 + $Q4) / $lambda;

printf("Rpassprt: %10.4f Secs.\n", $R);
printf("Rpassprt: %10.4f Hrs.\n", $R / 3600);
printf("----------------------------\n");
```

If the arrival rate at the registration *window 1* is 15 applicants per hour, the results of running the program are:

```
 Arrival:     15.0000 per Hr.
 lambda :      0.0042 per Sec.
----------------------------
 lambda1:      1.0000 * lambda
 lambda2:      0.3776 * lambda
 lambda3:      0.7755 * lambda
 lambda4:      1.0000 * lambda
----------------------------
Uwindow1:     20.0000 * lambda
Uwindow2:    226.5306 * lambda
Uwindow3:    232.6531 * lambda
Uwindow4:     60.0000 * lambda
----------------------------
Qwindow1:      0.0909
Qwindow2:     16.8182
Qwindow3:     31.6667
Qwindow4:      0.3333
----------------------------
Rpassprt: 11738.1818 Secs.
Rpassprt:      3.2606 Hrs.
----------------------------
```

Given these performance predictions, it might be more prudent to mail in your passport application. The passport office queueing circuit was solved here, without any assistance from PDQ, by explicitly coding the fundamental queue length formula from Chap. 2 into `passcalc.pl`. The corresponding PDQ model `passport.pl`, which takes of all that for you, is presented in Sect. 6.7.8 of Chap. 6.

3.4.6 Multiple Workloads in Open Circuits

In Fig. 3.3 we see that it was possible to have both open and closed circuits combined and therefore they involve mixed workloads. The same queueing centers service two different types of workloads. In this sense, the type of workload determines the type of queueing circuit.

By extension, it is possible to have an open circuit of queues with more than one stream of arrivals impinging on each server. Fig. 3.11 shows two different streams of work in a tandem queueing circuit. This might be applicable for a simple queueing circuit that accounts for the fact that the CPU and the disk must service requests from both the operating system (kernel) and an application, e.g., a database. The two streams of arrivals A and B depicted

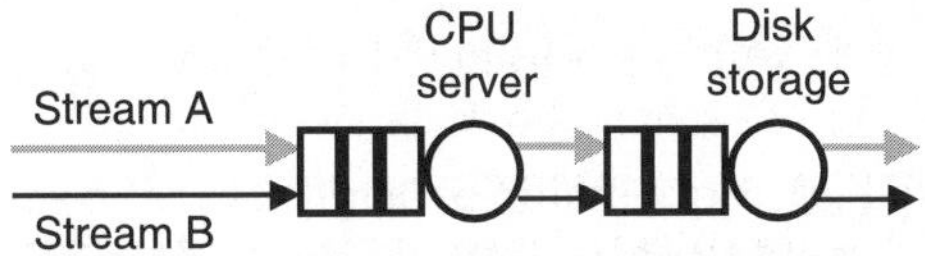

Fig. 3.11. An open queueing circuit with two streams of arrivals

in Fig. 3.11 are characterized by their different arrival rates λ^{A} and λ^{B} and their respective service demands D_k^{A} and D_k^{B} at each of the $k = 2$ queueing centers in the circuit. The total utilization at queueing center k is simply the sum of the utilizations due to each stream:

$$\rho_{\mathrm{k}} = \rho_{\mathrm{k}}^{\mathrm{A}} + \rho_{\mathrm{k}}^{\mathrm{B}} . \tag{3.21}$$

By virtue of Jackson's theorem (Sect. 3.4.4), the response time at each queue in the circuit in Fig. 3.11 can be calculated in a way analogous to the definition of response time (2.35) for an $M/M/1$ queue in Chap. 2. Applying (3.21), the response time for stream A at the CPU is given by

$$R_{\mathrm{cpu}}^{\mathrm{A}} = \frac{D_{\mathrm{cpu}}^{\mathrm{A}}}{1 - (\rho_{\mathrm{cpu}}^{\mathrm{A}} + \rho_{\mathrm{cpu}}^{\mathrm{B}})} , \tag{3.22}$$

and similarly for stream A at the disk queue the response time is:

$$R_{\mathrm{disk}}^{\mathrm{A}} = \frac{D_{\mathrm{disk}}^{\mathrm{A}}}{1 - (\rho_{\mathrm{disk}}^{\mathrm{A}} + \rho_{\mathrm{disk}}^{\mathrm{B}})} . \tag{3.23}$$

The difference between (2.35) and (3.22) or (3.23) is the utilization term in the denominator which takes into account the sharing of each resource by both streams A and B.

From the viewpoint of stream A, for example, the service rate at the CPU (or the disk) appears *degraded* by the consumption of service cycles because of the presence of stream B in the circuit. The greater the utilization by stream B, the longer the wait for stream A, and this will be reflected in a larger value of $R^{\mathrm{A}}_{\mathrm{cpu}}$ in (3.22).

The response time R^A for stream A:

$$R^{\mathrm{A}} = R^{\mathrm{A}}_{\mathrm{cpu}} + R^{\mathrm{A}}_{\mathrm{disk}} , \tag{3.24}$$

is simply the sum of the two contributions from (3.22) and (3.23) and similarly for stream B. We shall apply these concepts of multiple open workloads to the client/server model in Chap. 9.

3.5 Closed-Circuit Queues

So far, in this chapter we have considered open queueing circuits. When we turn to closed circuits of queues, however, we run into a problem. Since, by definition, there can only be a finite number of requests distributed throughout a closed circuit, the state of each queue is *interdependent* on the state of all the other queues. As a consequence, the previous assumption that each queue in the circuit can be solved *separately* (à la Jackson's theorem in Sect. 3.4.4) is no longer valid, and there is no closed-form analytic solution.

Historically, Gordon and Newell [1967], as well as Buzen [1973], developed analytical techniques for solving separable closed queueing circuits (see Appendix B), which have come to be known as the *convolution method* [See e.g., Jain 1990, Chap. 35 and references therein]. A more detailed discussion of separability criteria for general queueing networks is given at the end of this chapter in Sect. 3.8. Unfortunately, the convolution technique suffers from potential numerical instabilities. The modern approach uses a more robust *iterative* solution technique based on the following observation.

3.5.1 Arrival Theorem

Recall from Chap. 2 what happens to arrivals into an open queue. Under the assumption that all requests have mean service demand D_k, we can rewrite (2.32) as:

$$R_k = Q_k \, D_k + D_k , \tag{3.25}$$

so that (3.25) includes the possibility of there being $0 \leq k \leq K$ queues in the open circuit. When a request arrives at queueing center k, its expected time in the system is determined by the sum of two contributions:

- The first term in (3.25), which is the product of the average number of requests Q_k in the system ahead of the arriving request and the average service demand D_k of each request
- The second term in (3.25), which is the new arrival's own service demand D_k once it finally reaches the server

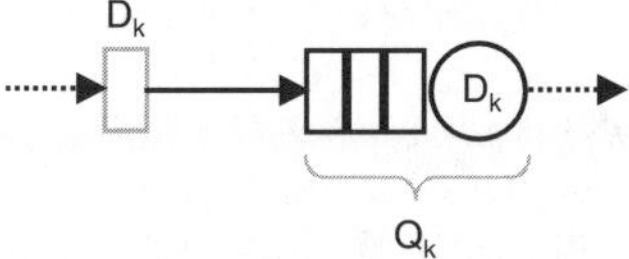

Fig. 3.12. Arrivals into an open queueing circuit see the time-averaged queue length at queue k ahead of them, determines the response time given by (3.25)

The first term in (3.25) is simply the *waiting* time W_k at queue k. Equation (3.25) holds no matter whether the new arrival has come from outside the open circuit, as the departure from an upstream queue, as a branch of departures that split into multiple streams, or combining with previously serviced requests that are being fed back into the tail of the queue. We could refer to (3.25) as the Arrival Theorem for open circuit queues.

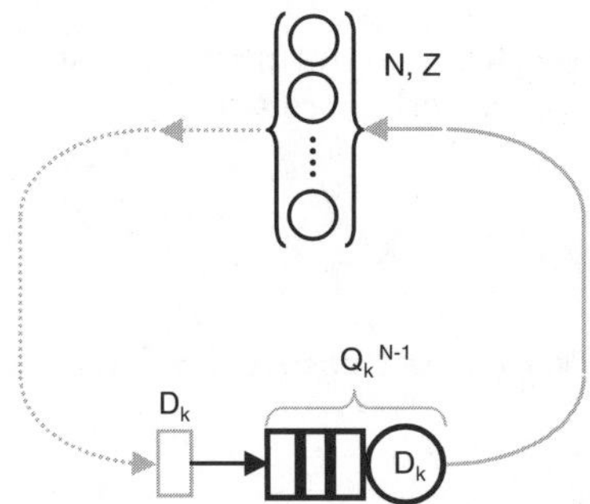

Fig. 3.13. Arrivals into a closed queueing circuit see the time-averaged queue length caused by $(N-1)$ requests at queue k, which determines the response time given by (3.27)

A generalization of this open Arrival Theorem originally formulated by [Reiser and Lavenberg 1980] and [Sevcik and Mitrani 1981] leads to the corresponding closed-circuit version of the Arrival Theorem [Allen 1990, Thm. 6.2.2]. Referring to Fig. 3.13, it states:

> The instantaneous queue length $Q_k(t)$ seen by an arrival in a closed queueing circuit is the same as the time-averaged queue length with one less request Q_k^{N-1} in the system.

The time-averaged queue length (4.12) also arises in the context of the UNIX load average metric in Chap. 4. More formally, the following replacement:

$$Q_k(t) \equiv Q_k^{N-1} \tag{3.26}$$

holds, and the average response time at the kth center can be expressed as:

$$R_k^N = D_k + D_k\, Q_k^{N-1} \,. \tag{3.27}$$

We examine the relationship between *instantaneous* queue length $Q(t)$ and the *time-averaged* queue length Q in Sect. 4.4.1.

An intuitive justification for (3.27) follows from the fact that at the instant the new request is arriving at the service center, it cannot also be in the queue, that is, it cannot "see" itself in the queue. Hence, there can only be $(N-1)$ other requests that could possibly interfere with the new arrival. The number of requests actually enqueued can be regarded as the average queue length when there were only $(N-1)$ requests in the system.

The recursive nature of the relationship between queueing metrics indexed by N requests on the left side of (3.27) and $(N-1)$ requests on the right side provides the basis of the iterative algorithm known as the *Mean Value Algorithm* or simply MVA.

3.5.2 Iterative MVA Algorithm

The MVA algorithm for a closed circuit iterated over $l \leq K$ queues and $n \leq N$ requests can be written as a Perl subroutine.

```
# mvasub.pl

sub mva
{
    # Reset queue length and response time arrays
    @Q = ();
    @R = ();

    for ($n = 1; $n <= $N; $n++) {

      # 1. Calculate the residence time at k
      for ($k = 1; $k <= $K; $k++) {
         $R[$k] = $D[$k] * (1.0 + $Q[$k]);
      }

      # 2. Calculate system response time
      $rtt = $Z;
      for ($k = 1; $k <= $K; $k++) {
         $rtt += $R[$k];
      }

      # 3. Calculate system throughput
      $X = ($n / $rtt);

      # 4. Calculate new queue length at k
      for ($k = 1; $k <= $K; $k++) {
         $Q[$k] = $X * $R[$k];
      }
```

```
    }
}
```

The algorithm consists of four essential steps that are repeated iteratively for each request n in the system, starting at $n = 1$, and incremented by one request at a time until the specified population $n = N$ is reached.

1. Calculate the response time given by (3.27) at each queue based on the number of requests in the previous iteration with $(n - 1)$ requests.
2. Calculate the response time for the entire system by adding the response times in step 1.
3. Calculate the throughput X for the entire system by applying the Response Time law (2.89) from Chap. 2.
4. Calculate the new number of requests Q_k^n at each queue by applying Little's macroscopic law given by (2.14) in Chap. 2.

When applied to the closed queueing circuit in Fig. 2.19 of Chap. 2, the MVA algorithm produces the throughput characteristic seen in Fig. 2.21 and the typical *hockey stick* characteristic for the response time seen in Fig. 2.20. For a single queue circuit, these results are in complete agreement with those obtained by using the Perl script `repair.pl` in Sect. 2.8.3. The MVA algorithm, of course, is much more general because it is valid for closed circuits with multiple queues, not just a single queue. Recent attempts to extend MVA to parallel computation are discussed in [Gennaro and King 1999].

3.5.3 Approximate Solution

There is a way to avoid the loop over $n \leq N$ by approximating the queue lengths. Assuming that N is large, the queue lengths at each node increase in the following proportion:

$$Q_k(N) \propto N \,, \tag{3.28}$$

or equivalently

$$Q_k(N-1) \propto (N-1) \,. \tag{3.29}$$

Then we have

$$\lim_{N \to \infty} Q_k(N-1) = \left(\frac{N-1}{N} \right) Q_k(N) \,. \tag{3.30}$$

Substituting into (3.27) produces the following approximation for the response time at queueing node k:

$$R_k = D_k + \left(\frac{N-1}{N} \right) D_k \, Q_k(N) \,, \tag{3.31}$$

For a closed circuit comprising K nodes and N users, the algorithm in Perl code looks like this:

```
# mvaapproxsub.pl

sub approx
{
   # Reset queue lengths and response times
   @Q = (); # number of requests at queue k
   @R = (); # residence time at queue k
   $tolerance = 0.0010; # stopping condition

   for ($k = 1; $k <= $K; $k++) {
      $Q[$k] = $N / $K;
   }

   while ( max($Q[$k] - ($X[$k] * $R[$k])) > $tolerance ) {
      for ($k = 1; $k <= $K; $k++) {
         $R[$k] = $D[$k] * (1.0 + $Q[$k] * ($N - 1) / $N);
      }

      $rtt = $Z;
      for ($k = 1; $k <= $K; $k++) {
         $rtt += $R[$k];
      }
      $X = ($n / $rtt);

      for ($k = 1; $k <= $K; $k++) {
         $Q[$k] = $X * $R[$k];
      }
   }
}
```

In PDQ the exact MVA solution and this approximation are distinguished by the flags `EXACT` and `APPROX`, respectively (Sect. 6.5.1 in Chap. 6).

Example results using the `approx` subroutine are plotted in Figs. 3.14 and 3.15. We see that the approximate method tends to slightly *underestimate* the throughput near the knee in the curve at $N_{\text{opt}} \approx 21$ (defined in Sect. 5.3.3). Conversely, the approximate algorithm tends to slightly *overestimate* the response time near $N_{opt} \approx 21$ in Fig. 3.15. Nonetheless, these small deviations in accuracy from the exact MVA algorithm can represent a wise trade-off when hundreds or thousands of users or processes (as is often the case with Web servers) must to be analyzed.

3.6 Visit Ratios and Routing Probabilities

Now that we have discussed both open and closed circuits, we revisit the concept of *visit ratios* introduced in Sect. 2.4.5 from the perspective of the *branching probabilities* p_k associated with routing requests between queues.

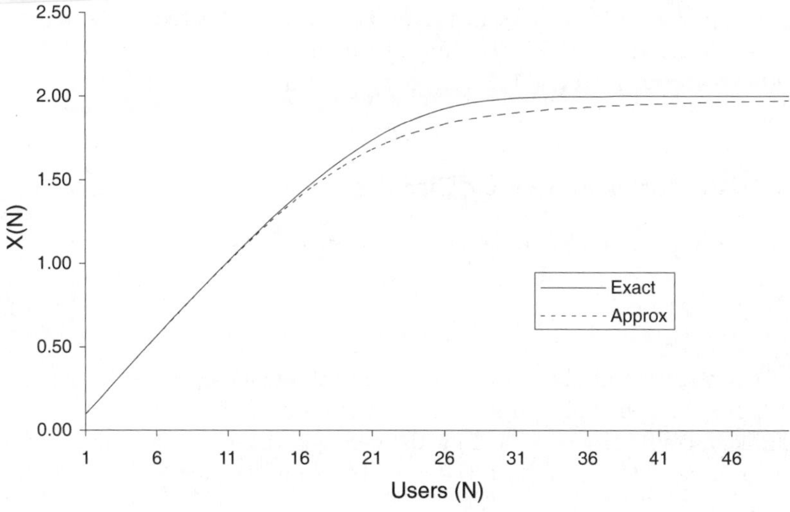

Fig. 3.14. Comparison of exact and approximate throughput curves

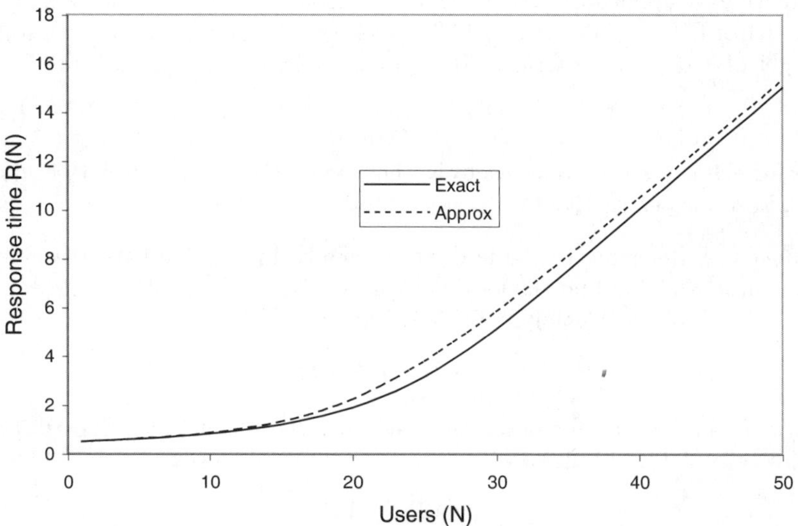

Fig. 3.15. Comparison of exact and approximate response time curves

In Chap. 2 we introduced the notion of counting repeated visits to a server to define the service demand D_k in (2.9). In that case, the visit count can be thought of an *integer* $V_k = 1, 2, \ldots$. However, this concept can be made more general.

3.6.1 Visit Ratios and Open Circuits

In Sects. 2.4.5 and 3.4.3, we defined the *visit ratio* as:

$$V_k = \frac{C_k}{C_{\text{sys}}} , \tag{3.32}$$

where C_k is the count of completions at the kth queueing center in the circuit, and C_{sys} is the count of completions for the entire circuit.

Unlike a count of visits, (3.32) is defined as a *ratio* and thus does not have to be an integer. Dividing both the numerator and the denominator in (3.32) by T produces:

$$V_k = \frac{C_k/T}{C_{\text{sys}}/T} = \frac{X_k}{X_{\text{sys}}} , \tag{3.33}$$

where we have applied the definition of the throughput in (2.3) and (2.4) from Sect. 2.4 of Chap. 2. Based on (3.33), we see that the visit ratio can also be thought of a *relative throughput.* Rearranging terms simplifies (3.33) to:

$$X_k = V_k X_{\text{sys}} \tag{3.34}$$

This form is sometimes referred to as the *Forced Flow Law* [Allen 1990, Jain 1990, Lazowska et al. 1984].

Example 3.4. Referring to the feedback queue in Fig.3.6, we have the global throughput $X_{\text{sys}} = \lambda$ and the local throughput $X_k = \lambda_1$. At the input branch (near the tail of the waiting line), (3.4) implies:

$$\lambda = (1 - p)\lambda_1 ,$$

with p the probability for branching back into the waiting line. Substituting all this into (3.33) produces

$$V_k = \frac{\lambda_1}{\lambda} = \frac{1}{1-p} ,$$

in agreement with (3.9). This result also shows how the visit ratio (or relative throughput) is related to the branching probability p. □

To maintain the flow of traffic at the fundamental branch intersections shown in Fig. 3.4, there can never be any accumulation or dissipation of requests. Any accumulation occurs at queues, and the only dissipation of requests occurs when they leave the system altogether. This is the reason for the reference to forced flow.

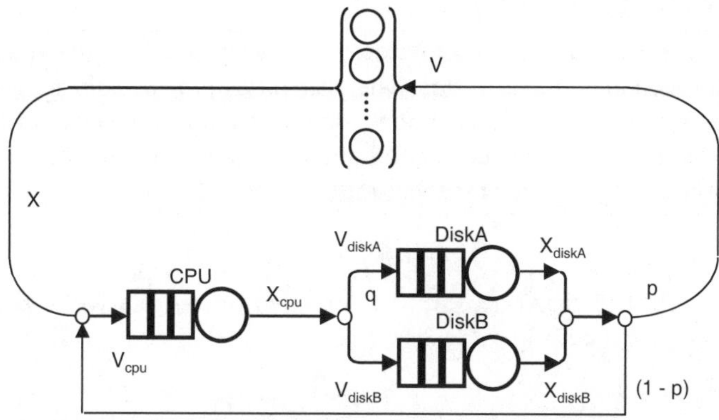

Fig. 3.16. Closed queueing circuit with routing probabilities p and q

3.6.2 Visit Ratios and Closed Circuits

Consider the closed circuit in Fig. 3.16. We write the system throughput as $X \equiv X_{\text{sys}}$ and the system visit ratio as $V \equiv V_{\text{sys}}$. The visit ratios for the remaining queueing nodes in the circuit can be written as:

$$
\begin{aligned}
V_{\text{cpu}} &= \frac{X_{\text{cpu}}}{X} , \\
V_{\text{dkA}} &= \frac{X_{\text{dkA}}}{X} , \\
V_{\text{dkB}} &= \frac{X_{\text{dkB}}}{X} ,
\end{aligned}
\tag{3.35}
$$

in accordance with the definition in (3.33). Furthermore, applying the Poisson branching rules in Fig. 3.4, the flow equations are:

$$
\begin{aligned}
X_{\text{cpu}} &= X + (1-p)(X_{\text{dkA}} + X_{\text{dkB}}) , \\
X_{\text{dkA}} &= q X_{\text{cpu}} , \\
X_{\text{dkB}} &= (1-q) X_{\text{cpu}} ,
\end{aligned}
\tag{3.36}
$$

where the branching ratios p and q in Fig. 3.16 are independent of each other.

Example 3.5. If the branching ratios $p = 0.20$ and $q = 0.60$, the flow equations (3.36) can be solved for the system throughput in terms of the CPU throughput: $X = 0.2X_{cpu}$. The resulting visit ratios (3.35):

$$
V = 1,\ V_{\text{cpu}} = 5,\ V_{\text{dkA}} = 3,\ V_{\text{dkB}} = 2, \tag{3.37}
$$

are produced by each integral user request, or equivalently, each integral system completion. Since they are all integers, this is how things might actually appear in monitored performance data. □

> As we have seen, both open and closed queueing circuits can be solved using relative throughputs or visit ratios. The visit ratios provide sufficient information to calibrate and solve a PDQ model even when the branching ratios are not known. This one of the virtues of the analytic approach; simulations cannot be solved without the explicit branching ratios.

Example 3.6. If the visit ratios in (3.35) are expressed relative to each visit to the CPU, $V_{\text{cpu}} = 1$ and:

$$V = \frac{1}{5}, \; V_{\text{cpu}} = 1, \; V_{\text{dkA}} = \frac{3}{5}, \; V_{\text{dkB}} = \frac{2}{5}. \tag{3.38}$$

These are the visit ratios produced by each integral visit to the CPU. For every CPU completion, the request returns to the user 20% of the time, i.e., $V = 0.20$. Note that the overall ratios are in the same proportion as in Example 3.5. □

3.7 Multiple Workloads in Closed Circuits

In this section we construct a closed-circuit queueing model of a simple computer system that is due for a processor upgrade. This example emphasizes the importance of multiclass workload analysis—even on a simple computer system. It also reveals the importance of looking for effects that might otherwise not be perceived with common sense. Failure to do this type of performance analysis can lead to incorrect performance projections.

3.7.1 Workload Classes

In the queueing theory literature a workload associated with an open queueing circuit is often referred to as a *transaction* workload class. Similarly, workloads associated with closed queueing circuits come in two varieties, often called *terminal* and *batch*. Each of these workload classes are distinguished as follows:

- A *terminal* workload is characterized by a constant number of users N or user processes and their mean think time Z. The arrival rate into the queueing circuit is not constant. It is reduced in proportion to the number of requests already in service or waiting for service. Historically, this terminology arose out of applying queueing theory to a time-share computer system where a finite number of users were connected literally by a fixed number of terminals.
- A *batch* workload is characterized by the number N of batch processes. The objective for a batch workload is to maximize its utilization of processor and I/O time so that it completes within a specified time—the

batch window. Since batch processes do not involve any delay due to user interaction, the think time parameter is not applicable.

- A *transaction* workload is characterized by the arrival rate λ. This is the characterization used in Chap. 2 and Sect. 3.4. It applies when the number of users is unknown. Such a situation arose historically with ATM banking systems, while today it also applies to HTTP-based Web servers (see Chap. 10). The effective population making requests can be regarded as infinite because the rate at which requests arrive into a queue is unaffected by the number of requests already in service or waiting for service.
- A *mixed* workload is a combination of the above workload classes.

Although these terms hark back to the historical application of queueing theory to time-share computers and banking systems, they are still very useful because they force you to think about what type of workload you are trying to represent in your performance analysis with PDQ (see Chap. 6).

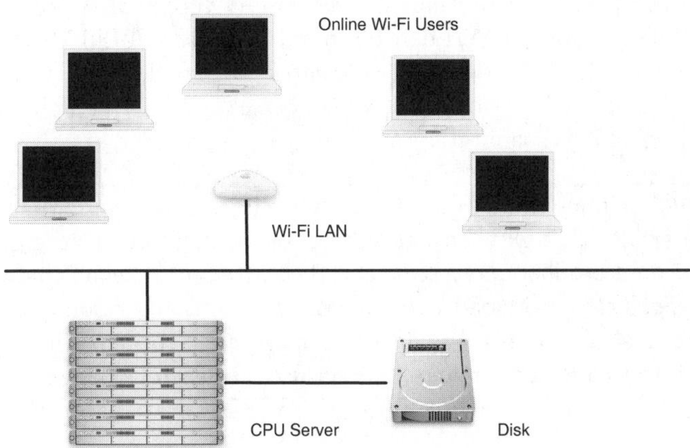

Fig. 3.17. Wireless networked compute-server architecture

3.7.2 Baseline Analysis

The computer system we investigate consists of the single processor compute-server shown in Fig. 3.17. It supports 25 online users simultaneously sharing a server that is also running 10 batch tasks. A batch task is represented by a closed workload with zero think time $Z = 0$. The corresponding queueing circuit for this wireless compute-server architecture is shown in Fig. 3.18. The 100Base-T wireless network has been determined not to be a bottleneck and therefore is not included in the performance model. The concurrent workloads are depicted schematically in black for interactive work and in grey for batch work. The measured performance metrics for the batch and online workloads

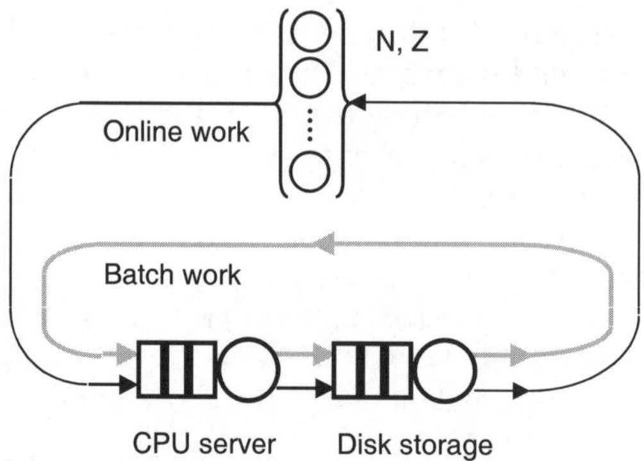

Fig. 3.18. Queueing circuit for wireless compute-server architecture

are summarized in Table 3.2. We use the MVA algorithm incorporated into PDQ to do the performance analysis but simply report the results for now. The actual PDQ model in Perl can be found in Sect. 6.7.9 in Chap. 6.

First, we consider a single-class *aggregated* workload. Then, we repeat the analysis with a *multiclass* workload, where each of the online and batch components are considered separately at each queueing center.

> This sequence mimics what would typically occur in a real performance analysis study. One would start with an aggregated set of measurements e.g., as might be obtained on a production system, and then attempt to refine that analysis by measuring significant workload components that consume resources. Of course, refining the analysis in this way involves more effort because it requires that additional performance parameters be measured for each workload component.

Here, we are assuming that those detailed measurements have already been made for Batch computation and Online users (Table 3.2), and we synthesize the effect of the aggregate workload from those more detailed measurements (third column in Table 3.2). In other words, this is the reverse of the sequence as it would occur in a real study. The data in Table 3.2 show the individual workload parameters, as well as the aggregated workload synthesized from those workload components. The aggregate think-time is calculated in the next section. The aggregate busy times for both the CPU and the disk (bottom two rows of the table) are the sums of the component busy times.

3.7.3 Aggregate Analysis

Returning to the discussion in Sect. 3.4.6 for multiple workloads in an open circuit (Fig. 3.11), and applying Little's law to (3.21) we have:

$$\lambda_{\mathrm{k}} D_k = \lambda_{\mathrm{k}}^{\mathrm{A}} D_k^{\mathrm{A}} + \lambda_{\mathrm{k}}^{\mathrm{B}} D_k^{\mathrm{B}} \,, \tag{3.39}$$

Table 3.2. Baseline workload parameters (times in seconds)

	Workloads		
Parameter	Batch	Online	Aggregate
N	10	25	35
Z	0	30.0	13.27
C	600	476	1076
B_{cpu}	600.1	47.6	647.7
B_{dsk}	54.0	428.4	482.4

from which it follows:

$$D_k = \left(\frac{\lambda_{\text{k}}^{\text{A}}}{\lambda_{\text{k}}}\right) D_k^{\text{A}} + \left(\frac{\lambda_{\text{k}}^{\text{B}}}{\lambda_{\text{k}}}\right) D_k^{\text{B}} . \tag{3.40}$$

This result states that the total service demand D_k at queueing center k, subject to arrivals from multiple workload streams A and B, is the weighted sum of the service demands due to each stream. The weights are given by the individual stream arrival rates relative to the total arrival rate

$$\lambda_{\text{k}} = \lambda_{\text{k}}^{\text{A}} + \lambda_{\text{k}}^{\text{B}} . \tag{3.41}$$

Since λ_{k} is equivalent to a single aggregated workload, and that workload must the same at each queueing center k, we can write:

$$\lambda_{\text{agg}} = \left(\lambda^{\text{A}} + \lambda^{\text{B}}\right)_k , \tag{3.42}$$

because $\lambda_{\text{k}} \equiv \lambda_{\text{agg}}$, no matter where the arrival streams are measured. Hereafter, we drop the k subscript unless it is needed for clarification.

For the closed circuit in Fig. 3.18, there will be a finite number of processes belonging to each stream such that:

$$N_{\text{agg}} = N^{\text{A}} + N^{\text{B}} , \tag{3.43}$$

and (3.42) is replaced by

$$X_{\text{agg}} = X^{\text{A}} + X^{\text{B}} . \tag{3.44}$$

Similarly, the total service demand (3.40) at queueing center k becomes

$$D_k^{\text{agg}} = \left(\frac{X^{\text{A}}}{X_{\text{agg}}}\right) D_k^{\text{A}} + \left(\frac{X^{\text{B}}}{X_{\text{agg}}}\right) D_k^{\text{B}} , \tag{3.45}$$

and the aggregate think-time for interactive workloads is

$$Z_{\text{agg}} = \left(\frac{X^{\text{A}}}{X_{\text{agg}}}\right) Z^{\text{A}} + \left(\frac{X^{\text{B}}}{X_{\text{agg}}}\right) Z^{\text{B}} , \tag{3.46}$$

where the weights are now expressed in terms of the relative throughputs. Equation (3.46) follows from the fact that the think-time is a special kind of service time where the utilization per terminal,

$$\rho_Z = XZ = \rho_Z^A + \rho_Z^B ,$$

follows from Little's law. These weights should not be confused with the visit ratios defined in Sect. 3.6.2. In particular,

$$\frac{X^A}{X_{agg}} + \frac{X^B}{X_{agg}} = 1 ,$$

which is not true for visit ratios.

We are now in a position to apply these aggregation formulas to the component data in Table 3.2. The results are as follows:

- Aggregate processes: From (3.43):

$$\begin{aligned} N_{agg} &= N^{batch} + N^{online} \\ &= 10 + 25 = 35. \end{aligned}$$

- Weight factors: We do not have throughput measurements, but we do have completion counts C, and applying the fundamental definition of throughput as, $X = C/T$ from Sect. 2.4, we can replace all throughputs by the appropriate completion counts. Then,

$$\begin{aligned} W_{batch} &= \frac{C_{batch}}{C_{batch} + C_{online}} \\ &= \frac{600}{1076} \\ &= 0.558 , \end{aligned}$$

and

$$\begin{aligned} W_{online} &= \frac{C_{online}}{C_{batch} + C_{online}} \\ &= \frac{476}{1076} \\ &= 0.442 . \end{aligned}$$

- CPU service demand: Using the definition of the service time, $S = B/C$ from Chap. 2, and applying it to (3.45), we have:

$$\begin{aligned} D_{cpu} &= W_{batch} \left(\frac{B_{cpu}^{batch}}{C_{cpu}^{batch}} \right) + W_{online} \left(\frac{B_{cpu}^{online}}{C_{cpu}^{online}} \right) \\ &= 0.558 + 0.044 \\ &= 0.602 \text{ s}. \end{aligned}$$

- Disk service demand: Similarly, from (3.45) the service demand at the disk is:

$$\begin{aligned} D_{\text{dsk}} &= W_{\text{batch}} \left(\frac{B_{\text{dsk}}^{\text{batch}}}{C_{\text{dsk}}^{\text{batch}}} \right) + W_{\text{online}} \left(\frac{B_{\text{dsk}}^{\text{online}}}{C_{\text{dsk}}^{\text{online}}} \right) \\ &= 0.050 + 0.398 \\ &= 0.448 \text{ s.} \end{aligned}$$

- Aggregate thinktime: From (3.46) the aggregate think-time is:

$$\begin{aligned} Z_{\text{agg}} &= W_{batch}\ Z_{\text{batch}} + W_{\text{online}}\ Z_{\text{online}} \\ &= (0.5576 \times 0) + (0.4424 \times 30) \\ &= 13.27 \text{ s.} \end{aligned}$$

This is the value that appears as an input parameter in Table 3.2.

These values can now be used as *input* parameters for a single-stream PDQ model. We postpone the details of that model until Chap. 6. The enthusiastic reader, however, will find the Perl code in Sect. 6.7.9. In Table 3.3 we summarize the important outputs from that PDQ model for the purposes of comparison with the component-level analysis presented in the next section.

Table 3.3. Performance predictions for aggregate system

Metric	Baseline	Upgrade
R	**8.11**	**3.31**
X	1.64	2.11

The baseline throughput and response time, computed by PDQ, are shown in the middle column of Table 3.3 for $N_{\text{agg}} = 35$. These values can be compared with the PDQ report in Sect. 6.7.9. The aggregate response time can also be calculated manually as the weighted sum:

$$R_{\text{agg}} = W_{batch}\ R_{\text{batch}} + W_{\text{online}}\ R_{\text{online}} \,. \tag{3.47}$$

The proposed upgrade involves replacing the current processor with one that is five times faster. Those results, shown in the rightmost column of Table 3.3, are produced by rerunning the PDQ model with the appropriate change for the CPU speed parameter. The predicted impact on response times is plotted in Fig. 3.19. Based on the bold numbers in Table 3.3, it is clear in Fig. 3.19 that a CPU upgrade would reduce the average response time by about 60%, if the system were measured with 35 active processes.

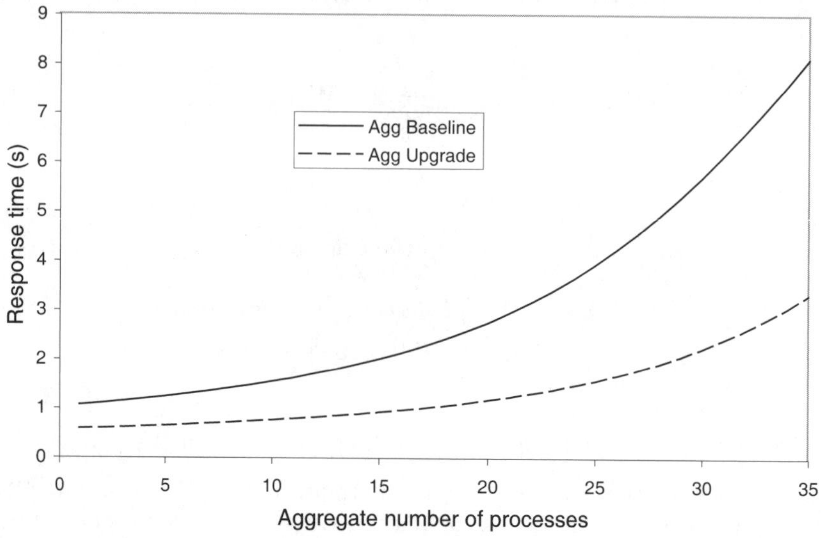

Fig. 3.19. Aggregate workload analysis. Comparison of baseline and CPU-upgrade performance predicts a 60% general *decrease* in the average response time for 35 processes

3.7.4 Component Analysis

Next, we repeat the study using a PDQ model with two workload streams: one for batch processes and the other representing interactive users. In order to make the comparison with the aggregated workload, it is useful to combine the performance projections for the batch and online components in the same plot (Fig. 3.20). This can be done easily within the PDQ program `mwl.pl` in Sect. 6.7.9. The outputs of that model are summarized in Table 3.4.

Examining the multiclass projections in Fig. 3.19, we see that the single class and multiclass projections are in good agreement for the for the baseline system. The completion time for 10 batch processes is improved by 80%. However, based on the bold numbers in Table 3.4, the 25 interactive users suffer more than a 150% *degradation* in response time! To make the crossover effects more visible, an enlargement of that region in Fig. 3.20 is shown in Fig. 3.21.

This striking difference in the performance analysis predictions arises from the fact that in the aggregated workload, the amount of time each averaged request spends at the CPU will be diminished significantly by the CPU speedup. The longer queue will be at the disk. In the two-class performance model, however, the batch component of the workload is processor bound while the interactive users are disk bound. Hence, the batch component benefits more from the processor upgrade by increasing its throughput. Additionally, the in-

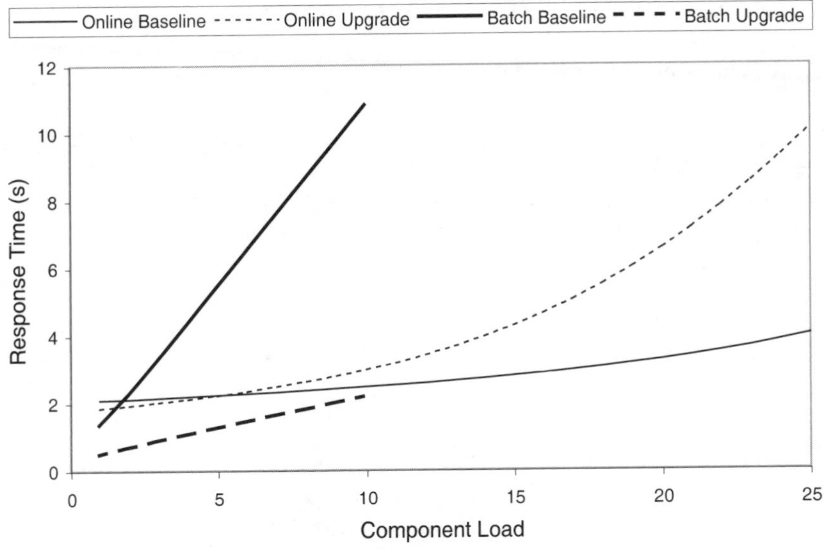

Fig. 3.20. Component workload analysis. Comparison of baseline and CPU-upgrade performance predicts an 80% *decrease* in batch completion time with 10 processes, but at the expense of the interactive users. 25 users will see a potentially disasterous 150% *increase* in their mean response time

teractive users spend some time thinking whereas the batch processes do not. This results in the interactive users typically finding many batch processes ahead of them when they reach the CPU queue. They not only do not benefit from the processor upgrade, they suffer increased contention from the batch component at the disk.

Table 3.4. Performance predictions for upgraded system

	Workload					
	Batch (10)		Interactive (25)		Combined (35)	
Metric	Baseline	Upgrade	Baseline	Upgrade	Baseline	Upgrade
R	10.79	2.16	**3.99**	**10.11**	7.52	3.16
X	0.93	4.65	0.74	0.62	1.67	5.27

3.8 When Is a Queueing Circuit Solvable?

In this section we identify the general rules for the applicability of MVA. In general, the queueing circuit must be separable or product-form. This means

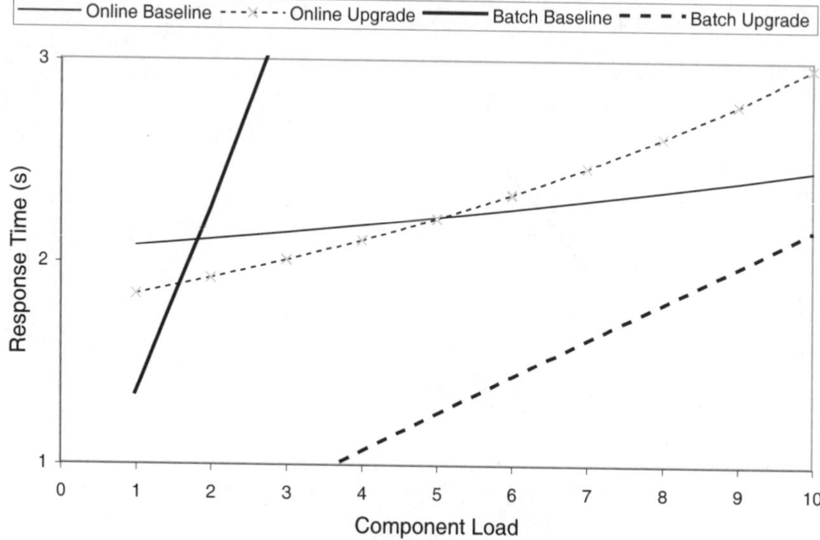

Fig. 3.21. Enlargement of the crossover region (*left hand side*) near 5 processes in Fig. 3.20. Fewer than 5 interacive users show a small improvement in their mean response time while more than 5 users begin to suffer. Contrast this with batch completion times which already show a significant improvement in this range of loads

that it must be possible to evaluate the performance measures of the complete circuit of queueing centers as though each of the centers were evaluated separately in isolation. The performance of the circuit as a whole is then constructed by combining these separate solutions.

3.8.1 MVA Is a Style of Thinking

The construction of queueing circuits in PDQ that use the MVA algorithm can often appear impenetrable to many performance analysts, especially those familiar with simulation techniques. The reasons for this can be identified as follows:

Dependency arrows. Although queueing circuits, such as Fig. 3.18, are conventionally drawn with *arrows* to represent what look like *dependency arcs* representing the flow between the queues, those arrows have no bearing on how PDQ performs its calculations. As you will discover in Chap. 6, no arrows are present in the Perl code. Why not? The only thing that matters is the *intensity* or *magnitude* of the workloads at each queueing center. These intensities are *scalar* quantities, not vectors or tensors. All associations are made by name. This is both the beauty, and for some, the mystery of this kind of queueing performance analysis.

Steady state. PDQ performs its calculations as though the queueing circuit was in *equilibrium* or *steady state.* In other words, the circuit has to be visualized as though requests have been witnessed over a long duration. Then, the flow of requests resembles a continuous *fluid* or electric current, rather than a series of instantaneous *fluctuations* caused by discrete requests or electrons. Such visualization is easy to say but sometimes hard to do in practice. This, of course, is the basis of the Arrival Theorem in Sect. 3.5.1. We expand on this view with respect to the determination of instantaneous and averaged queue length in Chap. 4.

Servicing policy. You do not tell MVA what service policy to use, MVA tells you! For example, a server being accessed by two different workload classes, each characterized by their different service times, cannot be a FIFO queue. This is because the workload with the shorter service demand will tend to preempt the other workload. Sections 3.9.1 and 3.9.2 present examples of this effect in the context of CPU schedulers. The service policy that is calculated ends up being *last-come-first-served with preempt-resume* or LCFS-PRs. Therefore, you need to check what it is that you are trying to represent in the physical computer system and whether or not that assumed service policy is being reflected by the MVA algorithm.

In this sense, MVA and its implementation in PDQ are really a style of thinking.

3.8.2 BCMP Rules

How can we know when the MVA algorithm is applicable? More formally, a separable queueing circuit is one which satisfies the following criteria known as BCMP rules [Baskett et al. 1975]:

In order. Customers are serviced in the order in which they arrive. This policy was denoted FIFO or FCFS in Chap. 2. The service times are exponentially distributed. If there are multiple customer classes, they must all have the same mean service time at a particular queueing center. They may have different visit counts or visit ratios. Service rate can be load-dependent, but it can only depend on the total number of customers at the queueing center and not on the number in any particular customer class.

Round robin. Denoted RR in Chap. 2. Customers receive a fixed amount of service time. This time allotment is also known as a *quantum* when used in reference to timeshare operating system schedulers, such as those used in UNIX. If the customer does not complete service within the allotted quantum, they return to the end of the queue to await further service.

Processor sharing. Denoted PS in Chap. 2. If there are N customers at the queueing center, they receive $1/N$ of their mean service time. Each class may have a distinct service time distribution. In the limit as $N \to \infty$, the RR policy becomes the same as the PS policy.

Delay centers. If an infinite supply of servers is available at a queueing center, then a queue will never form and there is no waiting time. This center is also called an infinite server (IS). In the case where the delay center is associated with human input, such as typing, the service time is called the *think-time.*

Preempt-resume priority. In this policy, the current customer (if any) has its servicing preempted by the newly arriving customer. When that customer completes, the server resumes service on the previously preempted customer. In this sense, the queue acts more like a stack, and we shall depict it as such in our queueing center diagrams. Also denoted last-come first-served preempt resume (LCFS-PR).

3.8.3 Service Classes

Requests belong to a particular workload class while enqueued or receiving service at a center. Requests are permitted to change class according to fixed probabilities after completion of service. A workload is defined in terms of its service time distribution and scheduling policy.

- Service time distributions. For FCFS or FIFO queueing centers, the service time distribution must be exponentially distributed for all workload classes.
- State-dependent service. For FIFO queues, the service time can depend only on the queue length at the center. For PS, LIFO-PR and IS centers, the service time for a given class can also depend on the queue length for that class but not that of other classes. The effective service rate of a subcircuit can depend only on the total number of customers in that subcircuit.
- Arrival processes. For open circuits, the interarrival period for a workload class must be exponentially distributed. There cannot be any bulk (group) arrivals. The arrival rates may be state-dependent. A queueing system maybe open with regard to certain classes of work and closed with respect to others.
- Flow balance. For each workload class, the number of arrivals at a center must equal the number of completions at the center.
- One-step behavior. No two customers finish being serviced at a service center, arrive into or depart from the queueing system at exactly the same time.
- Device homogeneity. The service rate at a center does not depend on the state of the queueing system other than through the total queue length at the center or the designated workloads queue length. From this assumption a number of other things follow:
  - Single resource possession. A request may not be waiting or receiving service at two or more centers simultaneously.

- No blocking. The service is rendered when a request is present and is not controlled or conditioned by the state of any other queue.
- No synchronization. The interaction among customers or requests occurs only through queueing for a physical resource.
- Fair service. Servers do not discriminate against one workload class based on the length of queues in other classes.
- Routing homogeneity. Routing patterns between centers have no influence of the performance measures of the queueing circuit.

The above requirements are needed to ensure that the queueing circuit can be solved. Obviously, many of them are often violated in real computer systems. For example, a UNIX process may fork a child process to be serviced simultaneously. Blocking and synchronization of requests are commonplace in application architectures. The skill that needs to be developed for doing performance analysis is discovering how to construct solvable queueing models in spite of these apparent technical violations. The remaining chapters in this book are intended to convey some of that skill by example, but like any skill, practice makes perfect!

3.9 Classic Computer Systems

We now turn to the application of queueing circuits for the performance analysis of computer systems.

The simplest closed-circuit queueing model we presented earlier, was first used by Scherr [1967] to model the *Multics* time-sharing computer with multiple users (See Appendix B for a chronology). In formal queueing theory, this model is called the *repairman model* [Allen 1990]. It also represents a bridge between the theory of single queueing centers and circuits containing multiple queues. The repairman model can be adapted to represent the performance of multiprocessor systems, and we pursue that topic further in Chap. 7.

3.9.1 Time-Share Scheduler

It is possible to construct an elementary queueing model of a UNIX time-share scheduler. As depicted in the closed queueing circuit of Fig. 3.22, consider N UNIX processes that are either *runnable* and therefore waiting in the run-queue, *running* on a CPU, or *suspended* for a mean time Z. The association with the queueing parameters can be summarized as:

Z: Average time spent in suspended state
X: Rate of job completions
S: CPU user time quantum
V: Number of returns visits to run-queue to complete the work
D: CPU user service demand $D = V \times S$

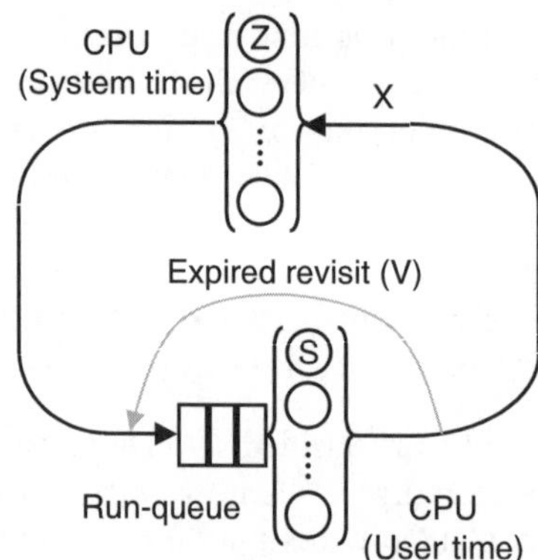

Fig. 3.22. PDQ model of a generic time-share CPU scheduler

In UNIX parlance [Vahalia 1996], the CPU busy time is partitioned into *user* time when the application or program is running, and the *system* time due to the execution of kernel code e.g., disk I/O device drivers discussed in Chap. 1. We need to apportion this service time dichotomy correctly in Fig. 3.22.

The CPU user-time is associated with the service demand at the nodes servicing the run-queue at the bottom of Fig. 3.22. The CPU system-time must be assigned to the Z value in the nodes at the top of the diagram. This accounts for the situation where a UNIX device driver is furiously burning CPU system time in the suspended state, but the run-queue length is essentially zero, and therefore the system load average (see Chap. 4 for a more detailed discussion of this point) would appear low.

Time-share (TS) operating systems, like UNIX, Linux, and Windows aim at providing responsive service to multiple interactive users. Put simply, the goal is to create the illusion for each user that they are the only one accessing system resources. This is to be contrasted with batch scheduling, where maximum throughput is the goal rather than minimum response time.

The TS scheduler attempts to give all active processes equal access to the CPU by employing a *round-robin* processor allocation policy. Put simply, each process gets a fixed amount of time to run on the processor. This fixed time is called a service *quantum* (commonly on the order of 10 ms).

We can also reach a simple understanding of how the UNIX *nice* command [Vahalia 1996] works. Its effect is simply to provide a small bias to the priority level of a process, which then influences where the process is placed in the run-queue when it returns after the CPU service time-quantum expires. In the real operating system, there is actually more than one queue. As we show in Chap. 6, our simple queueing model can be extended to include such details.

3.9.2 Fair-Share Scheduler

The time-share (TS) scheduler described in Sect. 3.9.1 has an inherent loophole that can be exploited under certain conditions. Processes that demand less than the fixed service *quantum* at the CPU generally complete processor service without being interrupted. A process that exceeds its service quantum, however, has its processing interrupted and is returned toward the back of the run-queue to await further CPU time. A natural consequence of the TS scheduling policy is that processes with processing demands that are shorter than the time quantum are favored over processes with longer demands because they tend to be preempted when their service quantum expires.

Herein lies a loophole. The UNIX scheduler is biased intrinsically in favor of a greedy user who runs many short-demand processes. This loophole is not a defect, rather it is a property of the round-robin scheduler that implements time-sharing, which in turn guarantees responsiveness to the shorter processing demands associated with multiple interactive users. One way to close this loophole is to employ a scheduler that implements a *fair share* scheduling policy [See Vahalia 1996, Chap. 5]. In contrast to TS, the fair share (FS)

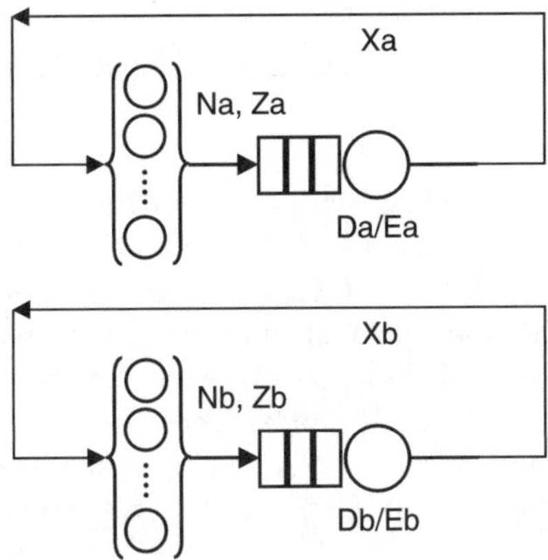

Fig. 3.23. A queueing model of the fair share scheduler for user classes N_{a} and N_{b} with respective entitlements E_{a} and E_{b} each running on their own *virtual* CPU with an *effective* service demand $D_{\mathrm{a}}^{\mathrm{FS}}$ and $D_{\mathrm{b}}^{\mathrm{FS}}$ defined by (3.48)

scheduler has two levels of scheduling: process level and user level. Process-level scheduling is essentially the same as that in standard UNIX, and *nice* values can be applied there as well. The user-level scheduler is the new component, which can be thought of as sitting on top of the TS scheduler in order to make associations between users and the processes they own. Process service demands are compared with resource *entitlements* granted to users by the system administrator via the literal allocation of resource tokens called *shares.* In this way, resource consumption can be partitioned and constrained in a *fair* manner, thereby removing the round-robin loophole present in the TS scheduler.

In terms of queueing circuits, the FS scheduler can be thought of as follows. For each user class or group of users $(N_{\rm a}, N_{\rm b}, N_{\rm c}, \ldots)$ with resource entitlement $(E_{\rm a}, E_{\rm b}, E_{\rm c}, \ldots)$, the FS scheduler allocates to each of them a *virtual* CPU such that their *effective* service demand $(D_{\rm a}^{\rm FS}, D_{\rm b}^{\rm FS}, D_{\rm c}^{\rm FS}, \ldots)$ is their actual service demand scaled by their respective entitlements. For class (a) users, we could write specifically:

$$D_{\rm a}^{\rm FS} = \frac{D_{\rm a}^{\rm Actual}}{E_{\rm a}^{\rm FS}} , \tag{3.48}$$

and similarly for each of the other classes. Figure 3.23 depicts the correspond-

Table 3.5. Some UNIX operating systems that implement fair share scheduling

O/S	Vendor	Open Source	Fair Share Scheduler
AIX	IBM		WorkLoad Manager (WLM)
FreeBSD		`www.freebsd.org/`	Proportional Share (PS)
HP-UX	HP		Process Resource Manager (PRM)
Irix	SGI		SHARE II
Multiple		`www.supercluster.org/`	Maui
Solaris	Sun		Solaris Resource Manager (SRM)

ing queueing circuits, and this provides a way to succinctly state the key principle of operation of fair share scheduling [Gunther 1999]. We see that each group of users appears to have their own TS scheduler with a *virtual* CPU that determines the actual responsiveness of the system. The greater their entitlement, the shorter will be their effective service time at the CPU and vice versa. Hence, the system will appear most responsive to those users who have been granted the greatest entitlement to resources. Table 3.5 provides a list of operating systems that implement FS scheduling.

3.9.3 Priority Scheduling

In our discussion of queues so far, we have generally assumed that the service policy is either FIFO (FCFS) or preemptive due to service demands that differ markedly. The FIFO assumption is valid for single workloads because we have assumed each request or customer has the same average service demand. If there are multiple workload classes, distinguished by their service demands, the server behaves as if it is following a last-come-first-served-preempt resume (LCFS-PR) policy. In more realistic situations these assumptions can be less than satisfactory and we need to include the effects of *explicit* priority scheduling. We demonstrate how such explicit priorities can be implemented within the queueing paradigms we have discussed in the last two chapters.

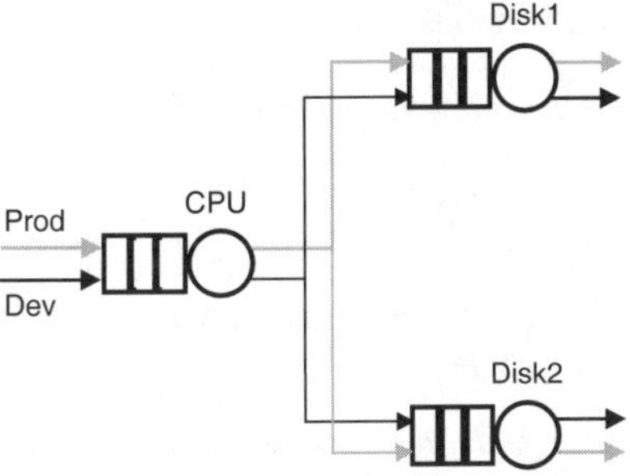

Fig. 3.24. The physical CPU and disks belonging to the central subsystem of an otherwise closed circuit (not shown) servicing the *Production* and *Development* workloads

The technical approach is a variant of the method developed in Sect. 3.4.6 for determining the response time at an open queue subjected to multi-class arrivals.

Assume for simplicity that there are two workload classes, *Production* and *Development*. In the current time-share system (Fig. 3.24), *Production* is not meeting its subsecond service level objectives for average response times. This situation can be corrected by giving *Production* higher priority at the CPU. We want to make performance estimates of the impact on the response times of both workloads.

We proceed by first building the no-priority performance model in Fig. 3.24 and calibrate it against the measured demands, utilizations, and response times. A numerical example is given in Example 3.7.

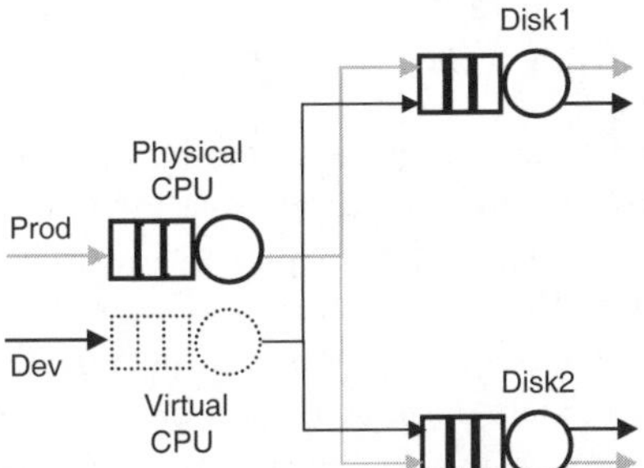

Fig. 3.25. Same diagram as Fig. 3.24 but with the high-priority *Production* workload executing on the physical CPU and the lower priority *Development* workload executing on a *virtual* CPU with inflated service demand given by (3.49)

We next determine the utilization $\rho_{\text{cpu}}^{\text{prod}}$ of the *Production* workload at the CPU. We then construct the *priority* model in Fig. 3.25, which allows *Production* to have exclusive access to the physical CPU and introduces a *virtual*

CPU to run only the *Development* workload. Although there is another CPU, albeit a virtual CPU, there is a cost to *Development.* The service demand on virtual CPU,

$$\tilde{D}_{\text{cpu}}^{\text{dev}} = \frac{D_{\text{cpu}}^{\text{dev}}}{1 - \rho_{\text{cpu}}^{\text{prod}}}, \tag{3.49}$$

is *inflated* by $\rho_{\text{cpu}}^{\text{prod}}$, the utilization from the *Production* workload. Note the similarity with (3.22) and (3.48).

Example 3.7. With 15 *Production* processes and 20 *Development* workstations having respective service demands: $D_{\text{cpu}}^{\text{prod}} = 300$ ms and $D_{\text{cpu}}^{\text{dev}} = 1000$ ms, the average *Production* response time of 2.69 s is above the acceptable subsecond service level agreement. *Development* response time is acceptable at 8.19 s. We apply (3.49) to determine the impact of giving *Production* a higher CPU priority. As the results in Table 3.6 indicate, explicitly giving higher priority to Production does not penalize Development significantly. The corresponding PDQ model is presented in Sect. 6.7.10 of Chap. 6. □

Table 3.6. Comparison of response times (in seconds) together with the percentage differences when high priority is given to the Production workload

Work stream	No priority	High priority	Percent difference
Production	2.69	0.62	+ 77
Development	8.19	8.66	-6

3.9.4 Threads Scheduler

The main difference between a *threaded* scheduler and the schedulers discussed in Sects. 3.9.1 and 3.9.2 is that the number of available threads corresponds to a *finite* resource in the presence of requests that may be unbounded (open circuit), such as would be the case for Internet-based traffic. Although a finite resource is closer to the commonly understood notion of a *buffer*, this is something simple queueing models do not accommodate, as we explain further in Sect. 3.10. As depicted in Fig. 3.26, idea is to treat the finite resource as a submodel, calculate its effects on various performance metrics (e.g., throughput) *independently*, and then use those results to determine the impact on the composite model.

The submodel looks exactly like the TS model of Sect. 3.9.1 except that it refers to service demands that operate at a finer time granularity than generic UNIX processes. Therefore, the submodel can be solved as a separate Perl *subroutine* in PDQ. We leave the details of how this submodel decoupling works until Chap. 6.

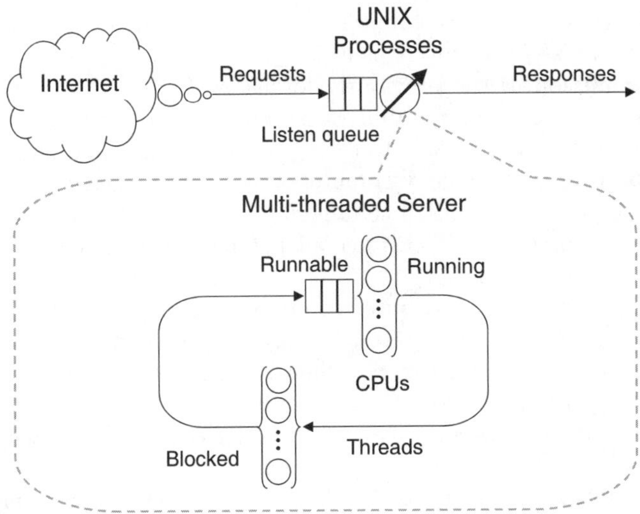

Fig. 3.26. A queueing model of threads-based scheduler showing the composite model with the load-dependent server indicated by an *arrow*. The details of the load-dependent server are determined by the threads submodel shown inside the exploded view (*dashed boundary*)

3.10 What Queueing Models Cannot Do

The material presented in this chapter is limited by the assumptions that have been invoked in order to obtain results that are useful in practice. With knowledge comes the responsibility of being careful how it gets applied.

Blocking: In the preceding discussions, we have assumed that queue lengths can be arbitrary. In real computer systems, however, queues or buffers often require allocation of a finite amount of storage. When a finite buffer becomes full, it may inhibit or block processing at other resources. Put differently, the service rate at a particular queueing center depends on the state (queue lengths) of the entire circuit. Since this situation lies outside the BCMP Rules, the separability assumption is lost. Various approximation have been devised.

Bulk arrivals: Arrivals occur in batches or groups. This is a common phenomenon in communication systems with so-called *bursty* traffic marked by long periods of quiescence punctuated by bursts of heavy traffic. Bulk arrivals can be modeled under certain restricted assumptions such as exponential distribution of group arrivals.

Contention resolution: Networks such as ALOHA and Ethernet incorporate sophisticated service disciplines that apply back-off and retry algorithms under heavy traffic conditions. These algorithms are not easy to render using queueing models [Gunther 2000a, Part III].

Fork/Join primitives: Forking child processes is used to achieve certain kinds of process-level parallelism. The join primitive is used to synchronize the completion of the previously forked processes. Prima facie, forking children violates the separability assumption of job independence.

Game-theoretic strategies: Cheating, bribery, and baulking.

Load-dependent arrivals: Computer systems with adaptive load-balancing strategies that shepherd incoming tasks to one of a number of under-utilized resources are difficult to model with queueing circuits. See Sect. 3.9.4 and Chap. 6.

Mutual exclusion: In distributed computer systems, several tasks attempting to access a common resource may be excluded while one task has possession. This policy can be achieved with such primitives as locks or combining networks. For example, only one task can acquire a lock to update a database record. This effect is not easy to model with queueing circuits.

Non-exponential service times: A major requirement for separability of queueing circuits is service times that are exponentially distributed. It has been demonstrated that MVA techniques are robust to mild departures from this assumption. This follows from the BCMP rules observation that performance measures such as utilizations and response times are determined by the mean of the service time only and not the higher moments. Accuracy of queue length-dependent measures such as response time may be more sensitive to this assumption.

Queueing defections: This is the sort of thing that happens in the grocery store. A customer gets impatient with the service rate of the current queue and defects to one that appears to be moving faster (see Chap. 2). A similar strategy appears in certain computer networks. Essentially, a packet carries timeout information on how long it will persist in any queue. After that time, the packet is dropped from the queue under that assumption that it has already been retransmitted by the source and received service elsewhere in the network.

Response-dependent arrivals: This is similar to the situation for Queueing Defections except that packet timeout and packet dropping is missing. Rather, the source just retransmits the packets. This in turn can cause further congestion at already congested resources. Even worse, such a positive feedback loop can make the entire system unstable to large transient fluctuations, causing sudden escalation in response times.

Sharing Finite Resources: Example of such computer resources include main memory, virtual memory, and networks.

Simultaneous resource possession: An example of this effect is known as asynchronous I/O in computer systems. The job continues to compute while having issued a request to the I/O subsystem. In this sense, the job is simultaneously holding more than one resource and is a violation of the job independence assumption. This is difficult to model in queueing circuits, but can sometimes be addressed with an appropriate choice of request granularity and mixed workload models.

Think time: This concept of a computer job waiting for human input from a terminal is becoming arcane in an era where modern workstations are based on window interfaces that allow a moderate degree of interactive concurrency to take place.

Transient analysis: As mentioned in Sect. 1.8.4, this is a very difficult problem that can be handled to some degree within the context of queueing circuit models. See [Gunther 2000a, Part III] and [Trivedi 2000] for differing approaches to this problem.

Concurrency and synchronization have become widespread with the advent of distributed computer systems. We shall show how these difficulties can be addressed in the context of client/server computer systems in Chap. 9.

3.11 Review

In this chapter we extended the characterization of single queueing centers to include a flow of customers or requests through a circuit of queues. This was necessary because real computers involve more than one subsystem, e.g., CPU, memory, and I/O subsystems. We discussed both series and parallel circuits of queues that can be both open and closed. This also includes possibility of flows feeding back into a queue. We also saw that flows of requests can be merged into a single queue as well as how they can split into multiple flows once they have been serviced.

For open-circuit queues, the solution is generally straightforward when the centers are $M/M/m$; each center can be solved separately, and the response time is the sum of the individual response times for each center. Jackson's Theorem guarantees this solution technique even although the arrivals do not necessarily conform to a Poisson process.

Closed-circuit queues are complicated by the state of each queueing center being dependent of the state of all the other queueing centers in the circuit. The Arrival Theorem provides a way to solve this problem iteratively for each value of N and gives rise to the Mean Value Analysis (MVA) algorithm. In general, MVA can be applied to any circuit of queues that obey the so-called BCMP rules. The MVA formulas also provide a useful way of bounding performance.

We examined queueing circuits where more than one workload is serviced. This is necessary because many computer systems, especially application servers, run more than one task at a time. Finally, we showed how queueing circuits can be applied to some classic computer systems viz. time-share scheduling, fair-share scheduling, time-share with priority scheduling, and threaded servers.

Exercises

3.1. Use the visit ratios in Example 3.5 to prove that the branching probabilities must be $p = 0.20$ and $q = 0.60$.

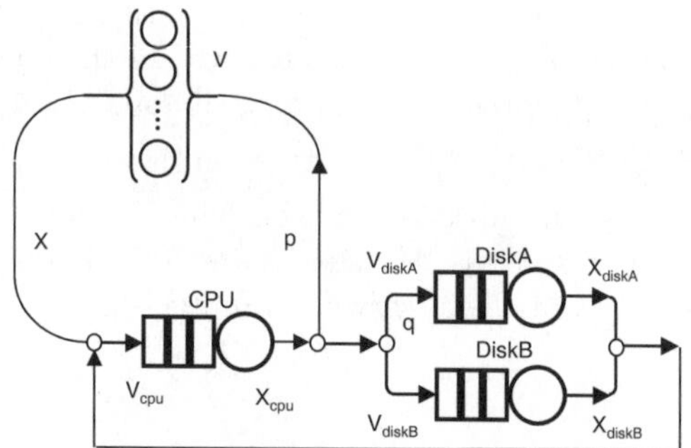

Fig. 3.27. Closed queueing circuit for Exercise 3.2

3.2. Figure 3.27 shows a closed queueing circuit with routing probability p returning some faction of serviced reuqests to users and routing probability q belonging to requests going to disk A. The visit ratios are: $V_{\text{cpu}} = 181$, $V_{\text{dkA}} = 80$ and $V_{\text{dkB}} = 100$.

(**a**) Show $V_{cpu} = 1 + V_{\text{dkA}} + V_{\text{dkB}}$.
(**b**) Show $p = 1/V_{\text{cpu}}$.
(**c**) Show $q = V_{\text{dkA}}/(V_{\text{cpu}} - 1)$.
(**d**) Show the branching ratios $p + q \neq 1$.

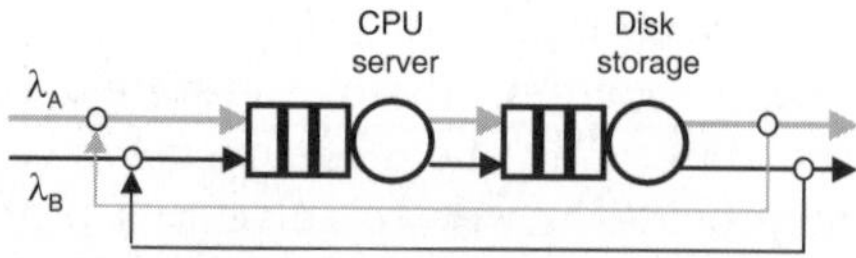

Fig. 3.28. Open queueing circuit for Exercise 3.3

3.3. Figure 3.28 shows an open queueing circuit with two workload streams denoted by the arrivals λ_A and λ_B.

Stream A		Stream B	
$V_{\text{cpu}} = 10.0$	$V_{\text{dsk}} = 9.0$	$V_{\text{cpu}} = 5.0$	$V_{\text{dsk}} = 4.0$
$S_{\text{cpu}} = 0.10$	$S_{\text{dsk}} = 0.333$	$S_{\text{cpu}} = 0.4$	$S_{\text{dsk}} = 1.0$
$D_{\text{cpu}} = 1.0$	$D_{\text{dsk}} = 3.0$	$D_{\text{cpu}} = 2.0$	$D_{\text{dsk}} = 4.0$
$\lambda_A = 0.158$		$\lambda_B = 0.105$	

Use the tabulated circuit inputs to solve for the residence times, queue lengths, and response times for both workloads.

3.4. Networked Storage. Two storage arrays reside on a network to service aggregate I/O traffic of 600,000 physical disk I/Os per h. One storage array is faster than the other. The fast array takes 5 ms to complete an I/O operation, the slow array takes 15 ms. What fraction of the total I/O traffic should go to the fast array in order to minimize the average response time of an IO operation?

4

Linux Load Average—Take a Load Off!

4.1 Introduction

The term *load* means different things to different people. For example, it might imply the number of *active users* or *throughput* to a system administrator, whereas we saw in Chap. 2 that it tends to imply *utilization* to a performance analyst.

A well-known indicator of the "load" on a UNIX server is the *load average* reported by a variety of UNIX shell commands. But which of the possible definitions of *load* is used in the load average report? Moreover, where and how is the load average calculated, and how does it relate to the queueing theory concepts presented in Chaps. 2 and 3? This chapter, which is based on a personal detective story, endeavors to address all these questions.

Although the load average appears on most UNIX systems, the source code for those UNIX kernels is usually proprietary and therefore not available for public inspection. A major exception is the Linux kernel, where the source code is not only annotated (see e.g., [Bovet and Cesati 2001]), but it is available online as an HTML document (`lxr.linux.no/blurb.html`) complete with cross-reference hyperlinks for easy navigation and enhanced readability. We therefore refer mostly to Linux code throughout this chapter while recognizing that similar implementations of the load average metric exist on UNIX kernels. Microsoft Windows 2000® does not have a formal load average metric, although it does monitor the processor queue length.

In this chapter we explore how the load average performance metric is calculated by several different UNIX shell commands. The details are presented with reference to the Linux operating system because that kernel source code is available online. For those readers not familiar with the formal queueing concepts discussed in Chaps. 2 and 3, this is a good place to start because, as you will see, the load average is related to the average size of the run-queue.

A function called `CALC_LOAD` contains the central algorithm. It computes a special time-dependent average of the run-queue size using fixed-point arithmetic. The reported 1-, 5-, and 15-min load averages correspond to three different weighting factors which put more emphasis on the most recent run-queue samples than older samples.

Finally, we look at some novel extensions of the conventional load average metrics that can provide better visual trend information and forecasting for distributed workloads running on computational GRIDs. We begin our journey by reviewing how the load average is typically reported.

4.1.1 Load Average Reporting

The load average comprises three metrics that appear in the ASCII output of certain UNIX operating system commands. For example, it appears as part of the `uptime` or network `ruptime` command:

```
[pax:~]% uptime
9:40am  up 9 days, 10:36,  4 users,  load average: 0.02, 0.01, 0.00
```

On Linux systems it appears as part of the `procinfo` command:

```
[pax:~]% procinfo
Linux 2.0.36 (root@pax) (gcc 2.7.2.3) #1 Wed Jul 25 21:40:16 EST 2001

Memory:      Total        Used        Free      Shared     Buffers      Cached
Mem:         95564       90252        5312       31412       33104       26412
Swap:        68508           0       68508

Bootup: Sun Jul 21 15:21:15 2002    Load average: 0.15 0.03 0.01
...
```

So, the metric `Load average: 0.15 0.03 0.01` we are interested in contains three numbers. Why are there three numbers and not just one? The usual way to find out on a UNIX system is to read the relevant manual pages.

```
[pax:~]% man "load average"
No manual entry for load average
```

This happens because the load average is not its own command. If, however, you read the UNIX online manual ("man") pages for the `uptime` or `procinfo` command, you quickly find that the three numbers correspond to the 1-minute, 5-minute, and 15-minute averages. But averages of what?

For further explanation, we turn to some of the many available UNIX reference books. For example, Peek et al. [1997, p. 726] warn:

> The load average tries to measure the number of active processes at any time. As a measure of CPU utilization, the load average is simplistic, poorly defined, but far from useless.

As we shall see shortly, the load average is not a measure of *CPU utilization* at all. But what is meant by *active* processes? Cockcroft and Pettit [1998, p. 229] are a little more explicit:

> The load average is the sum of the run queue length and the number of jobs currently running on the CPUs. In Solaris 2.0 and 2.2 the load average did not include the running jobs but this bug was fixed in Solaris 2.3.

However, they also indicate that the implementation of the load average calculation may not always be correct if quality assurance is not properly applied with each new release of the operating system.

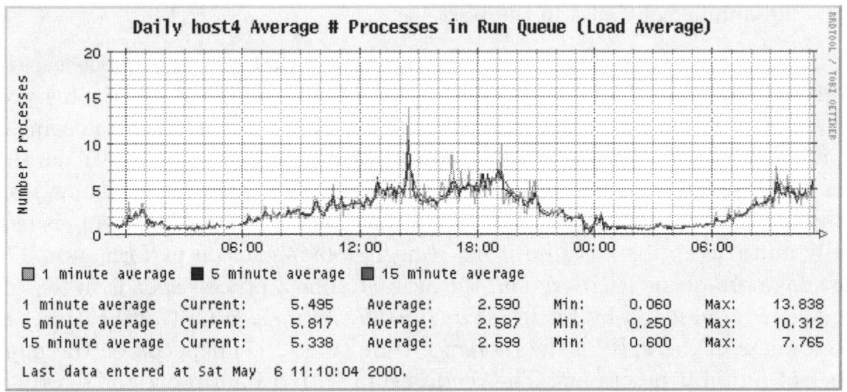

Fig. 4.1. Load average presented graphically as a time series over a 24-hour window. This screenshot shows three overlapping curves correspond to regularly scheduled samples of the 1-minute, 5-minute, and 15-minute load averages plotted in different colors

The quality of data presentation can be improved immensely by employing a graphical representation to display sampled load average data as a time series, like that produced by the ORCA tool (`www.orcaware.com/orca/docs/orcallator.html`) in Fig. 4.1. The relative significance of each load average sample can then be viewed across a broad window of time, in a way that is not possible with the generic UNIX performance tools.

4.1.2 What Is an "Average" Load?

So, it seems that *load*, in this context, means run queue length. But what is an "average" load? Peek et al. [1997, p. 720] tend to answer this question with a question:

> What's high? As usual, that depends on your system. Ideally, you'd like a load average under, say, 3, ... Ultimately, "high" means high enough so that you don't need uptime to tell you that the system is overloaded.

They continue:

> ...different systems will behave differently under the same load average. ...running a single CPU-bound background job ...can bring response to a crawl even though the load avg remains quite low.

Blair Zajac, author of the ORCA tool (Fig. 4.1), points out (`www.orcaware.com/orca/docs/orcallator.html#processes_in_run_queue_system_load`):

> If long term trends indicate increasing figures, more or faster CPUs will eventually be necessary unless load can be displaced. For ideal utilization of your CPU, the maximum value here should be equal to the number of CPUs in the box.

This is a nice statement because it recognizes that the run queue can be serviced by more than one processor. If the load average of all running processes exactly matches the number of physical processors, then queueing is unlikely to occur. That is an ideal state that may be achieveable with parallel or batch processing. For general purpose workloads, however, we know from the $M/M/m$ queue analysis in Chap. 2 that some amount of queueing is usually quite acceptible because it has a negligible impact on performance. The average run-queue length Q and the average time a process spends in the run queue R are related by Little's law $Q = \lambda R$. At a given CPU utilization, the sharpness of the knee in the residence time (Fig. 2.17) depends on the number of physical processors. The relationship with a multiprocessor scheduler is discussed in more detail in Sect. 4.4.2.

From the diversity of opinions expressed in Sects. 4.1.1 and 4.1.2, we might reasonably conclude that there is some noticeable confusion. That is because the load average metric is not your average kind of average. As we shall discover in this chapter, not only is the load average not a typical kind of average, it is a *time-dependent* average, indeed, a special kind of time-dependent average. We commence our deeper investigations into the nature of the load average with some controlled performance measurements.

4.2 A Simple Experiment

A controlled experiment was performed over a one-hour period on an otherwise quiescent single-CPU Linux box. The test comprised two phases:

- Two CPU-intensive processes were initiated in the background and allowed to execute for 2,100 s.
- The two processes were stopped simultaneously but measurements continued for another 1,500 s.

The following Perlscript was used to sample the load average every 5 s using the `uptime` command.

```
#! /usr/bin/perl
# getload.pl
```

```
$sample_interval = 5; # seconds

# Fire up 2 cpu-intensive tasks in the background
system("./burncpu &");
system("./burncpu &");

# Perpetually monitor the load average via the uptime
# shell command and emit it as tab-separated fields.
while (1) {
    @uptime = split (/ /, `uptime`);
    foreach $up (@uptime) {
        # collect the timestamp
        if ($up =~ m/(\d\d:\d\d:\d\d)/) {
            print "$1\t";
        }
        # collect the three load metrics
        if ($up =~ m/(\d{1,}\.\d\d)/) {
            print "$1\t";
        }
    }
    print "\n";
    sleep ($sample_interval);
}
```

The CPU-intensive workload in the following C code makes references that can cause cache-line replacement on many machines:

```
// burncpu.c

#include<stdio.h>
#include<stdlib.h>
#include<math.h>

#define MAXARRAY    100
long int        m[MAXARRAY];
double          a[MAXARRAY];

int main(void) {
  int               i;
  void              StuffMatrices();
  StuffMatrices();
  for (i = 0; i < MAXARRAY; i++) {
    a[i] = a[100 - i] * m[i];
    if (i == MAXARRAY - 1) {
      i = 0;
    }
  }
}  // end of main
```

```
void StuffMatrices () {
  int            k;
  for (k = 0; k < MAXARRAY; k++) {
    a[k] = (double) random ();
    m[k] = random ();
  }
}  //end of StuffMatrices
```

The following (edited) output from the `top` program confirms that the two workload instances initiated by the `getload` script ranked as the highest CPU-consuming processes.

```
  PID USER    SIZE  RSS SHARE STAT %CPU %MEM   TIME CPU COMMAND
20048 neil     256  256   212 R    30.6  0.0   0:32   0 burncpu
20046 neil     256  256   212 R    29.3  0.0   0:32   0 burncpu
15709 mir     9656 9656  4168 R    25.6  1.8  45:32   0 kscience.kss
 1248 root   66092  10M  1024 S     9.5  2.1 368:25   0 X
20057 neil    1068 1068   808 R     2.3  0.2   0:01   0 top
 1567 mir    39228  38M 14260 S     1.3  7.6  40:10   0 mozilla-bin
 1408 mir      340  296   216 S     0.7  0.0  50:33   0 autorun
 1397 mir     2800 1548   960 S     0.1  0.3   1:57   0 kdeinit
20044 neil    1516 1516  1284 S     0.1  0.2   0:00   0 perl
    1 root     156  128   100 S     0.0  0.0   0:04   0 init
    2 root       0    0     0 SW    0.0  0.0   0:01   0 keventd
    3 root       0    0     0 SW    0.0  0.0   0:02   0 kapmd
    4 root       0    0     0 SWN   0.0  0.0   0:00   0 ksoftirqd_CPU
    9 root       0    0     0 SW    0.0  0.0   0:00   0 bdflush
    5 root       0    0     0 SW    0.0  0.0   0:02   0 kswapd
    6 root       0    0     0 SW    0.0  0.0   0:00   0 kscand/DMA
```

4.2.1 Experimental Results

Figure 4.2 shows that the 1-min load average reaches a value of 2.0 after 300 s into the test, the 5-min load average reaches 2.0 around 1,200 s, while the 15-min load average would reach 2.0 at approximately 4,500 s but the processes were *killed* at 2100 s. Electrical engineers will immediately notice the resemblance to the voltage curve produced by a charging and discharging RC-circuit. This important analogy will be utilized in Sect. 4.3.4.

Notice that the maximum load is equivalent to the number of CPU-intensive processes running at the time of the measurements. If there was just a single process running, you could be forgiven for thinking that load average is a direct measure of CPU utilization. Our next goal is to explain why the load average data from these experiments exhibit the characteristics seen in Fig. 4.2. We begin by looking at the Linux kernel code that calculates the load average metrics.

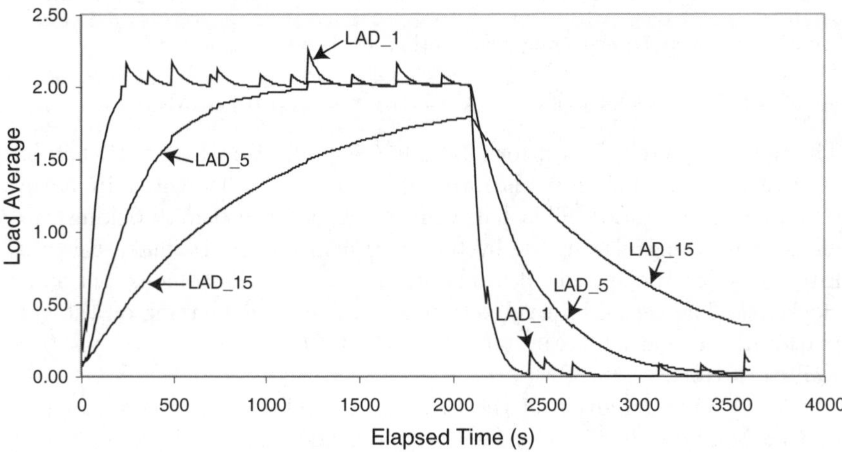

Fig. 4.2. Time series plot of data from load average experiments on a Linux platform

4.2.2 Submerging Into the Kernel

As mentioned in the introduction to this chapter, the source code for the Linux kernel is available online and this facilitates a studying it in detail. If we look at the code for the CPU scheduler in `lxr.linux.no/source/include/linux/sched.h`, we see the following C function called `calc_load()`:

```
unsigned long avenrun[3];

static inline void calc_load(unsigned long ticks)
{
        unsigned long active_tasks; /* fixed-point */
        static int count = LOAD_FREQ;

        count -= ticks;
        if (count < 0) {
                count += LOAD_FREQ;
                active_tasks = count_active_tasks();
                CALC_LOAD(avenrun[0], EXP_1, active_tasks);
                CALC_LOAD(avenrun[1], EXP_5, active_tasks);
                CALC_LOAD(avenrun[2], EXP_15, active_tasks);
        }
}
```

This is the primary routine for calculating the load average metrics. Essentially, `calc_load()` checks to see if the sample period has expired, resets the sampling counter, and calls the subroutine `CALC_LOAD` to calculate each of the

1-minute, 5-minute, and 15-minute metrics respectively. The array `avenrun[]`, and the constant `LOAD_FREQ` used by `calc_load()` are defined elsewhere as:

```
58 extern unsigned long avenrun[]; /* Load averages */
...
62 #define LOAD_FREQ       (5*HZ)  /* 5 sec intervals */
```

The sampling interval used for `LOAD_FREQ` is `5*HZ`. How long is that interval?

Every UNIX or Linux platform has a clock implemented in hardware (Chap. 1, Sect. 1.3.6). This hardware clock has a constant ticking rate by which everything else in the system is synchronized. To make this ticking rate known to the system, it sends an interrupt to the UNIX kernel on every clock *tick*. The actual interval between ticks differs depending on the type of platform, e.g., most UNIX systems have the CPU tick interval set to 10 ms of wall-clock time.

The specific definition of the tick rate is contained in a constant labeled `HZ` that is maintained in a system-specific header file called `param.h`. For the online Linux source code we are using here, you can see the value is 100 for an Intel platform in `lxr.linux.no/source/include/asm-i386/param.h`, and for a SPARC-based system in `lxr.linux.no/source/include/asm-sparc/param.h`. However, it is defined differently for a MIPS processor in `lxr.linux.no/source/include/asm-mips/param.h`. The statement:

```
#define HZ     100
```

in the header file means that one second of wall-clock time is divided into 100 ticks. In other words, we could say that a clock interrupt occurs with a *frequency* of once every 100th of a second, or 1 tick $= 1$ s$/100 = 10$ ms. Conversely, the C macro at line 73:

```
73 #define CT_TO_SECS(x)   ((x) / HZ)
```

is used to convert the number of ticks to seconds.

The constant labeled `HZ` should be read as the frequency *divisor* and not literally as the SI unit of frequency *cycles per second*, the latter actually having the symbol Hz. Thus, `5 * HZ` means five times the value of the constant called `HZ`. Furthermore, since `HZ` is equivalent to 100 ticks, 5×100 ticks $= 500$ ticks, it follows that 500 ticks is the same as 500×10 ms or an interval of 5 s. So, `CALC_LOAD` is called once every 5 s, and not 5 times per second as some people mistakenly think. Also, be careful not to confuse this sampling period of 5 s with the *reporting* periods of 1, 5, and 15 minutes.

4.3 Load Calculation

The C macro `CALC_LOAD` does the real work of calculating the load average, and it is defined in lines 67–70 of the following code fragment:

```
extern unsigned long avenrun[ ];          /* Load averages */

#define FSHIFT          11                /* nr of bits of precision */
#define FIXED_1         (1<<FSHIFT)       /* 1.0 as fixed-point */
#define LOAD_FREQ       (5*HZ)            /* 5 sec intervals */
#define EXP_1           1884              /* 1/exp(5sec/1min) */
#define EXP_5           2014              /* 1/exp(5sec/5min) */
#define EXP_15          2037              /* 1/exp(5sec/15min) */

#define CALC_LOAD(load,exp,n) \
        load *= exp; \
        load += n*(FIXED_1-exp); \
        load >>= FSHIFT;
```

Several questions immediately come to mind when reading this code:

1. Where do those strange numbers 1884, 2014, 2037 come from?
2. What role do they play in calculating the load averages?
3. What does the `CALC_LOAD` code actually do?

We attempt to address these questions in the subsequent sections. First, we need to make a brief diversion into the *fixed-point* representation of numbers.

4.3.1 Fixed-Point Arithmetic

The following, slightly cryptic comment in the code:

```
 * These are the constant used to fake the fixed-point load-average
 * counting. Some notes:
 * - 11 bit fractions expand to 22 bits by the multiplies: this gives
 *   a load-average precision of 10 bits integer + 11 bits fractional
 * - if you want to count load-averages more often, you need more
 *   precision, or rounding will get you. With 2-second counting freq,
 *   the EXP_n values would be 1981, 2034 and 2043 if still using only
 *   11 bit fractions.
```

alerts us to the fact that fixed-point, rather than floating-point operations are used to calculate the load average. Since the load average calculations are done in the kernel, the presumption is that fixed-point arithmetic is more efficient than floating-point routines, although no explicit justification is given for that assumption.

Fixed-point representation means that only a fixed number of digits, either decimal or binary, are permitted to express any number, including those that have a fractional part (mantissa) following the decimal point. Suppose, for example, that 4 bits of precision were allowed in the mantissa. Then, numbers like:

$$0.1234,\ -12.3401,\ 1.2000,\ 1234.0001$$

can be represented exactly. On the other hand, numbers like:

$$0.12346, \ -8.34051$$

cannot be represented exactly and would have to be rounded to:

$$0.1235, \ -8.3405$$

As the embedded comment starting at line 54 warns us, too much successive rounding can cause insignificant errors to become compounded into significant errors. One way around this is to increase the number of bits used to express the mantissa, assuming the storage is available to accommodate the greater precision.

Line 52 of the comment in the kernel source indicates that there are 10 bits allowed for the integer part of the number and 11 bits for the fractional part called an $M.N = 10.11$ format. The basic rules of fixed-point addition are the same as for integers. The important difference occurs with fixed-point multiplication. The product of multiplying two $M.N$ fixed-point numbers is:

$$M.N \times M.N = (M + M).(N + N) \tag{4.1}$$

To get back to $M.N$ format, the lower-order bits are dropped by shifting N bits.

4.3.2 Magic Numbers

There are several fixed-point constants used in the `CALC_LOAD` routine. The first of these is the number '1' itself, which is labeled `FIXED_1` on line 61 of the kernel code. In the following layout:

←10 bits→		← 11 bits →	
0000000001	.	0 0 0 0 0 0 0 0 0 0 0	(a)
1		0 0 0 0 0 0 0 0 0 0 0	(b)
11		10 9 8 7 6 5 4 3 2 1 0	(c)

row (a) shows `FIXED_1` expressed in 10.11 format, while the leading zeros and the decimal point have been dropped from row (b). The resulting binary digits 100000000000_2 are indexed 0 through 11 in row (c), which establishes that `FIXED_1` is equivalent to 2^{11} or 2048_{10} in decimal notation.

Using the C language bitwise left-shift operator (<<), 100000000000_2 can be written as $1 << 11$ in agreement with line 61 of the kernel code:

```
60 #define FSHIFT    11             /* nr of bits of precision */
61 #define FIXED_1   (1<<FSHIFT) /* 1.0 as fixed-point */
```

Alternatively, we can write `FIXED_1` as a decimal integer:

$$\texttt{FIXED\_1} = 2048_{10}\,, \tag{4.2}$$

to simplify calculation of the remaining constants: EXP_1, EXP_5, and EXP_15, for the 1-, 5-, and 15 min metrics, respectively.

Consider the 1-min metric as an example. If we denote the sample period as σ and the reporting period as τ, then:

$$\text{EXP\_1} \equiv \mathrm{e}^{-\sigma/\tau} \,. \tag{4.3}$$

We have already established that $\sigma = 5$ s and for the 1-min metric, $\tau = 60$ s. Furthermore, the decimal value of EXP_1 is:

$$\mathrm{e}^{-5/60} = 0.92004441463. \tag{4.4}$$

To convert (4.4) to a 10.11 fixed-point fraction, we only need to multiply it by the fixed-point constant FIXED_1 (i.e., '1'):

$$\lfloor 2048 \times 0.92004441463 \rfloor = 1884_{10} \,, \tag{4.5}$$

and round it to the nearest 11-bit integer. Each of the other magic numbers can be calculated in the same way, and the results are summarized in Table 4.1.

Table 4.1. Default magic numbers for 5-s sampling period

Parameter	Seconds	1. exp$(-5/\tau)$	Rounded	Binary
τ_1	60	1884.25	1884_{10}	11101011100_2
τ_5	300	2014.15	2014_{10}	11111011110_2
τ_{15}	900	2036.65	2037_{10}	11111110101_2

These results are seen to agree with the kernel definitions:

```
#define EXP_1      1884  /* 1/exp(5sec/1min)  */
#define EXP_5      2014  /* 1/exp(5sec/5min)  */
#define EXP_15     2037  /* 1/exp(5sec/15min) */
```

If the sampling rate was decreased to 2-s intervals, the constants would need to be changed to those summarized in Table 4.2. These values are seen to be in agreement with the embedded comment, "With 2-second counting freq, the EXP_n values would be 1981, 2034 and 2043."

Table 4.2. Magic numbers for a 2-s sampling period

Parameter	Seconds	1. exp$(-2/\tau)$	Rounded	Binary
τ_1	60	1980.86	1981_{10}	11110111101_2
τ_5	300	2034.39	2034_{10}	11111110010_2
τ_{15}	900	2043.45	2043_{10}	11111111011_2

So far, we can explain where those magic constants come from. They are an integral part of doing calculations in 10.11 format fixed-point arithmetic.

Now, we would like to understand how the CALC_LOAD function actually uses these constants to determine the load average. From Sect. 4.3, we see that this macro:

```
67 #define CALC_LOAD(load,exp,n) \
68          load *= exp; \
69          load += n*(FIXED_1-exp); \
70          load >>= FSHIFT;
```

comprises lines 67–70. Line 67 is the name of the macro together with its requisite three parameters `load`, `exp`, and `n`. Line 68 is equivalent to taking the current fixed-point value of the variable `load` and multiplying it by a factor called `exp`. That new value of `load` is then added to a term comprising the number of active processes `n` multiplied by another variable called `FIXED_1-exp` in line 69. Line 70 decimalizes the `load` variable.

However, in Sect. 4.3.2 we also established that `exp` is equivalent to $e^{-\sigma/\tau}$ by virtue of (4.3) and `FIXED_1-exp` is equivalent to $1 - e^{-\sigma/\tau}$ by virtue of (4.2) and (4.3). Consequently, the C code in the CALC_LOAD macro can be written in more conventional mathematical notation as:

$$load(t) = load(t-1)\, e^{-\sigma/\tau} + n(t)\,(1 - e^{-\sigma/\tau}) \,, \tag{4.6}$$

where $load(t)$ is the current estimate of the load average, $load(t-1)$ is the estimate of the load average from the previous sample, and $n(t)$ is number of currently active Linux processes. In other words, CALC_LOAD is the fixed-point arithmetic version of (4.6). How it works is best understood by examining some special cases.

4.3.3 Empty Run-Queue

First, we consider the case where the run-queue is empty, i.e., $n(t) = 0$. Recall our definition of *queue* from Chap. 2 includes not just those Linux processes that are waiting in the run-queue (*runnable*), but also those executing (*running*) on CPUs.

Setting $n(t) = 0$ in (4.6) produces:

$$load(t) = load(t-1)\, e^{-\sigma/\tau} \,. \tag{4.7}$$

If we iterate (4.7) between $t = t_0$ and $t = T$ we get:

$$load(T) = load(t_0)\, e^{-\sigma t/\tau} \,. \tag{4.8}$$

By plotting this function for the three reporting periods τ in Fig. 4.3, we see that it clearly exhibits time-dependent exponential *decay*. In other words, (4.7) is responsible for the fall-off in the observed load between $t_0 = 2,100$ and $T = 3,600$ in Fig. 4.2.

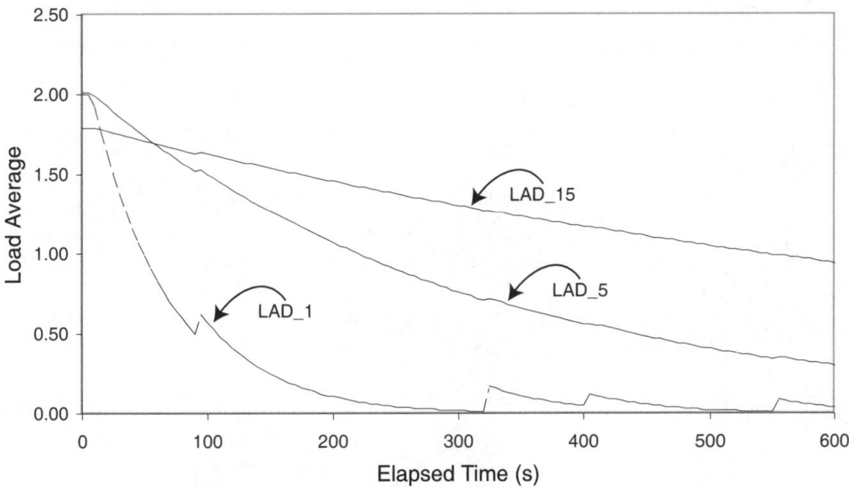

Fig. 4.3. Decaying load phase in Fig. 4.2

4.3.4 Occupied Run-Queue

The second special case is one in which the run-queue is consistently occupied with two processes. Then, the second term dominates in (4.6), and iterating between $t = t_0$ and $t = T$ produces:

$$load(T) = 2\, load(t_0)\, (1 - \mathrm{e}^{-\sigma t/\tau})\ . \tag{4.9}$$

Plotting this function in Fig. 4.4 for the three reporting periods (τ) shows monotonically increasing functions. We see that (4.9) is responsible for the observed *rise* in load between $t_0 = 0$ and $T = 2,100$ in Fig. 4.2.

Table 4.3. Characteristic rise times for the experiments in Fig. 4.2

Load avg. parameter	Time constant	Estimated rise time
τ_1	60	300
τ_5	300	1500
τ_{15}	900	4500

Having previously noted in Sect. 4.2.1 that the curves in Fig. 4.2 resemble the voltage characteristic of an RC-circuit, we take that analogy a step further. In circuit theory, it is known that the rise time is approximately five times the characteristic time constant τ. In CALC_LOAD, $\tau_1 = 60$ s, therefore the rise time can be estimated as $5\tau_1 \approx 300$ s. The other rise times are summarized in Table 4.3.

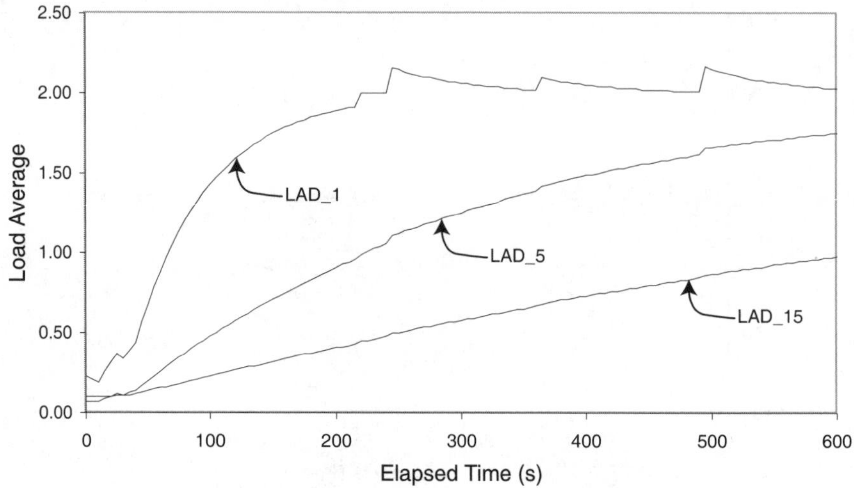

Fig. 4.4. Rising load phase in Fig. 4.2

4.3.5 Exponential Damping

A common technique used to preprocess highly variable raw data for subsequent analysis is to apply some kind of smoothing function to that data. The general relationship between the raw input data and the smoothed output data is given by:

$$\underbrace{Y(t)}_{\text{smoothed}} = Y(t-1) + \underbrace{\alpha}_{\text{constant}} \left[\underbrace{X(t)}_{\text{raw}} - Y(t-1) \right] . \tag{4.10}$$

This smoothing function (4.10) is an *exponential filter* or *exponentially-smoothed moving average* of the type used in financial forecasting and other forms of statistical regression. Such smoothing functions are readily available in data analysis tools such as: Excel, *Mathematica*, R, S^+. There is also a Perlpackage called Statistics::DEA (Discontiguous Exponential Averaging) available on CPAN.

Although the parameter α is commonly called the *smoothing constant*, we prefer to call it the *correction constant*, and $(1 - \alpha)$ the *damping factor*. The magnitude of the correction constant $(0 \leq \alpha \leq 1)$ determines how much the current forecast must be corrected for error in the previous forecast iteration. The `CALC_LOAD` algorithm in (4.6) can be rearranged to read:

$$\mathit{load}(t) = \mathit{load}(t-1) + (1 - \mathrm{e}^{-\sigma/\tau}) \left[n(t) - \mathit{load}(t-1) \right] , \tag{4.11}$$

which reveals that (4.11) is identical to (4.10) if we choose the correction factor to be $\alpha = 1 - \exp(-\sigma/\tau)$. The corresponding damping factors for each of the three load average metrics are shown in Table 4.4 and a comparison with the experimental data from Sect. 4.2 is shown in Fig. 4.5.

More detailed views for the rising phase are shown in Fig. 4.6(a) and for the falling phase in Fig. 4.6(b). Notice that the exponential damping factor

Table 4.4. Damping factors for `CALC_LOAD`.

Timebase parameter	Damping factor $e^{-\sigma/\tau}$	Correction factor α
τ_1	0.9200	0.0800 ($\approx$ 8%)
τ_5	0.9835	0.0165 ($\approx$ 2%)
τ_{15}	0.9945	0.0055 ($\approx$ 1%)

for τ_1 agrees with the value in (4.4) to four decimal places. The 1-min load average metric has the least damping, or about 8% correction, because it is the most responsive to instantaneous changes in the length of the run-queue. Conversely, the 15-min load average has the most damping, or only 1% correction, because it is the least responsive metric.

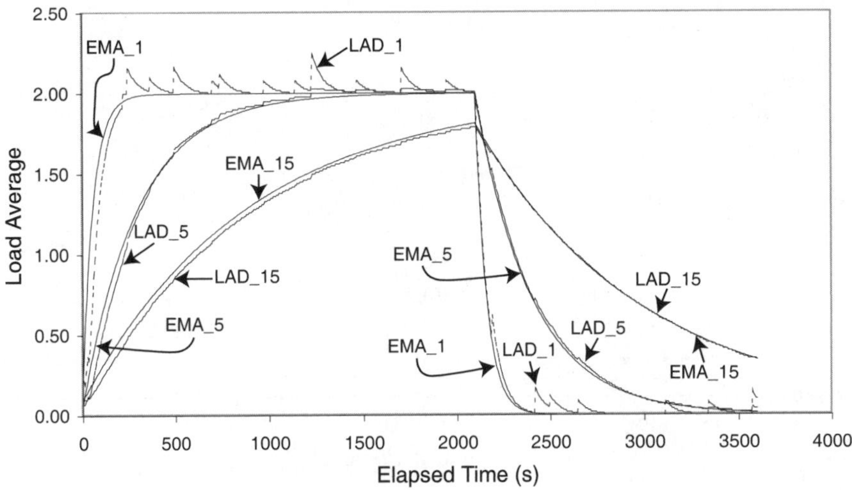

Fig. 4.5. Comparison of the exponentially damped moving average model given by (4.11) with the complete set of 1, 5, and 15 m experimental data in Fig. 4.2

> Pulling together all the diverse pieces from Sect. 4.3, we see that `CALC_LOAD` actually computes the exponentially-damped moving average of the run-queue length using 10.11 fixed-point format.

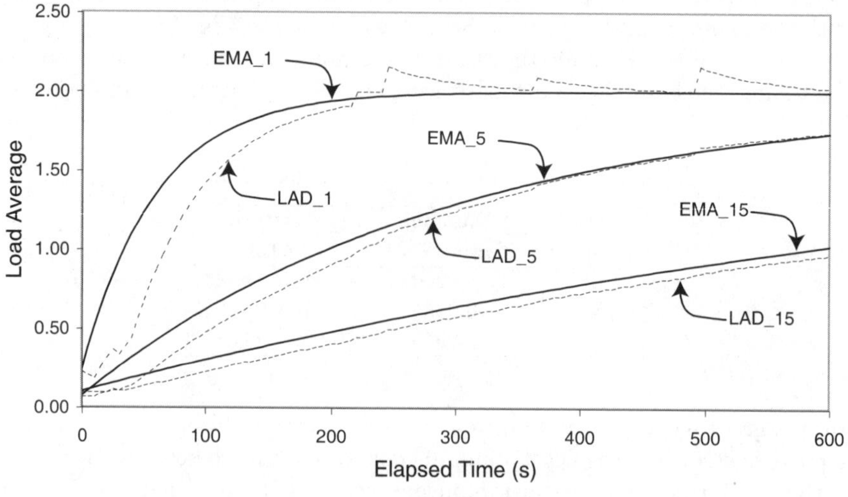

(a) Rising load phase (Fig. 4.4)

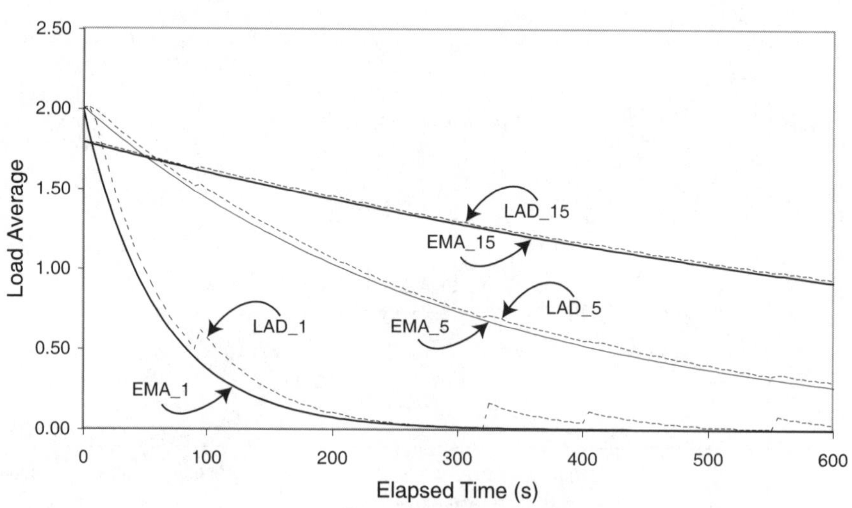

(b) Decaying load phase (Fig. 4.3)

Fig. 4.6. Detail of model fit for both rising and falling experimental phases

There is evidence that the choice of an exponentially damped moving average for the UNIX load average may have been inspired by similar instrumentation developed for the experimental multiuser time-share computer system called Multics [Saltzer and Gintell 1970]. Multics is often viewed as an historical precursor to the UNIX operating system (Appendix B). It is also the same computer system for which Scherr [1967] developed the first computer performance model discussed in Sect. 3.9.1.

4.4 Steady-State Averages

As mentioned in Sect. 4.3.5, smoothing is used in an effort to reveal trends in data that are otherwise highly variable or noisy. The smoothing technique incorporated into CALC_LOAD is an exponentially damped moving average of the sampled run-queue data. The usual arithmetic average is just the sum

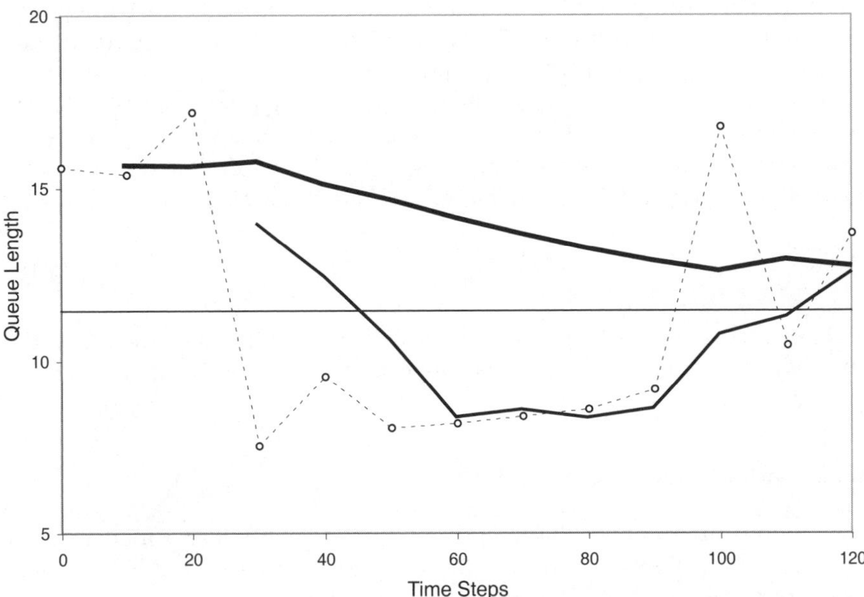

Fig. 4.7. Different types of average runqueue length. The *dotted curve* is the runqueue length measured at each time step or sample period. The *horizontal* line shows the arithmetic time average Q taken over the entire period. The *black curve* (middle) is the corresponding moving average with lag 4. The *thick black curve* (top) is the corresponding exponentially damped moving average with a damping factor chosen to match the 15-minute Linux load average

of all the data points normalized by the number of data points. The *moving average* is the arithmetic average with lag k (Fig. 4.7). For example, if $k = 4$, successive groups of 4 data points are summed and divided by 4.

This method works well if the data contain no obvious trends or cyclic patterns. The higher the value of the lag k, the greater the smoothing effect. Conversely, the arithmetic average can be viewed as the moving average with the lag equal to the number of data points. The exponentially damped moving average is applicable if the data contains no trends or cyclic patterns and the most recent data points are more significant than earlier points. In this sense, the exponential damping factor $(1 - \alpha)$ acts as a *weighting* factor.

4.4.1 Time-Averaged Queue Length

How do these various averaging definitions relate to the kind of averages discussed previously in Chaps. 2 and 3? Consider the load average displayed as a time series in Fig. 4.1 over a long measurement period, e.g., $T = 24$ h. A portion of that time series would appear something like Fig. 2.8 when viewed at higher resolution, and that time series in turn looks like a series of vertical columns. Each column sits at a position on the time-axis that corresponds to a sample step of width Δt. The value of the queue length $Q(\Delta t)$ at any sample time step is given by the height of that column.

The subarea contained in a column is given by $Q(\Delta t) \times \Delta t$ (i.e., height multiplied by width). Adding up all these column subareas $\sum Q(\Delta t) \times \Delta t$ gives the total area under the curve. The ratio of this total area to the total measurement period T is the time-averaged queue length Q:

$$\frac{\sum Q(\Delta t) \times \Delta t}{T} \rightarrow Q \,. \tag{4.12}$$

If $\Delta t \rightarrow 1$ then $T \rightarrow k$ (the total number of sampled points), then Q is the same as the arithmetic average that appears in Little's law (2.14) defined in Chap.2.

4.4.2 Linux Scheduler Model

The steady-state run-queue of the Linux time-share scheduler can be modeled along the lines discussed in Sect. 3.9.1. In Fig. 4.8, each of the N Linux processes are in one of the following scheduler states:

1. Runnable, and therefore waiting in the run-queue for CPU service
2. Running, and therefore executing on a CPU
3. Suspended or *uninterruptible*, in Linux parlance [Bovet and Cesati 2001, p. 67], for some other external condition

The queueing parameters of Chap. 2 can be associated with this scheduler model according to Table 4.5. The relationship between the average queue length Q and the number of active processes N is given by:

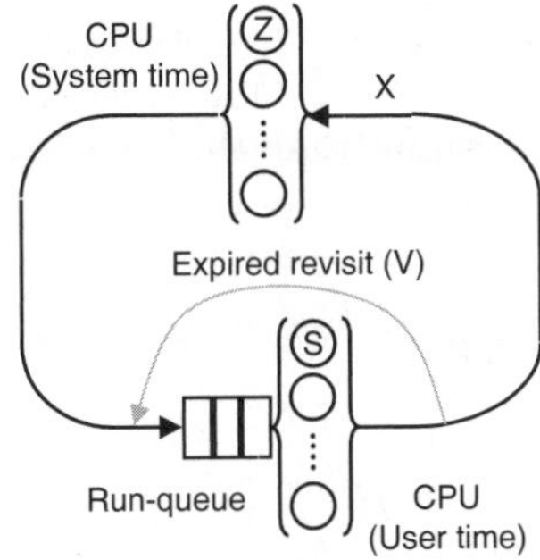

Fig. 4.8. Simple closed queueing model of the Linux scheduler

Table 4.5. Queueing parameters for the model depicted in Fig. 4.8

Parameter	Meaning for scheduler
N	Total number of active processes
Z	Average time a processes is suspended
X	Rate of CPU completions
S	CPU time quantum measured in Ticks.
V	Number of CPU visits required to complete the work
D	Total CPU execution demand $D = V \times S$ measured in ticks or ms
m	Number of CPU processors
Q	Average run-queue length (not the instantaneous length)

$$Q = N - X\,Z\,. \tag{4.13}$$

This is actually a variant of Little's law (2.14) where the arrival rate λ has been replaced by the CPU throughput X. Since only a finite number of Linux processes are active in the system, the scheduler can never have more than N requests enqueued. On average, however, there will be less than N processes enqueued because some of them will be in a *suspended* state. The average number in the *suspended* state is the product of how long Z they spend in the state and the rate X at which they become suspended. This is yet another variant of Little's microscopic law (2.15).

The length of the waiting line Q_{w} is distinct from the queue length Q. In general, it will be a function of the number of CPUs in the system and how busy they are:

$$Q_{\mathrm{w}} = Q - \rho\,, \tag{4.14}$$

where $\rho = U/m$ is the per-CPU utilization. Unfortunately, because of the feedback nature of the closed queueing model in Fig. 4.8, it is not easy to determine (4.13) or (4.14) without making the model. This can be accomplished most easily by modifying the code for `repair.pl` in Sect. 2.8.3 to become `timeshare.pl`.

The experiments of Sect. 4.2 were performed on a uniprocessor (i.e., $m = 1$) with two processes (i.e., $N = 2$) and essentially zero suspension time. In what follows, we shall assume that the workload is CPU intensive with $Z = 1$ ms and the CPU execution time is $D = 5$ s. Using these input values, the `timeshare.pl` model produces the following modified output:

```
M/M/1//2 Time-Share Model
--------------------------------
CPU processors      (m):   1
Total processes     (N):   2
Execution time      (D):   5.0000
Suspended time      (Z):   0.0010
Execution rate         :   0.2000
Utilization         (U):   1.0000
Utilzn. per CPU   (rho):   1.0000

Average load        (Q):   1.9998
Average in service     :   1.0000
Average enqueued   (Qw):   0.9998
Throughput          (X):   0.2000
Waiting time        (W):   4.9990
Completion time     (R):   9.9990
```

We see that the model predicts the CPU should run at 100% busy and the average load is $Q = 1.9998$, showing that one process is running while the other is waiting but runnable in the run-queue. Here, Q is not exactly 2 because some small amount of time (i.e., 1 ms) is spent in a suspended state. On average, any process will find the other process ahead of it at the CPU, and therefore will have to wait for 5 s before receiving service at the CPU. All this is in good agreement with what we observed on the experimental platform in Sect 4.2.

```
M/M/2//2 Time-Share Model
--------------------------------
CPU processors      (m):   2
Total processes     (N):   2
Execution time      (D):   5.0000
Suspended time      (Z):   0.0010
Execution rate         :   0.2000
Utilization         (U):   1.9996
Utilzn. per CPU   (rho):   0.9998

Average load        (Q):   1.9996
Average in service     :   1.9996
Average enqueued   (Qw):   0.0000
Throughput          (X):   0.3999
Waiting time        (W):   0.0000
Completion time     (R):   5.0000
```

How would things change if we added another CPU? The answer can be determined by simply changing the number of processors to $m = 2$ and rerunning the model. We see that the average load $Q = 1.9996$ is the same, but now the number enqueued is zero because each process can find its own CPU; a result that supports the comment of Zajac in Sect. 4.1.2.

4.5 Load Averages and Trend Visualization

Finally, we evaluate how well the standard load average does as a trend indicator. The intent of the load average metrics is to provide information about the trend in the growth of the length of the run queue. That is why it reports three metrics rather than one. The three metrics try to capture some historical information, viz. the run-queue length as it was 1, 5, and 15 min ago.

4.5.1 What Is Wrong with Load Averages

We concur with the comments of Peek et al. [1997] in Sect. 4.1.1 that the load average is simplistic and poorly defined. In fact, we take the position that three major flaws can be identified in the conventional load average metrics when it comes to presenting trend information to the performance analyst:

1. The three metrics are reported at some random instant in time whenever the corresponding shell command is invoked. They represent a snapshot or a slice in time of the averaged loads at that reporting instant. Imagine a vertical line at some arbitrary location on the time axis intersecting the three curves in Fig. 4.2.
2. The reporting order is inconsistent with time flow conventions. The 1-, 5-, 15-min metrics correspond to *recent*, *past*, and *distant past* averages. For trending purposes, however, time conventionally flows from left to right along the x-axis, e.g., in Fig. 4.2. It would be preferable, therefore, to have the reporting order of the metrics *reversed.*
3. The three load averages are reported at *unequal* intervals of time. This lack of uniformity makes trend projection awkward. A better choice might be: 0, 5, 10, 15 min where the '0' metric corresponds to *now* (no damped average).

These shortcomings lead us to consider a visual representation of the load average metrics.

4.5.2 New Visual Paradigm

Figure 4.9 shows two possible graphical representations of the load average sampled over a period of $T = 300$ time steps. The sampled data are for a workload that initially causes the load average to increase abruptly and then decay away more slowly. Figure 4.9(a) shows the conventional load average triplet of numbers in 1, 5, and 15 m order, while Fig. 4.9(b) shows the same sequence with the triplet ordering reversed, i.e., 15, 5, and 1 m.

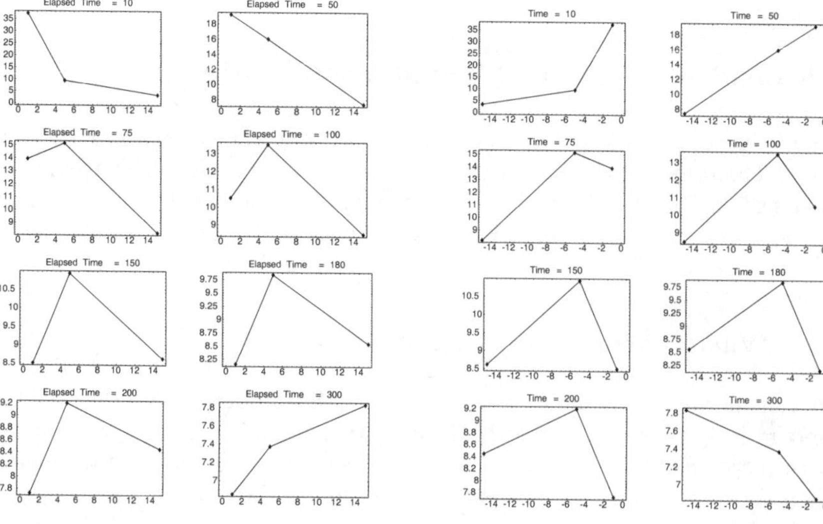

(a) Conventional 1, 5, and 15 m load average triplets plotted on a postive time axis gives the wrong trend cues

(b) The same load average triplets reversed on a negative time axis gives the correct trend cues

Fig. 4.9. Graphical representation of the 1, 5, and 15 m load average triplets plotted at successive time periods from $T = 10$ to $T = 300$ (a) in conventional order, and (b) in reversed time order. Each sequence is read from *top left* to *bottom right*. The reversed time ordering 15, 5, and 1 m in sequence (b) gives the correct visual cues because it shows the trend initially increasing and then slowly decreasing

Each sequence comprises eight plots in two columns with each plot representing a load average triplet sampled at some random time. The x-axis spans the range 0 to 15 min. Within each plot, there are three dots connected by straight lines to aid in revealing any load trends. The three dots, reading left to right in the plot, correspond to the 1-, 5- and 15-min load average metrics. The first plot shows the loads at 10 min after the load sampling process was commenced. The next sample was taken 50 min after sampling was commenced, and so on, up to the last sample taken 300 min into the sampling process.

Reading the first plot from left to right, the visual cue based on the line segments suggests that the load is initially *decreasing*. The first dot (highest), however, corresponds to the most recent load average—the 1-min average—

while the third dot (lowest) corresponds to the oldest load average—the 15-min average. So, this is back-to-front from the visual cue, and the load is actually *increasing.*
This visual paradox can be resolved easily by merely reversing the time-axis in the sequence of plots in Fig. 4.9(b). With this visual correction in place, it becomes much easier to see that the load is rapidly increasing and then gradually decreases. This effect can be achieved with the use of existing tools such as MRTG (`people.ee.ethz.ch/~oetiker/webtools/mrtg/`) because they have an option to reverse the x-axis presentation. An example of MRTG applied to monitoring system load average in a platform-independent way by using SNMP (Simple Network Management Protocol) is available at `howto.aphroland.de/HOWTO/MRTG/SystemMonitoringLoadAverage`.

Moreover, the visual paradigm in Fig. 4.9(b) could be taken a step further to improve the *cognitive impedence match* between the system analyst and the system under test. Plots of the load average triplets could be *animated* in a tiny area of screen real-estate that is less intrusive than the time series shown in Fig. 4.1. Any significant change in the load average trend is likely to be detected by the system analyst's peripheral vision rather than by poring over a complete trace of time series data [See Gunther 1992, for details].

4.5.3 Application to Workload Management

In keeping with the title of this chapter, we close by briefly reviewing some of the ways in which the load average metric has been used for monitoring and redistributing workloads. A novel example of load monitoring is described at `www.snowplow.org/tom/worm/worm.html`, where the load average metrics were affected by the presence of an Internet worm. It was well known that around 9:30 pm at night, the 1-min load average of the system should nominally be around 1. In the presence of the Internet worm, replication caused the 1-min load average to reach 37!

Understanding how host loads vary over time is important for predicting such things as the execution time of work that is under the control of dynamic load balancing [Franklin et al. 1994]. Dinda and O'Hallaron [1999] examined week-long traces of load averages on more than 35 different machines including production and research cluster machines, compute servers, and desktop workstations. Despite certain complex behaviors that were exhibited in the traces, it was found that relatively simple models based on (4.6) were sufficient for short-range load prediction. These ideas have also been extended to systems such as the computational GRID [Plale et al. 2002] and dispatchable load management [Wolski et al. 2000], performance management of Lotus Notes [Hellerstein et al. 2001], and an Apache web server [Diao et al. 2002].

4.6 Review

In this chapter we explored both the meaning and the generation of the load average performance metric reported by a variety of UNIX shell commands. A detailed understanding of how the load average is computed was accomplished by examining the relevant online kernel code for the Linux operating system.

The function called `CALC_LOAD` contains the central algorithm. It computes the exponentially damped moving average of the run-queue length using 10.11 fixed-point arithmetic. The reported 1-, 5-, and 15-min load averages correspond to three different damping factors shown in Table 4.4. These factors give more weight to the most recent run-queue length samples than to older data samples. Clearly, the Linux load average is not your average kind of average!

Finally, we looked at some novel extensions of the conventional load average metrics for providing better visual trend information and forecasting optimal placement of distributed workloads on systems such as the computational GRID.

Exercises

4.1. Definitions.
(**a**) How many definitions of the word *load* can you write down?
(**b**) Write down as many definitions of the word *average* as you can think of. Now, when you hear people using these words in a performance analysis or tuning context, you have no excuse for not asking what they mean.

4.2. What kind of averaging technique is used to calculate the Linuxload averages?

4.3. Fixed point arithmetic.
(**a**) Calculate 1.01×2.22 in 1.2 format.
(**b**) Calculate $1.01 \times (0.4 + 0.3)$ in 1.2 format.
(**c**) Calculate $1.01 \times 0.4 + 1.01 \times 0.3$ in 1.2 format.

4.4. (**a**) Repeat the experiment described in Sect. 4.2 but replace the Perlscript `burncpu.c` with one that performs disk-intensive I/O work.
(**b**) Compare your results with those obtained by `burncpu.c`.

5

Performance Bounds and Log Jams

5.1 Introduction

The material presented here comes from real case studies. Only the names, place, and numbers have been changed to protect the guilty. In this chapter you will see the power of bounds analysis based on the underlying queueing concepts presented in Chaps. 2 and 3. The main point is to demonstrate how much can be determined about *plausible* performance without knowing the detailed performance characteristics.

The first example comes from performance analysis that was done without being on site, without meeting the engineers involved, and without carrying out any new performance measurements on the actual system. Everything was done over the phone, and merely pointing out a simple inconsistency induced enough communal guilt to motivate everyone else to start looking for the cause of the problem. Eventually they found it. For me, in terms of doing the least amount of work, it doesn't get much better than that.

The second case study (commencing at Sect. 5.6), on the other hand, was exactly the opposite situation. It represents a lot of hard work in which I was very much involved in producing performance data, doing the performance analysis, and wandering down many primrose paths. Superlinear behavior in the response times measurements will be seen to arise from thrashing effects that are in conflict with the expected response time bounds. Although the amount of work was huge, so was the payoff: a three hundred percent performance improvement! Similarly, it doesn't come much better than that.

5.2 Out of Bounds in Florida

The title of this section is an oblique reference to the fact the system I shall describe was set up at a development center in Florida, whereas I was based in San Jose, California at the time. A third party had developed a custom application that was undergoing load and stress testing by an independent group of engineers on behalf of the customer in Florida. In the last phases of testing (where I came in), the system performance capabilities were being measured prior to beta release. All told, this development and testing had been going on for some 18 months.

5.2.1 Load Test Results

The following is a summary of the pertinent performance data with which I was presented by the group of test engineers in Florida. They had built a benchmarking platform with external client drivers. Using this platform, they had consistently measured a system throughput of around 300 transactions per second (TPS) with an average think-time of $Z = 10$ s between transaction requests. Moreover, during the course of development, they had also managed to have the application instrumented so as to be able to see where time was being spent internally when it was running. This is a good thing and a precious rarity!

The instrumented application had logged internal processing times. In the subsequent discussion we shall suppose that there were *three* sequential processing stages. In actual fact, there were many more. Enquiring about some examples of instrumented processing times, I was given a list of average values that we shall represent by the following three values: $3.5, 5.0$, and 2.0 ms; at which point I exclaimed, "Something is rotten in Denmark . . . er . . . Florida!"

5.2.2 Bottlenecks and Bounds

Before I explain my astonishment, we take a brief detour into some simple performance analysis techniques that are based on assessing performance *boundaries* rather than performance details. In other words, the following will show you how to do a lot with very little performance information. We shall return to the Florida story in Sect. 5.5.

The approach we shall take to understanding the performance limits of any computer system is sometimes referred to as the *bounds analysis* of the throughput and response time characteristics of the system. The three-stage tandem queueing circuit shown in Fig. 5.1 represents the three processing stages of the benchmark platform that existed in Florida. The service demands (in seconds) are:

$$\begin{aligned} D_{\mathrm{a}} &= 0.0035 \text{ s} , \\ D_{\mathrm{b}} &= 0.0050 \text{ s} , \\ D_{\mathrm{c}} &= 0.0020 \text{ s} . \end{aligned} \tag{5.1}$$

Of these service demands D_{b} is the largest; we shall subsequently also refer to it as $D_{\max}$.

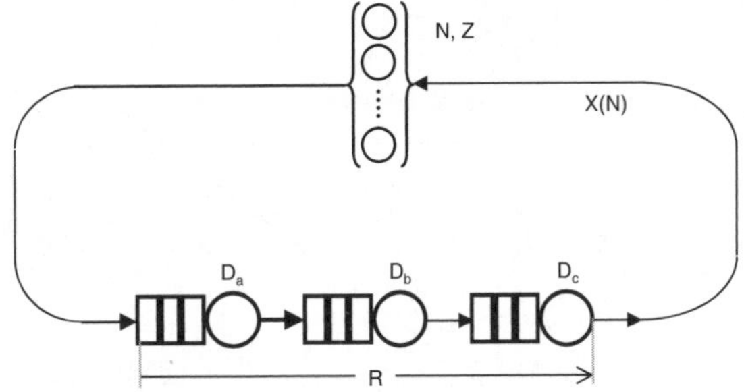

Fig. 5.1. A closed queueing circuit representing the three sequential processing stages, each with different service demands: D_{a}, D_{b}, and D_{c}, and an infinite server with think time Z representing the benchmark generators. The second queue is the bottleneck center (see discussion)

5.3 Throughput Bounds

In the next two sections, we consider the best and worst cases for the system throughput characteristic.

5.3.1 Saturation Throughput

We examine the *best case* throughput scenario first. At a *saturated* queueing center, the server is 100% busy, and therefore $\rho = 1$. Substituting into Little's law (2.15), we can write:

$$\rho \equiv 1 = X_{\max} D_{\max} \,. \tag{5.2}$$

At such a server in a queueing circuit, the throughput will be at a maximum because there are no cycles left to produce a higher completion rate. We denote the maximum throughput by $X_{\max}$.

In any queueing circuit under increasing request load, one queueing center will reach saturation before the others. That center is called the *bottleneck center* or just the *bottleneck*. It follows from (5.2) that the bottleneck is the center with the longest service demand $D_{\max}$. In other words, the *best* possible system throughput $X_{\max}$ is controlled by the bottleneck in the queueing circuit. This can be expressed more formally by rearranging (5.2) as:

$$X_{\max} = \frac{1}{D_{\max}} \,. \tag{5.3}$$

Note that $X_{\max}$ in (5.3) has no dependence on the load N, once the saturation point is reached; $X_{\max}$ is constant. If we plot it against the load N, it simply appears as a horizontal dashed line like that shown in Fig. 5.2.

The bottleneck will also have the longest queue or waiting line in a real system; this is a fact that can often be observed easily, e.g., message queues.

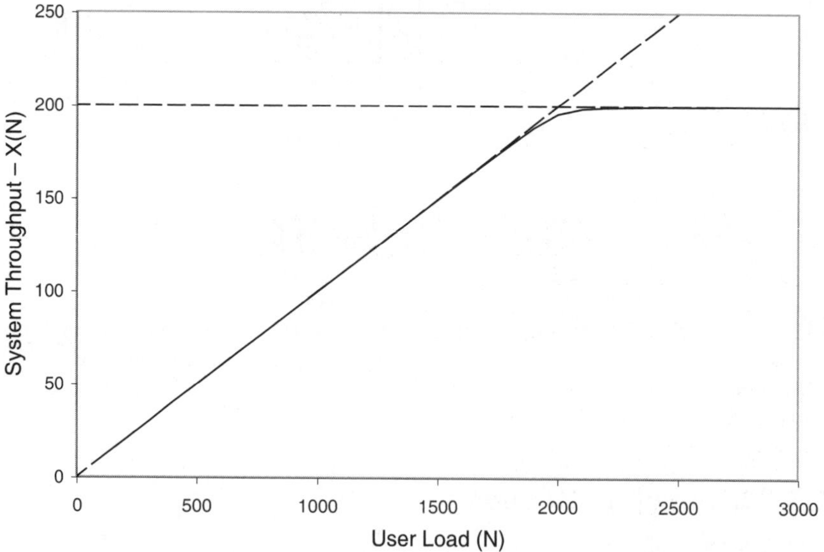

Fig. 5.2. Bounds on the throughput characteristic. The *horizontal dashed line* is the maximum possible throughput and is controlled by the bottleneck queue in the system. The *inclined dashed line* is the uncontended throughput bound. The optimal system load occurs where the two dashed lines intersect

This follows from the fact that all centers upstream from the bottleneck center (just D_{a} in Fig. 5.1) have service demands that are smaller than D_{b}. Therefore, all completions from the upstream queue simply pile up at the bottlenecked queue and will tend to make the bottlenecked queue grow. Similarly, all queues downstream from the bottleneck also have service demands that are shorter than D_{b}, but they can only service completed requests flowing from the bottlenecked queue, so they cannot shorten the bottleneck queue length.

5.3.2 Uncontended Throughput

We next bound the *subsaturated* throughput. The shortest possible time R_{min} it takes to get through the circuit in Fig. 5.1 occurs when there is no queueing to contend with. That time is simply the sum of the service demands at all the centers:

$$R_{\mathrm{min}} = D_{\mathrm{a}} + D_{\mathrm{b}} + D_{\mathrm{c}} \; . \tag{5.4}$$

If we substitute (5.4) into the Response Time Law give by (2.90) from Chap. 2 we find:

$$D_{\mathrm{a}} + D_{\mathrm{b}} + D_{\mathrm{c}} = \frac{N}{X} - Z \; . \tag{5.5}$$

Solving for the throughput X produces:

$$X = \frac{N}{D_{\mathrm{a}} + D_{\mathrm{b}} + D_{\mathrm{c}} + Z} . \tag{5.6}$$

This is the throughput under the special constraint of no contention. Following our previous inclinations for the saturated throughput, we plot the *uncontended* throughput against the load N, and see that it appears as the *inclined* straight line in Fig. 5.2. For this reason we denote it by X_{lin} and note that the general form is given by:

$$X_{\mathrm{lin}} = \frac{N}{\mathfrak{D} + Z} , \tag{5.7}$$

where we have introduced the symbol $\mathfrak{D}$ as shorthand for

$$\mathfrak{D} = D_{\mathrm{a}} + D_{\mathrm{b}} + D_{\mathrm{c}} , \tag{5.8}$$

the sum of the service demands.

We now see that the uncontended throughput is bounded by a linear function of N with a slope controlled by $1/(\mathfrak{D} + Z)$. As we increase the load N on a real system, the actual throughput begins to fall away from this ideal linear boundary because of increasing queueing contention in the system.

5.3.3 Optimal Load

The leading indicator of optimal load occurs at the point N_{opt} where the throughput bounds intersect in Fig. 5.2. From (5.3) and (5.7) we have:

$$\frac{1}{D_{\max}} = \frac{N}{\mathfrak{D} + Z} . \tag{5.9}$$

Solving for N produces:

$$N_{\mathrm{opt}} = \frac{\mathfrak{D} + Z}{D_{\max}} . \tag{5.10}$$

Since $D + Z$ is actually the minimum possible *round trip time* Min(RTT), we could also write (5.10) in the alternative form:

$$N_{\mathrm{opt}} = \frac{\mathrm{Min}(RTT)}{\mathrm{Max}(D_{\mathrm{a}}, D_{\mathrm{b}}, \ \ldots)} . \tag{5.11}$$

The value of (5.10) is that it enables us to interpret characteristics like Figs. 5.2 and 5.3 in terms of *light* and *heavy* load regimes.

Light load: The region where $N \leq N_{\mathrm{opt}}$. Resources are generally under-utilized. This may be appropriate if some head room is required for future capacity consumption. More typically, it is a sign of waste.

Heavy load: The region where $N \geq N_{\mathrm{opt}}$. Resources are generally over-burdened and the load tends to drive the system into saturation. This is when bottlenecks are observed and ranked for removal according to cost–benefit criteria.

We can carry out a similar analysis to evaluate the best-, and worst-case response times.

5.4 Response Time Bounds

We repeat the same kind of bounds analysis for the response time characteristic.

5.4.1 Uncontended Response Time

As we observed previously, the shortest possible time (5.4) to get through all the queueing centers occurs when there is only one customer in the system, since under those circumstances, there can be no queueing contention for common resources, viz.

$$R_{\min} = \mathfrak{D}. \tag{5.12}$$

Since $R_{\min}$ is not a function of N, it appears as a horizontal line in the middle of in Fig. 5.3.

5.4.2 Saturation Response Time

Beyond the saturation point N_{opt} there is no worst time. The response time just gets progressively worse with increasing load. For a closed system like that in Fig. 5.1, the only limit is the size of the finite request population N. Applying the Response Time Law in (2.90) once again, we have in saturation:

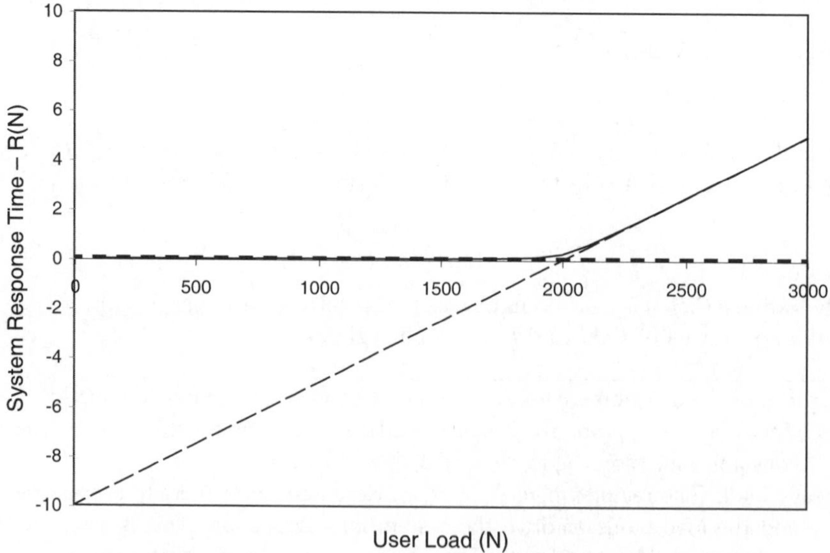

Fig. 5.3. Bounds on response time characteristic

$$R = \frac{N}{X_{max}} - Z , \tag{5.13}$$

and substituting (5.3) for $X_{\max}$ produces:

$$R_\infty = N \, D_{\max} - Z . \tag{5.14}$$

Beyond the saturation point N_{opt}, the response time is asymptotic to (5.14) with the *slope* controlled by $D_{\max}$ and a y-intercept at $-Z$ as shown in Fig. 5.3.

> Note that the increase in response time above N_{opt} is *linear*, not *exponential*, as some authors claim (see, e.g., [Wilson and Kesselman 2000, p. 6 ff.] and [Splaine and Jaskiel 2001, p. 241]).

5.4.3 Worst–Case Response Bound

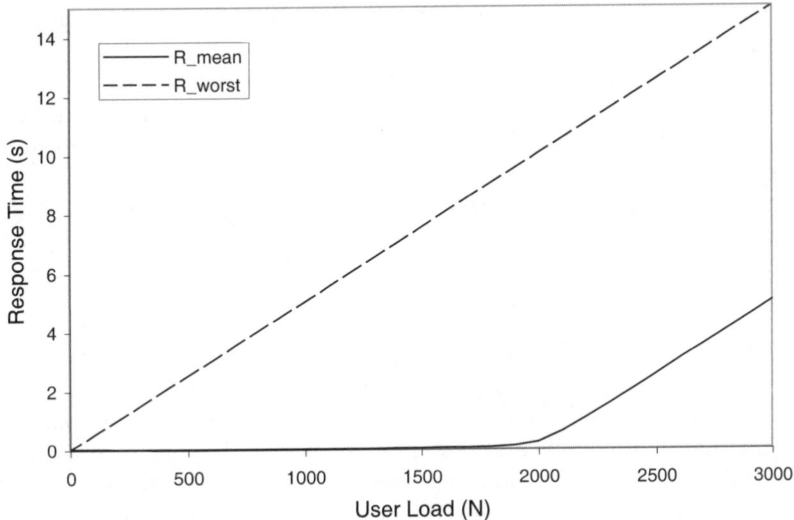

Fig. 5.4. Worst-case response time bound (*upper curve*) compared with the average response time (*lower curve*)

The worst-case response time bound (Fig. 5.4) corresponds to (5.14) with $Z = 0$. Then:

$$R_{\text{worst}} = N D_{\max} . \tag{5.15}$$

It is an asymptote with the same slope as (5.14) in Fig. 5.3 but translated to intersect the load axis N at the origin.

5.5 Meanwhile, Back in Florida ...

With the basic concepts of bounds analysis understood, we are now in a position to apply them to the data from the benchmark platform in Florida in Sect. 5.2.1. So, what is it that was rotten in Florida?

We know from the application instrumentation data that $D_{max} = 0.005$ s and the bounds analysis determines $X_{\max} = 200$ TPS from (5.3). We can also apply (5.10) with the data in (5.1) to predict:

$$N_{\text{opt}} = \frac{10.011}{0.005} = 2002.10 \text{ users} .$$

On the other hand, the benchmark data led the test engineers doing the measurements to claim 300 TPS performance. From this information we may hypothesize:

1. The benchmark measurement of 300 TPS is wrong.
2. The instrumented data from the application are wrong.

In light of this apparent inconsistency, the test engineers in Florida decided to thoroughly review their measurement methodology. Within 24 hours they found the problem.

The client code employed an `if()` statement to calculate the instantaneous think-time between each transaction in such a way that the statistical mean for Z was 10 s. The engineers discovered that this code was not being executed. The think-time was in fact precisely $Z = 0$.

In essence, it was as though the transaction measured at the client X_{client} was comprised of two contributions:

$$X_{\text{client}} = X_{\text{actual}} + X_{\text{errors}} ,$$

such that $X_{\text{actual}} = 200$ TPS and $X_{\text{errors}} = 100$ errors/s. In other words, the test platform was being overdriven into *batch* mode, where the undue intensity of arrivals caused the software to fail to complete some transactions successfully. Nonetheless, the application returned an ACK to the client driver, which then scored it as a correctly completed transaction. The instrumentation data were correct, but the benchmark measurements were wrong. This led to a performance claim for the throughput that was only in error by 50%!

> You should always have a performance model against which to compare with your measured data. To paraphrase a quote often attributed to Einstein, if your data disagrees with your model, change your data!

The PDQ model `florida.pl` that was used to do the performance analysis in this chapter can be found in Chap. 6.

5.5.1 Balanced Bounds

Tighter bounds on throughput and response times could be obtained by considering a *balanced* system. In Fig. 5.1 the service demand $D_{\rm b}$ is the bottleneck node, and it determines the system performance according to Sect. 5.2.2. Clearly, this performance limitation would be improved if we could reduce the magnitude of the service demand $D_{\rm b}$. For example, if we could arrange things such that $D_{\rm b} < D_{\rm a}$ then, $D_{\rm a}$ would become the new, but less severe bottleneck. In principal, this procedure could be continued until all the queues had identical service demands: $D_{\rm a} = D_{\rm b} = D_{\rm c}$. Then, we would have a *balanced* system where performance could not be improved any further.

5.5.2 Balanced Demand

Lazowska et al. [1984] present a detailed discussion of balanced systems. Here, we merely outline the formal concept by first defining the average of *all* the service demands over K queueing centers. That is,

$$D_{\rm avg} \equiv \frac{\mathfrak{D}}{K} = \frac{1}{K} \sum_{k}^{K} D_k \,, \tag{5.16}$$

where we shall make use subsequently of the explicit summation. For the circuit in Fig. 5.1:

$$D_{\rm avg} = \frac{D_{\rm a} + D_{\rm b} + D_{\rm c}}{3} \,. \tag{5.17}$$

The bottlenecked queue determines the saturation throughput $X_{\rm max}$. Forcing all the queues to have the same service demand $D_{\rm max}$ would certainly make the system balanced, but it would not reduce $X_{\rm max}$. That, however, is the most *pessimistic* choice.

The *ideal* throughput bound would be achieved if we forced all the servers to have the shortest service demand $D_{\rm min}$, e.g., 2 ms in Fig. 5.1. Realistically, however, the best attainable throughput lies somewhere between these two extremes and corresponds to setting all the service demands equal to $D_{\rm avg}$ in (5.16).

5.5.3 Balanced Throughput

More formally, consider a closed queueing circuit with K queues and a batch workload (i.e., think-time $Z = 0$). Applying the Response Time law in (2.90) the system throughput is:

$$X = \frac{N}{R} \,, \tag{5.18}$$

where the response time

$$R = \sum_{k}^{K} D_k \left[1 + Q_k^{N-1}\right] , \tag{5.19}$$

is expressed in terms of the *Arrival Theorem* given by (3.27) from Chap. 3.

In a balanced system, all queues will have the same queue length, viz. the number of requests in the system $(N - 1)$ averaged over the K queues. Therefore, we can rewrite (5.19) as:

$$R = \sum_{k} D_k \left[1 + \frac{N-1}{K}\right] , \tag{5.20}$$

which, upon factoring out $1/K$, gives:

$$R = \sum_{k} \frac{D_k}{K} \left[K + N - 1\right]. \tag{5.21}$$

But the summation over D_k in the first factor is just the definition of D_{avg} in (5.16). Consequently, (5.21) simplifies to:

$$R = D_{\text{avg}} \left[K + N - 1\right] . \tag{5.22}$$

Substituting this result into (5.18) produces the *balanced* bound:

$$X \leq X_{\text{balanced}} \equiv \frac{N}{D_{\text{avg}} \left[K + N - 1\right]} , \tag{5.23}$$

which should be compared with:

$$X \leq X_{bottleneck} \equiv \frac{1}{D_{\text{max}}} , \tag{5.24}$$

the *bottleneck* bound.

Example 5.1. Combining the measurement data in (5.1) with the parameters in (5.25) and substituting into (5.23) gives $X_{\text{balanced}} = 285.49$ TPS, whereas

$$\begin{aligned} N &= 2500 , \\ Z &= 10.00 , \\ K &= 3 , \\ D_{\text{avg}} &= 0.0035 , \\ D_{\text{max}} &= 0.0050 , \end{aligned} \tag{5.25}$$

and $X_{\text{bottleneck}} = 200$ TPS in Fig. 5.2. Therefore, $X_{\text{balanced}} > X_{\text{bottleneck}}$. □

For large K, the averaged service demand D_{avg} will be less than D_{max}, so the achievable throughput in a balanced system (5.23) will always be higher than that in an unbalanced system.

5.6 The X–Files: Encounters with Performance Aliens

We continue to demonstrate how the bounding techniques of Sect. 5.2 can be applied to the performance analysis and tuning of a large-scale clustered computing environment. The *alien* effects and performance *gremlins* that we uncover in this section were sufficiently evanescent that we could not resist presenting them with an oblique nod to the popular television show *The X-Files*, and Steven Spielberg's movie *Close Encounters of the Third Kind.*

5.6.1 X-Windows Architecture

The X-Windows system, or more colloquially just *X* or *X11*, is a ubiquitous windowing technology developed in the 1980s at MIT and primarily directed at providing a network-transparent graphical user interface (GUI) for the UNIX operating system.

X11 is possibly one of the longest and most successful open-source collaborations administered by the `www.x11.org` consortium, with a worldwide user community estimated to exceed 30 million. It is the de facto graphical engine for Linux and many UNIX platforms and provides the only common windowing environment spanning the heterogeneous platforms present in most enterprise computing environments.

Because of its network transparency and its independence from the operating system, hardware platform, all the major hardware vendors (e.g., Sun, HP, IBM) support the X11. Other X11-based technologies, such as Citrix and WinTerm, integrate X11 applications into desktop environments running Microsoft Windows and Apple MacOS. It is also the basis for many thin-client technologies `zdnet.com.com/2100-1104_2-5298751.html`. In this sense, it is more proven than many Web technologies.

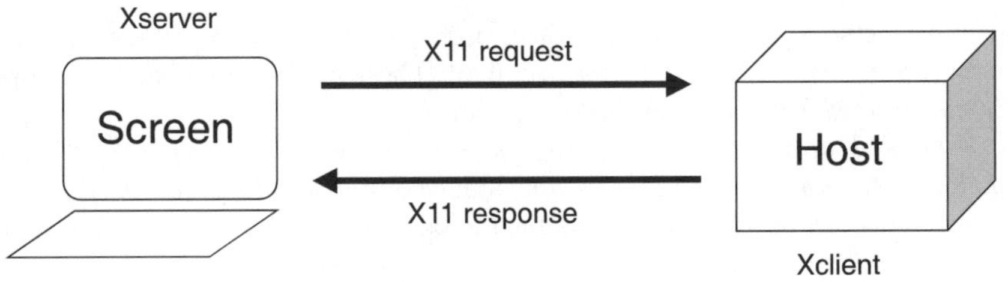

Fig. 5.5. X-window client/server protocol terminology

The version of the X windows described in this section is X11R5. The thin client architecture shown in Fig. 5.5 is described in terms that are the reverse of the conventional client/server terminology used in Chap. 9. A remote host, called the *X-client*, performs the windowing computations and tells the desktop display, called the *X-server*, how to draw on the screen. This is accomplished by X11 messages exchanged between X-client and X-server. Also included in the X11 architecture is the possibility of using remote services for file and font storage, as well as doing scheduled backups.

5.6.2 Production Environment

The production environment, shown schematically in Fig. 5.6, was hosted on a 200 node IBM SP-cluster platform which supported proprietary X11 applications running Tektronix (Tek) X-terminals. The X11 applications enabled

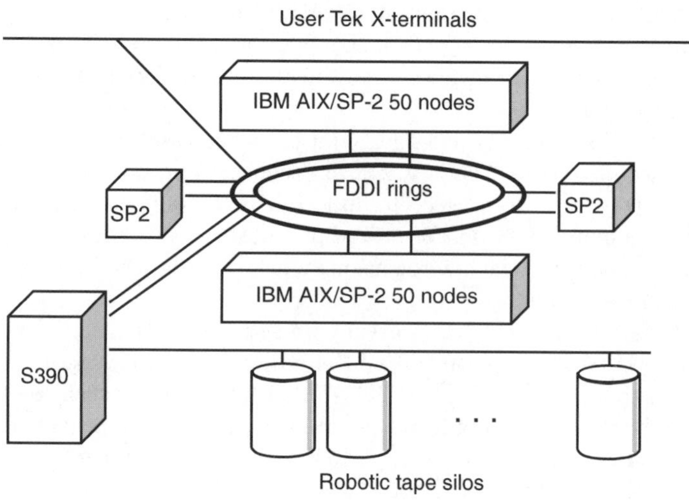

Fig. 5.6. SP-cluster X-window based production environment

geophysicists to perform seismic data processing using numerical transforms and graphics routines to the presence of oil. These applications were developed by an in-house software development group.

The X11 applications were sold both as an analytic service to other oil exploration companies and as a stand-alone commercial package. A significant investment had been made in this technology worldwide. There was only one problem: performance!

5.7 Close Encounters of the Performance Kind

5.7.1 Close Encounters I: Rumors

In UFO terminology, a close encounter of the *first* kind refers to a *sighting* without any physical evidence being left behind or actual contact being made.

In this case, the geophysicists who used the system had observed and were complaining about poor responsiveness of the application suite. Many users also agreed with one another that some applications had poorer performance than others. In particular, many users expressed frustration with the erratic nature of the poor responsiveness.

The two dominant performance perceptions were:

1. Application launch times could be very long (sometimes on the order of minutes).
2. Interactive response times, once the application was launched, could also be sluggish.

These conditions were also impossible to replicate on demand, so there was no physical evidence; just like a UFO, you either believed you saw it or not. In particular, there were no *quantitative* measurements. This leads us to close encounters of the *second* kind.

5.7.2 Close Encounters II: Measurements

A close encounter of the *second* kind refers to recovering *evidence* without making physical contact.

In this case, three of the most frequently used and poorest performing applications were reviewed. It turned out that some typical launch times had been measured with a wrist-watch! This is where the rumor of launch times of order a minute came from. In this sense, there were some quantitative measurements but they had not been recorded, so that information could never have a status higher than rumor or hearsay. With no supporting log files, the accuracy of someone's memory could not be validated.

Nonetheless, this led quickly to the idea of writing a *benchmark* script that emulated a user interacting with the three notorious applications. The initial benchmark was directed solely at launching each of the three X11 applications in succession every 10 min and logging the respective launch times to a file. A sample set of raw benchmark data is shown in Fig. 5.7. The corresponding time series representation in Fig. 5.8 is often more useful for recognizing patterns in the data. The large spike seen at around 6:15 p.m. belongs to the *seismoe* application and shows clearly that it took about 55 s to launch, thus corroborating the close encounter of the first kind.

We can also see clearly that all three of the applications of interest have launch times with a 10 s average and significant variance. A close encounter of the *third* kind, i.e., *contact*, requires analysis of the collected performance data.

5.7.3 Close Encounters III: Analysis

Statistical analysis can now be applied to the raw data. Unfortunately, in the this production environment no X11 statistical tools were available, so Perlscripts were constructed to produce relevant statistical plots (Fig. 5.9).

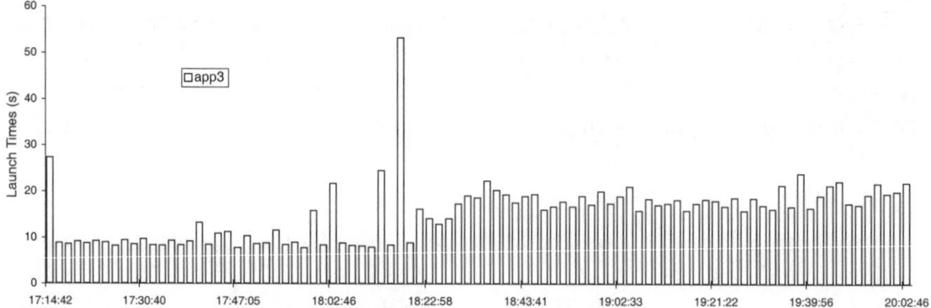

Fig. 5.7. Histogram plot of raw benchmark data for the application that suffered most frequently from prolonged launch times. An example of a large launch-time spike (almost 1 min) is seen near 18:20 h

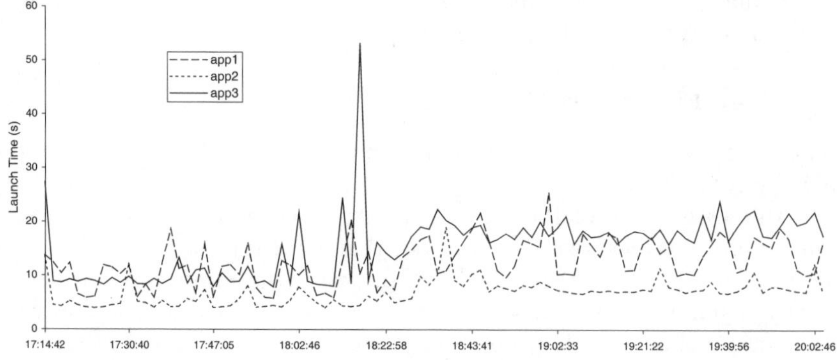

Fig. 5.8. Time series representation of raw benchmark data showing comparative launch-time fluctuations for all three measured applications

It occurred to the author to try and use the some of the seismic application software for performance analysis. There were indeed a large number of statistical tools, but they required a proprietary structured file format that would have been too time consuming to reproduce. Summary launch-time statistics based on benchmark data for each of the three applications of interest are shown in Table 5.1. In all cases, the asymmetric statistical distribution with

Table 5.1. Benchmark statistics with times reported in seconds

Application	Min.	Mean	SD	Max.
Seismoe	10	20	30	≥ 100
Multiflow	6	10	3	20
Grapho	6	15	5	50

a long tail is clearly evident. Physically, this means that any user launching an application would generally see a mean launch time in the range 10 to

```
App1 Stats for 728 samples in "bench.log.seismoe"
=================================================================
Minm:   5.69    Mean:  14.26    Maxm: 773.94    MDev:    4.35
Var:  811.65    SDev:  28.49    COV:    2.00
GamA:   0.25    GamB:  56.92
Secs |     5%  10%  15%  20%  25%  30%  35%  40%  45%  50%
-----|----+----+----+----+----+----+----+----+----+----+---------
 <  3|
 3- 6|*
 6- 9|****************
 9-12|*********************
12-15|****************************
15-18|**********************
18-21|****
21-24|**
24-27|*
27-30|
30-33|
33-36|
36-39|
39-42|
42-45|
45-48|
48-51|
51-54|
54-57|
 > 60|
```

Fig. 5.9. Example histogram of application response time profile

20 s, but occasionally launch times more than ten times that long could be observed. Although launching an application is typically only performed once per session, such a huge variation in launch times can already give the user the unnecessary perception of *erratic* application performance.

During the launch phase, the application was measured to be mostly in a wait state on the corresponding SP cluster node (i.e., it was neither CPU-bound nor I/O-bound). To resolve further how time was being spent during the launch phase, it was necessary to monitor the actual X-messages.

5.8 Performance Aliens Revealed

5.8.1 Out of Sight, Out of Mind

On the enterprise network were two remote and un-instrumented font servers that between them had approximately 15,000 fonts. The role of these two servers was to provide the best match to a font query from any X-client. Moreover, having the fonts loaded on just a couple remote servers is more efficient, from a system management standpoint, than replicating all those fonts on each one of the 200 nodes in the SP cluster.

The impact on performance of these remote services has to be measured. The open source tool called Xscope (provided with the X11R5 source distribution) was used for this purpose. Xscope uses the simple concept of interposing itself between the Xserver (terminal) and the Xclient (an SP cluster node) in such a way that the terminal thinks it is responding directly to the SP and the SP thinks it is talking to the terminal. This *ambushed* X-traffic is decoded on the fly and logged to a trace file. What is most important for many secure enterprises is that no *promiscuous* network packet-sniffing is required.

The following two UNIX commands:

```
> xscope -term121 -i0 -v1 >xscope.trace &
> seismoe -display host46:0 1>seismoe.rc.trace 2>/dev/null &
```

tell Xscope running on `host46` to record X-traffic generated by the application `seismoe` from the X-terminal `term121` and log it to a file called `xscope.trace`. Surprisingly, Xscope adds no more than about 2% to X-traffic latency. A fragment of a trace file looks like this:

```
............REQUEST: OpenFont
                     font-id: FNT 02000287
                        name: "*courier*medium-o-normal*-11-*"
         ............REQUEST: QueryFont
                        font: FTB 02000287
7.39:                       1460 bytes <-- X11 Server
7.39:                       1480 bytes <-- X11 Server
                                 ..............REPLY: QueryFont
                                 min-bounds:
                                 max-bounds:
                                   min-char-or-byte2: 0x0020
                                   max-char-or-byte2: 0x00ff
                                     default-char: 0x0000
                                    draw-direction: LeftToRight
                                       min-byte1: 0x00
                                       max-byte1: 0x00
                                    all-chars-exist: False
                                         font-ascent: 8
                                         font-descent: 2
```

Fig. 5.10. Tiny portion taken from a typical xscope trace file showing the point when the remote font service is called. A sporadic time stamp can be seen on the left-hand side

From Xscope traces (Fig. 5.10), it was determined that most of the launch time was spent resolving application font requests across the two remote X-font servers. The two numbers on the left-hand side of the file are actually wall-clock time in decimal seconds (cf. Chap. 1). They tell us that the X-conversation about remote fonts starts at 7.39 s into the application launch, in this particular measurement. That elapsed time is consistent with other performance instrumentation, particularly where the CPU appears to go into a wait state after about 10 s.

Seismoe, for example, required some 40 fonts to launch but there was an aggregate of more than 15,000 remote fonts were available. The 40 fonts that best fit the X-request must be searched for among the thousands of fonts available.

During these experiments, several font protocols were measured for their relative latencies. As well as the two font servers just mentioned (that use the X-protocol to resolve font queries), the Tek boot PROM provided another source (13 fonts), as did the Tek boot file system (96 fonts), and NFS-mounted files on Zeus and Kepler. The respective numbers of fonts were:

```
total fonts in Path tcp/fs001.big.seismic.com:7000   8371
total fonts in Path tcp/fs002.big.seismic.com:7000   7113
total fonts in Path /xterms/teknc305/boot/             96
total fonts in Path resident/                          13
total fonts in Path tcp/zeus.big.seismic.com:7100    4781
total fonts in Path tcp/kepler.big.seismic.com:7100  6237
```

The injection benchmark was reconfigured to rotate among these various font services. Each font path was reset dynamically in benchmark. Table 5.2 shows some of the resulting measurements. One immediate observation was that restricting queries to just one font server was faster than querying across two remote servers.

Table 5.2. Selected remote font services and the corresponding latencies

Font server	Number of fonts	Server type	Latency (s)
$XFS1$	8371	X font server	18.57
$XFS2$	7113	X font server	16.72
$NFS1$	4781	NFS mounted	17.01
$NFS2$	109	NFS mounted	9.41

5.8.2 Log–Jammed Performance

An extremely simple model can be constructed to confirm that the mean launch time R exhibits logarithmic scaling with the number of font files F on the remote font servers. Consider two font servers: a reference server S_o

loaded with F_o font files and a comparison server S_X loaded with F_X font files. The relative latency R_X/R_o of a font-query can be expressed as:

$$R_X = R_o \frac{\log_{10}(F_X)}{\log_{10}(F_o)} . \tag{5.26}$$

In fact, it is more convenient to normalize all the results to a reference serve with the least number of fonts, viz. $F_o = 109$ in Table 5.2.

> The insight of the model can be stated very simply. Suppose the reference font server is loaded with just $F_o = 100$ fonts while the remote server has $F_X = 1000$ fonts. Then the latency model given by (5.26) states that since the logarithm of the number of fonts is in the ratio 3/2, the average launch time for the remote font server will be 1.5 times longer than for the reference server.

Table 5.3 compares some typical measured latencies with estimates from the logarithmic latency model in (5.26).

Table 5.3. Comparison between measured font latencies and the logarithmic latency model R_X. All times are in seconds

Server	Data	R_X	Error (%)
$XFS1$	18.57	18.12	−2.50
$XFS2$	16.72	17.79	6.02
$NFS1$	17.01	16.99	−0.09
$NFS2$	9.41	9.41	N/A

The subscript notation $XFS1$ and $XFS2$ in Table 5.3 refers to the standard font servers, which happened to be two IBM RS6000 workstations. The alternative font paths with subscripts $NFS1$ and $NFS2$ refer to the NFS-mounted servers. Service from $NFS2$ gave the best typical launch time (R_{NFS2}) for seismoe, and that is why it was used as the basis for normalization. A minus sign in the percentage error column indicates that the model underestimated the measured time. Additional experiments bore out this conclusion within an error margin of less than ±10%, but why does this model work so well?

5.8.3 To Get a Log You Need a Tree

We can anticipate that the observed latency of any remote font service is determined by a large number of factors, including network latency, platform latency, caching, and so on. In addition, the font query in X11 is complicated. For example, rather than simply returning an explicitly nominated font, the font server tries to return the best match to the query based on the window geometry and a number of other factors. To explicitly measure the latency of all these factors would be horrendously complicated. There is an old adage

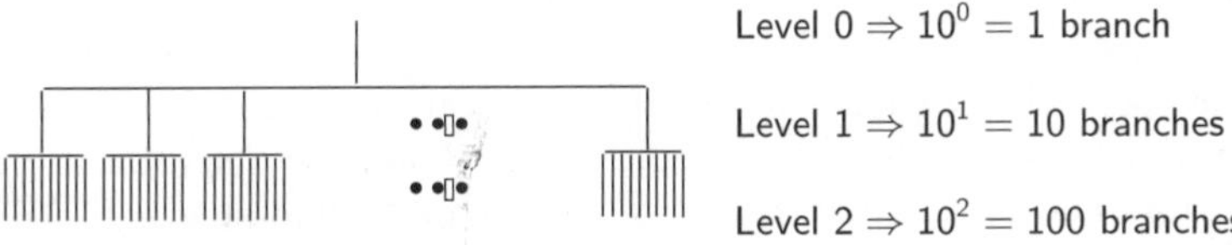

Fig. 5.11. Example tree structure responsible for logarithmic characteristic seen in the X11 font server latencies

in mathematics that says *to get a log, you need a tree.* If we take the very simple view that the fonts are organized in some kind of directory structure and that directory structure can be expressed as a simple tree such as depicted in Fig. 5.11, the logarithmic nature of (5.26) can be understood easily.

The depth of the tree can be enumerated as a number starting with zero at the root. At any level L every predecessor branch (above) has ten sibling branches. The total number of branches at that level is then given by 10^L. Since the time to search is determined by the depth of the tree, the latency will also be proportional to L, i.e., $R \propto L$. The model in (5.26) is the normalized version of this intuition. This simple model, however, only accounts for the average latency because some font queries may be addressed in less time if that font has been cached due to a previous query requesting the same font. Moreover, this caching effect also accounts for the erratic variation in observed application launch times.

The great value of this simple model is that it immediately suggests a simple and therefore very cheap fix, namely, paring back the number of fonts loaded on the primary font server. Given the complexity of the various subsystems needed to support the operation of X11, e.g., X-client software port, memory accesses, buffering, network load, it is surprising that none of these things plays a significant role in determining the mean launch time. As suggested by the log-model, the most important control parameter is the number of fonts on the font servers. Two corollaries follow immediately.

1. Restrict the number of fonts used by developers and verify the performance impact via *acceptance testing* procedures.
2. As part of overall of X11 system management the fonts loaded onto font servers at each new release should be *deliberately selected* to match those used by application developers.

These two points are important because they are not part of the prescription endorsed by the X11 consortium as part of system management, and the severe impact on performance of ignoring them should be clear from the results presented in this section. The performance gain was 300% for launch times.

5.9 X-Windows Scalability

Having made "contact" with the major performance *alien* responsible for the erratically poor launch times, the second performance issue that was observed in Sect. 5.7.1 was the significant interactive variance that occurred once the application was launched. The interactive responsiveness can depend on multiple users having multiple copies of the same application running concurrently. This is an issue directly related to application scalability. Quantification of such multi-user effects requires the measurement of X-window events within the context of sibling windows belonging to each user instance of an X-parent window.

5.9.1 Measuring Sibling X-Events

Capturing context-dependent X-events is difficult to do and is best left to commercial load testing tools designed for that purpose. In this case, Mercury Interactive's XRunner® product was selected. A set of experiments were performed using XRunner to measure the increase in launch times as the SP-cluster node was placed under increasing user load. The response time mea-

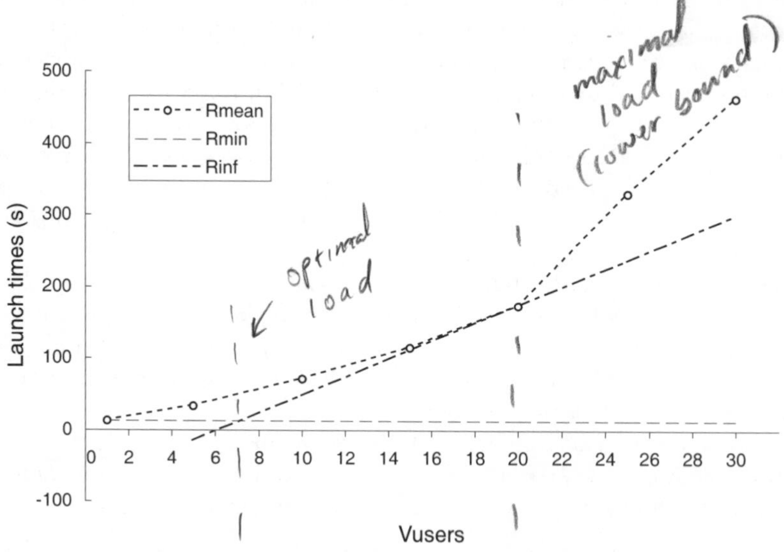

Fig. 5.12. Superlinear response time curve (cf. Fig. 5.3)

surements were expected to conform to the typical characteristic shown in Figs. 2.20 and 5.3 for a closed queueing circuit. The actual data, corresponding to the mean response time measurements, are plotted in Fig. 5.12. The general convex characteristic appears to be correct. However, when we plot the corresponding bounds:

- **Rmin:** The minimum possible response time with no contention present
- **Rinf:** The linear rise in response time as the number of users increases (assuming no other limit is reached).

we discover a significant deviation from this expected characteristic. Above an XRunner load of 20 $Vusers$ (Fig. 5.12), the mean seismoe launch times increase dramatically above the $Rmin$ asymptote. In fact, it is *superlinear*! This can only happen when secondary latency effects (e.g., virtual memory paging) begin to dominate the measured response times. Indeed, Fig. 5.13 shows that above 20 seismoe $Vusers$ the system begins to thrash, while above 30 seismoe $Vusers$ the local X host quietly pages itself into oblivion.

```
kthr     memory             page                    faults           cpu
----- ----------- ------------------------ ------------ -----------
 r  b    avm    fre  re  pi  po  fr    sr  cy   in    sy    cs us sy id
17  5 125304      8   0   0 319 330   362   0 2302 12278 3464 41 59  0
11  8 126177      9   0   0 306 320   371   0 2518 13072 3680 37 63  0
11 10 126959      8   0   1 321 336   381   0 2054 12472 3312 39 61  0
 8 11 127884      4   0   2 284 336   391   0 1688 10294 3921 38 43  0
13  4 128521     81   0   2 274 298   343   0 1728 10893 3344 45 47  0
 7 11 129328      6   0   1 276 317   397   0 1816 10702 3200 38 54  0
11  7 130235      5   0   1 285 357   427   0 1378  9194 3669 34 35  0
18  1 130189    521   0   1 126 112   128   0 1368 11547 2026 52 48  0
```

Fig. 5.13. A portion of AIX `vmstat` output showing a high degree of virtual-memory paging activity

5.9.2 Superlinear Response

Optimal loading is determined by the point where the asymptote intersects the lower bound, i.e., $Vusers = 7$. Recalling that these curves are based on mean response time values, this choice allows for the inevitable fluctuations (variance) around the optimum while trying to minimize their impact on the $Vusers$ response time.

Maximal loading is determined by the point where the response curve rises faster than the theoretical asymptote, i.e., $Vusers = 20$. Fluctuations above this point are likely to occur often and only recover in times that are relatively long compared with those about the optimum.

This interpretation is further corroborated by Seismoe interactive response time measurements. At 20 $Vusers$ the response times for the interactive seismoe operations of opening and saving a data file, suddenly escalate by an order of magnitude over the times measured for 15 $Vusers$. No time was available to investigate whether this was also a side effect of virtual memory paging or some other phenomenon.

5.10 Review

In this chapter we demonstrated the power of bounds analysis based on the underlying queueing theory presented in Chaps. 2 and 3. In particular, we saw that busywork doth not the truth make. Flaws in the performance data that had been collected previously on a remote benchmark platform were uncovered with minimal effort and the cost of a couple of phone calls. It doesn't get much better than that!

Similarly, the superlinear behavior of the measured response times on a large-scale cluster platform could be attributed to thrashing effects conflicting with the expected response time bounds. In this sense, some expectations are better than no expectations.

Exercises

5.1. Suppose the performance instrumentation in the software was broken on the Florida benchmark platform, rather than the driver script as was discovered in Sect. 5.5. What would the service demand of the bottleneck stage have to be for the system to produce the measured 300 TPS?

5.2. If all the service demands could be set to D_{min} in Example 5.1, what would be the balanced throughput bound?

Part II

Practice of System Performance Analysis

6

Pretty Damn Quick (PDQ)—A Slow Introduction

6.1 Introduction

This chapter introduces the PDQ© (Pretty Damn Quick) queueing analyzer and explains how to use it. We begin with some guidelines on how to build performance models and then move on to the specifics of the PDQ library in Perl. Finally, we present the actual PDQ codes for the examples discussed in Chaps. 2 and 3. Other PDQ model codes are embedded in the chapters of Part II. Instructions for installing PDQ and creating the corresponding Perl module can be found in Appendix F.

6.2 How to Build PDQ Circuits

Consistent with the notion of circuits presented in Chap. 3, every PDQ program should have a defined set of *inputs* and a set of *outputs*. The inputs are performance metrics such as traffic rates, active user population, and service rates. These come from the data you have collected from the system you are analyzing or estimates if no data exists. The role of PDQ is to provide a set of performance metrics, such as utilizations, queue lengths, and residence times, as outputs.

6.3 Inputs and Outputs

As an example of this procedure, recall the response time formula in (2.35) for an $M/M/1$ queue labeled with its respective input and output parameters:

$$(\textbf{output})\, R \quad \longleftarrow \quad \frac{D\ (\textbf{input})}{1 - \ \lambda\ (\textbf{input})\ \times\ D\ (\textbf{input})} \,. \tag{6.1}$$

This is also a model; an equational model but a model, nonetheless. The corresponding queueing circuit is shown in Fig. 6.1. Equation (6.1) is already contained in PDQ, so you will never have to write the code for this equation explicitly. To solve (6.1) *manually*, however, we need the appropriate inputs. These are the parameters on the right side of the formula, viz. the arrival rate λ and the service demand D. Those inputs are then used to calculate the output R on the left side of (6.1). That is precisely what PDQ does *algorithmically.*

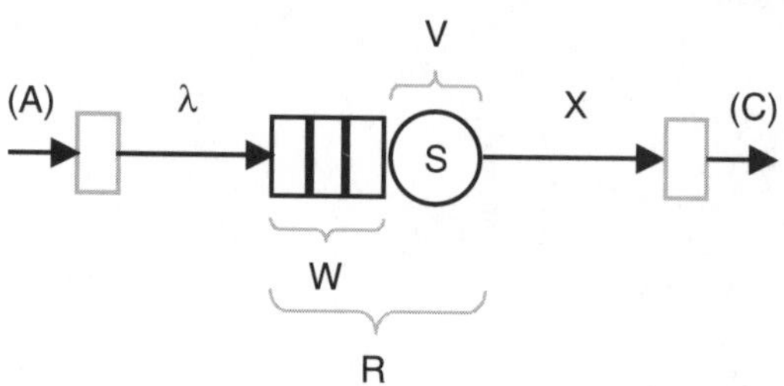

Fig. 6.1. Simple $M/M/1$ queueing circuit with conventional *inputs*: the arrival rate λ, the mean number of visits V, the mean service time S, or the service demand $D = VS$. The typical *outputs* are the waiting time W, the residence time R in (6.1), and the mean queue length $Q = \lambda R$

Of course, things are rarely this simple in real life. We may not have a direct measurement of the arrival rate λ or the average service demand D, so we have to resort to deducing it from other information we do have. For example, we may have to calculate the arrival rate by counting the number of arrivals A during the measurement period T and using the relation $\lambda = A/T$ from Chap. 2. Combining this calculated λ with the measured utilization of the server, we can use Little's law $\rho = \lambda D$ to determine the input service demands as $D = \rho/\lambda$.

Building PDQ models is merely an extension of this same process. We try to limit the number of input parameters required for the model and let PDQ do the work of computing numerous output metrics. Sometimes, the process of building a PDQ model can surprise you by telling you what parameters need to be measured as inputs that you had not thought of previously. An advantage of PDQ is that you do not have to construct the code for all the performance equations presented in Chaps. 2 and 3. Another advantage of PDQ is that the outputs can be computed for very complex queueing circuits with multiple workloads that would otherwise be debilitating, if not impossible, to carry out by hand.

6.3.1 Setting Up PDQ

PDQ is a queueing circuit solver, not a simulator. As part of its suite of solution methods, PDQ incorporates the MVA algorithm discussed in Chap. 3. The purpose is to enable the user to build queueing circuit representations of actual computer systems to do the kind of performance analysis described in Part I of this book.

Unlike similar queueing circuit solvers, PDQ is not a binary application constrained to run only on certain types of computers. Rather, PDQ is provided as *open source* so that it can be installed and run on the user's platform of choice. Naturally, all the other benefits of open-source development accrue. In particular, users are encouraged to extend the source and share it with others, and possibly find remaining bugs.

For efficiency, the underlying solver routines are written and maintained in the C language, but its functionality is also made available to the user through a Perl module interface. A new PDQ model is written in the Perl scripting language, and thus some programming is required. This approach imposes two simple demands on the user:

1. The first is that you are familiar with the Perl language. The choice of Perl facilitates the use of all the constructs of a modern programming language such as procedures, lists, associative arrays, subroutines, and recursion to solve potentially very elaborate performance models in PDQ.
2. Second, you need to have to access to a C compiler. It is necessary to compile the PDQ library *once* so that it can execute the PDQ Perl module on your system. C compilers are generally available with every UNIX and Linux platform but you might be advised to check with your local system administrator facilitate the installation of perl PDQ.

This choice of Perl is intended to maximize the portability and utility of PDQ.

Perl scripts do not need to be formally compiled, thereby enabling rapid prototyping and testing of performance models. The interested reader is also encouraged to see `home.pacbell.net/ouster/scripting.html`, which provides further compelling justifications for the use of scripting languages.

Setting up a PDQ model is very straightforward and may be summarized in the following simple sequence of programming steps:

1. Define each instance of a queue in the queueing circuit by calling the `PDQ::CreateNode()` function.
2. For an *open* circuit, define each instance of a traffic stream by calling the `PDQ::CreatOpen()` function.
3. For a *closed* circuit, define each instance of a batch or interactive user workload stream by calling the `PDQ::CreatClosed()` function.
4. Specify the service demand for each of the defined workloads on each of the previously defined queueing centers in the circuit by calling the `PDQ::SetDemand()` function.
5. Solve the PDQ model by calling the `PDQ::Solve()` function with the desired solution technique passed as parameter.
6. Generate a standard performance report by calling the `PDQ::Report()` function.

All PDQ performance models are constructed by following this same basic paradigm.

For those readers not familiar with the Perl language, PDQ offers a motivation to learn it. The classic introductory programming references are by Schwartz and Phoenix [2001], and Wall et al. [2003]. Many other excellent texts and other Perl resources can be found online at `www.perl.org`. Remember, any serious performance modeling is actually serious programming.

6.3.2 Some General Guidelines

Based on the concept of circuit inputs and outputs, a good starting point for creating a PDQ model is to draw a block diagram of the system. This might be a *functional* block diagram showing the workflow or a UML diagram [Smith and Williams 2001]. It is usually best to choose the high-level description with which you are most familiar.

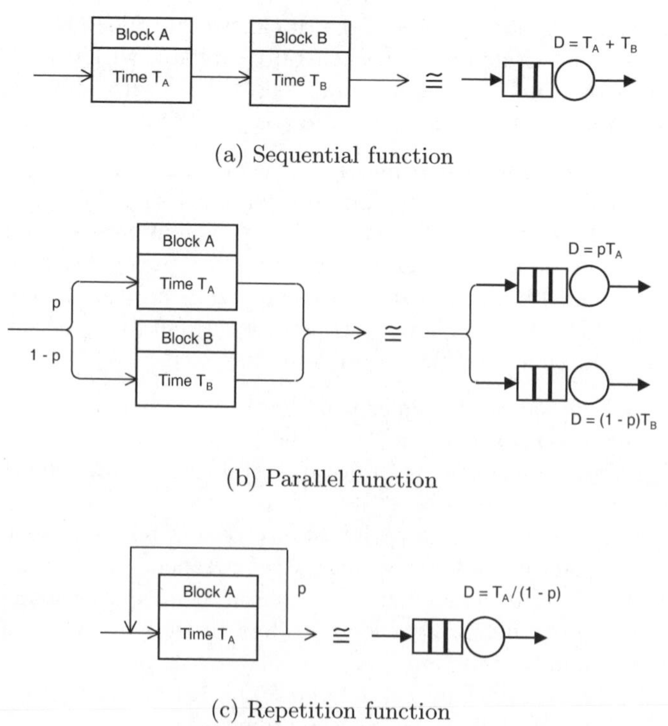

Fig. 6.2. Functional block primitives and their queueing equivalents

These functional blocks can then be translated into the appropriate queueing paradigms such as those shown in Figs. 6.2(a)– 6.2(c). Measured speeds and feeds for request rates, file sizes, CPU clock frequency, and so on are then used to parameterize the respective PDQ queueing nodes. These data may come from benchmark results, production systems, or simply as best engineering estimates. You should always be prepared to review these parameters in the future. The fact that you are documenting them in one place (the PDQ model) is itself an important contribution to any engineering effort.

You should try to estimate resource demands at the lowest levels in the presence of just one or a few requests, if possible. This one way to get reasonable estimates of service demands. These values can then be combined to get the application-level demands.

6.4 Simple Annotated Example

The annotated PDQ performance model in Sect. 6.4.1 is constructed by following the steps enumerated in Sect 6.3.1. In the case of more sophisticated PDQ models that represent more complex computer systems, it is often advisable to write separate Perl subroutines to represent the different computer subsystems being modeled.

6.4.1 Creating the PDQ Model

In this section we construct, run, and validate a PDQ model of the simple $M/M/1$ queue in Fig. 6.1. Measurement data and derived inputs for the PDQ model are summarized in Table 6.1. The time-base must be common to all

Table 6.1. Measured and derived input parameters for the PDQ model

Parameter (symbol)	Perl scalar variable
Measurement period (T)	`$MeasurePeriod = 3600;`
Arrival count (A)	`$ArrivalCount = 1800;`
Service visits (V)	`$ServiceVisits = 10;`
Service time (S)	`$ServiceTime = 0.10;`
Arrival rate (λ)	`$ArrivalRate = $ArrivalCount / $MeasurePeriod;`
Service demand (D)	`$ServiceDemand = $ServiceVisits * $ServiceTime;`

parameters. Here, the time-base is chosen to be *seconds*. We suppose that the period for which the $M/M/1$ queue was measured is one hour. The count of arrivals into the queue over that period was 1,800; and there were 10 repeated visits to the server. The corresponding PDQ outputs and their validation are summarized in Table 6.2. At this point, it might be worthwile for the reader to quickly review the compendium of queueing symbols and equations in Appendix E. From (2.27) the condition:

$$\lambda \leq D^{-1}$$

must be satisfied for the $M/M/1$ queue to be stable. In Perl, this becomes:

```
$ServiceCap = 1 / $ServiceDemand;
if( $ArrivalRate >= $ServiceCap ) { ...
```

which is a check for an error condition. See lines 17–23 in the following PDQ script.

```
1 #! /usr/bin/perl
2 # mm1.pl
3
4 use pdq;
5
6 ## INPUTS ##
7 # Measured parameters
8 $MeasurePeriod = 3600; # seconds
9 $ArrivalCount = 1800;
10 $ServiceVisits = 10;
11
12 # Derived parameters
13 $ArrivalRate = $ArrivalCount / $MeasurePeriod;
14 $ServiceTime = 0.10; # seconds
15 $ServiceDemand = $ServiceVisits * $ServiceTime; # seconds
16
17 # Check the queue meets stability condition
18 $ServiceCap = 1 / $ServiceDemand;
19 if($ArrivalRate > $ServiceCap) {
20     print "Error: Arrival rate $ArrivalRate ";
21     print "exceeds service capacity ServiceCap !!\n";
22     exit;
23 }
24
25 $NodeName = "FIFO";
26 $WorkName = "Work";
27
28 # Initialize PDQ internal variables
29 pdq::Init("FIFO Example");
30
31 # Change the units used by PDQ::Report()
32 pdq::SetWUnit("Requests");
33 pdq::SetTUnit("Seconds");
34
35 # Define the FIFO queue
36 $pdq::nodes = pdq::CreateNode($NodeName, $pdq::CEN, $pdq::FCFS);
37
```

```
# Define the queueing circuit type and workload
$pdq::streams = pdq::CreateOpen($WorkName, $ArrivalRate);

# Define service demand due to the workload at FIFO
pdq::SetDemand($NodeName, $WorkName, $ServiceDemand);

# Solve the PDQ model
pdq::Solve($pdq::CANON);
# NOTE: Must use CANON-ical method since this is an open circuit

## OUTPUTS ##
# Generate a report
pdq::Report();
```

The report generated by the call to `PDQ::Report()` (Sect. 6.6.14) is presented in the next section.

6.4.2 Reading the PDQ Report

The following report is produced by `mm1.pl` in Sect 6.4.1. Note the appearance of a Comments field described in Sect. 6.6.14.

```
        ***************************************
        ****** Pretty Damn Quick REPORT *******
        ***************************************
        ***  of : Sun Jan  4 15:43:18 2004  ***
        ***  for: FIFO Example              ***
        ***  Ver: PDQ Analyzer v2.7 080202  ***
        ***************************************
        ***************************************

         ******        Comments           *******

Just a simple FIFO queue for demonstration purposes.

         ***************************************
         ******    PDQ Model INPUTS      *******
         ***************************************

Node Sched Resource   Workload   Class     Demand
---- ----- --------   --------   -----     ------
CEN  FCFS  FIFO       Work       TRANS     1.0000

Queueing Circuit Totals:

    Streams:      1
    Nodes:        1

WORKLOAD Parameters
```

```

Source          per Sec         Demand
--------        -------         ------
Work            0.5000          1.0000

        ***************************************
        ******   PDQ Model OUTPUTS     *******
        ***************************************

Solution Method: CANON

        ******   SYSTEM Performance     *******

Metric                          Value   Unit
-----------------               -----   ----
Workload: "Work"
Mean Throughput               0.5000  Requests/Seconds
Response Time                 2.0000  Seconds

Bounds Analysis:
Max Demand                    1.0000      Requests/Seconds
Max Throughput                1.0000      Requests/Seconds

        ******   RESOURCE Performance   *******

Metric          Resource     Work               Value   Unit
---------       ------       ----               -----   ----
Throughput      FIFO         Work              0.5000   Requests/Secon
Utilization     FIFO         Work             50.0000   Percent
Queue Length    FIFO         Work              1.0000   Requests
Residence Time  FIFO         Work              2.0000   Seconds
```

The banner includes the PDQ model name of the model that was passed as an argument to `PDQ::Init()`. The banner is followed by the comment field, if any.

6.4.3 Validating the PDQ Model

Finally, we compare the PDQ outputs with those expected using the appropriate queueing formulae in Appendix E.

For more complex models that combine a flow of requests between many queues in a circuit, such manual calculations become extremely tedious and error-prone. Similarly, you might want to use the same model code but simply change the parameter values. In this sense, PDQ might be thought of as a *writes once, model anywhere* tool.

Table 6.2. Validation of outputs from the PDQ report. The numbers in the upper half of the table correspond to PDQ Inputs while the lower half corresponds to PDQ Outputs seen in the PDQ report

Parameter (symbol)	Calculated value
Arrival rate (λ)	$\lambda = 1800/3600 = 0.5$ TPS
Service demand (D)	$D = 10 \times 0.10 = 1.0$ s
Residence time (R)	$R = 1/(1 - 0.5) = 2.0$ s
Server utilization (ρ)	$\rho = 0.5$ or 50%
Queue length (Q)	$Q = 0.5 \times 2.0 = 1.0$
Waiting time (W)	$W = 2.0 - 0.5 = 1.5$ s

6.5 Perl PDQ Module

In this section we describe the public data types, global variables, and public procedures that are available in the PDQ Perl module. The PDQ module is invoked with the statement:

```
use pdq;
```

at the beginning of the Perl script that defines the PDQ model.

6.5.1 PDQ Data Types

The following types are used in conjunction with PDQ library functions. See the synopses of procedures for the correct syntax.

Nodes

`$pdq::CEN`	Queueing center. Parameter in `PDQ::CreateNode()`.
`$pdq::DLY`	Delay center. Parameter in `PDQ::CreateNode()`.

Service Disciplines

`$pdq::FCFS`	First-come first-served parameter in `PDQ::CreateNode()`.
`$pdq::LCFS`	Last-come first-served parameter in `PDQ::CreateNode()`.
`$pdq::ISRV`	Infinite server parameter in `PDQ::CreateNode()`.
`$pdq::PSHR`	Processor sharing. Parameter in `PDQ::CreateNode()`.

Workload Streams

Following Chap. 3, the workload associated with an open queueing circuit is called a *transaction* workload stream. Workloads associated with closed queueing circuits are called *terminal* or *batch* streams.

`$pdq::BATCH` A batch class workload is defined as having zero think time and is parameterized by the number of batch jobs. Only consistent in the context of a closed queueing circuit to distinguish from `$pdq::TERM`. Parameter in `PDQ::CreateClosed()`.

`$pdq::TERM` A terminal class workload has a think-time and is parameterized by the number of user processes. Only consistent in the context of a closed queueing circuit to distinguish from `$pdq::BATCH`. Parameter in `PDQ::CreateClosed()`.

`$pdq::TRANS` A transaction class workload for an open queueing circuit. This variable is now deprecated in PDQ. Parameter in `PDQ::CreateOpen()`.

Solution Methods

`$pdq::APPROX` Argument to `PDQ::Solve()` that causes PDQ to apply the approximate MVA solution method. See Chap. 3 for the conceptual background. Only consistent in the context of solving a *closed* queueing circuit. An approximation to the EXACT or iterative MVA solution method.

`$pdq::CANON` Argument to `PDQ::Solve()` that causes PDQ to apply the canonical solution method. See Chap. 2 for the conceptual background. Only consistent in the context of an *open* queueing circuit.

`$pdq::EXACT` Argument to `PDQ::Solve()` that causes PDQ to apply the iterative MVA solution method. Only consistent in the context of a *closed* queueing circuit.

6.5.2 PDQ Global Variables

The following global variables are apply to every PDQ model.

`$pdq::nodes;` Cumulative counter for the number of nodes returned by `PDQ::CreateNode()`.

`$pdq::streams;` Cumulative counter for the number of workload streams returned by `PDQ_CreateClosed()` and `PDQ::CreateOpen()`.

`$pdq::model;` String containing the model name. Initialized via `PDQ::Init()`.

`$pdq::DEBUG;` Flag to toggle PDQ debug facility. Default `DEBUG = FALSE`. Pass as an argument to `PDQ_SetDebug()`.

`$pdq::tolerance;` Terminates iteration in the *approximate* MVA solution method `$pdq::APPROX`.

6.5.3 PDQ Functions

All PDQ functions in the Perl module have the `PDQ::` prefix. Here, we group them in the order of typical invocation.

1. `PDQ::Init`
2. `PDQ::CreateOpen` or `PDQ::CreateClosed`
3. `PDQ::CreateNode` or `PDQ::CreateSingleNode`
4. `PDQ::SetDemand` or `PDQ::SetVisits`
5. `PDQ::SetWUnit`, `PDQ::SetTUnit`
6. `PDQ::Solve`
7. `PDQ::GetResponse`, `PDQ::GetThruput`
8. `PDQ::GetQueueLength`, `PDQ::GetResidenceTime`
9. `PDQ::GetUtilization`
10. `PDQ::Report`

The next section provides a complete synopsis for each of these functions.

6.6 Function Synopses

Each function is presented in alphabetical order by name.

6.6.1 PDQ::CreateClosed

Syntax
`PDQ::CreateClosed($workname, $class, $population, $think);`

Description
`PDQ::CreateClosed()` is used to define the characteristics of a workload in a closed-circuit queueing model. A separate call is required for each workload stream that has different characteristics.

Argument	*Description*
`$workname`	String identifying the workload name in report files.
`class`	Either `$pdq::TERM` or `$pdq::BATCH` type.
`$population`	Number of requests in the closed circuit.
`$think`	Think-time between requests.

Returns
`PDQ::CreateClosed()` returns the current number of workload streams created in the model.

See Also
`PDQ::CreateOpen()`, `PDQ::Init()`

Usage

```
PDQ::CreateClosed("DB_workers", $pdq::TERM, 57.4, 31.6);
PDQ::CreateClosed("fax_tasks", $pdq::BATCH, 10.0);
```

6.6.2 PDQ::CreateMultiNode

Syntax
`PDQ::CreateMultiNode($servers, $workname, $nodetype, $schedtype);`

Description
`PDQ::CreateMultiNode()` is used to define a multiserver queueing node in an open-circuit queueing model (See Sect. 6.7.3). A separate call is required for each instance of a multiserver queueing node.

Argument	*Description*
`$servers`	Integer number of servers.
`$workname`	String to identify node in reports.
`$nodetype`	Type of queue, e.g., `$pdq::CEN`.
`$schedtype`	Service discipline, e.g.,`$pdq::FCFS`.

Returns
`PDQ::CreateMultiNode()` returns the current number of queueing nodes created in the model.

See Also
`PDQ::CreateNode()`, `PDQ::CreateSingleNode()`

Usage

```
PDQ::CreateMultiNode(4, "cpu", $pdq::CEN, $pdq::FCFS);
PDQ::CreateNode("bus", $pdq::CEN, $pdq::ISRV);
PDQ::CreateNode("disk", $pdq::CEN, $pdq::FCFS);
```

6.6.3 PDQ::CreateNode

Syntax
`PDQ::CreateNode($workname, $nodetype, $schedtype);`

Description
`PDQ::CreateNode()` is used to define a queueing node in either a closed or an open-circuit queueing model. A separate call is required for each instance of a queueing node. `PDQ::CreateSingleNode()` is now preferred. `PDQ::CreateNode()` is maintained for backward compatibility but it may be deprecated in future releases of PDQ.

Argument	*Description*
`$workname`	String to identify node in reports.
`$nodetype`	Type of queue, e.g., `$pdq::CEN`.
`$schedtype`	Service discipline, e.g.,`$pdq::FCFS`.

Returns
`PDQ::CreateNode()` returns the current number of queueing nodes created in the model.

See Also
`PDQ::CreateSingleNode()`, `PDQ::PDQ::CreateMultiNode()`

Usage

```
PDQ::CreateNode("cpu", $pdq::CEN, $pdq::FCFS);
PDQ::CreateNode("bus", $pdq::CEN, $pdq::ISRV);
PDQ::CreateNode("disk", $pdq::CEN, $pdq::FCFS);
```

6.6.4 PDQ::CreateOpen

Syntax
`PDQ::CreateOpen($workname, $lambda);`

Description
`PDQ::CreateOpen()` defines a stream in an open-circuit queueing model. A separate call is required for each workload instance.

Argument	*Description*
`$workname`	String to identify workload in report files.
`$lambda`	Arrival rate per unit time into the open circuit.

Returns
`PDQ::CreateOpen()` returns the current number of open workloads created in the model.

See Also
`PDQ::CreateClosed()`, `PDQ::Init()`

Usage

```
PDQ::CreateOpen("IO_Cmds", 10.0);
```

6.6.5 PDQ::CreateSingleNode

Syntax
`PDQ::CreateSingleNode($workname, $nodetype, $schedtype);`

Description
`PDQ::CreateSingleNode()` is used to define a queueing node in either a closed or an open-circuit queueing model. Equivalent to `PDQ::CreateNode()`. A separate call is required for each instance of a single queueing node.

Argument	*Description*
`$workname`	String to identify node in reports.
`$nodetype`	Type of queue, e.g., `$pdq::CEN`.
`$schedtype`	Service discipline, e.g.,`$pdq::FCFS`.

Returns
`PDQ::CreateSingleNode()` returns the current number of queueing nodes created in the model.

See Also
`PDQ::CreateNode()`, `PDQ::CreateMultiNode()`, `PDQ::Init()`

Usage

```
PDQ::CreateSingleNode("cpu", $pdq::CEN, $pdq::FCFS);
PDQ::CreateSingleNode("bus", $pdq::CEN, $pdq::ISRV);
PDQ::CreateSingleNode("disk", $pdq::CEN, $pdq::FCFS);
```

6.6.6 PDQ::GetLoadOpt

Syntax
`PDQ::GetLoadOpt($class, $workname);`

Description
`PDQ::GetLoadOpt` is used to determine the optimal system load for the specified workload in a closed circuit.

Argument	*Description*
`$class`	Only `$pdq::TERM` or `$pdq::BATCH`.
`$workname`	String to identify workload in report files.

Returns
`PDQ::GetLoadOpt` returns the optimal user load as a decimal number. See Sect. 5.3.3 for the conceptual details.

See Also
PDQ::GetThruput, PDQ::GetResponse

Usage

```
$lopt = PDQ::GetLoadOpt("intranet", 10.0);
printf("N*(%s): %3.4f\n","intranet users", $lopt);
```

6.6.7 PDQ::GetQueueLength

Syntax
`PDQ::GetQueueLength($nodename, $workname, $class);`

Description
`PDQ::GetQueueLength()` is used to determine the queue length of the designated service node by the specified workload. It should only be called after the PDQ model has been solved.

Argument	*Description*
`$nodename`	Name of the queueing node.
`$workname`	Name of the workload.
`$class`	One of `$pdq::TRANS`, `$pdq::TERM`, or `$pdq::BATCH`.

Returns
`PDQ::GetQueueLength()` returns the queue length as a decimal value.

See Also
PDQ::GetResidenceTime(), PDQ::GetUtilization(),

Usage

```
PDQ::Solve();
...
$ql = PDQ::GetQueueLength("disk", "IO_Cmds", $pdq::TRANS);
printf("R(%s): %3.4f\n","IO_Cmds", $ql);
```

6.6.8 PDQ::GetResidenceTime

Syntax
`PDQ::GetResidenceTime($nodename, $workname, $class);`

Description
`PDQ::GetResidenceTime()` is used to determine the residence time at the designated queueing node by the specified workload. It should only be called after the PDQ model has been solved.

Argument	*Description*
`$nodename`	Name of the queueing node.
`$workname`	Name of the workload.
`$class`	One of `$pdq::TRANS`, `$pdq::TERM`, or `$pdq::BATCH`.

Returns

`PDQ::GetResidenceTime()` returns the residence time as a decimal value.

See Also

`PDQ::GetQueueLength()`, `PDQ::GetUtilization()`

Usage

```
PDQ::Solve();
...
$rez = PDQ::GetResidenceTime("disk", "IO_Cmds", $pdq::TRANS);
printf("R(%s): %3.4f\n","IO_Cmds", $rez);
```

6.6.9 PDQ::GetResponse

Syntax

`PDQ::GetResponse($class, $workname);`

Description

`PDQ::GetResponse()` is used to determine the system response time for the specified workload.

Argument	*Description*
`$class`	One of `$pdq::TRANS`, `$pdq::TERM`, or `$pdq::BATCH`.
`$workname`	Name of the workload.

Returns

`PDQ_GetResponse()` returns the system response time for the specified workload.

See Also

`PDQ::CreateClosed()`, `PDQ::Init()`, `PDQ::CreateOpen()`

Usage

```
$rtime = PDQ_GetResponse($pdq::TRANS, "IO_Cmds");
printf("R(%s): %3.4f\n","IO_Cmds", $rtime);
```

6.6.10 PDQ::GetThruMax

Syntax
`PDQ::GetThruMax($class, $workname);`

Description
`PDQ::GetThruMax` is used to determine the upper bound on the system throughput for the specified workload in a closed circuit.

Argument	*Description*
`$class`	Only `$pdq::TERM` or `$pdq::BATCH`.
`$workname`	String to identify workload in report files.

Returns
`PDQ::GetThruMax` returns the upper bound on throughput as a decimal number. See Chap. 5 for the conceptual details.

See Also
`PDQ::GetThruput`

Usage

```
$xmax = PDQ::GetThruMax(\$pdq::TERM, "database");
printf("N*(%s): %3.4f\n","database users", $xmax);
```

6.6.11 PDQ::GetThruput

Syntax
`PDQ::GetThruput($class, $workname);`

Description
`PDQ::GetThruput()` is used to determine the system throughput for the specified workload.

Argument	*Description*
`$class`	One of `$pdq::TRANS`, `$pdq::TERM`, or `$pdq::BATCH`.
`$workname`	A string containing the name of the workload.

Returns
`PDQ::GetThruput()` returns the system throughput for the specified workload.

See Also
PDQ::GetResponse()

Usage

```
$tput = PDQ::GetThruput(TRANS, "IO_Cmds");
printf("R(%s): %3.4f\n", "IO_Cmds", $tput);
```

6.6.12 PDQ::GetUtilization

Syntax
`PDQ::GetUtilization($nodename, $workname);`

Description
`PDQ::GetUtilization()` is used to determine the utilization of the designated queueing node by the specified workload. Should only be called after the PDQ model has been solved.

Argument	*Description*
`$nodename`	Name of the queueing node.
`$workname`	Name of the workload.

Returns
`PDQ::GetUtilization()` returns the utilization as a decimal fraction in the range 0.0 to 1.0.

See Also
`PDQ::GetResponse()`, `PDQ::GetThruput()`, `PDQ::Solve()`

Usage

```
PDQ::Solve();
...
$util = PDQ::GetUtilization("disk", "IO_Cmds");
printf("R(%s): %3.4f\n","IO_Cmds", $util);
```

6.6.13 PDQ::Init

Syntax
`PDQ::Init($modelname);`

Description
`PDQ::Init()` initializes all internal PDQ variables. Must be called prior to any other PDQ function. It also resets PDQ variables so that there is no separate cleanup function call required. Can be called an arbitrary number of times in the same model.

Argument	*Description*
`$modelname`	The name of the performance model that will appear in the PDQ report banner. String length should not exceed 24 characters (including spaces).

Returns
None.

See Also
`PDQ::Solve()`, `PDQ::Report()`

Usage

```
PDQ::Init("File Server");
...
PDQ::Solve($pdq::APPROX);
PDQ::Report();
...
PDQ::Init("Client Workstation");
...
PDQ::Solve($pdq::CANON);
PDQ::Report();
```

6.6.14 PDQ::Report

Syntax
`PDQ::Report();`

Description
`PDQ::Report()` generates a standardized output format which includes the total number of PDQ nodes and streams, system performance measures, such as throughputs and response times for each workload stream, together with nodal performance measures, such as node utilization and queue lengths. Example PDQ reports can be found in Sect. 6.7 and throughout the remainder of this book. The default output device for the PDQ report is the terminal window where the PDQ program is run. On a UNIX or Linux K platform, the most expeditious way to save a PDQ report to a file is to include the shell I/O redirect command (`>`) when the PDQ program is executed. Non-UNIX platforms may require the use of the Perl `open` and `close` functions [Wall et al. 2003]. The function `PDQ::Report` must not be called before `PDQ::Solve`. Comments can be included at the beginning of the report by including them in a file named `comments.pdq`.

Returns
None.

See Also
`PDQ::Init()`, `PDQ::Solve()`

Usage

```
...
PDQ::Solve(\$pdq::APPROX);
PDQ::Report();
```

6.6.15 PDQ::SetDebug

Syntax
`PDQ::SetDebug($flag);`

Description
`PDQ::SetDebug()` enables diagnostic printout of PDQ internal variables and procedures used in solving a model.

Argument	*Description*
`$flag`	Set to 1 or 0 to toggle the debug facility.

Returns None. Output is written to a file called `debug.log`.

Description
PDQ::Init()

Usage

```
PDQ::SetDebug(TRUE);
$nodes = PDQ::CreateNode("server", $pdq::CEN, $pdq::FCFS);
$streams = PDQ::CreateOpen("work", 0.5);
PDQ::SetDemand("server", "work", 1.0);
...
PDQ::SetDebug(FALSE);
```

Produces the following output in the file debug.log.

```
DEBUG: PDQ::CreateNode
        Entering
        Node[0]: CEN FCFS "server"
        Exiting
        Stream[0]:  TRANS       "work"; Lambda: 0.5
DEBUG: PDQ::SetDemand()
        Entering
DEBUG: getnode_index()
        Entering
        node:"server"  index: 0
        Exiting
```

```
DEBUG: getjob_index()
        Entering
        stream:"work"  index: 0
        Exiting
DEBUG: PDQ::SetDemand()
        Exiting
```

6.6.16 PDQ::SetDemand

Syntax

`PDQ::SetDemand($nodename, $workname, $time);`

Description

`PDQ::SetDemand()` is used to define the service demand of a specific workload. The named node and workload must exist. A separate call is required for each workload stream that accesses the same node. Note that because of the reporting structure in PDQ, use of `SetDemand` and `SetVisits` are mutually exclusive.

Argument	*Description*
`$nodename`	Name of the queueing node.
`$workname`	Name of the workload.
`$time`	Service demand due to workload `$workname`.

Returns

None.

See Also

`PDQ::CreateClosed()`, `PDQ::CreateNode()`, `PDQ::CreateOpen()`, `PDQ::SetVisits()`

Usage

```
PDQ::CreateClosed("DB_Workers", $pdq::TERM, 57.4, 31.6);
PDQ::CreateClosed("Fax_Report", $pdq::BATCH, 10.0);
...
PDQ::CreateNode("cpu", $pdq::CEN, $pdq::FCFS);
PDQ::CreateNode("cpu_dly", $pdq::CEN, $pdq::ISRV);
...
PDQ::SetDemand("cpu", "DB_Workers", 0.130);
PDQ::SetDemand("cpu_dly", "DB_Workers", 0.003);
PDQ::SetDemand("cpu", "Fax_Report", 3.122);
PDQ::SetDemand("cpu_dly", "Fax_Report", 0.001);
```

6.6.17 PDQ::SetTUnit

Syntax
`PDQ::SetTUnit($unitname);`

Description
`PDQ::SetTUnit()` changes the name of the time unit that appears in the PDQ report. The default time unit is seconds.

Argument	*Description*
`$unitname`	Name of the measurement unit.

Returns
None.

See Also
`PDQ::Report()`

Usage

```
PDQ::SetTUnit("Minutes");
```

6.6.18 PDQ::SetVisits

Syntax
`PDQ::SetVisits($nodename, $workname, $visits, $time);`

Description
`PDQ_SetVisits()` is used to define the service demand of a specific workload in terms of the explicit service time and visit count. The named node and workload must exist. A separate call is required for each workload stream that accesses the same node. The difference from `PDQ_SetDemand()` is in the way node-level performance metrics are formatted in the output from `PDQ_Report()`. The number of visits shows up in the PDQ `Model INPUTS` section and throughput in the `RESOURCE Performance` section shows up as counts per unit time. Note that because of the reporting structure in PDQ, use of `SetVisits` and `SetDemand` are mutually exclusive.

Argument	*Description*
`$nodename`	Name of queueing node.
`$workname`	Name of the workload.
`$visits`	Average number of visits to that node.
`$time`	Service time per visit by workload.

Returns
None.

See Also
PDQ::CreateClosed(), PDQ::CreateNode(), PDQ::CreateOpen(), PDQ::SetDemand()

Usage

```
$streams = PDQ::CreateClosed("DB_Workers", $pdq::TERM, 57.4, 31.6);
$nodes = PDQ::CreateNode("cpu", $pdq::CEN, $pdq::FCFS);
PDQ::SetVisits("cpu", "DB_Workers", 10.0, 0.013);
...
```

6.6.19 PDQ::SetWUnit

Syntax
PDQ::SetWUnit($unitname);

Description
PDQ::SetWUnit() changes the name of the work unit that appears in the PDQ report. The default unit of work is called *Job*.

Argument	*Description*
$unitname	Name of the measurement unit.

Returns
None.

See Also
PDQ::Report()

Usage

```
PDQ::SetWUnit("I/O_Reqs");
```

6.6.20 PDQ::Solve

Syntax
PDQ::Solve($method);

Description
PDQ::Solve() is called after the PDQ model has been created. An appropriate solution method must be passed as an argument or an error will be reported at run-time.

Argument	*Description*
$method	One of $pdq::EXACT, $pdq::APPROX or $pdq::CANON.

Returns

None.

See Also

`PDQ::Solve()`

Usage

```
PDQ::Solve($pdq::APPROX);
PDQ::Report();
```

6.7 Classic Queues in PDQ

The remaining sections of this chapter contain the actual Perl PDQ codes and resulting reports for both the single queues discussed theoretically in Chap. 2 and the circuits of queues presented in Chap. 3. Where appropriate, we use the Kendall notation of Sect. 2.9.2. The intent is to provide the reader with a broad view of the variety of applications for PDQ in analyzing computer systems. All the Perl sources can be downloaded from the PDQ section of the Web site `www.perfdynamics.com`.

6.7.1 Delay Node in PDQ

A delay node simply provides a constant service time without any queueing. One of the most common applications of a delay node in computer system performance analysis is the *think time* associated with the closed queueing circuit of Sect. 2.11.1. To set up an IS in PDQ there are two steps:

1. Create a PDQ node with service discipline `$pdq::ISRV` (see Sect. 6.5.1), instead of `$pdq::FCFS`.
2. Define the magnitude of the delay using the `SetDemand()` function.

Delay nodes are also commonly used in hardware-oriented performance analysis of the type discussed in Chap. 7.

6.7.2 $M/M/1$ in PDQ

Kendall notation (see Sect. 2.9.2):
M: Memoryless arrivals. Poisson process with rate λ
M: Memoryless service. Exponentially distributed with mean period S
1: Single server with unconstrained queue size.

Refer to the annotated PDQ model `mm1.pl` in Sect. 6.4.1.

6.7.3 $M/M/m$ in PDQ

Kendall notation (see Sect. 2.9.2):
M: Memoryless arrivals. Poisson process with rate λ
M: Memoryless service. Exponentially distributed with mean period S
m: Multiple servers each with mean utilization $\lambda S/m$

The current implementation of `PDQ::CreateMultiNode` described in Sect. 6.6.2 is evaluated using the approximation discussed in Sect. 2.7 of Chap. 2.

6.7.4 $M/M/1//N$ in PDQ

Kendall notation (see Sect. 2.9.2):
M: Memoryless arrivals. Poisson process with rate λ
M: Memoryless service. Exponentially distributed with mean period S
1: Single server.
N: Finite number of requests and finite queue length.

This is the classic single-server *repairman* model for the case $m = 1$ discussed in Sect. 2.8.3 of Chap. 2.

```
#!/usr/bin/perl
# mm1n.pl
use pdq;

# Model specific variables
$requests    = 100;
$thinktime   = 300.0;
$serviceTime = 0.63;
$nodeName    = "CPU";
$workName    = "compile";

# Initialize the model
pdq::Init("M/M/1//N Model");

# Define the queueing circuit and workload
$pdq::streams = pdq::CreateClosed($workName, $pdq::TERM, $requests,
$thinktime);

# Define the queueing node
$pdq::nodes  = pdq::CreateNode($nodeName, $pdq::CEN, $pdq::FCFS);

# Define service time for the work on that node
pdq::SetDemand($nodeName, $workName, $serviceTime);

# Solve the model
pdq::Solve($pdq::EXACT);
```

```
# Report the PDQ results
pdq::Report();
```

6.7.5 $M/M/m//N$ in PDQ

Kendall notation (see Sect. 2.9.2):
M: Memoryless arrivals. Poisson process with rate λ
M: Memoryless service. Exponentially distributed with mean period S
m: Multiple servers.
N: Finite number of requests and finite queue length.

This is the classic *repairman* model presented in Chap. 2. It can be solved in PDQ as a *load-dependent server* like the one discussed in Sect. 3.9.4, Chap. 3. The Perl code is essentially the same as `fesc.pl` in Sect. 6.7.11, so we do not reproduce it here.

6.7.6 Feedforward Circuits in PDQ

What follows is the PDQ code for the three-stage tandem circuit discussed in Sect. 3.4.2 of Chap. 3.

```
#!/usr/bin/perl
# feedforward.pl
use pdq;

$ArrivalRate = 0.10;
$WorkName = "Requests";
$NodeName1 = "Queue1";
$NodeName2 = "Queue2";
$NodeName3 = "Queue3";

pdq::Init("Feedforward Circuit");
$pdq::streams = pdq::CreateOpen($WorkName, $ArrivalRate);
$pdq::nodes = pdq::CreateNode($NodeName1, $pdq::CEN, $pdq::FCFS);
$pdq::nodes = pdq::CreateNode($NodeName2, $pdq::CEN, $pdq::FCFS);
$pdq::nodes = pdq::CreateNode($NodeName3, $pdq::CEN, $pdq::FCFS);
pdq::SetDemand($NodeName1, $WorkName, 1.0);
pdq::SetDemand($NodeName2, $WorkName, 2.0);
pdq::SetDemand($NodeName3, $WorkName, 3.0);
pdq::Solve($pdq::CANON);
pdq::Report();
```

The PDQ report looks like this.

```
        ***************************************
        ****** Pretty Damn Quick REPORT *******
        ***************************************
        ***  of : Mon Jan  5 12:38:25 2004  ***
        ***  for: Feedforward Circuit       ***
```

```
         ***  Ver: PDQ Analyzer v2.7 080202  ***
         ***************************************
         ***************************************

          ***************************************
          ******    PDQ Model INPUTS      *******
          ***************************************

Node Sched Resource   Workload   Class     Demand
---- ----- --------   --------   -----     ------
CEN  FCFS  Queue1     Requests   TRANS     1.0000
CEN  FCFS  Queue2     Requests   TRANS     2.0000
CEN  FCFS  Queue3     Requests   TRANS     3.0000

Queueing Circuit Totals:

    Streams:      1
    Nodes:        3

WORKLOAD Parameters

Source      per Sec      Demand
--------    -------      ------
Requests    0.1000       6.0000

          ***************************************
          ******   PDQ Model OUTPUTS      *******
          ***************************************

Solution Method: CANON

          ******   SYSTEM Performance     *******

Metric                        Value  Unit
-----------------             -----  ----
Workload: "Requests"
Mean Throughput          0.1000  Job/Sec
Response Time            7.8968  Sec

Bounds Analysis:
Max Demand               0.3333      Job/Sec
Max Throughput           0.3333      Job/Sec

          ******   RESOURCE Performance   *******

Metric           Resource     Work              Value   Unit
---------        ------       ----              -----   ----
Throughput       Queue1       Requests         0.1000   Job/Sec
Utilization      Queue1       Requests        10.0000   Percent
```

```
Queue Length      Queue1      Requests        0.1111   Job
Residence Time    Queue1      Requests        1.1111   Sec

Throughput        Queue2      Requests        0.1000   Job/Sec
Utilization       Queue2      Requests       20.0000   Percent
Queue Length      Queue2      Requests        0.2500   Job
Residence Time    Queue2      Requests        2.5000   Sec

Throughput        Queue3      Requests        0.1000   Job/Sec
Utilization       Queue3      Requests       30.0000   Percent
Queue Length      Queue3      Requests        0.4286   Job
Residence Time    Queue3      Requests        4.2857   Sec
```

We see that the PDQ values for the utilizations, residence times, and queue lengths are in complete agreement with those in Table 3.1 in Chap. 3.

6.7.7 Feedback Circuits in PDQ

The following PDQ model represents the feedback queue discussed in Sect. 3.4.3 of Chap. 3.

```
#! /usr/bin/perl
# feedback.pl

use pdq;

$rx_prob           = 0.30;
$inter_arriv_rate = 0.5;
$service_time      = 0.75;
$mean_visits       = 1.0 / (1.0 - $rx_prob);

# Initialize the model
pdq::Init("Open Feedback");

# Define the queueing center
$pdq::nodes = pdq::CreateNode("channel", $pdq::CEN, $pdq::FCFS);

# Define the workload and circuit type
$pdq::streams = pdq::CreateOpen("message", $inter_arriv_rate);

# Define service demand due to workload
pdq::SetVisits("channel", "message", $mean_visits, $service_time);

# Solve and generate a PDQ report
pdq::Solve($pdq::CANON);
pdq::Report();
```

The PDQ report looks like this:

```
        ***************************************
        ****** Pretty Damn Quick REPORT *******
        ***************************************
        ***  of : Tue Jan  6 11:02:24 2004  ***
        ***  for: Open Feedback             ***
        ***  Ver: PDQ Analyzer v2.7 080202  ***
        ***************************************

        ***************************************
         ******    PDQ Model INPUTS      *******
         ***************************************

Node Sched Resource   Workload  Class     Visits    Service     Demand
---- ----- --------   --------  -----     ------    -------     ------
CEN  FCFS channel    message   TRANS     1.4286     0.7500     1.0714

Queueing Circuit Totals:

    Streams:      1
    Nodes:        1

WORKLOAD Parameters

Source       per Sec       Demand
--------     -------       ------
message      0.5000        1.0714

        ***************************************
        ******   PDQ Model OUTPUTS      *******
        ***************************************

Solution Method: CANON

        ******   SYSTEM Performance     *******
Metric                        Value  Unit
-----------------             -----  ----
Workload: "message"
Mean Throughput          0.5000  Job/Sec
Response Time            2.3077  Sec

Bounds Analysis:
Max Demand               0.9333      Job/Sec
Max Throughput           0.9333      Job/Sec

        ******   RESOURCE Performance   *******
Metric           Resource      Work              Value   Unit
---------        ------        ----              -----   ----
Throughput       channel       message          0.7143   Visits/Sec
Utilization      channel       message         53.5714   Percent
```

```
50 Queue Length    channel    message         1.1538   Job
51 Residence Time  channel    message         2.3077   Sec
52 Waiting Time    channel    message         0.8654   Sec
```

We see that the residence time in the satellite telemetry channel, reported on line 51 of the PDQ report, is 2.3077 s, which agrees with the manual calculation performed in Example 3.2.

6.7.8 Parallel Queues in Series

The following PDQ queueing circuit represents the passport office discussed in Sect. 3.4.5 of Chap. 3.

```
#!/usr/bin/perl
# passport.pl

use pdq;

#### Input parameters
$ArrivalRate = 15.0 / 3600;
$WorkName = "Applicant";
$NodeName1 = "Window1";
$NodeName2 = "Window2";
$NodeName3 = "Window3";
$NodeName4 = "Window4";

#### Branching probabilities and weights
$p12 = 0.30;
$p13 = 0.70;
$p23 = 0.20;
$p32 = 0.10;

$L3 = ($p13 + $p23 * $p12) / (1 - $p23 * $p32);
$L2 = $p12 + $p32 * $w3;

#### Initialize and solve the PDQ model
pdq::Init("Passport Office");

$pdq::streams = pdq::CreateOpen($WorkName, $ArrivalRate);

$pdq::nodes   = pdq::CreateNode($NodeName1, $pdq::CEN, $pdq::FCFS);
$pdq::nodes   = pdq::CreateNode($NodeName2, $pdq::CEN, $pdq::FCFS);
$pdq::nodes   = pdq::CreateNode($NodeName3, $pdq::CEN, $pdq::FCFS);
$pdq::nodes   = pdq::CreateNode($NodeName4, $pdq::CEN, $pdq::FCFS);

pdq::SetDemand($NodeName1, $WorkName, 20);
pdq::SetDemand($NodeName2, $WorkName, 600 * $L2);
pdq::SetDemand($NodeName3, $WorkName, 300 * $L3);
pdq::SetDemand($NodeName4, $WorkName, 60);
```

```
pdq::Solve($pdq::CANON);

pdq::Report();
```

The PDQ report shows:

```
            ***************************************
            ****** Pretty Damn Quick REPORT *******
            ***************************************
            ***  of : Mon Jan  5 14:01:37 2004  ***
            ***  for: Passport Office            ***
            ***  Ver: PDQ Analyzer v2.7 080202  ***
            ***************************************
            ***************************************

            ***************************************
            ******    PDQ Model INPUTS      *******
            ***************************************

Node Sched Resource   Workload   Class     Demand
---- ----- --------   --------   -----     ------
CEN  FCFS  Window1    Applicant  TRANS    20.0000
CEN  FCFS  Window2    Applicant  TRANS   226.5306
CEN  FCFS  Window3    Applicant  TRANS   232.6531
CEN  FCFS  Window4    Applicant  TRANS    60.0000

Queueing Circuit Totals:

    Streams:        1
    Nodes:          4

WORKLOAD Parameters

Source        per Sec        Demand
--------      -------        ------
Applicant     0.0042       539.1837

            ***************************************
            ******   PDQ Model OUTPUTS      *******
            ***************************************

Solution Method: CANON

            ******   SYSTEM Performance     *******

Metric                        Value  Unit
-----------------             -----  ----
Workload: "Applicant"
Mean Throughput              0.0042  Job/Sec
```

```
Response Time         11738.1818  Sec

Bounds Analysis:
Max Demand                0.0043       Job/Sec
Max Throughput            0.0043       Job/Sec

           ******   RESOURCE Performance   *******

Metric           Resource    Work               Value   Unit
---------        ------      ----               -----   ----
Throughput       Window1     Applicant         0.0042   Job/Sec
Utilization      Window1     Applicant         8.3333   Percent
Queue Length     Window1     Applicant         0.0909   Job
Residence Time   Window1     Applicant        21.8182   Sec

Throughput       Window2     Applicant         0.0042   Job/Sec
Utilization      Window2     Applicant        94.3878   Percent
Queue Length     Window2     Applicant        16.8182   Job
Residence Time   Window2     Applicant      4036.3636   Sec

Throughput       Window3     Applicant         0.0042   Job/Sec
Utilization      Window3     Applicant        96.9388   Percent
Queue Length     Window3     Applicant        31.6667   Job
Residence Time   Window3     Applicant      7600.0000   Sec

Throughput       Window4     Applicant         0.0042   Job/Sec
Utilization      Window4     Applicant        25.0000   Percent
Queue Length     Window4     Applicant         0.3333   Job
Residence Time   Window4     Applicant        80.0000   Sec
```

From this PDQ report we see that the PDQ results are identical to those from the non-PDQ Perl program `passcalc.pl` constructed in Sect. 3.4.5 of Chap. 3.

6.7.9 Multiple Workloads in PDQ

What follows is the Perl code for the multicomponent wireless server upgrade analysis presented in Sect. 3.7 of Chap. 3. Since this PDQ model is a closed circuit, it uses the MVA algorithm incorporated into PDQ.

```
#!/usr/bin/perl
# mwl.pl

use pdq;

# ****************************************
#  Parameters from workload measurements *
# ****************************************
$maxBatJobs = 10;
```

```
$maxIntJobs = 25;
$intThink = 30;
$batThink = 0.0;
$cpuBatBusy = 600.0;
$dskBatBusy = 54.0;
$cpuIntBusy = 47.6;
$dskIntBusy = 428.4;
$batchCompletes = 600;
$interCompletes = 476;
$cpuSpeedup = 5; # CPU upgrade in relative units

$totCpuBusy = $cpuBatBusy + $cpuIntBusy;
$totDskBusy = $dskBatBusy + $dskIntBusy;
$totalCompletes = $batchCompletes + $interCompletes;
$maxAggJobs = $maxBatJobs + $maxIntJobs;
$aggThink = ($interCompletes / $totalCompletes) * $intThink;
$aggCpuDemand = $totCpuBusy / $totalCompletes;
$aggDskDemand = $totDskBusy / $totalCompletes;


# *********************************************************
#  Create and analyze models based on the aggregate workload *
# *********************************************************
pdq::Init("Aggregate BASELINE");

$pdq::nodes = pdq::CreateNode("cpu", $pdq::CEN, $pdq::FCFS);
$pdq::nodes = pdq::CreateNode("dsk", $pdq::CEN, $pdq::FCFS);
$pdq::streams = pdq::CreateClosed("aggwork", $pdq::TERM,
    $maxAggJobs, $aggThink);

pdq::SetDemand("cpu", "aggwork", $aggCpuDemand);
pdq::SetDemand("dsk", "aggwork", $aggDskDemand);

pdq::Solve($pdq::EXACT);
pdq::Report();


pdq::Init("Aggregate UPGRADE");

$pdq::nodes = pdq::CreateNode("cpu", $pdq::CEN, $pdq::FCFS);
$pdq::nodes = pdq::CreateNode("dsk", $pdq::CEN, $pdq::FCFS);
$pdq::streams = pdq::CreateClosed("aggwork", $pdq::TERM,
    $maxAggJobs, $aggThink);

pdq::SetDemand("cpu", "aggwork", $aggCpuDemand / $cpuSpeedup);
pdq::Solve($pdq::EXACT);
pdq::Report();
```

```
# ****************************************************
#  Now analyze models based on the workload components *
# ****************************************************
pdq::Init("Component BASELINE");

$pdq::nodes = pdq::CreateNode("cpu", $pdq::CEN, $pdq::FCFS);
$pdq::nodes = pdq::CreateNode("dsk", $pdq::CEN, $pdq::FCFS);
$pdq::streams = pdq::CreateClosed("batch", $pdq::BATCH,
    $maxBatJobs, $batThink);

pdq::SetDemand("cpu", "batch", $cpuBatBusy / $batchCompletes);
pdq::SetDemand("dsk", "batch", $dskBatBusy / $batchCompletes);

$pdq::streams = pdq::CreateClosed("online", $pdq::TERM,
    $maxIntJobs, $intThink);
pdq::SetDemand("cpu", "online", $cpuIntBusy / $interCompletes);
pdq::SetDemand("dsk", "online", $dskIntBusy / $interCompletes);

pdq::Solve($pdq::EXACT);
pdq::Report();


pdq::Init("Component UPGRADE");

$pdq::nodes = pdq::CreateNode("cpu", $pdq::CEN, $pdq::FCFS);
$pdq::nodes = pdq::CreateNode("dsk", $pdq::CEN, $pdq::FCFS);

$pdq::streams = pdq::CreateClosed("batch", $pdq::BATCH,
    $maxBatJobs, $batThink);
pdq::SetDemand("cpu", "batch",
    ($cpuBatBusy / $batchCompletes) / $cpuSpeedup);
pdq::SetDemand("dsk", "batch", $dskBatBusy / $batchCompletes);

$pdq::streams = pdq::CreateClosed("online", $pdq::TERM,
    $maxIntJobs, $intThink);
pdq::SetDemand("cpu", "online",
    ($cpuIntBusy / $interCompletes) / $cpuSpeedup);
pdq::SetDemand("dsk", "online", $dskIntBusy / $interCompletes);

pdq::Solve($pdq::EXACT);
pdq::Report();
```

The PDQ report that follows (mwlbase_agg.rpt) is for the baseline model with an aggregated workload parameterized in Table 3.3 of Sect. 3.7.3.

```
        ***************************************
        ****** Pretty Damn Quick REPORT *******
        ***************************************
        ***  of : Fri Jun 18 08:37:58 2004  ***
        ***  for: Aggregate BASELINE        ***
```

```
      ***  Ver: PDQ Analyzer v2.8 120803  ***
      ***************************************
      ***************************************

      ***************************************
      ******    PDQ Model INPUTS      *******
      ***************************************

Node Sched Resource   Workload   Class     Demand
---- ----- --------   --------   -----     ------
CEN  FCFS  cpu        aggwork    TERML     0.6019
CEN  FCFS  dsk        aggwork    TERML     0.4483

Queueing Circuit Totals:

 Clients:    35.00
 Streams:      1
 Nodes:        2

WORKLOAD Parameters

Client       Number       Demand   Thinktime
----         ------       ------   ---------
aggwork       35.00        1.0502    13.27

      ***************************************
      ******   PDQ Model OUTPUTS      *******
      ***************************************

Solution Method: EXACT

      ******   SYSTEM Performance     *******

Metric                      Value  Unit
-----------------           -----  ----
Workload: "aggwork"
Mean Throughput           1.6373      Job/Sec
Response Time             8.1056      Sec
Mean Concurrency         13.2711      Job
Stretch Factor            7.7182

Bounds Analysis:
Max Throughput        1.6615      Job/Sec
Min Response          1.0502      Sec
Max Demand            0.6019      Sec
Tot Demand            1.0502      Sec
Think time           13.2714      Sec
Optimal Clients      23.7956      Clients

```

```
55       ******    RESOURCE Performance    *******
56
57 Metric              Resource     Work               Value    Unit
58 ---------           ------       ----               -----    ----
59 Throughput          cpu          aggwork           1.6373    Job/Sec
60 Utilization         cpu          aggwork          98.5410    Percent
61 Queue Length        cpu          aggwork          10.6855    Job
62 Residence Time      cpu          aggwork           6.5264    Sec
63
64 Throughput          dsk          aggwork           1.6373    Job/Sec
65 Utilization         dsk          aggwork          73.4036    Percent
66 Queue Length        dsk          aggwork           2.5855    Job
67 Residence Time      dsk          aggwork           1.5792    Sec
```

The pertinent values of the aggregate throughput and response time can be read off from lines 42 and 43, respectively. The next PDQ report (`mwlbase_cmp.rpt`) is for the baseline model using the parameters for the component workloads in Table 3.4 of Sect. 3.7.4.

```
        ***************************************
        ****** Pretty Damn Quick REPORT *******
        ***************************************
        ***  of : Fri Jun 18 08:37:58 2004  ***
        ***  for: Component BASELINE         ***
        ***  Ver: PDQ Analyzer v2.8 120803  ***
        ***************************************
        ***************************************

        ***************************************
        ******     PDQ Model INPUTS     *******
        ***************************************

Node Sched Resource   Workload   Class     Demand
---- ----- --------   --------   -----     ------
CEN  FCFS  cpu        batch      BATCH     1.0000
CEN  FCFS  dsk        batch      BATCH     0.0900
CEN  FCFS  cpu        online     TERML     0.1000
CEN  FCFS  dsk        online     TERML     0.9000

Queueing Circuit Totals:
 Jobs:        10.00
 Clients:     25.00
 Streams:       2
 Nodes:         2

WORKLOAD Parameters
Job             MPL       Demand
---             ---       ------
batch         10.00       1.0900

```

```
Client       Number       Demand   Thinktime
----         ------       ------   ---------
online        25.00       1.0000     30.00

     ***************************************
     ******   PDQ Model OUTPUTS      *******
     ***************************************

Solution Method: EXACT

     ******   SYSTEM Performance     *******

Metric                      Value   Unit
-----------------           -----   ----
Workload: "batch"
Mean Throughput             0.9265  Job/Sec
Response Time              10.7937  Sec
Mean Concurrency           10.0000  Job
Stretch Factor              9.9025

Bounds Analysis:
Max Throughput              1.0000  Job/Sec
Min Response                1.0900  Sec
Max Demand                  1.0000  Sec
Tot Demand                  1.0900  Sec
Optimal Jobs                1.0900  Jobs

Workload: "online"
Mean Throughput             0.7353  Job/Sec
Response Time               3.9978  Sec
Mean Concurrency            2.9397  Job
Stretch Factor              3.9978

Bounds Analysis:
Max Throughput              1.1111  Job/Sec
Min Response                1.0000  Sec
Max Demand                  0.9000  Sec
Tot Demand                  1.0000  Sec
Think time                 30.0000  Sec
Optimal Clients            34.4444  Clients

     ******   RESOURCE Performance   *******

Metric          Resource     Work               Value   Unit
---------       ------       ----               -----   ----
Throughput      cpu          batch             0.9265   Job/Sec
Utilization     cpu          batch            92.6466   Percent
Queue Length    cpu          batch             9.7173   Job
Residence Time  cpu          batch            10.4886   Sec
```

```
81 Throughput      dsk          batch           0.9265   Job/Sec
82 Utilization     dsk          batch           8.3382   Percent
83 Queue Length    dsk          batch           0.2827   Job
84 Residence Time  dsk          batch           0.3051   Sec
85
86 Throughput      cpu          online          0.7353   Job/Sec
87 Utilization     cpu          online          7.3534   Percent
88 Queue Length    cpu          online          0.8496   Job
89 Residence Time  cpu          online          1.1553   Sec
90
91 Throughput      dsk          online          0.7353   Job/Sec
92 Utilization     dsk          online         66.1808   Percent
93 Queue Length    dsk          online          2.0902   Job
94 Residence Time  dsk          online          2.8424   Sec
```

The batch throughput and response time can be read off respectively from lines 47 and 48, while the online throughput and response time appear respectively on lines 60 and 61.

6.7.10 Priority Queueing in PDQ

This is the Perl code that compares priority queueing using the virtual server approximation presented in Sect. 3.9.3.

```
#!/usr/bin/perl
# shadowcpu.pl
use pdq;

$PRIORITY = 1;  # Turn priority queueing on or off
$noPri = "CPU Scheduler with No Priority";
$priOn = "CPU Scheduler with Priority On";

sub GetProdU {
   pdq::Init(""); # Don't need a name string here
   $pdq::streams = pdq::CreateClosed("Production", $pdq::TERM, 20.0, 20.
   $pdq::nodes   = pdq::CreateNode("CPU", $pdq::CEN, $pdq::FCFS);
   $pdq::nodes   = pdq::CreateNode("DK1", $pdq::CEN, $pdq::FCFS);
   $pdq::nodes   = pdq::CreateNode("DK2", $pdq::CEN, $pdq::FCFS);
   pdq::SetDemand("CPU", "Production", 0.30);
   pdq::SetDemand("DK1", "Production", 0.08);
   pdq::SetDemand("DK2", "Production", 0.10);

   pdq::Solve($pdq::APPROX);
   return(pdq::GetUtilization("CPU", "Production", $pdq::TERM));
}

if ( $PRIORITY ) {
    $Ucpu_prod = GetProdU();
}
```

```
pdq::Init(PRIORITY ? $priOn : $noPri);


#### Workloads
$pdq::streams = pdq::CreateClosed("Production", $pdq::TERM, 20.0, 20.0);
$pdq::streams = pdq::CreateClosed("Developmnt", $pdq::TERM, 15.0, 15.0);

#### Nodes
$pdq::nodes = pdq::CreateNode("CPU", $pdq::CEN, $pdq::FCFS);

if (PRIORITY) {
    $pdq::nodes = pdq::CreateNode("shadCPU", $pdq::CEN, $pdq::FCFS);
}
$pdq::nodes = pdq::CreateNode("DK1", $pdq::CEN, $pdq::FCFS);
$pdq::nodes = pdq::CreateNode("DK2", $pdq::CEN, $pdq::FCFS);

#### Service demands
pdq::SetDemand("CPU", "Production", 0.30);

if ($PRIORITY) {
    pdq::SetDemand("shadCPU", "Developmnt", 1.00/(1 - $Ucpu_prod));
} else {
    pdq::SetDemand("CPU", "Developmnt", 1.00);
}

pdq::SetDemand("DK1", "Production", 0.08);
pdq::SetDemand("DK1", "Developmnt", 0.05);
pdq::SetDemand("DK2", "Production", 0.10);
pdq::SetDemand("DK2", "Developmnt", 0.06);

pdq::Solve($pdq::APPROX);

pdq::Report();
```

What follows is the PDQ report for the case of preemptive queueing.

```
***************************************
****** Pretty Damn Quick REPORT *******
***************************************
***  of : Fri May  3 18:48:31 2002  ***
***  for: CPU Scheduler - No Pri    ***
***  Rel: PDQ Analyzer v2.6 032202  ***
***************************************
***************************************

 ***************************************
 ******    PDQ Model INPUTS     *******
 ***************************************
```

```
Node Sched Resource   Workload   Class     Demand
---- ----- --------   --------   -----     ------
CEN  FCFS  CPU        Production TERML     0.3000
CEN  FCFS  DK1        Production TERML     0.0800
CEN  FCFS  DK2        Production TERML     0.1000
CEN  FCFS  CPU        Developmnt TERML     1.0000
CEN  FCFS  DK1        Developmnt TERML     0.0500
CEN  FCFS  DK2        Developmnt TERML     0.0600

Queueing Circuit Totals:

    Generators: 35.00
    Streams   :   2
    Nodes     :   3

WORKLOAD Parameters

Gens          Number       Demand   Thinktime
----          ------       ------   ---------
Production     20.00        0.4800    20.00
Developmnt     15.00        1.1100    15.00

        ***************************************
        ******   PDQ Model OUTPUTS      *******
        ***************************************

Solution Method: APPROX (Iterations: 15; Accuracy: 0.1000%)

        ******   SYSTEM Performance     *******

Metric                       Value  Unit
-----------------            -----  ----
Workload: "Production"
Mean Throughput         0.8813      Job/Sec
Response Time           2.6944      Sec
Mean Concurrency        2.3745      Job
Stretch Factor          5.6134
Bounds Analysis:
Max Throughput          3.3333      Job/Sec
Min Response            0.4800      Sec

Workload: "Developmnt"
Mean Throughput         0.6468      Job/Sec
Response Time           8.1914      Sec
Mean Concurrency        5.2981      Job
Stretch Factor          7.3796
Bounds Analysis:
Max Throughput          1.0000      Job/Sec
Min Response            1.1100      Sec
```

```
62
63          ******   RESOURCE Performance   *******
64
65 Metric          Resource     Work              Value    Unit
66 ---------       ------       ----              -----    ----
67 Throughput      CPU          Production       0.8813    Job/Sec
68 Utilization     CPU          Production      26.4382    Percent
69 Queue Length    CPU          Production       2.1958    Job
70 Residence Time  CPU          Production       2.4916    Sec
71
72 Throughput      DK1          Production       0.8813    Job/Sec
73 Utilization     DK1          Production       7.0502    Percent
74 Queue Length    DK1          Production       0.0783    Job
75 Residence Time  DK1          Production       0.0888    Sec
76
77 Throughput      DK2          Production       0.8813    Job/Sec
78 Utilization     DK2          Production       8.8127    Percent
79 Queue Length    DK2          Production       0.1004    Job
80 Residence Time  DK2          Production       0.1140    Sec
81
82 Throughput      CPU          Developmnt       0.6468    Job/Sec
83 Utilization     CPU          Developmnt      64.6792    Percent
84 Queue Length    CPU          Developmnt       5.2179    Job
85 Residence Time  CPU          Developmnt       8.0673    Sec
86
87 Throughput      DK1          Developmnt       0.6468    Job/Sec
88 Utilization     DK1          Developmnt       3.2340    Percent
89 Queue Length    DK1          Developmnt       0.0360    Job
90 Residence Time  DK1          Developmnt       0.0556    Sec
91
92 Throughput      DK2          Developmnt       0.6468    Job/Sec
93 Utilization     DK2          Developmnt       3.8808    Percent
94 Queue Length    DK2          Developmnt       0.0443    Job
95 Residence Time  DK2          Developmnt       0.0685    Sec
```

The response times of interest are on lines 47 and 56, respectively, of the PDQ report. The next PDQ report is for the case where the *Production* workload is given explicit priority over *Development*.

```
1          ***************************************
2          ****** Pretty Damn Quick REPORT *******
3          ***************************************
4          ***  of : Fri May  3 18:49:41 2002  ***
5          ***  for: CPU Scheduler - Pri On    ***
6          ***  Rel: PDQ Analyzer v2.6 032202  ***
7          ***************************************
8          ***************************************
```

```

         ***************************************
         ******    PDQ Model INPUTS      *******
         ***************************************

Node Sched Resource   Workload   Class     Demand
---- ----- --------   --------   -----     ------
CEN  FCFS  CPU        Production TERML     0.3000
CEN  FCFS  shadCPU    Production TERML     0.0000
CEN  FCFS  DK1        Production TERML     0.0800
CEN  FCFS  DK2        Production TERML     0.1000

CEN  FCFS  CPU        Developmnt TERML     0.0000
CEN  FCFS  shadCPU    Developmnt TERML     1.4106
CEN  FCFS  DK1        Developmnt TERML     0.0500
CEN  FCFS  DK2        Developmnt TERML     0.0600

Queueing Circuit Totals:

    Generators: 35.00
    Streams   :   2
    Nodes     :   4

WORKLOAD Parameters

Gens           Number        Demand   Thinktime
----           ------        ------   ---------
Production      20.00         0.4800    20.00
Developmnt      15.00         1.5206    15.00

         ***************************************
         ******    PDQ Model OUTPUTS     *******
         ***************************************

Solution Method: APPROX (Iterations: 13; Accuracy: 0.1000%)

         ******    SYSTEM Performance    *******

Metric                          Value   Unit
-----------------               -----   ----
Workload: "Production"
Mean Throughput             0.9700      Job/Sec
Response Time               0.6190      Sec
Mean Concurrency            0.6004      Job
Stretch Factor              1.2896
Bounds Analysis:
Max Throughput              3.3333      Job/Sec
Min Response                0.4800      Sec

```

```
58 Workload: "Developmnt"
59 Mean Throughput          0.6340      Job/Sec
60 Response Time            8.6611      Sec
61 Mean Concurrency         5.4907      Job
62 Stretch Factor           5.6957
63 Bounds Analysis:
64 Max Throughput           0.7089      Job/Sec
65 Min Response             1.5206      Sec
66
67         ******   RESOURCE Performance   *******
68
69 Metric           Resource      Work              Value    Unit
70 ---------        ------        ----              -----    ----
71 Throughput       CPU           Production       0.9700    Job/Sec
72 Utilization      CPU           Production      29.0993    Percent
73 Queue Length     CPU           Production       0.4022    Job
74 Residence Time   CPU           Production       0.4146    Sec
75
76 Throughput       DK1           Production       0.9700    Job/Sec
77 Utilization      DK1           Production       7.7598    Percent
78 Queue Length     DK1           Production       0.0867    Job
79 Residence Time   DK1           Production       0.0894    Sec
80
81 Throughput       DK2           Production       0.9700    Job/Sec
82 Utilization      DK2           Production       9.6998    Percent
83 Queue Length     DK2           Production       0.1115    Job
84 Residence Time   DK2           Production       0.1150    Sec
85
86 Throughput       shadCPU       Developmnt       0.6340    Job/Sec
87 Utilization      shadCPU       Developmnt      89.4276    Percent
88 Queue Length     shadCPU       Developmnt       5.4114    Job
89 Residence Time   shadCPU       Developmnt       8.5360    Sec
90
91 Throughput       DK1           Developmnt       0.6340    Job/Sec
92 Utilization      DK1           Developmnt       3.1698    Percent
93 Queue Length     DK1           Developmnt       0.0355    Job
94 Residence Time   DK1           Developmnt       0.0560    Sec
95
96 Throughput       DK2           Developmnt       0.6340    Job/Sec
97 Utilization      DK2           Developmnt       3.8037    Percent
98 Queue Length     DK2           Developmnt       0.0438    Job
99 Residence Time   DK2           Developmnt       0.0691    Sec
```

The relevant response times appear on lines 51 and 60, respectively, of the PDQ report. As summarized in Table 3.6, the response times confirm that *Production* can be given higher priority to meet subsecond SLA requirements while impacting *Development* in only a minimal way.

The `Stretch Factor` reported on lines 53 and 62 (above) is the ratio of the system response time under load to the system response time when it is uncontended (i.e., no queueing). For a single queue, the stretch factor is simply the ratio of the residence time R to the service time S.

6.7.11 Load-Dependent Servers in PDQ

We present the detailed code for PDQ models with load-dependent servers, such as the threads model of Sect. 3.9.4. The example presented here is for the *memory-constrained* time-share system presented in Lazowska et al. [1984, Sect. 9.3]. We consider that model in order to check the correctness of our PDQ representation.

Consider the closed queueing circuit shown in Fig. 6.3. It contains a waiting line connected to a server with an arrow through it. In Chap. 3 we learned that such a server has a service rate that is dependent on the length of the waiting line. In the case of Fig. 6.3, the load dependency is associated with

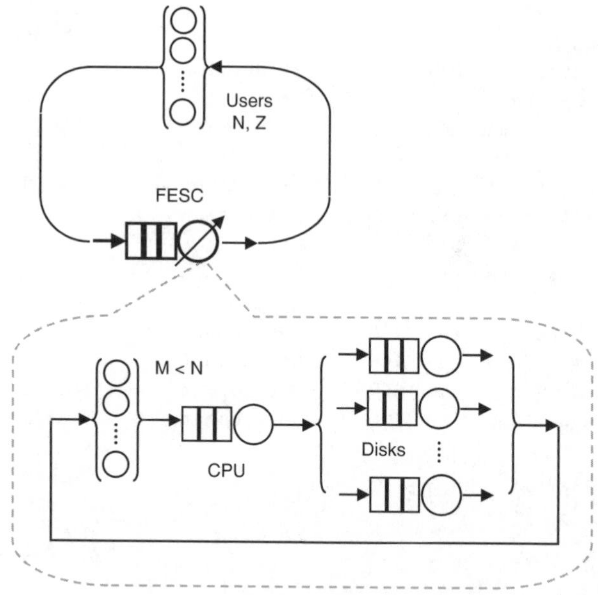

Fig. 6.3. Flow-equivalent service center model of a memory-constrained computer system

the finite number of requests that can be serviced by the memory subsystem bounded by the dotted line in the diagram.

There are N users making requests to the time-share computer, but only a maximum number ($M < N$) are permitted to access the finite size memory resource. When the maximum occupancy M is reached in the memory subsystem, all other user requests must remain waiting outside the region marked by the dotted line until that resource is freed by the departure of a serviced request. The waiting requests enqueue at the waiting line attached to the load-dependent server with the arrow in Fig. 6.3. Since that queue does not conform to the BCMP rules in Sect. 3.8.2, this queueing circuit is not formally *separable*, and therefore cannot be solved using PDQ in the usual way. How are we to approach the problem of a queueing circuit that does not fulfill the conditions for separability?

The solution is quite easy to understand if we approach it from a programming standpoint. The memory-limited subsystem (in the exploded view) is represented and solved as a separate Perl subroutine in PDQ. We think of all of the queueing centers in the subcircuit as acting like a *single server* for those requests waiting outside the subcircuit. It is as though we literally short out the subcircuit that will act as the server, solve it separately, then reconnect it and solve the composite system with the load-dependent server. This is the queueing circuit equivalent of *Norton's theorem* for passive electrical circuits [Jain 1990, Chap. 36], and is known in queueing theory as the *Chandy–Herzog–Woo theorem*. This is another reason we have adopted the term queueing *circuit* rather than the more conventional queueing *network*.

```
#!/usr/bin/perl
# fesc.pl

use pdq;

# Model parameters
$USERS = 15;
$pq[0][0] = 1.0;
$max_pgm = 3;
$think   = 60.0;

#  Composite (FESC) Model
$pq   = []; # joint probability dsn.
$sm_x = []; # throughput characteristic of memory submodel

mem_model($USERS, $max_pgm); # Call the submodel first

for ($n = 1; $n <= $USERS; $n++) {
   $R = 0.0;  # reset
   # Response time at the FESC
   for ($j = 1; $j <= $n; $j++) {
      $R += ($j / ($sm_x[$j]) *
        $pq[$j - 1][$n - 1]);
   }
   # Thruput and queue-length at the FESC
   $xn = $n / ($think + $R);
   $qlength = $xn * $R;

   # Compute queue-length distribution at the FESC
```

```
    for ($j = 1; $j <= $n; $j++) {
       $pq[$j][$n] = ($xn / $sm_x[$j]) *
         $pq[$j - 1][$n - 1];
    }
    $pq[0][$n] = 1.0;

    for ($j = 1; $j <= $n; $j++) {
       $pq[0][$n] -= $pq[$j][$n];
    }
}

#  Memory-limited Submodel
sub mem_model
{
   my ($n, $m) = @_;
   $x = 0.0;

   for ($i = 1; $i <= $n; $i++) {
      if ($i <= $m) {
         pdq::Init("");
         $pdq::nodes = pdq::CreateNode("CPU",
            $pdq::CEN, $pdq::FCFS);
         $pdq::nodes = pdq::CreateNode("DK1",
            $pdq::CEN, $pdq::FCFS);
         $pdq::nodes = pdq::CreateNode("DK2",
            $pdq::CEN, $pdq::FCFS);
         $pdq::streams = pdq::CreateClosed("work",
            $pdq::BATCH, $i);
         pdq::SetDemand("CPU", "work", 3.0);
         pdq::SetDemand("DK1", "work", 4.0);
         pdq::SetDemand("DK2", "work", 2.0);
         pdq::Solve($pdq::EXACT);
         $x = pdq::GetThruput($pdq::TERM, "work");
         $sm_x[$i] = $x; # use current value
      } else {
         $sm_x[$i] = $x; # use last computed value
      }
   }

}  # end of mem_model

#  Report selected FESC metrics
printf("\n");
printf("Max Tasks: %2d\n", $USERS);
printf("X at FESC: %3.4f\n", $xn);
printf("R at FESC: %3.2f\n", $R);
printf("Q at FESC: %3.2f\n\n", $qlength);

# Joint Probability Distribution
```

```
printf("QLength\t\tP(j | n)\n");
printf("-------\t\t--------\n");

for ($n = 0; $n <= $USERS; $n++) {
    printf(" %2d\t\tp(%2d|%2d): %3.4f\n",
     $n, $n, $USERS, $pq[$n][$USERS]);
}
```

The throughput characteristic of the isolated subcircuit is solved as a subroutine (called `sub mem_model`) for each of the $n \leq M$ permitted customers. This memory-limited subcircuit throughput characteristic, shown schematically in Fig. 6.4, is then used as the n-dependent service rate in the high-level model. Since the service rate now depends on the number of permitted customers

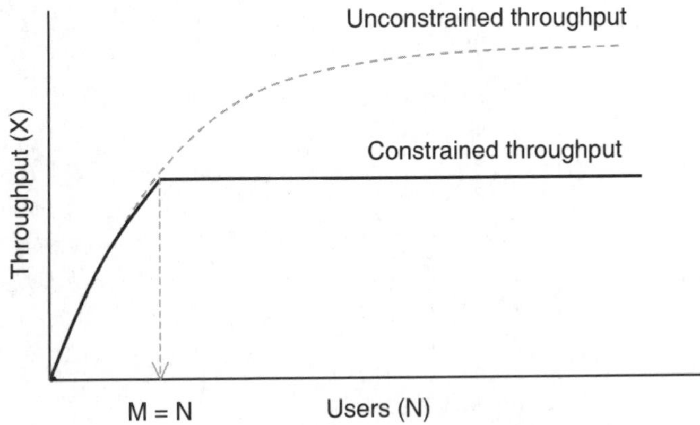

Fig. 6.4. FESC throughput characteristic for the memory-constrained time-share system

$n \leq M$ in the memory-limited subcircuit, it is as though we have replaced the complex server circuit with a single load-dependent server in Fig. 3.26. Moreover, since we calculate the load-dependent server throughput characteristic explicitly, it is known as a *flow-equivalent service center* or *FESC*, denoted by the arrow through the server in the composite model.

Example 6.1. Consider a multitasking PC with one CPU, two disks and 512 MB of RAM. An average 100 MB task requires 3 CPU-seconds, 4 ms of service at one disk and 2 ms at the other. The operating system requires 150 MB, so that at most 3 tasks can be resident simultaneously in memory. There are a maximum number of 15 task threads available, and the think-time between task initiation is 60 ms. Running the program `fesc.pl` with these parameters produces the following results:

```
Max Tasks: 15
X at FESC: 0.1750
R at FESC: 25.70
Q at FESC: 4.50
```

The average queue at the FESC contains 4.5 tasks. □

At a slightly more detailed level, we need to concern ourselves with the *queue length distribution* associated with the waiting line outside the subcircuit. Unlike most of the other PDQ models we have considered so far, calculating the *mean* queue length is simply no longer sufficient. This is the price we must pay to solve what is otherwise a nonseparable queueing circuit. So, to accurately model the queueing subcircuit with a FESC, we need to know the queue length with $n \leq N$ customers in the composite system.

The PDQ model `fesc.pl` also reports the queue length at the FESC and the corresponding joint probability distribution as:

```
QLength      P(j | n)
-------      --------
   0         p( 0|15): 0.0381
   1         p( 1|15): 0.0857
   2         p( 2|15): 0.1222
   3         p( 3|15): 0.1372
   4         p( 4|15): 0.1422
   5         p( 5|15): 0.1350
   6         p( 6|15): 0.1166
   7         p( 7|15): 0.0907
   8         p( 8|15): 0.0626
   9         p( 9|15): 0.0379
  10         p(10|15): 0.0196
  11         p(11|15): 0.0085
  12         p(12|15): 0.0029
  13         p(13|15): 0.0008
  14         p(14|15): 0.0001
  15         p(15|15): 0.0000
```

which is in precise agreement with Table 9.6 of Lazowska et al. [1984, Sect. 9.3]. It tells us that 3.81% of the time the memory submodel is idle, 8.57% of the time there is a single active task, and 12.22% of the time there are two active tasks. The remainder of the time (75.40%) there are three or more tasks ready. Consequently, there are:

$$(0.0381 \times 1) + (0.0857 \times 2) + (0.7540 \times 3) = 2.592 \tag{6.2}$$

active tasks, on average, in the memory submodel.

Example 6.2. Using these results, we can determine the memory access time. We have that $X = 0.1750$ from `fesc.pl` and $N_{\text{mem}} = 2.592$ from (6.2). Writing Little's law (2.14) as $N_{\text{mem}} = XR_{\text{mem}}$, we find the time spent in the memory sub-model is:

$$R_{\text{mem}} = \frac{2.592}{0.1750} = 14.81 \text{ ms} .$$

Since we have already calculated the task response time as 25.70 ms at the high-level composite model, we conclude that a tasks must wait for $25.70 - 14.81 = 10.89$ ms to access memory. □

The reader should be aware that a FESC is not the only algorithm to accommodate the constraint of a finite size queue or buffer. Another approach is to construct a hybrid model where the finite states are computed using the appropriate Markov chain [Trivedi 2000, Ajmone-Marsan et al. 1990]. This approach works best when the number of buffer states is relatively small.

Having demonstrated the basic concept of load-dependent servers in PDQ, we shall apply it to PDQ models of multicomputer performance in Chap. 7 and Web application performance in Chap. 10.

6.7.12 Bounds Analysis with PDQ

This is the Perl code for the bounds analysis presented in Chap. 5.

```
#!/usr/bin/perl
# florida.pl
use pdq;

$STEP = 100;
$MAXUSERS = 3000;
$think = 10;          #seconds
$srvt1 = 0.0050;      #seconds
$srvt2 = 0.0035;      #seconds
$srvt3 = 0.0020;      #seconds
$Dmax = $srvt1;
$Rmin = $srvt1 + $srvt2 + $srvt3;

# print the header ...
printf("%5s\t%6s\t%6s\t%6s\t%5s\t%6s\t%6s\t%6s\n",
    "  N  ", "  X  ", "  Xlin ", " Xmax ",
    "  N  ", "  R  ", "  Rmin ", " Rinf ");

# iterate up to $MAXUSERS ...
for ($users = 1; $users <= $MAXUSERS; $users++) {
    pdq::Init("Florida Model");
    $pdq::streams = pdq::CreateClosed("benchload",
        $pdq::TERM, $users, $think);
    $pdq::nodes  = pdq::CreateNode("Node1", $pdq::CEN, $pdq::FCFS);
    $pdq::nodes  = pdq::CreateNode("Node2", $pdq::CEN, $pdq::FCFS);
    $pdq::nodes  = pdq::CreateNode("Node3", $pdq::CEN, $pdq::FCFS);
    pdq::SetDemand("Node1", "benchload", $srvt1);
    pdq::SetDemand("Node2", "benchload", $srvt2);
    pdq::SetDemand("Node3", "benchload", $srvt3);
```

```
    pdq::Solve($pdq::APPROX);

    if ( ($users == 1) or ($users % $STEP == 0) ) {
        # print as TAB separated columns ...

        printf("%5d\t%6.2f\t%6.2f\t%6.2f\t%5d\t%6.2f\t%6.2f\t%6.2f\n",
            $users,
            pdq::GetThruput($pdq::TERM, "benchload"),
            $users / ($Rmin + $think),
            1 / $Dmax,
            $users,
            pdq::GetResponse($pdq::TERM, "benchload"),
            $Rmin,
            ($users * $Dmax) - $think
        );
    }
}
```

6.8 Review

All the performance models discussed in this book are constructed using the Perl PDQ module described in this chapter. The open-source PDQ software can be downloaded from www.perfdynamics.com. The mathematical background for this chapter is presented in Chaps. 2 and 3.

Exercises

6.1. Build and solve an $M/M/1$ model in PDQ using the following parameters:

Parameter	Value
$MeasurePeriod	7200 s
$ArrivalCount	3450
$ServiceVisits	12.25
$ServiceTime	0.010 s

6.2. Build and solve a PDQ model for a computer system comprising a CPU and two disks running three workload streams, two online and one batch, with the following parameters:

Stream	N	Z	Node	Demand
OnlineA	5	20	CPU	0.50 s
OnlineA	5	20	DK1	0.04 s
OnlineA	5	20	DK2	0.06 s
OnlineB	10	30	CPU	0.40 s
OnlineB	10	30	DK1	0.20 s
OnlineB	10	30	DK2	0.30 s
Batch	5	0	CPU	1.20 s
Batch	5	0	DK1	0.05 s
Batch	5	0	DK2	0.06 s

7

Multicomputer Analysis with PDQ

7.1 Introduction

In this chapter we turn to the subclass of multicomputer architectures known as *symmetric multiprocessors* (SMP). Because of their intrinsic economy, expandability, performance, and reliability, SMPs have found their way into a wide range of applications. In particular, commercial applications, and that is the focus of this chapter. Distinct from scientific requirements, the emphasis in the commercial arena is on high levels of coarse-grain concurrency rather than fine-grain parallelism.

In terms of queueing circuit models, we shall see how the time-share model of N users queueing to access a CPU or a central computing resource (the closed queueing circuit in Sect. 3.9.1 of Chap. 3 can be "inverted" to construct a model of a multiprocessor computer. The notion is a simple one: the N users become N processors, and the queueing center represents a shared-memory bus rather than a CPU. The think-time then, becomes the mean execution time between memory requests across the bus. The same SMP queueing-circuit paradigm can be used to assess the performance of clusters of SMPs [Buyya 1999], and distributed-memory SMPs, such as non-uniform memory architectures (NUMA) [Westall and Geist 1997].

In this chapter you will see how to apply PDQ to the performance analysis of symmetric multiprocessors (SMPs) and distributed multicomputer clusters. For SMPs, caching effects and cache protocols can be a significant determinant for performance and scalability. This is particularly true for workloads that involve shared writeable data, e.g., online transaction processing databases.

Later in this chapter, you will learn that for read-intensive workloads, e.g., data mining or decision support, multicomputer clusters offer better response time performance than SMPs. Since the data is not being updated, previously read data can be cached and queries can be processed in parallel across a striped database. The optimal back-end parallel configuration can be determine by examining the saturation throughput for each configuration.

7.2 Multiprocessor Architectures

We saw in Chap. 2 that under the same conditions the fastest available uniprocessor offered the highest performance. Unfortunately, the fastest available uniprocessor is also likely to use the most expensive technology, e.g., bipolar logic. There may also be other technical limitations to the fastest technology such as packaging and cooling.

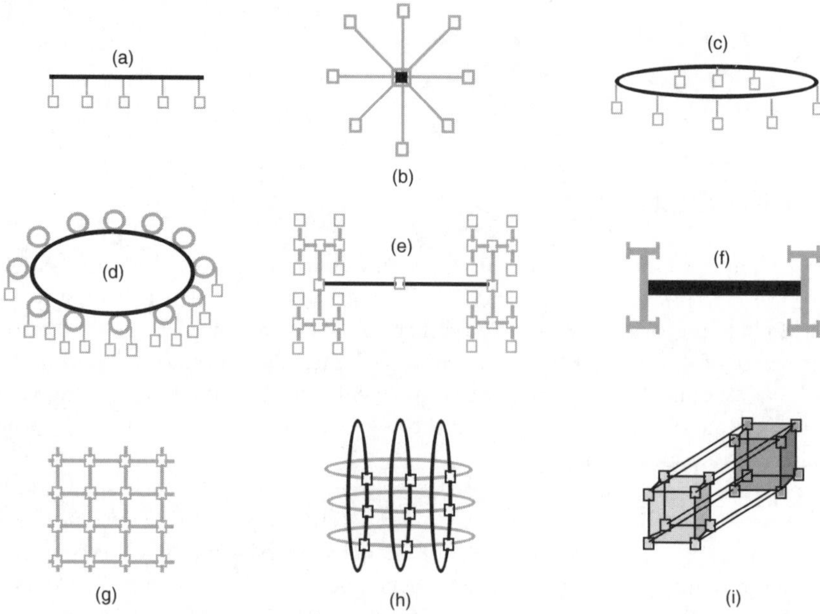

Fig. 7.1. Schematic representation of some commonly used multicomputer interconnect topologies: (a) linear bus, (b) crossbar, (c) ring, (d) hierarchical ring, (e) binary tree, (f) fat tree, (g) mesh, (h) 2-dimensional torus, (i) 4-dimensional hypercube. Computing nodes are depicted as squares

There is clearly an economy of scale that attends when multiple, relatively cheap, processors can be directed at a workload rather than being limited to a single processor. The real problem is how to combine these multiple processors into a useful computing machine. At the hardware level there is a large variety of topologies (Fig. 7.1) available to provide an interconnection between processors and storage [Gunther 2000a, Chap. 5].

At the software level, one of the most effective solutions is supported by having the multiple processors share a common global memory. This leads to the multiple instruction multiple data (MIMD) subclass of multicomputers in Fig. 7.2. The run-time environment can be made to look the same as it would on a uniprocessor, and neither the programmer nor the application

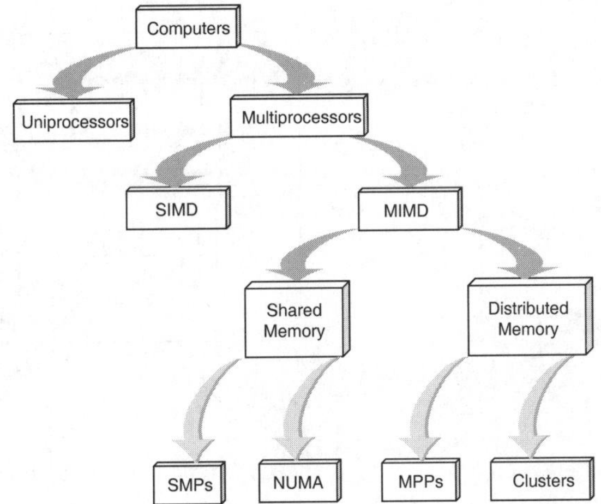

Fig. 7.2. A taxonomy of multicomputer architectures

need be aware of which CPU the program will run on at any time. The is the meaning of "symmetric" in SMP. Standard programming paradigms remain largely intact so that applications require only minimal modification to run on an SMP.

7.2.1 Symmetric Multiprocessors

The classic SMP has a single shared-memory bus like that depicted in Fig. 7.3(a). Typical commercial SMP architectures now have multiple memory buses like that depicted in Fig. 7.3(b) that can enhance memory throughput. They can also be combined with multiple operating system images to achieve a cost-effective form of high availability.

Simply adding more processors to the memory bus consumes bus bandwidth dramatically. Also processor speeds are usually much higher than memory and bus speeds (see Table 1.1). These problem can be alleviated via the use of memory subsystems that are more local to the processor. These memories are called caches. The proximity of the cache to the CPU is sometimes called its level, e.g., a level-one (L1) cache is closest to the CPU and is often included on the microprocessor chip. A level-two (L2) cache sits between the L1 cache and the bus. It has been demonstrated that higher levels of caching do not significantly improve the price–performance metric.

Processor caches may store data and instructions separately or together, the latter often being referred to as a *unified* cache. The presence of caches leads to a number of architectural performance determinants. The local memories improve access times if the necessary data (or instructions) are present. The relative speed of the processor, the cache size, and the locality of memory references in the code all conspire to determine overall performance. If

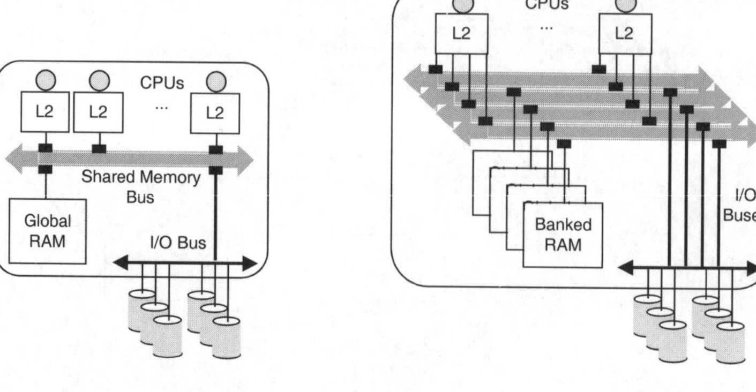

(a) Single memory bus interconnect

(b) Multiple memory bus interconnect

Fig. 7.3. Typical SMP memory bus architectures. (a) A single shared-memory bus with second-level cache memories and a separate I/O subsystem. (b) Banked or interleaved memory busses

the cache is too small or the reference locality is poor, then the number of references that must be passed to main memory will be high and little will be achieved with respect to reducing bus utilization. In a multiprocessor system, since each CPU has its own cache or caches, any references that have been copied to caches must be kept consistent with each other and with main memory. This house keeping activity must also be kept efficient if bus loading is to be kept at a minimum. The degree to which memory references are not available in the cache is called the *miss rate* [Flynn 1995, Appendix A] or *miss ratio.*

7.2.2 Multiprocessor Caches

A cache can be thought of as comprising a number of rows or lines (also known as *blocks*). Cache lines need to be replaced from time to time due to the presence of *stale data* that needs to be made consistent with other cached copies or because new lines need to be brought into the cache and other lines must be removed to make way for them. These cache lines or rows can also be broken into smaller segments (like columns in a spreadsheet). The former is called a *direct-mapped* cache, while the latter is called a *set-associative* cache. The number of columns in the cache is called the *degree of set associativity.*

When references are made to main memory, a request has to be generated by the cache (e.g., the *L2* cache) and placed on the bus. The memory bus can be either circuit-switched or packet-switched. In a circuit-switched bus, the bus is usually held during the time of the request being sent to and processed by main memory, and also during the time when the requested data is being returned from main memory. During this bus-holding period, no other requests can be placed on the bus. This approach keeps the implementation rather simple but, it severely limits the ability to place more than a few processors on the bus.

An alternative is the packet-switched bus protocol, also known as a *split-cycle* bus or *transaction* bus. There, requests are placed on the bus asynchronously and the data is returned to the requestor when it becomes available. In the meantime, the cache can continue servicing processor (or other cache) requests. Most large-scale SMP servers employ some variant of a split-cycle in order to assist scalability. UNIX SMP scalability is discussed in Gunther [2000a, Chap. 6 and 14] and Windows 2000 scalability is discussed in Friedman and Pentakalos [2002, p. 225].

The way data is kept consistent across caches also requires an intricate protocol in order to achieve SMP scalability. A *write-through* protocol is one where updates are immediately transmitted to main memory at the time they are written to the cache. This keeps main memory as the holder of the most current state, but it creates a lot of write traffic on the bus. A more efficient scheme is called *write-back* or *copy-back*. There, only the local copy is updated, with the change reflected in main memory only when the line is removed from the cache. We construct a PDQ performance model for each of these cache protocols in Sect. 7.3.4. Local caches are kept consistent with each other by listening to requests on the bus and taking appropriate action. This monitoring of the bus is called a *snooping* protocol [Flynn 1995, Appendix F].

The performance characteristics of a cache memory have a lot in common with virtual memory. In particular, locality of references is determined by compiler optimizations (i.e., the number of instructions per computational task). It has also been shown that successive memory references can exhibit a long-term *fractal*-like behavior. Other important performance determinants include control algorithms such as *preemption control* and *processor affinity* [Gunther 2000a, Appendix C].

7.2.3 Cache Bashing

Caches can be defeated quite simply by poor programming practice. Consider a linked list with a large number of entries. Traversing the links in the list to find a certain datum requires relatively few instructions. These few instructions are repeated until the datum is found. The instructions will therefore remain resident in the cache so it serves its intended purpose for instruction accesses. The picture is different for data caching, however. For each link the corresponding datum must be read. But these data will not be in the same cache line, so a read miss will occur and there will be a high (relative to the processor) latency to obtain a replacement cache line from main memory. The way out is to change the search algorithm from a linear search to a hashed or tree-type search.

Another problem for direct-mapped caches occurs when copying arrays that are separated by a multiple of the cache size. The source and destination addresses become resident in the same cache line. These examples apply to either uniprocessor or multiprocessor codes. Specifically for SMPs is the problem of *ping-pong* synchronization locks between processor caches [Gunther 1996]. If a processor modifies a memory location via an atomic *test-and-set* operation, the lock will end up resident exclusively in that processor's cache (whether the lock is free or not). Another processor performing the same test-and-set operation will then cause the lock to be moved to its cache. Since the test-and-set operation must be applied until the lock is acquired, the lock can "bounce" between the waiting processors. More processors contending for the same lock degrades performance further. One solution to this problem is to test the lock state before applying the test-and-set operation. This is know as *test-and-test-and-set* operation.

A similar effect can occur when adjacent words in a cache line are modified by different processors. The first occurrence of a write moves the line to that processor's cache, while the next write is issued by another processor, which moves the line to that processor's cache. We can identify three basic rules of thumb:

- Perform all operations on the same datum in the same CPU to avoid interprocessor communication.
- Align data to prevent words that are frequently accessed by different processors being adjacent.
- Localize the use of data and avoid sweeping through all data items.

There is also the broader issue of *symmetrization* (the 'S' in SMP). Symmetrizing application code to run efficiently on SMPs is a more difficult problem. A set of performance guidelines for symmetrizing applications can be found in Gunther [2000a, Appendix C]. Next, we consider some methods for estimating the performance of these multiprocessor architectures.

7.3 Multiprocessor Models

The simplest performance model might be constructed using an $M/M/m$ queueing center discussed in Chap. 2 and shown in Fig. 7.4. In this case, the servers represent the processors, and the waiting line represents the run-queue feeding the CPUs. While this simple approach might be of value in some cases, it suffers several drawbacks:

- This is an open-circuit queueing center. As we saw in Chap. 2, if the circulating population of requests is not more than an order of magnitude greater than the queue length, an open-circuit model may not be a very accurate representation.

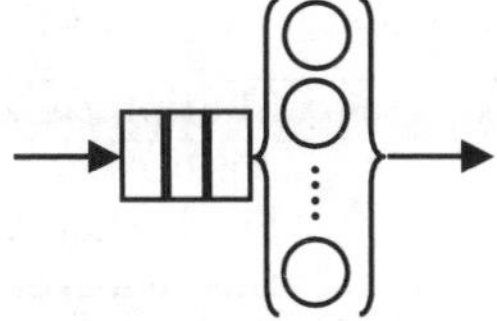

Fig. 7.4. A simple $M/M/m$ representation of an SMP

- It may not be an accurate way to assess the impact of multiple users on the SMP system.
- The throughput is unbounded and proportional to server load ρ.
- There must be an asymptote where the throughput saturates.
- The model does not include memory or I/O contention.

These limitations notwithstanding, Figure 7.4 may still be useful elementary tool for setting initial SMP performance expectations.

7.3.1 Single-Bus Models

We can incorporate the effects of multiple users and the effects of bus saturation by applying the repairman model (discussed in Chaps. 2 and 3) to construct a closed-circuit queueing model (Fig. 7.5) of an SMP [Ajmone-Marsan et al. 1990]). The mapping between the repairman model and the

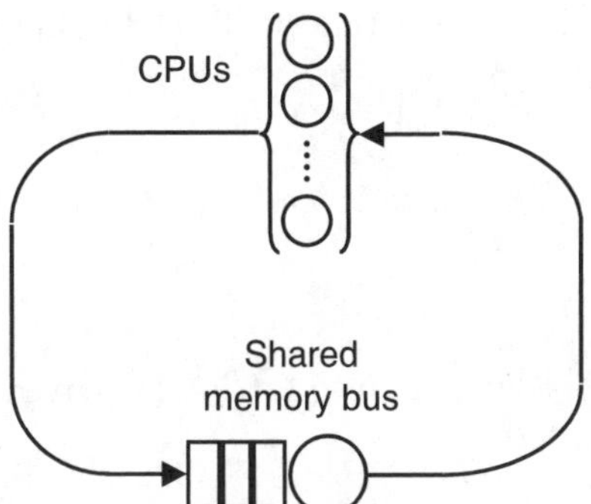

Fig. 7.5. Repairman model of a single shared-memory bus SMP

SMP multiprocessor is summarized in Table 7.1. The SMP model in Fig. 7.5 is pessimistic in that:

- memory service is exponentially distributed rather than deterministic
- memory requests are not returned in order

A hybrid model [Tsuei and Vernon 1992] is needed to include such effects. On the other hand, Fig. 7.5 is optimistic in that:

Table 7.1. Mapping between Repairman and SMP models

Repairman model	Multiprocessor model
N user terminals	p processors (N/p users per CPU)
Central CPU	Single shared-memory bus
Programs	Bus requests
Think time	Compute time
Response time	Execution time
System throughput	Bus bandwidth

- no disk I/O
- no cache intervenes
- no retries
- no software locking

Again, a hybrid model can be used to address these aspects.

7.3.2 Processing Power

A common metric used to assess SMP performance is the *processing power* [Ajmone-Marsan et al. 1990]. The mean processing power $\mathfrak{P}$ is defined as the average number of actively computing processors (Fig. 7.6). This metric is useful because other performance measures can be derived from it, as we now demonstrate.

The mean number of *active* processors is the total number of physical processors reduced by the number that have outstanding requests on the bus:

$$\mathfrak{P} = p - Q \,. \tag{7.1}$$

Applying the *Response Time Law* given by (2.90) from Chap 2, the average bus delay for a request is:

$$R = \frac{p}{X} - Z \,. \tag{7.2}$$

Substituting this expression for R into Little's law given by (2.14) produces:

$$Q = XR = p - XZ \,, \tag{7.3}$$

from which we obtain a more transparent definition of processing power, viz:.

$$\mathfrak{P} = XZ \,. \tag{7.4}$$

In other words, $\mathfrak{P}$ can also be interpreted as the total processor utilization, where the processors are treated as an infinite server (IS) node (cf. Sect. 2.11.1). Rewriting the bus delay (7.2) as:

$$R = \frac{p}{X} - \frac{ZX}{X} \,, \tag{7.5}$$

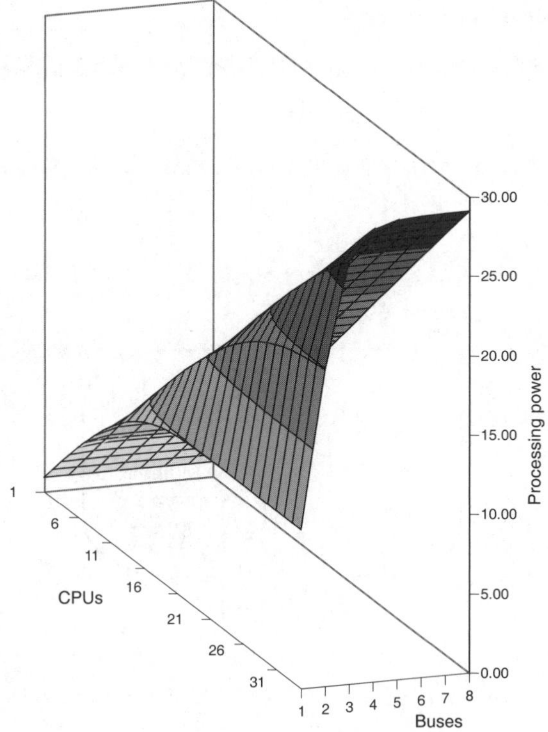

Fig. 7.6. Processing power for a 32-way SMP with up to 8 busses

and noting that $X = \mathfrak{P}/Z$, by rearrangment of (7.4) we have:

$$R = \left(\frac{p - \mathfrak{P}}{\mathfrak{P}} \right) Z \tag{7.6}$$

after the appropriate substitution.

By defining $\Omega = S/Z$, the mean waiting time ($W = R - S$) for a bus request is determined to be:

$$W = \left(\frac{p - (1 + \Omega)\mathfrak{P}}{\mathfrak{P}} \right) Z \,, \tag{7.7}$$

and the mean memory-bus cycle time $T_{\text{bus}} = R + Z$ is:

$$T_{\text{bus}} = \left(\frac{p}{\mathfrak{P}} \right) Z \,. \tag{7.8}$$

From these definitions, it is possible to construct other SMP performance indices. See Exercise 7.1.

7.3.3 Multiple-Bus Models

The effect of adding more buses and memories can be determined by replacing the uniserver bus center with a multiserver center like that shown in Fig. 7.7. This $M/M/b/p/p$ model gives an upper bound from bus contention only. Similarly, a $b(M/M/1)$ model will give a lower bound because of memory contention only.

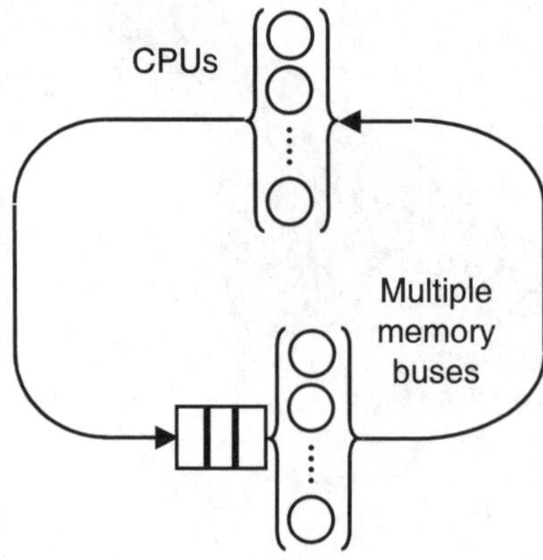

Fig. 7.7. Repairmen model for an SMP with multiple shared-memory buses

The following PDQ model uses a load-dependent server (See Chaps. 3 and 6) to compute the effects of multiple buses:

```
#! /usr/bin/perl
#  multibus.pl
use pdq;

# System parameters
$BUSES  =     9;
$CPUS   =    64;
$STIME  =   1.0;
$COMPT  =  10.0;
printf("multibus.out\n");

# Compute the submodel first
multiserver($BUSES, $STIME);
# Now, compute the composite model
$pq[0][0] = 1.0;

for ($n = 1; $n <= $CPUS; $n++) {
   $R = 0.0;            # reset
   for ($j = 1; $j <= $n; $j++) {
```

```
      $h  = ($j / $sm_x[$j]) * $pq[$j - 1][$n - 1];
      $R += $h;
   }
   $xn = $n / ($COMPT + $R);
   $qlength = $xn * $R;

   for ($j = 1; $j <= $n; $j++) {
      $pq[$j][$n] = ($xn / $sm_x[$j]) * $pq[$j - 1][$n - 1];
   }
   $pq[0][$n] = 1.0;

   for ($j = 1; $j <= $n; $j++) {
      $pq[0][$n] -= $pq[$j][$n];
   }
}

# Processing Power
printf("Buses:%2d, CPUs:%2d\n", $BUSES, $CPUS);
printf("Load %3.4f\n", ($STIME / $COMPT));
printf("X at FESC: %3.4f\n", $xn);
printf("P %3.4f\n", $xn * $COMPT);

sub multiserver {
   my  ($m, $stime) = @_;
   $work = "reqs";
   $node = "bus";
   $x = 0.0;

   for ($i = 1; $i <= $CPUS; $i++) {
      if ($i <= $m) {
         pdq::Init("multibus");
         $streams = pdq::CreateClosed($work, $pdq::TERM, $i, 0.0);
         $nodes   = pdq::CreateNode($node, $pdq::CEN, $pdq::ISRV);
         pdq::SetDemand($node, $work, $stime);
         pdq::Solve($pdq::EXACT);
         $x = pdq::GetThruput($pdq::TERM, $work);
         $sm_x[$i] = $x;
      } else {
         $sm_x[$i] = $x;
      }
   }
}  # end of multiserver
```

Multibus scaling for a 64-way multiprocessor is shown in Fig 7.8. Notice that the saturation throughput values are equally spaced along the y-axis. The corresponding efficiency characteristics are shown in Fig. 7.9. For a fixed number of CPUs, adding more buses beyond the third or fourth has little impact on system throughput.

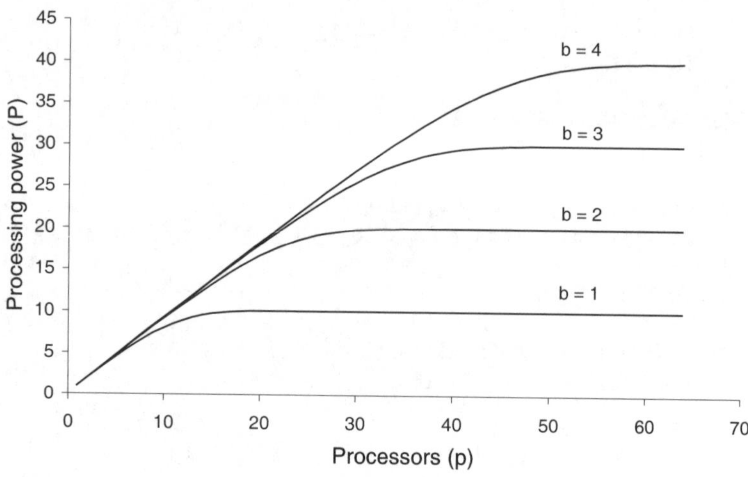

Fig. 7.8. Scalability for a 64-way SMP with b buses at $\rho = 0.1$

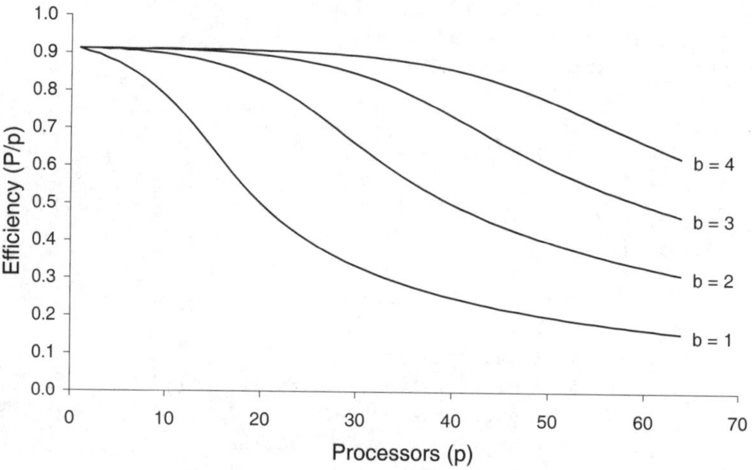

Fig. 7.9. Efficiency curves for a 64-way SMP with b buses

More elaborate bus models that distinguish between the (possibly) different service times for bus-reads and bus-writes can be developed using multiclass workloads like that shown in Fig. 7.10.

7.3.4 Cache Protocols

As we mentioned earlier, processor caches are an important architectural consideration for reducing shared bus contention. Their effectiveness is determined by many subtle factors (some of which we have already discussed), but in this section we extend our previous SMP performance models to include the effects of the cache update policy. The two policies we consider are:

1. Write-through: A cache write is simultaneously sent to main memory.
2. Write-back: Main memory is updated only when a cache line is replaced.

A detailed analysis using PDQ would take us too far afield. Instead, we con-

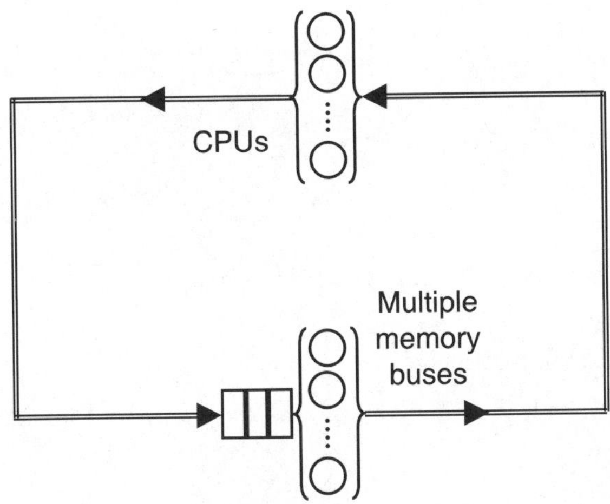

Fig. 7.10. PDQ bus model with multiclass workload

sider the simpler PDQ model in Fig 7.10 to give an idea of what can be achieved with relatively little labor compared to that which might be required for a simulation. The model depicts a single shared-memory bus with the p CPUs supported by $0, \ldots, p-1$ private second-level (L2) caches. The caches are assumed to be unified, i.e., there is no distinction between the data and instruction content. In the case of the *write-through* protocol there are *three* PDQ workload classes:

- reads and writes that are hits in the L2 cache
- reads that are misses in the L2 cache that cause a memory read bus operation
- writes that are misses in the L2 cache that cause a write-through bus operation

The *write-back* policy requires *four* PDQ workload classes:

- reads and writes that are hits in the L2 cache
- reads that are misses in the L2 cache that cause a memory read bus operation
- Writes that are misses in the L2 cache that cause a memory write bus operation

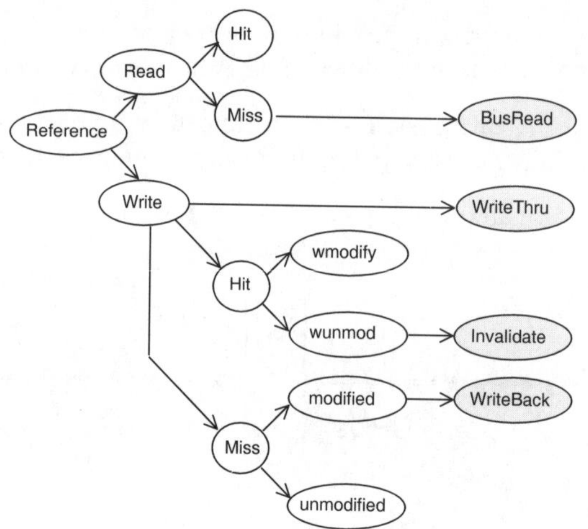

Fig. 7.11. SMP model bus operations

- an Invalidate bus operation

The references that lead to bus operations are shown in Figs. 7.11 and 7.12.

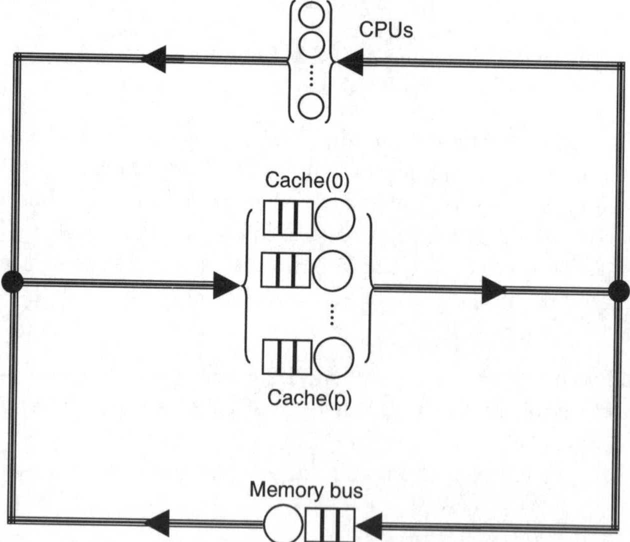

Fig. 7.12. PDQ bus model including multiclass workloads and separate CPU caches

The remainder of the description of the model appears in the following PDQ source code:

```
#! /usr/bin/perl
```

```
#  abcache.pl

use pdq;
# Main memory update policy
# The main-memory update policy is selected to be write-through here.
$WBACK   =  1;
# Globals
$MAXCPU  =   15;
$ZX      =  2.5;

# Cache parameters
$RD      =  0.85;
$WR      =  (1 - $RD);
$HT      =  0.95;
$WUMD    =  0.0526;
$MD      =  0.35;

# Bus and L2 cache ids
$L2C     = "L2C";
$BUS     = "MBus";

# Aggregate cache traffic
$RWHT    = "RWhit";
$gen     =  1.0;

# Bus Ops
$RDOP    = "Read";
$WROP    = "Write";
$INVL    = "Inval";

# per CPU intruction stream intensity
# The following variables are used to assign the per CPU intruction stream
# intensity for write-through.

$Prhit = ($RD * $HT);
$Pwhit = ($WR * $HT * (1 - $WUMD)) + ($WR * (1 - $HT) * (1 - $MD));
$Prdop = $RD * (1 - $HT);
$Pwbop = $WR * (1 - $HT) * $MD;
$Pwthr = $WR;
$Pinvl = $WR * $HT * $WUMD;

$Nrwht = 0.8075 * $MAXCPU;
$Nrdop = 0.0850 * $MAXCPU;
$Nwthr = 0.15 * $MAXCPU;

$Nwbop = 0.0003 * $MAXCPU * 100;
$Ninvl = 0.015 * $MAXCPU;

$Srdop = (20.0);
```

```
$Swthr = (25.0);
$Swbop = (20.0);

$Wrwht = 0.0;
$Wrdop = 0.0;
$Wwthr = 0.0;
$Wwbop = 0.0;
$Winvl = 0.0;

$Zrwht = $ZX;
$Zrdop = $ZX;
$Zwbop = $ZX;
$Zinvl = $ZX;
$Zwthr = $ZX;

$Xcpu  = 0.0;
$Pcpu  = 0.0;
$Ubrd  = 0.0;
$Ubwr  = 0.0;
$Ubin  = 0.0;
$Ucht  = 0.0;
$Ucrd  = 0.0;
$Ucwr  = 0.0;
$Ucin  = 0.0;


pdq::Init("ABC Model");

# More appopriate units are assigned for assessing bus performance.
pdq::SetWUnit("Reqs");
pdq::SetTUnit("Cycs");

## Create single bus queueing center
$nodes = pdq::CreateNode($BUS, $pdq::CEN, $pdq::FCFS);

## Create per CPU cache queueing centers
for ($i = 0; $i < $MAXCPU; $i++) {
   $cname = sprintf "%s%d", $L2C, $i;
   $nodes = pdq::CreateNode($cname, $pdq::CEN, $pdq::FCFS);
   #printf "i %2d  cname %10s  nodes %d\n", $i, $cname, $nodes;
}

## Create CPU nodes, workloads, and demands
# In this PDQ model the proportion of each workload (read-write hits,
# reads, writes, invalidates) is partitioned amongst the total number of
# processors by a call to intwt().  In the event that the number of CPUs
# belonging to a workload is less than one, the number of CPUs is taken to
# be one with a weight factor assigned to its throughput and utilization.
```

```
printf "       Nrwht %s, Zrwht %s\n", $Nrwht, $Zrwht;
$no = intwt($Nrwht, \$Wrwht);
printf "no %d %f  Nrwht %d, Zrwht %d\n", $no, $no, $Nrwht, $Zrwht;
for ($i = 0; $i < $no; $i++) {
   $wname   = sprintf "%s%d", $RWHT, $i;
   #printf "wname %s  Nrwht %d, Zrwht %d\n", $wname, $Nrwht, $Zrwht;
   $streams = pdq::CreateClosed($wname, $pdq::TERM, $Nrwht, $Zrwht);
   $cname   = sprintf "%s%d", $L2C, $i;
   #printf "cname %s\n", $cname;
   pdq::SetDemand($cname, $wname, 1.0);
   pdq::SetDemand($BUS, $wname, 0.0);       # no bus activity
   printf "i %2d  cname %10s  nodes %2d  streams %d\n", $i, $cname,
      $nodes, $streams;
}

$no = intwt($Nrdop, \$Wrdop);
printf "no %d  Nrdop %d, Zrdop %d\n", $no, $Nrdop, $Zrdop;
for ($i = 0; $i < $no; $i++) {
   $wname   = sprintf "%s%d", $RDOP, $i;
   $streams = pdq::CreateClosed($wname, $pdq::TERM, $Nrdop, $Zrdop);
   $cname   = sprintf "%s%d", $L2C, $i;
   pdq::SetDemand($cname, $wname, $gen);    # generate bus request
   pdq::SetDemand($BUS, $wname, $Srdop);    # req + async data return
   printf "i %2d  cname %10s  nodes %2d  streams %d\n", $i, $cname,
      $nodes, $streams;
}

if (WBACK) {
   $no = intwt($Nwbop, \$Wwbop);
   printf "no %d  Nwbop %d, Zwbop %d\n", $no, $Nwbop, $Zwbop;

   for ($i = 0; $i < $no; $i++) {
      $wname   = sprintf "%s%d", $WROP, $i;
      $streams = pdq::CreateClosed($wname, $pdq::TERM, $Nwbop, $Zwbop);
      $cname   = sprintf "%s%d", $L2C, $i;
      pdq::SetDemand($cname, $wname, $gen);
      pdq::SetDemand($BUS, $wname, $Swbop);      # asych write to memory ?
      printf "w %2d  cname %10s  nodes %2d  streams %d\n", $i, $cname,
         $nodes, $streams;
   }
} else {  # write-thru
   $no = intwt($Nwthr, \$Wwthr);
   printf "no %d  Nwthr %d, Zwthr %d\n", $no, $Nwthr, $Zwthr;

   for ($i = 0; $i < $no; $i++) {
      $wname   = sprintf "%s%d", $WROP, $i;
      $streams = pdq::CreateClosed($wname, $pdq::TERM, $Nwthr, $Zwthr);
      $cname   = sprintf "%s%d", $L2C, $i;
      pdq::SetDemand($cname, $wname, $gen);
```

```
            pdq::SetDemand($BUS, $wname, $Swthr);
            printf "i %2d  cname %10s  nodes %2d  streams %d\n", $i, $cname,
               $nodes, $streams;
        }
    }

    if (WBACK) {
        $no = intwt($Ninvl, \$Winvl);
        printf "no %d  Ninvl %d, Zinvl %d\n", $no, $Ninvl, $Zinvl;

        for ($i = 0; $i < $no; $i++) {
            $wname   = sprintf "%s%d", $INVL, $i;
            $streams = pdq::CreateClosed($wname, $pdq::TERM, $Ninvl, $Zinvl);
            $cname   = sprintf "%s%d", $L2C, $i;
            pdq::SetDemand($cname, $wname, $gen);   # gen + intervene
            pdq::SetDemand($BUS, $wname, 1.0);
            printf "w %2d  cname %10s  nodes %2d  streams %d\n", $i, $cname,
               $nodes, $streams;
        }
    }
    pdq::Solve($pdq::APPROX);

    ## Calculate bus utilizations
    $no = intwt($Nrdop, \$Wrdop);
    for ($i = 0; $i < $no; $i++) {
        $wname   = sprintf "%s%d", $RDOP, $i;
        $Ubrd += pdq::GetUtilization($BUS, $wname, $pdq::TERM);
    }
    $Ubrd *= $Wrdop;

    if (WBACK) {
        $no = intwt($Nwbop, \$Wwbop);
        for ($i = 0; $i < $no; $i++) {
            $wname   = sprintf "%s%d", $WROP, $i;
            $Ubwr += pdq::GetUtilization($BUS, $wname, $pdq::TERM);
        }
        $Ubwr *= $Wwbop;
        $no = intwt($Ninvl, \$Winvl);

        for ($i = 0; $i < $no; $i++) {
            $wname   = sprintf "%s%d", $INVL, $i;
            $Ubin += pdq::GetUtilization($BUS, $wname, $pdq::TERM);
        }
        $Ubin *= $Winvl;
    } else {  # write-thru
        $no = intwt($Nwthr, \$Wwthr);
        for ($i = 0; $i < $no; $i++) {
            $wname   = sprintf "%s%d", $WROP, $i;
            $Ubwr += pdq::GetUtilization($BUS, $wname, $pdq::TERM);
```

```
    }
    $Ubwr *= $Wwthr;
}

## Cache measures at CPU[0] only
$i     = 0;
$cname = sprintf "%s%d", $L2C, $i;

$wname = sprintf "%s%d", $RWHT, $i;
$Xcpu  = pdq::GetThruput($pdq::TERM, $wname) * $Wrwht;
$Pcpu += $Xcpu * $Zrwht;
$Ucht  = pdq::GetUtilization($cname, $wname, $pdq::TERM) * $Wrwht;

$wname = sprintf "%s%d", $RDOP, $i;
$Xcpu  = pdq::GetThruput($pdq::TERM, $wname) * Wrdop;
$Pcpu += $Xcpu * $Zrdop;
$Ucrd  = pdq::GetUtilization($cname, $wname, $pdq::TERM) * $Wrdop;

$Pcpu *= 1.88;
if ($WBACK) {
   $wname = sprintf "%s%d", $WROP, $i;
   $Ucwr = pdq::GetUtilization($cname, $wname, $pdq::TERM) * $Wwbop;
   $wname = sprintf "%s%d", $INVL, $i;
   $Ucin = pdq::GetUtilization($cname, $wname, $pdq::TERM) * $Winvl;
} else {          # write-thru
   $wname = sprintf "%s%d", $WROP, $i;
   $Ucwr = pdq::GetUtilization($cname, $wname, $pdq::TERM) * $Wwthr;
}
printf "\n**** %s Results ****\n", $model;
printf "PDQ nodes: %d  PDQ streams: %d\n", $nodes, $streams;
printf "Memory Mode: %s\n", $WBACK ? "WriteBack" : "WriteThru";
printf "Ncpu:  %2d\n", $MAXCPU;

$no = intwt($Nrwht, \$Wrwht);
printf "Nrwht: %5.2f (N:%2d  W:%5.2f)\n", $Nrwht, $no, $Wrwht;
$no = intwt($Nrdop, \$Wrdop);
printf "Nrdop: %5.2f (N:%2d  W:%5.2f)\n", $Nrdop, $no, $Wrdop;

if (WBACK) {
   $no = intwt($Nwbop, \$Wwbop);
   printf "Nwbop: %5.2f (N:%2d  W:%5.2f)\n", $Nwbop, $no, $Wwbop;
   $no = intwt($Ninvl, \$Winvl);
   printf "Ninvl: %5.2f (N:%2d  W:%5.2f)\n", $Ninvl, $no, $Winvl;
} else {
   $no = intwt($Nwthr, \$Wwthr);
   printf "Nwthr: %5.2f (N:%2d  W:%5.2f)\n", $Nwthr, $no, $Wwthr;
}

printf "\n";
```

```
printf "Hit Ratio:   %5.2f %%\n",  $HT * 100.0;
printf "Read Miss:   %5.2f %%\n",  $RD * (1 - $HT) * 100.0;
printf "WriteMiss:   %5.2f %%\n",  $WR * (1 - $HT) * 100.0;
printf "Ucpu:        %5.2f %%\n",  ($Pcpu * 100.0) / $MAXCPU;
printf "Pcpu:        %5.2f\n",     $Pcpu;
printf "\n";
printf "Ubus[reads]: %5.2f %%\n",  $Ubrd * 100.0;
printf "Ubus[write]: %5.2f %%\n",  $Ubwr * 100.0;
printf "Ubus[inval]: %5.2f %%\n",  $Ubin * 100.0;
printf "Ubus[total]: %5.2f %%\n",  ($Ubrd + $Ubwr + $Ubin) * 100.0;
printf "\n";
printf "Uca%d[hits]:  %5.2f %%\n", $i, $Ucht * 100.0;
printf "Uca%d[reads]: %5.2f %%\n", $i, $Ucrd * 100.0;
printf "Uca%d[write]: %5.2f %%\n", $i, $Ucwr * 100.0;
printf "Uca%d[inval]: %5.2f %%\n", $i, $Ucin * 100.0;
printf "Uca%d[total]: %5.2f %%\n", $i, ($Ucht + $Ucrd + $Ucwr + $Ucin)
  * 100.0;

sub itoa {
   my ($n, $s) = @_;
   if (($sign = $n) < 0) {
      $n = -$n;
   }
   $i = 0;

   do {  # generate digits in reverse order
      $s[$i++] = '0' + ($n % 10);
   } while (($n /= 10) > 0);
   if ($sign < 0) {
      $s[$i++] = '-';
   }
   $s[$i] = '\0';
   # reverse order of bytes
   for ($i = 0, $j = strlen($s) - 1; $i < $j; $i++, $j--) {
      $c = $s[$i];
      $s[$i] = $s[$j];
      $s[$j] = $c;
   }
}

sub intwt {
   my ($N, $W) = @_;
   my($i);

   if ($N < 1.0) {
      $i = 1;
      $$W = $N;
   }
   if ($N >= 1.0) {
```

```
        $i = $N;
        $$W = 1.0;
    }
    return int($i);
}
```

The throughput projections from the SMP cache model `abcache.pl` are shown in Fig. 7.13. The advantages of the write-back memory update policy are clear.

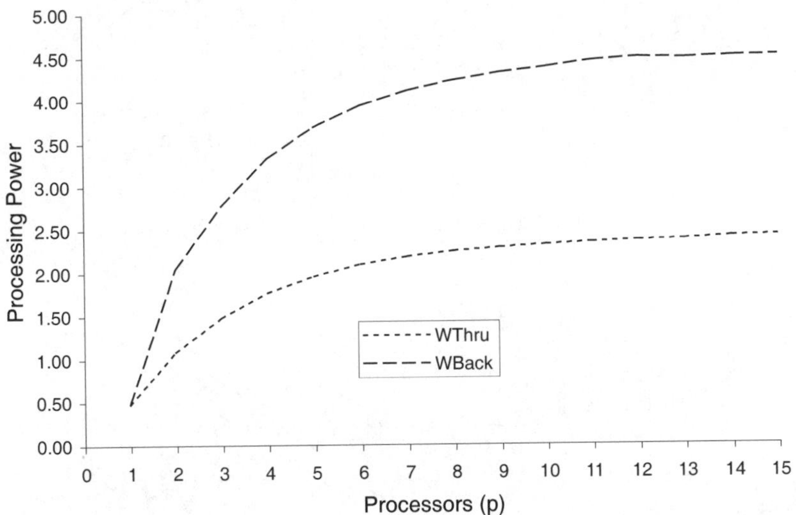

Fig. 7.13. Relative scalability for caches using a write-through and write-back protocol

Projected bus utilizations for the write-through policy are shown in Fig. 7.14. The write-through policy means that the bus utilization is clearly dominated by writes to main memory. Projected bus utilizations for the write-back policy are shown in Fig. 7.15. The write-back policy means that the bus utilization is dominated by reads that are caused by the increasing amount of invalidation traffic.

7.3.5 Iron Law of Performance

The most common performance rating applied to a microprocessor is the millions of instructions per second (MIPS) it can execute. Since MIPS has the engineering dimensions of a throughput, or rate, it can rightfully be regarded as a legitimate unit of performance in the sense of (2.3). The problem arises when the MIPS rating is used to compare different microprocessors. Different microprocessors use different instruction sets, and those instructions exhibit different cycle times per instruction (CPI) to complete.

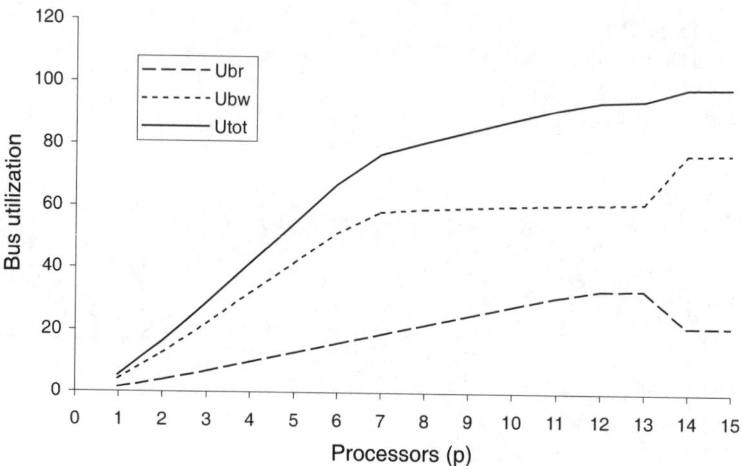

Fig. 7.14. Bus utilizations for the write-through protocol

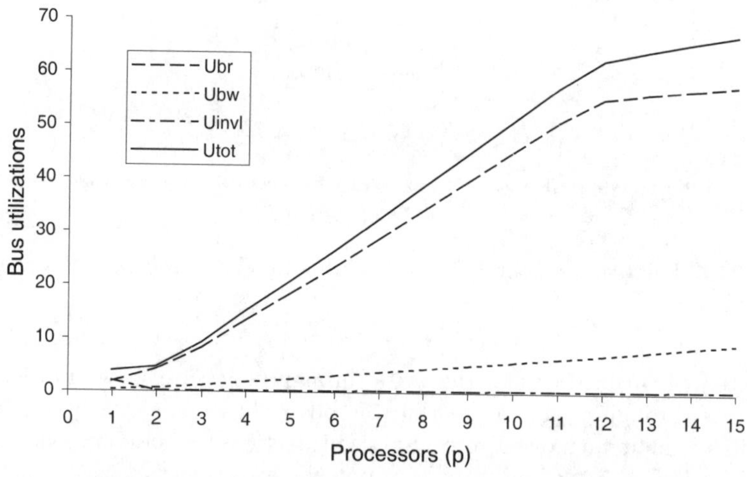

Fig. 7.15. Bus utilizations for the write-back protocol

A somewhat more realistic performance measure can be arrived at by incorporating the *path length* (PL) which measures the number of instructions in a program. The elapsed time to complete a entire program can then be written as:

$$\frac{\text{time}}{\text{pgm}} = \left(\frac{\text{instr}}{\text{pgm}}\right)\left(\frac{\text{cycle}}{\text{instr}}\right)\left(\frac{\text{time}}{\text{cycle}}\right). \tag{7.9}$$

This relationship is used by microprocessor architects. It is sometimes referred to as the *iron law of performance* because it involves such fundamental parameters as the number of instructions executed and the number of CPU cycles to execute an instruction; it appears to be immutable. Inverting this equation and rearranging the order of the factors in the denominator produces:

$$\frac{\text{pgm}}{\text{time}} = \frac{\left(\frac{\text{cycle}}{\text{time}}\right)}{\left(\frac{\text{cycle}}{\text{instr}}\right)\left(\frac{\text{instr}}{\text{pgm}}\right)} . \tag{7.10}$$

The number of programs completed per unit time is just the system throughput, X_{sys} defined by (2.3). Then:

$$X_{\text{sys}} = \frac{\left(\frac{\text{cycle}}{\text{time}}\right)}{\left(\frac{\text{cycle}}{\text{instr}}\right)\left(\frac{\text{instr}}{\text{pgm}}\right)} . \tag{7.11}$$

If the time-base is taken to be measured in seconds, for example, then the numerator can be measured in cycles per second or Hz. Moreover, modern microprocessors run at clock frequencies in the GHz range. Abbreviating cycle/instr as CPI, and instr pgm by the *path length*, PL, (7.11) can be rewritten as:

$$X_{\text{sys}} = \frac{\text{GHz}}{\text{CPI} \times \text{PL}} . \tag{7.12}$$

We can also interpret (7.12) in terms of the queueing theory in Chap. 2 as follows. Think of a simple $M/M/1$ queueing center with the CPI representing the service time per instruction and the PL as the number of visits to the CPU in order to execute one program (e.g., a database transaction). From (2.9) the average service demand D_{cpu} at the CPU is the product of the service time S_{cpu} and the visit count V_{cpu} at the CPU device. In other words, we have:

$$X_{\text{sys}} = \frac{\text{MHz}}{S_{\text{cpu}} \times V_{\text{cpu}}} = \frac{\text{MHz}}{D_{\text{cpu}}} . \tag{7.13}$$

The CPU clock frequency in the numerator simply translates the throughput units into transactions per second. We immediately recognize this as the saturation throughput of the CPU in agreement with the assumption that the workload is CPU-intensive.

7.4 Multicomputer Models

Having discussed scalability models for multiprocessors, we now turn to a scalability analysis for multicomputers. We introduce an empirical method (first presented in [Gunther 2000a]) for determining the optimal query processing configuration based on knowledge of the saturation throughput.

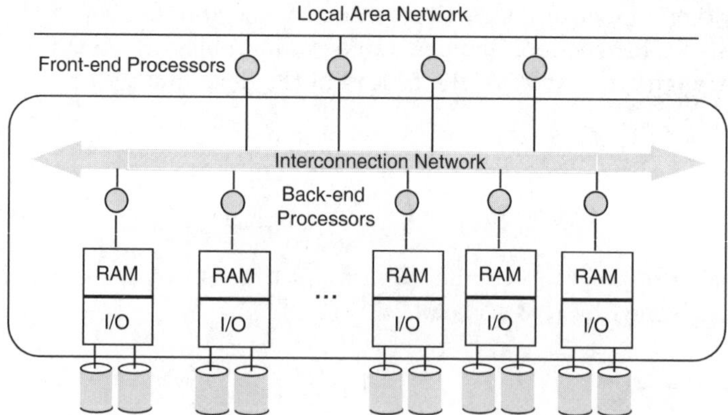

Fig. 7.16. Typical architecture of a parallel query cluster

7.4.1 Parallel Query Cluster

The following analysis is based on a massively parallel database cluster architecture represented schematically in Fig. 7.16. The essential architectural subsystems are labelled as follows:

CLI: The number of client submitting queries into the cluster
FEP: Front-end processors that manage communications with network clients
BEP: Back-end processors
DSU: Disk storage units on the back-end processors
NET: High-speed interconnect to facilitate parallel query processing between the FEPs and the BEPs

Even with the availability of large-scale clusters at relatively good price–performance, performance tuning is not always straightforward because of sensitivities to data partitioning and load balancing. Optimal tuning techniques are specific to the particular cluster platform.

A more significant general problem is how to determine the optimal number of parallel BEP processors for a given size of the database, and that is the problem we shall address here using PDQ. A simple rule of thumb suggests that scaling the number of parallel processors should reduce the uniprocessor response time according to:

$$R(p) = \frac{R(1)}{p}, \tag{7.14}$$

where $R(1)$ is the uniprocessor query time, and p is the number of physical processors or the size of the BEP configuration in the SMP cluster.

Intuitively, we expect that the parallel query time should be reduced in inverse proportion to the number of parallel processors applied to the query,

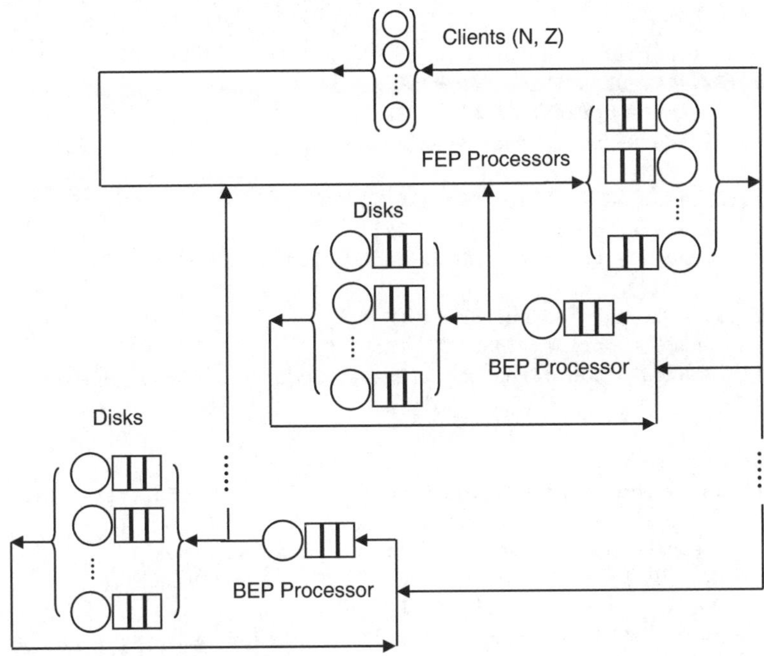

Fig. 7.17. Simple PDQ model of a multicomputer cluster architecture (Fig. 7.16) running a homogeneous query workload

assuming the data is partitioned more or less uniformly across the DSUs. We can use PDQ to see how well this intuition is supported.

The Perlscript for the PDQ queueing model in Fig. 7.17 follows. Identifying our previous nomenclature with the associated Perlvariables, the model parameters are: 800 CLIs (`$users`), 15 FEPs (`$Nfep`), 50 BEPs (`$Nbep`) and 100 DSUs (`$Ndsu`). In Sect. 7.4.2, we shall use the same PDQ model to determine the optimal parallel processing configuration for the multicomputer cluster.

```
#!/usr/bin/perl
#cluster.pl
use pdq;
$think = 10.0;
$users = 800;
$Sfep  = 0.10;
$Sbep  = 0.60;
$Sdsu  = 1.20;
$Nfep  = 15;
$Nbep  = 50;
$Ndsu  = 100;

pdq::Init("Query Cluster");
```

```
# Create parallel centers
for ($k = 0; $k < $Nfep; $k++) {
      $name = sprintf "FEP%d", $k;
      $nodes = pdq::CreateNode($name, $pdq::CEN, $pdq::FCFS);
}
for ($k = 0; $k < $Nbep; $k++) {
      $name = sprintf "BEP%d", $k;
      $nodes = pdq::CreateNode($name, $pdq::CEN, $pdq::FCFS);
}
for ($k = 0; $k < $Ndsu; $k++) {
      $name = sprintf "DSU%d", $k;
      $nodes = pdq::CreateNode($name, $pdq::CEN, $pdq::FCFS);
}

# Create the workload
$streams = pdq::CreateClosed("query", $pdq::TERM, $users, $think);

# Set service demands using visits to parallel nodes
for ($k = 0; $k < $Nfep; $k++) {
      $name = sprintf "FEP%d", $k;
      pdq::SetVisits($name, "query", 1 / $Nfep, $Sfep);
}
for ($k = 0; $k < $Nbep; $k++) {
      $name = sprintf "BEP%d", $k;
      pdq::SetVisits($name, "query", 1 / $Nbep, $Sbep);
}
for ($k = 0; $k < $Ndsu; $k++) {
      $name = sprintf "DSU%d", $k;
      pdq::SetVisits($name, "query", 1 / $Ndsu, $Sdsu);
}

pdq::Solve($pdq::APPROX);
pdq::Report();
```

A drastically abbreviated initial section of the associated PDQ report shows only the service demands for some of the 165 PDQ nodes.

```
***************************************
****** Pretty Damn Quick REPORT *******
***************************************
***  of : Tue Jun 22 11:08:26 2004  ***
***  for: Query Cluster             ***
***  Ver: PDQ Analyzer v2.8 120803  ***
***************************************
***************************************
```

```
***************************************
******    PDQ Model INPUTS      *******
***************************************

Node Sched Resource   Workload   Class     Demand
---- ----- --------   --------   -----     ------
CEN  FCFS  FEP0       query      TERML     0.0067
CEN  FCFS  FEP1       query      TERML     0.0067
...
CEN  FCFS  BEP0       query      TERML     0.0120
CEN  FCFS  BEP1       query      TERML     0.0120
...
CEN  FCFS  BEP48      query      TERML     0.0120
CEN  FCFS  BEP49      query      TERML     0.0120
CEN  FCFS  DSU0       query      TERML     0.0120
CEN  FCFS  DSU1       query      TERML     0.0120
...
CEN  FCFS  DSU98      query      TERML     0.0120
CEN  FCFS  DSU99      query      TERML     0.0120
```

Next, the SYSTEM Performance section of the PDQ report for the 50-BEP cluster model reveals that the expected response time is 5.0923 s (line 24) with 800-CLI queries in the system. This same response time also appears in Table 7.2.

```
1 Queueing Circuit Totals:
2     Clients:    800.00
3     Streams:      1
4     Nodes:      165
5
6 WORKLOAD Parameters
7
8 Client       Number       Demand   Thinktime
9 ----         ------       ------   ---------
10 query        800.00        1.9000    10.00
11
12         ***************************************
13         ******    PDQ Model OUTPUTS      *******
14         ***************************************
15
16 Solution Method: APPROX (Iterations: 10; Accuracy: 0.1000%)
17
18         ******    SYSTEM Performance      *******
19
20 Metric                          Value  Unit
21 -----------------               -----  ----
22 Workload: "query"
23 Mean Throughput          53.0073       Job/Sec
```

```
Response Time              5.0923       Sec
Mean Concurrency         269.9270       Job
Stretch Factor             2.6801

Bounds Analysis:
Max Throughput            83.3333       Job/Sec
Min Response               1.9000       Sec
Max Demand                 0.0120       Sec
Tot Demand                 1.9000       Sec
Think time                10.0000       Sec
Optimal Clients          991.6667       Clients
```

Running the PDQ model with successively larger BEP/DSU configurations produces the results in Table 7.2. The first column shows the number of processors in the BEP complex. The second column shows the predicted query time based on the PDQ queueing model, and the third column is an estimate based on (7.14).

Although the differences are not great, the results in Table 7.2 indicate that the query response times predicted by the simple hyperbolic model are more pessimistic (longer) than those predicted by PDQ. This occurs because the hyperbolic model is simply scaling the query time $R(1)$ for a single-processor configuration, and that configuration has maximal queueing. The additional servers of the parallel queues in the PDQ model, on the other hand, have the effect of scaling the service demand at each type of processing node, i.e., FEP, BEP or DSU, as explained in Sect. 2.6.4. Nonetheless, we see that hyperbolic scaling can provide a reasonable rule of thumb when estimating parallel query response times for the cluster.

Another drawback of the hyperbolic model is that it cannot not tell us anything about the optimal cluster hardware configuration. All we see in Fig. 7.18 is a region of diminishing performance gain somewhere around 60 BEP processors. Is there any way to determine the optimal cluster database configuration?

7.4.2 Query Saturation Method

In Chap. 5 we discussed the concepts of asymptotic bounds and balanced bounds on system performance. In this section we introduce a similar idea, the *query saturation method*, and show how it can be used to determine the optimal configuration for a parallel query platform, assuming a homogeneous aggregate query workload.

We begin with a variant of the balanced bounds techniques introduced in Chap. 5 where we learned that a balanced system has the best performance. In the simple case of two queueing centers arranged in tandem, a balanced system requires that the utilizations be equal: $U_1 = U_2$. Since the throughput X is the same at both queueing centers, it follows that the service demands

Table 7.2. Query times for 800 CLI-ents as a function of BEP cluster configuration

	Predicted query time (s)	
BEPs	PDQ	Hyperbolic
1	471.23	471.23
10	40.18	47.12
20	16.85	23.56
30	9.68	15.71
40	6.60	11.78
50	5.09	9.42
60	4.25	7.85
70	3.75	6.73
80	3.42	5.89
90	3.18	5.24
100	3.02	4.71
110	2.89	4.28
120	2.79	3.93

must also be equal: $D_1 = D_2$ (Little's law). Otherwise, the queueing center with the largest service demand $D_{\max}$ becomes the bottleneck and limits the system throughput according to $X_{\max} = 1/D_{\max}$.

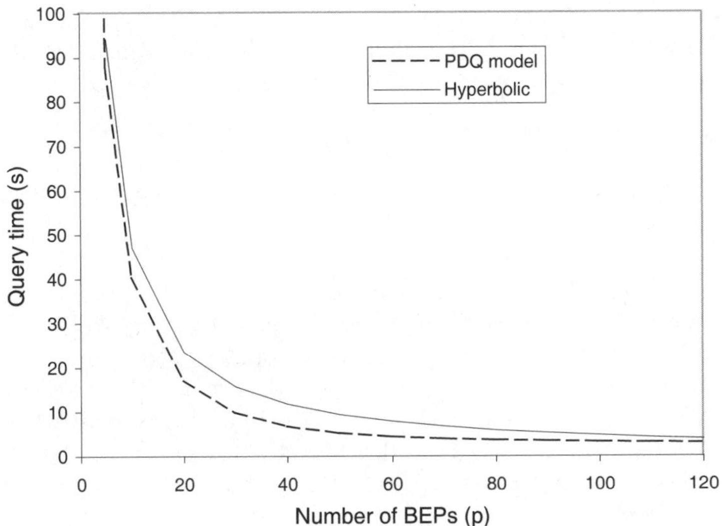

Fig. 7.18. Comparison of the hyperbolic and PDQ models

By analogy, consider the cluster to be comprised of two logical subsystems in tandem: the FEP (front end) and a BEP (back end). If each subsystem consists of just a single queueing center, then we expect the the BEP queue to have a larger service demand due to its longer processing time: $D_{\text{BEP}} > D_{\text{FEP}}$.

However, as the BEP configuration is scaled up with more parallel queues (Fig. 7.17) the service demand at each parallel node will be reduced. This happens because the successive inclusion of more parallel queues in the BEP subsystem, together with the requisite repartitioning of the data tables, means fewer visits to each of the p BEP nodes in order to complete a query (cf. Chap. 2). The BEP service demand at node p can be written in terms of the visists as:

$$D_p = V_p \, S_p \,, \tag{7.15}$$

where $V_p = 1/p$. As p becomes larger, the corresponding service demand is reduced. The performance optimum occurs when the tandem subsystems become balanced with $D_{\text{BEP}} = D_{\text{FEP}}$. How can we find this configuration?

In our discussion so far, we have focused on response time as the primary performance metric for query workloads. Now, however, we shall find it useful to include the query *throughput* as an aid in determining optimal cluster configurations. For each BEP processor configuration in Table 7.2, there is a saturation throughput value $X_{\text{sat}}(p)$ corresponding to the point at which the primary bottleneck occurs. That point is determined by $D_{\max}$ in the BEP subsystem.

Since X_{sat} is a direct measure of the maximum processing capacity of each BEP configuration, it follows that X_{sat} must scale with p, the number of processing nodes. In other words, $X_{\text{sat}}(p)$ is a linear function of p. The saturation throughput of any BEP configuration is simply p times the saturation throughput $X_{\text{sat}}(1)$ with a single BEP node:

$$X_{\text{sat}}(p) = p \, X_{\text{sat}}(1) \,. \tag{7.16}$$

An important point is that $X_{\text{sat}}(1)$ can be measured directly. Note also, that $X_{\text{sat}}(1)$ refers to the entire database back end including processors and disks.

In the PDQ model we have been considering the FEP capacity as fixed at 15 processors. As the capacity of the BEP configuration is scaled up, $D_{\max}$ in the BEP is effectively decreased. At some point, $D_{\max}$ will become smaller than that for the FEP. At that point, the FEP becomes the bottleneck that limits query throughput and there is no virtue in adding more BEP capacity. The saturation curve for the BEP develops a plateau in Fig. 7.19. We shall refer to this point as the saturation optimum and the corresponding BEP configuration as p_{opt}.

The value of p_{opt} can be determined as the point at which the saturation line saturates, i.e., where it reaches the maximum global throughput of the system. For the query cluster, the absolute global maximum in the system throughput occurs when there is no BEP processing at all. For an isolated and balanced FEP the minimum response time can be written as:

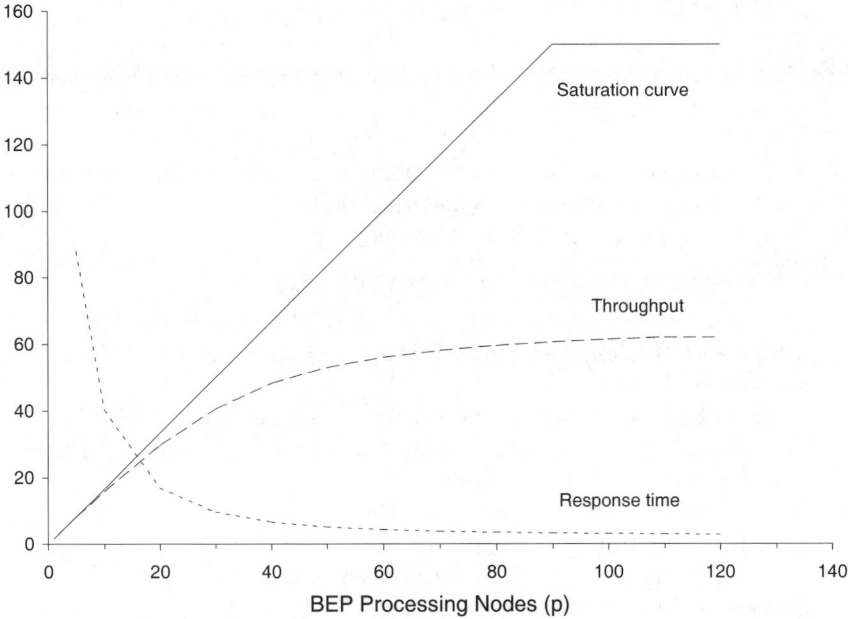

Fig. 7.19. The saturation throughput curve (*upper*) with the knee defining the optimal BEP cluster configuration at $p = 90$ nodes. The average throughput (*middle*) provides no guidance because it depends on the amount of work in the system. Here, the work is fixed at 800 CLI queries, but adding more queries into the system would push the average throughput up toward the saturation curve

$$D_{FEP} = \sum_{k}^{\text{stages}} D_k \bigg|_{p=0} , \tag{7.17}$$

where k represents the number of sequential pre-processing stages in the FEP and the evaluation at $p = 0$ indicates that the BEP is isolated from the FEP. Equation (7.17) corresponds to the isolated overhead for query pre-processing time. The plateau in the X_{sat} line must therefore occur at the point where the two curves intersect in Fig. 7.19. The two curves are given respectively by (7.16) and (7.17). The intersection can be found by solving

$$p\, X_{\text{sat}}(1) = \frac{1}{D_{\text{FEP}}} \tag{7.18}$$

so that the optimal BEP configuration is given by:

$$p_{\text{opt}} = \frac{1}{X_{\text{sat}}(1)\, D_{\text{FEP}}} \,. \tag{7.19}$$

The knee in the query saturation curve corresponding to p_{opt} can be seen in Fig. 7.19.

Example 7.1. The knee in the saturation throughput curve defines the optimal BEP cluster configuration at $p = 90$ nodes. The average throughput in Fig. 7.19 provides no guidance for finding this optimum because there not enough work in the system. The amount of work is *fixed* at 800 concurrent CLI queries and $X(50) = 53.03$ QPS. Adding more BEP capacity (increasing p) does not increase the mean throughput. However, adding more queries into the system does increase the mean throughput. For example, with 2800 concurrent CLI queries, $X(50) = 77.56$ QPS. □

Why does the query saturation method work?

1. For a small query cluster with only one BEP processor the FEP service demand is much less than the BEP processing time, i.e., the FEP overhead is relatively small.
2. As more BEP processors are added with their associated DSU disks, and the database tables restriped, the BEP processing time is reduced because of fewer visits to each BEP node.
3. As more BEP processors are added their service demand is scaled down by p according to (7.15).
4. Eventually, the reduced BEP service demand matches the FEP service demand and the knee in Fig. 7.19 occurs.
5. Adding more BEP processors beyond this knee increases the cost of the cluster without increasing performance (the plateau in Fig. 7.19) because the FEP is now the system bottleneck.

Such is the power of parallelism (when you can get it!).

Example 7.2. Using (7.19), the query saturation method predicts the optimum for the query cluster back ends as follows. We already know that $D_{FEP} = 0.0067$ at the front-end. Taking this value together with the single BEP saturation throughput $X_{sat}(1) = 1.67$, we calculate the optimal configuration as:

$$p_{opt} = \frac{1}{1.67 \times 0.0067} = 89.83 \text{ BEPs}\,,$$

which agrees with the PDQ result ($p = 90$) in Table 7.3. □

The PDQ model of the query cluster can be used to directly compute the optimal BEP. We see from Table 7.3 that the optimal BEP processing configuration occurs at $p = 90$ BEPs (and 180 DSU disks). With the optimal database BEP configuration determined, the response times for a multiuser query workload can be estimated. The results of running the PDQ model as a function of different interquery arrival times (modeled as different think-times) on the query cluster are summarized in Table 7.4.

7.5 Review

In this chapter we saw how to apply PDQ to the performance analysis of symmetric multiprocessors (SMPs) and distributed multicomputer clusters.

Table 7.3. Selected PDQ throughput estimates. The average query throughput $X(p)$ (*center column*) corresponds to the *concave curve* in Fig. 7.19. The *knee* occurs at $p = 90$ for which the query time is 3.18 *s* (Table 7.2)

p	$X(p)$	$X_{\text{sat}}(p)$
1	1.66	1.67
10	15.94	16.67
50	53.03	83.33
70	58.19	116.67
90	**60.69**	**150.00**
100	61.45	150.00
120	62.07	150.00

Table 7.4. Predicted multiuser query times for various think times. The last row corresponds to the number of CLI-ents in the PerlPDQ model of Sect. 7.4.1

	Optimized query performance (s)				
Users	$Z = 10$	$Z = 20$	$Z = 30$	$Z = 40$	$Z = 50$
1	1.89	1.89	1.89	1.89	1.89
200	2.13	2.02	1.98	1.96	1.94
400	2.41	2.15	2.07	2.02	2.00
600	2.76	2.31	2.16	2.09	2.05
800	3.18	2.48	2.27	2.17	2.11

For SMPs, caching effects and cache protocols can be a significant determinant for performance and scalability. This is particularly true for workloads that involve shared writeable data, e.g., online transaction processing databases.

For read-intensive workloads, e.g., data mining or decision support, multicomputer clusters offer better response time performance. Since the data is not being updated, previously read data can be cached and queries can be processed in parallel across a striped database. The optimal back-end parallel configuration can be determine by examining the saturation throughput for each configuration.

Exercises

7.1. Using the definition of processing power $\mathfrak{P}$ in Sect. 7.3.2, show:
(**a**) The mean number of enqueued processors is $p - \mathfrak{P}(1 + \Omega)$.
(**b**) The mean number of processors accessing memory is $\Omega\,\mathfrak{P}$.

7.2. A 1.25-GHz CPU executes a TPC-C transaction with a path length of 965,000 instructions, and the measured CPI is 0.71 cycles per instruction. What is the transaction per second (TPS) rate?

7.3. Calculate the optimal back-end configuration for a data mining cluster for which a single node has a maximum throughput of 19.7 QPS (queries per second) and the front-end processing is capable of 500 QPS.

8

How to Scale an Elephant with PDQ

8.1 An Elephant Story

There is a story about three blind men and an elephant that goes like this.

> The first blind man touches the elephant's trunk and exclaims, "This is a huge tree!" The second blind man happens to be holding onto the elephant's tail so he counters with, "No, it's a snake!" The third blind man who is touching the elephant's flank rejoins, "You're both wrong! It's a wall."

Each blind man thinks he is right and the others are wrong, even though all three of them are touching the same elephant.

Similarly, three performance engineers—who were not blind (at least, not in the above sense)—were reviewing performance data collected from a large-scale application server. At some point, the following conversation ensued:

Engineer 1: "Wow! This system scales linearly!"
Engineer 2: "No it doesn't! The system becomes maxed out."
Engineer 3: "You're both wrong! The server supports the desired number of users."

As you'll soon *see*, all three engineers are correct because they are talking about different aspects of the same performance characteristic, just like the blind men and the elephant.

Performance data that are produced by load tests and benchmarks are not the same thing as information. Extracting performance information out of performance measurements requires knowing what to look for, which in turn requires knowing where to look, or, perhaps more importantly, knowing *how* to look at performance measurements. Knowing where and how to look is akin to having the right kind of geographical *map*. In this chapter you will learn how PDQ can be used like a *performance* map.

This chapter shows you how the queueing concepts in Chaps. 2, 3, and 5 can be applied to the scalability analysis of load test and benchmark data. In particular, we examine the SPEC SDM multiuser benchmark. A key lesson is that in order to carry out performance analysis with PDQ, it is essential to obtain steady-state measurements of the throughput (and the corresponding response time) at each user load. These time-averaged values can then be used to parameterize a PDQ model.

In addition, you will see that Amdahl's law provides a functional definition of application scalability. In particular, it corresponds to worst-case synchronous queueing, and therefore represents another type of bound on throughput performance in addition to those discussed in Chap. 5.

8.1.1 What Is Scalability?

Scalability is a perennial hot topic, most recently of interest for newer application architectures based on technologies such as peer-to-peer networks (see, e.g., `www.ececs.uc.edu/~mjovanov/Research/gnutella.html`), PHP, Java (see e.g., `www.onjava.com/pub/a/onjava/2003/10/15/ php_scalability.html`), and Linux (see e.g., `lse.sourceforge.net`).

Scalability is an abstract notion that too often remains either poorly defined [Joines et al. 2002, Chap.1] or remains undefined altogether. Simply put, *scalability* is a relation among performance metrics that characterizes the rate of diminishing returns as the dimensions of the system are increased. This means that scalability can actually be expressed in a mathematical form. Therefore, scalability is not a number, but a *function*. An example of a well-known scalability function is Amdahl's law [Amdahl 1967] for processor *speed-up*:

$$S_{\mathrm{A}}(p) = \frac{p}{1 + \alpha(p-1)} \,. \tag{8.1}$$

Equation (8.1) expresses scalability very simply in terms of the number of physical processors p in the server configuration and a single parameter α that quantifies the degree of diminishing returns at each processor configuration. The relative speed-up $S_A(p)$ is defined by the ratio of the execution time on p processors to the execution time on a single processor.

Since the value of α lies in the range $0 \leq \alpha \leq 1$, it can be interpreted alternatively as:

1. a measure of the level of *contention* in the system
2. the fraction of time spent waiting for a resource, e.g., a database lock
3. the percentage of serial execution time in the workload
4. the degree of single-threadedness in the workload

It turns out that item 1 is most significant for the subsequent discussion.

In an ironic twist of history, the original argument by Gene Amdahl [1967] has been doubly misunderstood. First, (8.1), usually attributed to him, does not appear in his paper, which is a purely empirical account. Second, his original argument was an attempt to convince people that multiple processors were less cost effective than the fastest available single processors. Ironically, these days, (8.1) always appears in the context of parallel processing performance.

History notwithstanding, (8.1) can be generalized in two ways.

1. Another parameter β can be introduced to quantify the degree of *incoherency* in the system (e.g., cache-miss latency). The generalized scalability function is:

$$S_G(p) = \frac{p}{1 + \alpha(p-1) + \alpha\beta p(p-1)} , \tag{8.2}$$

   and is discussed in more detail in Gunther [2000a, Eqn. 6.24 on p. 189], and [Gunther 2002b].
2. Application scalability can be expressed by modifying (8.1) to be a function of user load N with the processor configuration p held fixed. See (8.9) in Sect. 8.3.2.

If there is no delay for maintaining coherency, the β parameter vanishes, and (8.2) reduces to Amdahl's law (8.1).

Another important point to note about (8.2) and (8.1) is that neither of these scalability functions contains any explicit reference to the platform architecture, the interconnect technology, the operating system, or the application that is running. All this complexity is hidden in the measurable values of α and β. Therefore, these scalability functions must be *universally applicable*!

We now turn to some public-domain benchmark data from the `www.spec.org` Web site to see how these scalability concepts can be applied.

8.1.2 SPEC Multiuser Benchmark

The SPEC benchmark, most relevant for our scalability analysis, is called *SDET* from the SDM (System Development Multitasking) suite `www.spec.org/osg/sdm91` which is currently part of the OSG (Open Systems Group) working group within the SPEC organization.

The SDET workload simulates a group of UNIX software developers doing compiles, and edits, as well as exercising other shell commands. These multi-user activities are emulated by concurrently running multiple copies of scripts containing the shell commands. The relevant performance metric is the *throughput* measured in *scripts per hour*. A very important distinguishing feature of the benchmark is that it does not rely on reporting a single metric in the way that `www.spec.org/osg/cpu2000/` does. Arguably, the SPEC CPU2000 metric has replaced the notion of nominal MIPS (cf. Sect. 7.3.5). Rather, the reporting procedure requires that a graph showing a significant portion of the

Table 8.1. SPEC SDET benchmark data for a 16-way SPARCcenter 2000

Concurrent generators	Throughput (scripts/hour)	Normalized throughput
0	0.00	0.00
1	64.90	1.00
18	995.90	15.35
36	1,652.40	25.46
72	1,853.20	28.55
108	1,828.90	28.18
144	1,775.00	27.35
216	1,702.20	26.23

throughput characteristic must be constructed. The SPEC SDET run rules indicate how this throughput data must be collected and presented.

The results used in the subsequent analysis come from the SPEC SDET benchmark for a 16-way Sun SPARCcenter2000. The full report can be downloaded from `www.spec.org/osg/sdm91/results/res9506/`. Those benchmark data are summarized here in Table 8.1 and Fig. 8.1. The most significant fea-

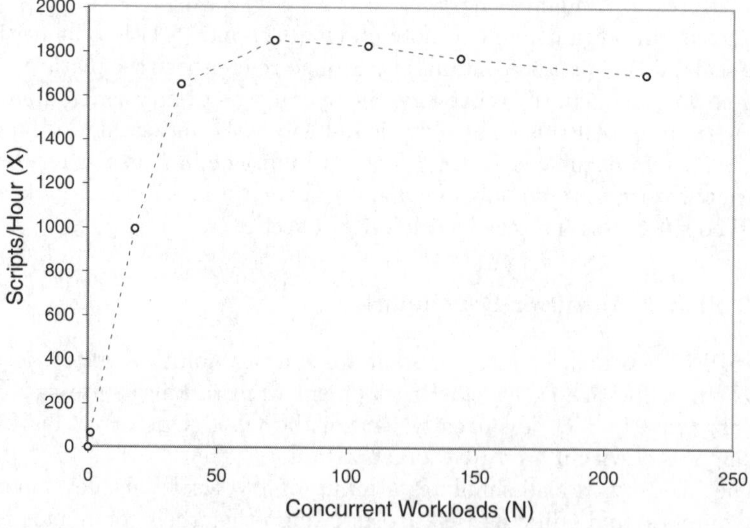

Fig. 8.1. A plot of the throughput measurements in Table 8.1 which a reporting requirement of the SPEC SDET benchmark

tures of this benchmark are:

1. The throughput characteristic has a maximum.

2. The maximum throughput is 1,853.20 scripts/h.
3. The maximum throughput occurs at 72 generators or emulated users.
4. Beyond the peak, the throughput becomes retrograde.

These benchmark results are obtained by applying the following steady-state measurement methodology.

8.1.3 Steady-state Measurements

An important but hidden feature of benchmark results like those plotted in Fig. 8.1 is that each point on the plot corresponds to the average throughput evaluated when the throughput rate reaches *steady state.* The relationship

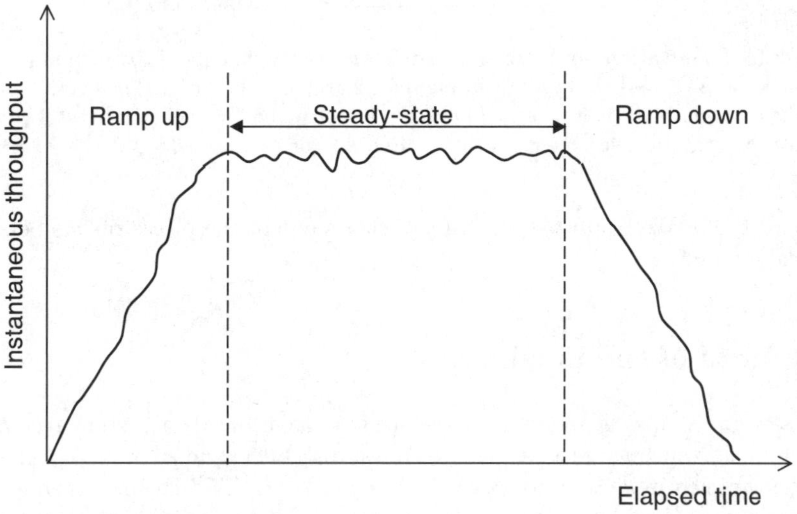

Fig. 8.2. Steady-state measurements of instantaneous throughput for a fixed user load. The steady-state throughput (*center*) is measured as a function of time by first ramping-up the workload (*left*) and later ramping-down (*right*) once the statistical average throughput has been determined

between steady-state (Fig. 8.2) measurements of the *instantaneous* throughput and the average throughput at each user load level is shown in Fig. 8.3. The steady-state average for a given user load is determined by taking measurements over some measurement period T and eliminating any ramp-up or ramp-down periods from the data.

By way of contrast, the SPEC jAppsServer2002 benchmark requires that such ramp-up and ramp-down data be reported along with the steady-state throughput values.

To get the most information out of benchmark or load testing data like these, you need a performance model. This is another performance-by-design

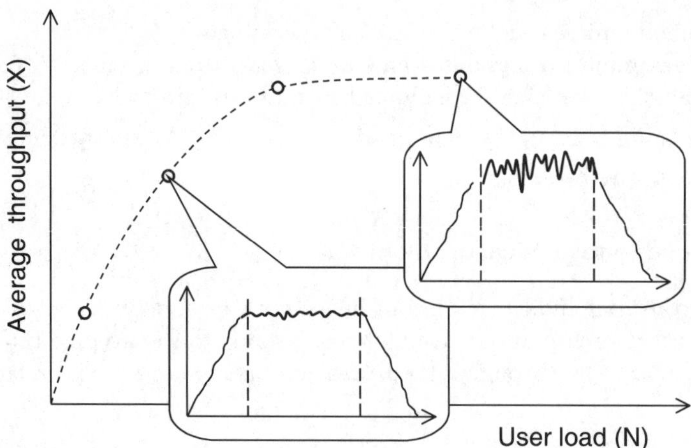

Fig. 8.3. The relationship between steady-state measurements of the instantaneous throughput $X(t)$ and the system throughput characteristic $X(N)$. The overall mean throughput characteristic (*dashed curve*) is determined by repeating (*inset plots*) the steady-state measurement process in Fig. 8.2 for each user load N

role for PDQ. We begin by putting together some of the pieces of this benchmark elephant.

8.2 Parts of the Elephant

We saw in Chaps. 2 and 3 that we need to have data on system resource consumption such as: process service times, disk busy, and so on, to construct a performance model. Unfortunately, the SPEC SDET benchmark rules do not require the reporting of such performance metrics, so we cannot proceed directly in that fashion. Instead, we need to deduce that information from the data we do have.

The maximum measured throughput in Table 8.2 is 1,853.20 scripts/h. You should not take the decimal places in these measurements too literally. Typical performance measurements have an error range of about $\pm 5\%$, which would put the maximum throughput $X_{\max}$ anywhere between 1,760 and 1,945 scripts/h. The benchmark platform would have been configured and tuned to generate this maximum throughput number, after all, that is what serious benchmarking is about. Moreover, part of the tuning process is to make the system processor-bound, rather than memory-bound or disk-bound. Using the concepts presented in Chap. 5, we can presume that throughput performance was bottlenecked by saturated CPUs, and this will be usefl for constructing our PDQ model.

Table 8.2. Summary of SPEC benchmark analysis

Performance metric	Value	Unit
Max. throughput X_{max}	1,853.20	Scripts per hour
Peak loading N_{peak}	72	Concurrent generators
Bottleneck demand D_{max}	0.00054	Hours per script
Average think-time Z	0.01487	Hours (free parameter)

8.2.1 Service Demand Part

We start with the relationship:

$$X_{\text{max}} = \frac{1}{D_{\text{max}}} , \tag{8.3}$$

from Chap. 2 where D_{max} is the service demand at the bottleneck resource, the CPU in this case. Inverting this equation, we get:

$$D_{\text{max}} = \frac{1}{X_{\text{max}}} . \tag{8.4}$$

Since we know $X_{\text{max}} = 1,853.20$ scripts/h from Table 8.1, we can calculate that:

$$D_{\text{max}} = \frac{1}{1,853.20} = 0.00054 \text{ hours per script} , \tag{8.5}$$

which is equivalent to 1.94 seconds per script.

8.2.2 Think Time Part

We cannot determine the value of the thinktime parameter Z directly from the benchmark data but we can estimate it using the response time law:

$$X(N) = \frac{N}{R+Z} , \tag{8.6}$$

from Chap. 2. The uncontended throughput occurs when $N = 1$, and in the absence of any queueing $R = D_{\text{max}}$. Therefore:

$$X(1) = \frac{1}{D_{\text{max}} + Z} . \tag{8.7}$$

We can simply read off $X(1) = 64.90$ scripts/h from Table 8.1, and since we have already calculated $D_{max} = 0.00054$ h, we can use (8.7) to calculate Z. The result is $Z = 0.01487$ h.

8.2.3 User Load Part

Based on Sect. 5.3.3 in Chap. 5, a simple estimator of the optimal number of users that the system can support is given by:

$$N_{\text{opt}} = \left\lfloor \frac{D_{\max} + Z}{D_{\max}} \right\rfloor , \tag{8.8}$$

where $\lfloor \cdot \rfloor$ means the *floor* function that rounds down to the nearest integer. Substituting the appropriate values from our performance model, we find $N_{\text{opt}} = 28$, which is much lower than the peak measured throughput at 72 generators.

If the average user load is maintained too far below this optimum (i.e., $N \ll N_{\text{opt}}$) the system capacity is under-utilized, i.e., resources that have already been paid for are not being utilized efficiently. Conversely, if the user load is maintained too much above this optimum (i.e., $N \gg N_{\text{opt}}$) the system will become saturated and response times will increase dramatically.

8.3 PDQ Scalability Model

Now we are in a position to construct a simple queueing model of this benchmark system using PDQ. Since the benchmark is driven near its peak capability, we assume that the performance is controlled primarily by the bottleneck resource represented by the single PDQ node (Fig. 8.4). To construct this

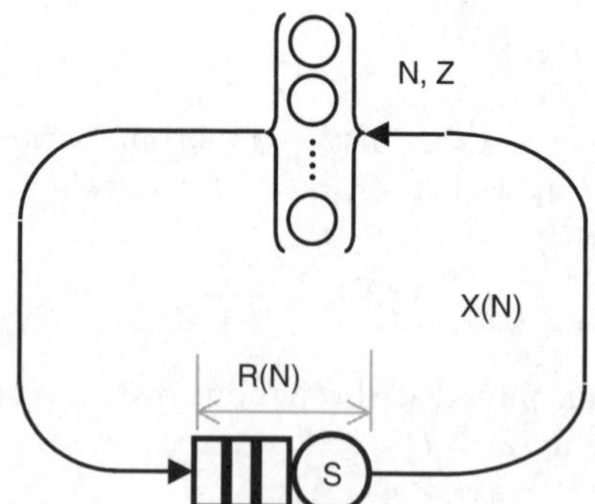

Fig. 8.4. Simple queueing model of the SPEC benchmark

simple model we use the following benchmark parameters:

1. The maximum throughput: $X_{\max} = 2000$ scripts/h
2. The maximum service demand: $D_{\max} = 0.0005$ h
3. The thinktime for each user: $Z = 0.0149$ h

Here, we are allowing (perhaps optimistically) for the fact that if there was no throughput degradation above the peak load at 72 clients, the achievable throughput might be closer to 2000 scripts/h. We do this by adjusting $D_{\max}$ to be slightly smaller (line 9 below) than was determined in Table 8.2. We also set the number of clients at 50, so as to be above the expected value of N_{opt}.

```
1 #! /usr/bin/perl
2 # elephant.pl
3
4 use pdq;
5
6 $clients = 50;    # load generators
7 $think = 0.0149; # hours
8 $Dmax = 0.0005;  # hours
9
10 pdq::Init("SPEC SDET Model");
11
12 $pdq::streams = pdq::CreateClosed("BenchWork", $pdq::TERM, $clients, $think)
13 $pdq::nodes  = pdq::CreateNode("BenchSUT", $pdq::CEN, $pdq::FCFS);
14 pdq::SetDemand("BenchSUT", "BenchWork", $Dmax);
15
16 pdq::SetWUnit("Scripts");
17 pdq::SetTUnit("Hour");
18
19 pdq::Solve($pdq::EXACT);
20 pdq::Report();
```

The normalized results shown in Fig. 8.5 are derived from the following PDQ report:

```
        ***************************************
        ****** Pretty Damn Quick REPORT *******
        ***************************************
        ***  of : Tue Feb 10 11:55:45 2004  ***
        ***  for: SPEC SDET Model           ***
        ***  Ver: PDQ Analyzer v2.8 120803  ***
        ***************************************
        ***************************************

        ***************************************
        ******    PDQ Model INPUTS      *******
        ***************************************

Node Sched Resource   Workload   Class     Demand
---- ----- --------   --------   -----     ------
CEN  FCFS  BenchSUT   BenchWork  TERML     0.0005

Queueing Circuit Totals:

```

```
20     Clients:    50.00
21     Streams:        1
22     Nodes:          1
23
24 WORKLOAD Parameters
25
26 Client        Number        Demand   Thinktime
27 ----          ------        ------   ---------
28 BenchWork      50.00         0.0005     0.01
29
30         ***************************************
31         ******    PDQ Model OUTPUTS      *******
32         ***************************************
33
34 Solution Method: EXACT
35
36         ******    SYSTEM Performance     *******
37
38 Metric                           Value  Unit
39 -----------------                -----  ----
40 Workload: "BenchWork"
41 Mean Throughput          1999.6137      Scripts/Hour
42 Response Time               0.0101      Hour
43 Mean Concurrency           20.2058      Scripts
44 Stretch Factor             20.2097
45
46 Bounds Analysis:
47 Max Throughput           2000.0000      Scripts/Hour
48 Min Response                0.0005      Hour
49 Max Demand                  0.0005      Hour
50 Tot Demand                  0.0005      Hour
51 Think time                  0.0149      Hour
52 Optimal Clients            30.8000      Clients
53
54         ******    RESOURCE Performance   *******
55
56 Metric          Resource     Work              Value   Unit
57 ---------       ------       ----              -----   ----
58 Throughput      BenchSUT     BenchWork     1999.6137   Scripts/Hour
59 Utilization     BenchSUT     BenchWork       99.9807   Percent
60 Queue Length    BenchSUT     BenchWork       20.2058   Scripts
61 Residence Time  BenchSUT     BenchWork        0.0101   Hour
```

The optimal load is reported on line 52 as 30.80 clients; this is slightly higher than the 28 clients estimated in Sect. 8.2.3 because we manually adjusted the bottleneck service demand D_{max}. The PDQ node in Fig. 8.4 is saturated at 99.98% busy (line 59 above).

The PDQ prediction (the upper curve in Fig. 8.5) represents the best possible outcome that one could expect from this benchmark platform. The measured data adheres fairly closely to the PDQ prediction until it gets above CPU saturation, at which point the throughput falls slightly below theoretical expectations and heads toward the Amdahl bound (the lower curve in Fig. 8.5).

8.3.1 Interpretation

This very simple queueing model of the SPEC benchmark data reveals a tremendous amount of information about the performance of this UNIX *elephant*. Where one might have expected to build a simulation model of this otherwise complicated multiprocessor platform, we have actually arrived at a

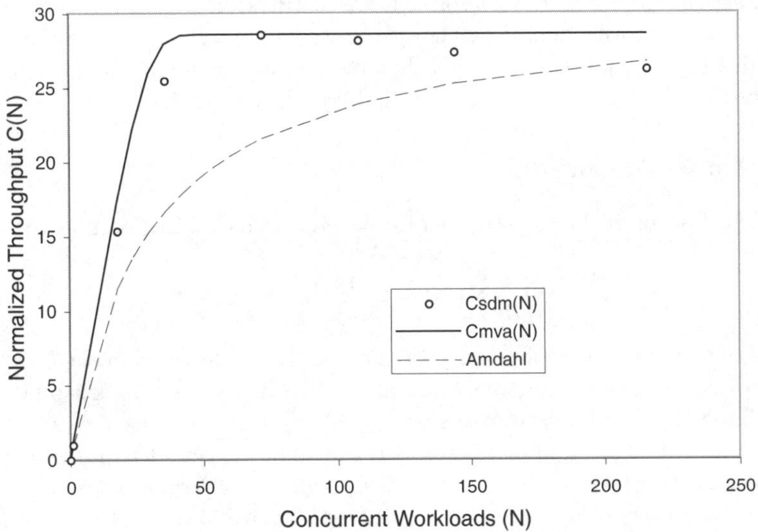

Fig. 8.5. SPEC benchmark data shown together with the PDQ prediction (*upper curve*) and the Amdahl bound (*lower curve*)

very close approximation to its SPEC benchmark performance characteristics using a PDQ queueing model with just a single contention point (Fig. 8.4). A real multiprocessor system has many contention points, e.g., memory bus arbitration, spin-locks, and i-node locks, just to name a few. Remarkably, we have subsumed all those details into a single queue without too much loss of generality or accuracy. How did we get away with it?

> The key concept to recognize is the single queue corresponds precisely to the benchmark goal of making the workload CPU-bound. Recall that the workload represents multiple UNIX software developers, and the benchmark is a stress test. This single point of contention has the side effect of making the measured throughput characteristic (the upper curve in Fig. 8.5) rise almost linearly up to the saturation plateau. It is this linear characteristic in the measured throughput that validates our choice of a single PDQ queueing node in Fig. 8.4.

Real software developers would have significant think-times, and a real multiprocessor platform would have multiple contention points. Those additional contention points (represented as additional queueing nodes in PDQ) would tend to reduce the measured throughput. In other words, the real throughput characteristic would tend to approach the saturation plateau with a much slower rise. The lower bound on the system throughput is shown as the lower curve in Fig. 8.5. It turns out that this lower bound is identical to the curve produced by Amdahl's law (8.1) in a slighlty different guise.

8.3.2 Amdahl's Law

Amdahl's law in (8.1) can be reexpressed in terms of the number of user *processes* N:

$$S_{\mathrm{A}}(N) = \frac{N}{1 + \alpha(N-1)} , \tag{8.9}$$

instead of the number of physical processors p. This follows from the fact that the processor configuration was fixed at $p = 16$ in the benchmark platform, while the number of user processes was varied in the range $1 \leq N \leq 216$ (Table 8.2). The throughput in Fig. 8.1 was then measured as a function of N, or concurrent user scripts in the SPEC benchmark terminology.

The author has shown elsewhere [Gunther 2002a, 2004] that the α parameter in (8.1) is determined by the bottleneck demand (D_{max}) and the thinktime (Z) in the queueing circuit by virtue of the relationship:

$$\alpha = \frac{D_{\max}}{D_{\max} + Z} . \tag{8.10}$$

Equation (8.10) contains the following two special cases:

1. $\alpha = 0$: No serialization of the workload; this condition is guaranteed when there is no service demand ($D_{\max} = 0$) in (8.10). With this condition, all the virtual users are purely in a think state and there is zero serialization.

2. $\alpha = 1$: A single-threaded workload with no available concurrency; this condition is guaranteed when there is no thinking delay ($Z = 0$) in (8.10). With this condition, the virtual users are always waiting for service because they are 100% serialized.

These cases correspond precisely to the extreme values of α. For the values of $D_{\max}$ and Z from the SPEC benchmark data, it can be determined that $\alpha = 0.0325$, or the workload is serialized is 3.25% of the time. Here, however, we have provided a queueing theory interpretation of α. But what is the queueing theory interpretation of the Amdahl bound?

Following Sect. 8.1.3, the PDQ model assumes that the benchmark system is in *steady state* at each user configuration N where measurements are taken. That means some client users (i.e., benchmark workload generators) are being serviced while others are in a thin state. The PDQ model also assumes that no user can have more than one outstanding request being serviced, i.e., another request cannot be issued by the same user script until the previous request has been serviced.

The Amdahl bound represents a worst-case scenario where all the users issue their requests *simultaneously*! Consequently, all N requests become piled up at the CPU queue in Fig. 8.4. Rather than the asynchronous queueing implied in Chap. 3, the Amdahl bound (8.9) corresponds to worst-case *synchronous* queueing, i.e., an all-or-nothing situation with all requests either waiting in the queue or thinking. Either case represents low throughput. The relative proportions of thinking time Z and service time $D_{\max}$ determine the actual value of α in equation 8.10. In the SPEC SDET benchmark Z is near zero (Table 8.2).

An analogous situation arises for the hardware version of Amdahl's law (8.1). The serial fraction of the workload can be thought of as follows. A processor makes a request for data. It could make such a request in different ways. An efficient process would be for the requesting processor to contact each of the other processors successively until it gets the needed response. The remaining $(p - 2)$ processors would continue to compute uninterrupted. In this way, the outstanding request and computation would overlap asynchronously. But Amdahl's law is not a represention of maximum efficiency.

Instead, the dynamics expressed by Amdahl's law means the requesting processor *broadcasts* its request to all the other processors simultaneously [Gunther 2000a, Chap. 14], thereby interrupting them all simultaneously. In order to process the request, all the other processors must stop computing, listen to, and process the request to see if they are the processor that needs to respond before continuing with their own computation. Once again, this is an all-or-nothing situation, just like synchronous queueing.

The important conclusion of this section is that Amdahl's law corresponds to synchronous queueing of requests and represents another bound on throughput performance in addition to those discussed in Chap. 5.

Amdahl's law cannot account for the retrograde throughput present in the SDET benchmark data of Fig. 8.1. It is possible, however, to enhance our simple queueing models to include it. We have assumed that the service demand $D_{\max}$ is constant (e.g., 1.94 s). This gives rise to the saturation plateau (upper curve) in Fig. 8.5. If we relax that assumption and permit the service demand to increase with the load, long queues will persist and the throughput will begin to fall. One way to achieve this effect is through the use of a load-dependent server described in Chaps. 6 and 10.

8.3.3 The Elephant's Dimensions

So, how big is this UNIX elephant? We collect all the various estimates from our queueing model analysis (Sect. 8.3) in Table 8.3.

Table 8.3. Predicted dimensions of our benchmarked elephant

Performance metric	Value	Unit
Max. throughtput X_{max}	2,000.00	Scripts per hour
Bottleneck demand D_{max}	0.0005	Hours per script
Average thinktime Z	0.0149	Hours (free parameter)
Optimal loading N_{opt}	31	Concurrent users
Serial fraction α	3.25	Percent

In this particular case, a great deal of the CPU service demand is being spent in *system* time by the UNIX kernel. Further reduction in those times might be achieved by implementing such changes as:

- improving streams-queue management
- using finer granularity locks for threads
- converting singly linked lists to doubly linked lists
- using a `malloc()` on `fork()` rather than expensive page faults
- using more efficient hashing
- applying processor affinity

This level of performance enhancement typically requires detailed investigation of both the operating system and the application. The average think-time is not a number that is easy to identify by direct measurement. It is often set to zero in the benchmark scripts and should be treated here as a modeling parameter.

Finally, we review how well our intrepid performance engineers in Sect. 8.1 fared in assessing this UNIX elephant.

- Engineer 1 was essentially correct as far as he went. But the remainder of the throughput characteristic tells the real story.
- Engineer 2 was not wrong, but was perhaps guilty of being too literal. The benchmark system is being overdriven. This may indeed be a requirement either for stress testing or for "bench-marketing," where a single peak number looks more impressive when quoted out of context from the other measurements.
- Engineer 3 was too optimistic. The optimal load of 28 users is less than half that expected from the benchmark data (i.e., the peak at 72 users).

As can be seen in Fig. 8.1, the application of 72 generators has already driven the system into saturation and the engineer did not take this into account.

Needless to say, they are all talking about the same benchmark elephant.

The Amdahl bound (which the benchmark data does indeed approach) is the more likely throughput characteristic of a general multiprocessor application. There is usually a lot more runtime serialization in an application than most people realize, which makes writing efficient applications or multiprocessors (Chap. 7) a difficult task [Gunther 2000a, Appendix C, *Guidelines for Making Multiprocessor Applications Symmetric*].

8.4 Review

This chapter has shown you how some of the queueing concepts presented in Chaps. 2, 3, and 5 can be applied to the performance analysis of load test and benchmark data. In particular, we considered an example application based on SPEC SDM multiuser benchmark data.

The SDM benchmark source codes are available for a nominal fee from the SPEC Web site at `www.spec.org/osg/sdm91/`. If this benchmark looks at all relevant, you might consider purchasing it and tailoring the scripts to create your own customized benchmark harness.

In order to carry out performance analysis with PDQ it is essential to obtain steady-state measurements of the throughput (and the response time) at each user load point. These time-averaged values can then be used to parameterize a PDQ model of the type discussed in Sect. 8.3.

Amdahl's law provides a functional definition of application scalability. In Sect. 8.3.2 we showed that it also corresponds to worst-case synchronous queueing of requests, and therefore represents another bound on throughput performance in addition to those discussed in Chap. 5.

Our single contention point PDQ model does not account for the data falling away from the saturation plateau toward the Amdahl bound (the lower curve in Fig. 8.5). However, the PDQ model could include such effects, and a more detailed discussion of that technique is given in Chap. 10.

Exercises

8.1. (**a**) Substitute the expression (8.10) for α into (8.9) and show that it reduces to

$$S_{\mathrm{A}}(N) = \left(\frac{N}{N D_{\max} + Z} \right) (D_{\max} + Z). \tag{8.11}$$

(**b**) Convince yourself that $ND_{\max}$ in the denominator of (8.11) can be interpreted as $R_{\max}$ i.e., maximal residence time due to maximal queueing.
(**c**) Defining

$$X_{sync}(N) = \frac{N}{R_{\max} + Z},$$

apply (8.7) to (8.11) and show that

$$S_{\mathrm{A}}(N) = \frac{X_{sync}(N)}{X(1)}.$$

(**d**) Interpret the expression in part (c). (Hint: Read Sect. 8.3.2)

8.2. Who was the original author of the SDET benchmark?

8.3. Derive Amdahl's law.

8.4. What changes would need to be reflected in the parameters of the PDQ model `elephant.pl` to move the optimal load point to the measured peak load point, i.e., $N_{\mathrm{opt}} = 72$?

8.5. Plot $S_{\mathrm{G}}(p)$ in (8.2) for integral processor configurations in the range $0 \leq p \leq 100$, with $\alpha = 0.10$, and incrementing β by 0.10 in the range $0 \leq \beta \leq 1$. How do these curves compare with $S_{\mathrm{A}}(p)$?

9

Client/Server Analysis with PDQ

9.1 Introduction

In this chapter we present performance analysis for client/server architectures using PDQ. This material is the most complex use of PDQ so far in that it draws on the techniques presented in previous chapters and extends them to software and communication network analysis.

Many modern computing environments are moving to a more distributed paradigm, with client/server being one of the most common distributed architectures in use today (Fig. 9.1). But the fragmentation of computer resources across networks has also broken the notion of centralized performance management that worked for mainframe applications. Consequently, performance

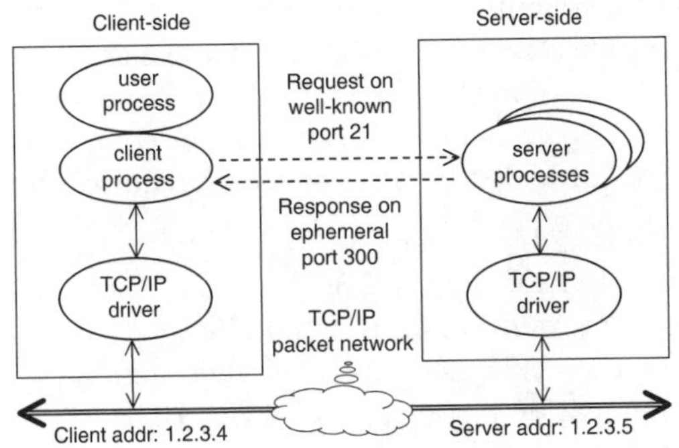

Fig. 9.1. Classical client/server process architecture

management is a major problem once again, and those business operations that have been quick to adopt client/server, technology are now starting to recognize the hidden costs of providing services with consistent performance. Those implementing client/server applications are learning to demand assurance about performance in terms of *service level agreements* (SLAs).

In this chapter, you will learn how to apply PDQ to the performance analysis of a multitier B2C client/server environment. A key point to note is that PDQ can be used to predict the scalability of distributed *software* applications, not just hardware as in Chap. 7. This is achieved by using the workflow analysis of Sect. 9.3.3.

Moreover, the approach presented here shows you how to make benchmarking and load testing more cost-effective. Load test results only need to be obtained on a relatively sparse set of smaller test platform configurations. These data can be used to parameterize a PDQ model which, in turn, can be used to predict the performance of the client/server application once it is deployed into production. Thus, PDQ offers another way to keep the cost of load testing complex distributed applications under control.

9.2 Client/Server Architectures

From the standpoint of computer technology, client/server refers to a software interface specification shown schematically in Fig. 9.1. The client/side of the interface makes requests and the server side of the interface provides the service usually without the client process understanding how the service is actually implemented. From the standpoint of the services provided, it is irrelevant where the client and server processes are physically located and which resources they consume in order to do the processing. This creates a very flexible computing environment.

So how does the client/server software interface work? The rules that the client and server processes communicate are called a protocol. Client/server is a special case of distributed computing.

Client/server applications can be implemented using a variety of protocols, but Transmission Control Protocol over Internet Protocol (TCP/IP) is among the most commonly chosen. Any TCP/IP network connection between a client process and services provided by a remote host requires the following items:

- Client-side IP host address, e.g., 1.2.3.4
- Server-side host address, e.g., 1.2.3.5
- Server process on a well-known port number, e.g., 21
- Client process on an ephemeral port number, e.g., anything above 255
- Process communication protocol, e.g., TCP, UDP

All this information gets encapsulated in one or more IP packets, which are then transmitted over the network, along with either the request message or the data response. This is the basis of the transparency offered by client/server architectures.

From the performance analyst's standpoint, however, knowing which software processes are executing and on which remote hardware resources is vital to any kind of performance analysis. As we shall see shortly, this is the Achilles' heel of many client/server applications.

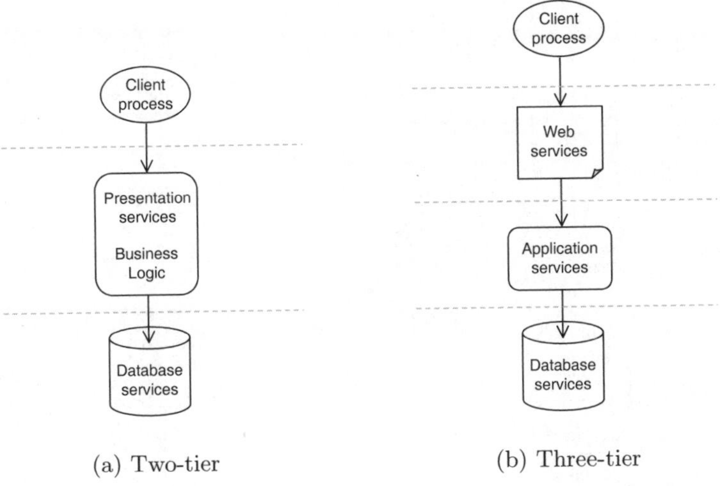

Fig. 9.2. Comparison of (a) two-tier and (b) three-tier client/server architectures

The kind of distributed performance measurements required are discussed in Gunther [2000a, Chap. 4], but this level of integrated performance monitoring is still in a rather immature state. A whimsical analogy with remotely monitored pizza delivery in Gunther [2000a, Chap. 8] highlights the requirements. The upshot of that analysis is that you need a client/server architecture (tools) to manage a client/server architecture (application). This is easy to say, but hard to do.

9.2.1 Multitier Environments

The classic client/server model is a master/slave relationship, where the client process resides in one physical location, e.g., on a desktop, hand-held personal digital assistant (PDA), or cell phone, and the server process resides in a different physical location. Both processes are connected via a network. Figure 9.2(a) exemplifies this is the basic *two-tier* architecture.

9.2.2 Three–Tier Options

In a three-tier approach, like that shown in Fig. 9.2(b), another layer of servers is inserted between the clients and the data servers. These second-tier servers provide dual functionality: they can act as clients that make requests to the appropriate data sources (application servers), and they function as servers for the desktop clients (function servers). A three-tiered architecture divides applications into parts that run on different types of platforms.

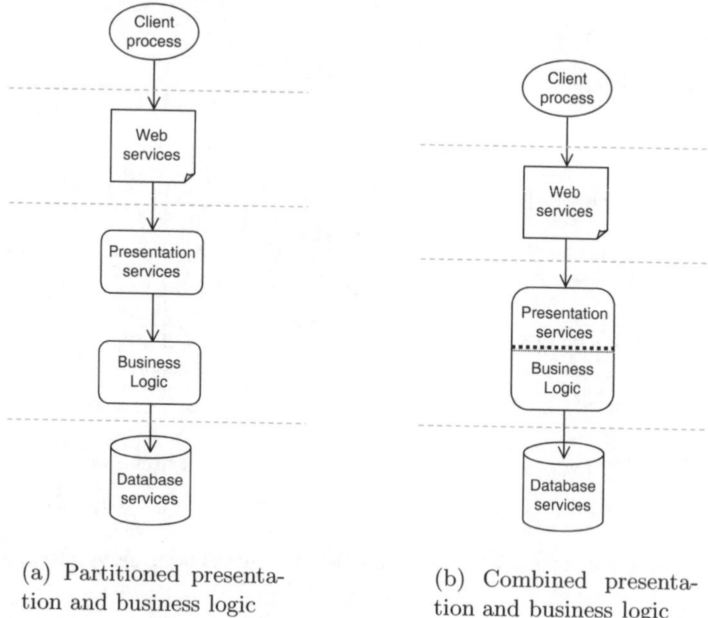

(a) Partitioned presentation and business logic

(b) Combined presentation and business logic

Fig. 9.3. Comparison of logical three-tier client/server architectures. In (a) the presentation logic and business logic separated across tiers, while in (b) they are combined on the same tier and interact through an API

The clients support the presentation layer of the application to display data retrieved from the server side, e.g., databases. The application servers process business applications such as financial transactions and marketing queries. The data sources range from SQL databases to legacy application programs. A client/server architecture also lets the system administrator or architect separate the business logic from the actual processing logic (Fig. 9.3). This modularity enables business changes to be rapidly incorporated into applications.

A three-tier architecture can also be expanded horizontally by adding different types of application servers and different types of databases. This additional capacity and functionality can be enhanced in a way that is quite transparent to the clients.

The flexibility and scalability of a three-tiered (or n-tiered) architecture comes at the price of greater complexity of applications and management. Modern client/server development environments offer facilities such as object libraries, 4GL development languages, and dynamic directories to assist in dealing with multitiered complexity. A primary goal of these tools is to facilitate changes in the environment without rebuilding the client applications.

In practice, the performance of a multitiered application will also be determined by such factors as:

- How much of the client user interface runs on the application server.
- Whether or not presentation services and business logic reside on the same physical server. (Fig. 9.3)
- How much of the application logic runs on the database servers.
- How much data is placed on the application server.

For more on the impact of business logic placement on performance and scalability is `www.onjava.com/pub/a/onjava/2003/10/15/php_scalability.html`.

9.3 Benchmark Environment

In this section we demonstrate how to construct and evaluate performance models of modern three-tier client/server architectures. The environment to be analyzed is a *business-to-consumer* (B2C) application intended to support 1,000 to 2,000 concurrent Web-based users. The analysis is to be made against the benchmark platform in Fig. 9.4, which is on the scale of a TPC-W-type benchmark. The application spans a distributed architecture involv-

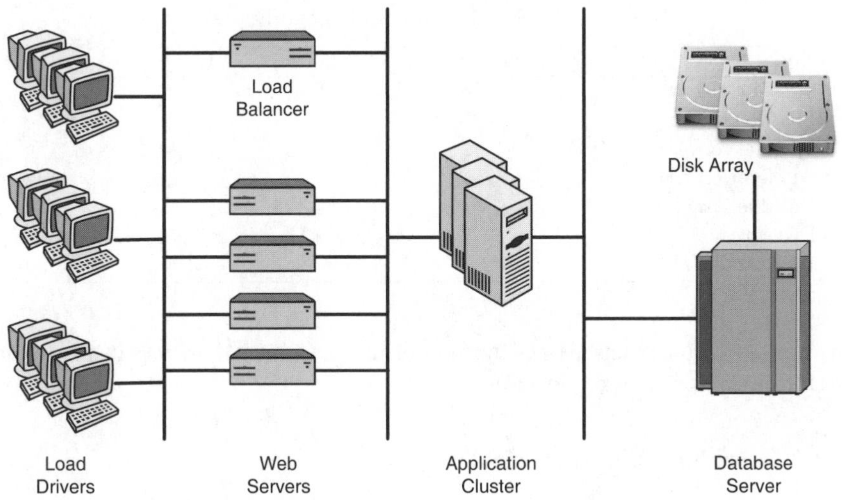

Fig. 9.4. Multitier client/server benchmark environment

ing PC benchmark drivers, multiple Web servers, an application cluster, a database server, and attached storage array. All the services are connected via a 100Base-T switched Ethernet. The hardware resources together with some relevant performance measures are listed in Table 9.1.

9.3.1 Performance Scenarios

The objectives of the benchmark are to assess scalability of the application prior to deployment. The primary performance criterion is that the 95th percentile of user response times for Web-based transactions should not exceed 500 ms.

The performance scenarios that we shall consider are:

- 100 client generators on the baseline benchmark platform (Sect. 9.4.1)
- 1,000 client generators predicted by PDQ (Sect. 9.4.2)
- 1,500 client generators predicted by PDQ (Sects. 9.4.3, 9.4.4, and 9.4.5)
- determine the client generator load at saturation (Sect. 9.4.6)

In reality, different load points can be chosen. The key idea is to predict many points using PDQ, but only benchmark a few for validation. Using PDQ in this way is intended to be more cost effective than reconfiguring the real platform to measure each load point.

The various speeds and feeds of the benchmark platform are summarized in Table 9.1 where CPU2000 refers to the integer SPEC CPU benchmark ratings available online at `www.spec.org`. Arguably, the SPEC CPU2000 metric has replaced the notion of nominal MIPS (cf. Sect. 7.3.5). With these assumptions

Table 9.1. Baseline benchmark configuration ratings

Node	Number	CPU2000	Ops/s	MB/s
Desktop driver	100	499	–	–
Load balancer	1	499	–	–
Web server	2	–	400	–
Application cluster	1	792	–	4.00
Database server	1	479	–	–
Disk arrays	4	–	250	5.72
100Base-T LAN	1	–	–	0.40

in mind, we construct a baseline model in PDQ and then use it to predict performance for a target level of 2,000 clients.

9.3.2 Workload Characterization

The same client application runs on all of the PC drivers, and it can initiate any of three transactions types with the mean request rates shown in Table 9.1. These rates also determine the multiclass workload mix as discussed in Chap. 3. A *business work* unit is a high-level measure appropriate for both business analysis and system-level performance analysis. For example, the three transactions listed in Table 9.2 might be used to process claims

Table 9.2. Client transactions

Transaction name	Prefix symbol	Rate (per minute)
Category display	CD	4
Remote quote	RQ	8
Status update	SU	1

at an insurance company. The number of claims processed each day is a quantity that measures both business performance and computational performance since it is also a measure of aggregate throughput.

The underlying distributed processes that support the three key transactions in Table 9.2 are listed in Table 9.3. The prefixes in the process names (first column) identify which transaction each process supports. The process identification number (PID) can be obtained using performance tools such as the UNIX `ps -aux` command. The third column shows how many kilo-instructions are executed by each process. These numbers will be used to calculate the process service demands. For compiled applications written in C or C++, for example, the assembler instruction counts for each software component of the application can be obtained from compiler output as outlined in Example 9.1. For J2EE applications, other tools are available for determining component service demands (see Appendix D). The last two columns of Table 9.3 show I/O rates and caching effects that will also be used as parameters in the PDQ model.

Example 9.1. To demonstrate how instruction counts in Table 9.3 can be obtained, we took the source code for the C version of the *baseline* PDQ model (`baseline.c` is included in the PDQ download) in Sect. 9.4.1 and compiled it using `gcc` with the `-S` switch. The command is:

```
gcc -S baseline.c
```

This produced a corresponding file `baseline.s` containing assembler code only. The UNIX `wc` command was then applied to that file to count the number of assembler instructions (assuming 1 assembly code instruction per line).

```
wc -l baseline.c 477
wc -l baseline.s 1583
```

The latter number corresponds to the values appearing in the third column of Table 9.3. The only difference is that each client/server component corresponds not to 1.58 k-instructions, but to hundreds of k-instructions. □

The service demand given in (2.9), defined in Chap. 2, can be derived from Tables 9.1 and 9.3 for each type of workload by using a variant of the *iron law of performance* in (7.9) in Chap. 7. The service demand for process c executing on resource k is given by:

$$D_k(c) = \frac{(\text{instruction count})_{\text{c}}}{\text{MIPS}_{\text{k}}}\,, \tag{9.1}$$

Table 9.3. Workload parameters for client/server processes

Process name	Process PID	Assembler k-instructions	Disk I/Os	Percent cached
CD_Request	1	200	0	0
CD_Result	15	100	0	0
RQ_Request	2	150	0	0
RQ_Result	16	200	0	0
SU_Request	3	300	0	0
SU_Result	17	300	0	0
ReqCD_Proc	4	500	1.0	50
ReqRQ_Proc	5	700	1.5	50
ReqSU_Proc	6	100	0.2	50
CDMsg_Proc	12	350	1.0	50
RQMsg_Proc	13	350	1.5	50
SUMsg_Proc	14	350	0.5	50
DBCD_Proc	8	5000	2.0	0
DBRQ_Proc	9	1500	4.0	0
DBSU_Proc	10	2000	1.0	0
LB_Send	7	500	0	0
LB_Recv	11	500	0	0
LAN_Inst	18	4	0	0

where $(\text{instruction count})_c$ refers to the number of executable instructions belonging to workload c, and MIPS_k is the throughput rating of hardware resource k in *mega instructions per second.* Expressing (9.1) as thousands of instructions per process and replacing MIPS by 10^6 instructions/s produces:

$$D_k(c) = (10^3 \times \text{instructions})_c \times \left(\frac{\text{seconds}}{10^6 \times \text{instructions}} \right)_k , \tag{9.2}$$

which renders the service demand in units of milliseconds.

In the PDQ model `baseline.pl` presented in Sect. 9.4, the service demand is represented by a two-dimensional array, denoted **`$demand`**[ ][ ], where the first entry is a process and then second is a physical resource. The *Category Display* process, for example, has a service demand defined by:

```
$demand[$CD_Req][$PC] = 200 * $K / $PC_MIPS;
```

when executing in the PC benchmark driver. Here, `$K` is a Perlscalar representing the constant 1024, and the scaler `$PC_MIPS` represents the MIPS rating of the PC driver.

9.3.3 Distributed Workflow

To build a useful performance model in PDQ, the flow of work between the queueing nodes must be expressed in terms of the processes that support the B2C transactions. For example, processing the CD transaction incurs the following workflow:

1. A process on the PC driver (representing the user) issues a request `CD_Request` to the web sever. The web server `Req_CD` in turn activates a process `App_CD` on the application server that propagates a request to the database server `DB_CD`.
2. The database server is activated by this request, some data are read, and are sent back to the application server.
3. Upon receipt of the data, another Web server process updates the transaction status and routes the result back to the originating user. The user's display is then updated with the retrieved data.

The complete chain of processes and the hardware resources that support the CD transaction are shown in Fig. 9.5. The right-pointing arrows represent

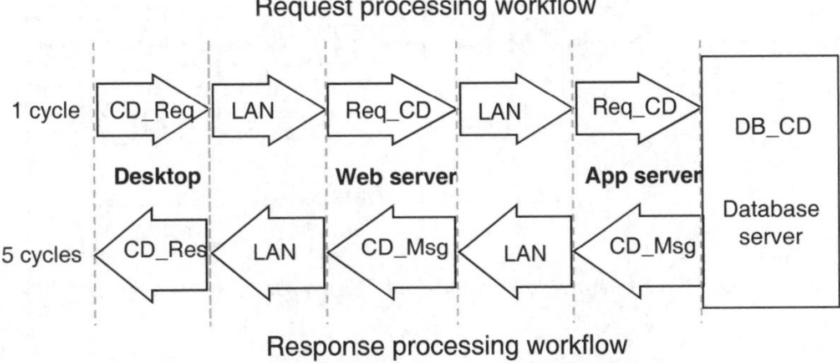

Fig. 9.5. The processing workflow required by the category display transaction

the client request being processed, while the left-pointing arrows represent the response data being returned to the client process. The response arrows are wider to reflect the fact that the database server issues multiple requests to the application server in order return the necessary volume of data. The CD transaction invokes five calls to the application server which are then propagated back to the client process. This is similar to the situation in the NFS timing chain discussed in Chap. 1.

As each process executes it consumes both CPU cycles and generates physical disk I/O. Table 9.3 summarizes the resource demands for each process, including physical I/O. Knowledge of such detailed performance information—including instruction traces and cached I/O rates—can be critical for meaningful performance analysis of client/server applications.

9.4 Scalability Analysis with PDQ

We construct a baseline model with 100 desktops, which we then use to evaluate the impact of a 10-fold increase in users. The PDQ model (Fig. 9.6),

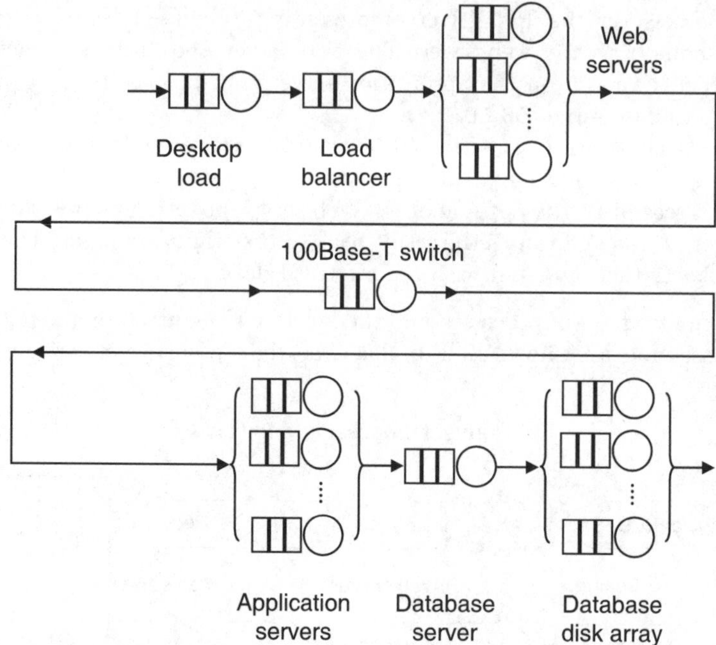

Fig. 9.6. PDQ performance model of client/server system in Fig 9.4

called `baseline.pl`, is constructed as an open-circuit model. Although 100 users suggests there is a finite number of requests in the system and that therefore a *closed* PDQ queueing model would be appropriate, we can use the result of Sect. 2.8.7 to justify the use of an open PDQ model. Moreover, in a Web or intranet environment requests can be submitted asynchronously without waiting for the response to a previous request.

We also note, in passing, that the LAN is a shared resource and could be modeled more accurately using a *load-dependent* PDQ queue (Chap. 10), but we found that it did not appreciably alter our results.

9.4.1 Benchmark Baseline

The following Perlcode contains the PDQ model for the baseline system in Fig. 9.6. We present the complete PDQ baseline model without reviewing the corresponding PDQ output in this section. Instead, we review the certain PDQ outputs for the upgrade scenarios in Sect. 9.3.1 while omitting the respective PDQ scripts.

```
#!/usr/bin/perl
# cs_baseline.pl
use pdq;
```

```
#-------------------------------------------------------
# PDQ model parameters
#-------------------------------------------------------
$scenario           = "Client/Server Baseline";

#  Useful constants
$K                  =  1024;
$MIPS               =   1E6;

$USERS              =   100;
$WEB_SERVS          =     2;
$DB_DISKS           =     4;
$PC_MIPS            =  499 * $MIPS;
$AS_MIPS            =  792 * $MIPS;
$LB_MIPS            =  499 * $MIPS;
$DB_MIPS            =  479 * $MIPS;
$LAN_RATE           =  100 * 1E6;
$LAN_INST           =     4;
$WEB_OPS            =   400;
$DB_IOS             =   250;

$MAXPROC            =    20;
$MAXDEV             =    50;

$PC                 =     0;    # PC drivers
$FS                 =     1;    # Application cluster
$GW                 =     2;    # Load balancer
$MF                 =     3;    # Database server
$TR                 =     4;    # Network
$FDA                =    10;    # Web servers
$MDA                =    20;    # Database disks

##  Process PIDs
$CD_Req             =     1;
$CD_Rpy             =    15;
$RQ_Req             =     2;
$RQ_Rpy             =    16;
$SU_Req             =     3;
$SU_Rpy             =    17;
$Req_CD             =     4;
$Req_RQ             =     5;
$Req_SU             =     6;
$CD_Msg             =    12;
$RQ_Msg             =    13;
$SU_Msg             =    14;
$GT_Snd             =     7;
$GT_Rcv             =    11;
$MF_CD              =     8;
$MF_RQ              =     9;
```

```
$MF_SU              =    10;
$LAN_Tx             =    18;

# Initialize array data structures
for ($i = 0; $i < $WEB_SERVS; $i++) {
   $FDarray[$i]->{id}    = $FDA + $i;
   $FDarray[$i]->{label} = sprintf("WebSvr%d", $i);
}
for ($i = 0; $i < $DB_DISKS; $i++) {
   $MDarray[$i]->{id}    = $MDA + $i;
   $MDarray[$i]->{label} = sprintf("SCSI%d", $i);
}

$demand[$CD_Req][$PC] = 200 * $K / $PC_MIPS;
$demand[$CD_Rpy][$PC] = 100 * $K / $PC_MIPS;
$demand[$RQ_Req][$PC] = 150 * $K / $PC_MIPS;
$demand[$RQ_Rpy][$PC] = 200 * $K / $PC_MIPS;
$demand[$SU_Req][$PC] = 300 * $K / $PC_MIPS;
$demand[$SU_Rpy][$PC] = 300 * $K / $PC_MIPS;

$demand[$Req_CD][$FS] =  500 * $K / $AS_MIPS;
$demand[$Req_RQ][$FS] =  700 * $K / $AS_MIPS;
$demand[$Req_SU][$FS] =  100 * $K / $AS_MIPS;
$demand[$CD_Msg][$FS] =  350 * $K / $AS_MIPS;
$demand[$RQ_Msg][$FS] =  350 * $K / $AS_MIPS;
$demand[$SU_Msg][$FS] =  350 * $K / $AS_MIPS;

$demand[$GT_Snd][$GW] =  500 * $K / $LB_MIPS;
$demand[$GT_Rcv][$GW] =  500 * $K / $LB_MIPS;

$demand[$MF_CD][$MF]  =  5000 * $K / $DB_MIPS;
$demand[$MF_RQ][$MF]  =  1500 * $K / $DB_MIPS;
$demand[$MF_SU][$MF]  =  2000 * $K / $DB_MIPS;

#  Packets generated at each of the following sources
$demand[$LAN_Tx][$PC] = 2 * $K * $LAN_INST / $LAN_RATE;
$demand[$LAN_Tx][$FS] = 2 * $K * $LAN_INST / $LAN_RATE;
$demand[$LAN_Tx][$GW] = 2 * $K * $LAN_INST / $LAN_RATE;

# Parallel web servers
for ($i = 0; $i < $WEB_SERVS; $i++) {
   $demand[$Req_CD][$FDarray[$i]->{id}] = (1.0 * 0.5 /
        $WEB_OPS) / $WEB_SERVS;
   $demand[$Req_RQ][$FDarray[$i]->{id}] = (1.5 * 0.5 /
        $WEB_OPS) / $WEB_SERVS;
   $demand[$Req_SU][$FDarray[$i]->{id}] = (0.2 * 0.5 /
        $WEB_OPS) / $WEB_SERVS;
   $demand[$CD_Msg][$FDarray[$i]->{id}] = (1.0 * 0.5 /
        $WEB_OPS) / $WEB_SERVS;
```

```
   $demand[$RQ_Msg][$FDarray[$i]->{id}] = (1.5 * 0.5 /
        $WEB_OPS) / $WEB_SERVS;
   $demand[$SU_Msg][$FDarray[$i]->{id}] = (0.5 * 0.5 /
        $WEB_OPS) / $WEB_SERVS;
}

# RDBMS disk arrays
for ($i = 0; $i < $DB_DISKS; $i++) {
   $demand[$MF_CD][$MDarray[$i]->{id}] = (2.0 / $DB_IOS) /
        $DB_DISKS;
   $demand[$MF_RQ][$MDarray[$i]->{id}] = (4.0 / $DB_IOS) /
        $DB_DISKS;
   $demand[$MF_SU][$MDarray[$i]->{id}] = (1.0 / $DB_IOS) /
        $DB_DISKS;
}

#  Start building the PDQ model
pdq::Init($scenario);

#  Define physical resources as queues
$nodes = pdq::CreateNode("PC", $pdq::CEN, $pdq::FCFS);
$nodes = pdq::CreateNode("LB", $pdq::CEN, $pdq::FCFS);
for ($i = 0; $i < $WEB_SERVS; $i++) {
   $nodes = pdq::CreateNode($FDarray[$i]->{label},
        $pdq::CEN, $pdq::FCFS);
}
$nodes = pdq::CreateNode("AS", $pdq::CEN, $pdq::FCFS);
$nodes = pdq::CreateNode("DB", $pdq::CEN, $pdq::FCFS);
for ($i = 0; $i < $DB_DISKS; $i++) {
   $nodes = pdq::CreateNode($MDarray[$i]->{label}, $pdq::CEN,
        $pdq::FCFS);
}
$nodes = pdq::CreateNode("LAN", $pdq::CEN, $pdq::FCFS);

#  Assign transaction names
$txCD =  "CatDsply";
$txRQ =  "RemQuote";
$txSU =  "StatusUp";
$dumCD  = "CDbkgnd ";
$dumRQ  = "RQbkgnd ";
$dumSU  = "SUbkgnd ";

#  Define focal PC load generator
$streams = pdq::CreateOpen($txCD, 1 * 4.0 / 60.0);
$streams = pdq::CreateOpen($txRQ, 1 * 8.0 / 60.0);
$streams = pdq::CreateOpen($txSU, 1 * 1.0 / 60.0);

#  Define the aggregate background workload
$streams = pdq::CreateOpen($dumCD, ($USERS - 1) * 4.0 / 60.0);
```

```
$streams = pdq::CreateOpen($dumRQ, ($USERS - 1) * 8.0 / 60.0);
$streams = pdq::CreateOpen($dumSU, ($USERS - 1) * 1.0 / 60.0);
#----------------------------------------------------
# CategoryDisplay request + reply chain  from workflow diagram
#----------------------------------------------------
pdq::SetDemand("PC", $txCD,
    $demand[$CD_Req][$PC] + (5 * $demand[$CD_Rpy][$PC]));
pdq::SetDemand("AS", $txCD,
    $demand[$Req_CD][$FS] + (5 * $demand[$CD_Msg][$FS]));
pdq::SetDemand("AS", $dumCD,
    $demand[$Req_CD][$FS] + (5 * $demand[$CD_Msg][$FS]));
for ($i = 0; $i < $WEB_SERVS; $i++) {
   pdq::SetDemand($FDarray[$i]->{label}, $txCD,
       $demand[$Req_CD][$FDarray[$i]->{id}] +
       (5 * $demand[$CD_Msg][$FDarray[$i]->{id}]));
   pdq::SetDemand($FDarray[$i]->{label}, $dumCD,
       $demand[$Req_CD][$FDarray[$i]->{id}] +
       (5 * $demand[$CD_Msg][$FDarray[$i]->{id}]));
}
pdq::SetDemand("LB", $txCD, $demand[$GT_Snd][$GW] +
    (5 * $demand[$GT_Rcv][$GW]));
pdq::SetDemand("LB", $dumCD, $demand[$GT_Snd][$GW] +
    (5 * $demand[$GT_Rcv][$GW]));
pdq::SetDemand("DB", $txCD, $demand[$MF_CD][$MF]);
pdq::SetDemand("DB", $dumCD, $demand[$MF_CD][$MF]);
for ($i = 0; $i < $DB_DISKS; $i++) {
   pdq::SetDemand($MDarray[$i]->{label}, $txCD,
       $demand[$MF_CD][$MDarray[$i]->{id}]);
   pdq::SetDemand($MDarray[$i]->{label}, $dumCD,
       $demand[$MF_CD][$MDarray[$i]->{id}]);
}
#  NOTE: Synchronous process execution causes data for the CD
#  transaction to cross the LAN 12 times as depicted in the
#  following parameterization of pdq::SetDemand.
pdq::SetDemand("LAN", $txCD,
      (1 * $demand[$LAN_Tx][$PC]) + (1 * $demand[$LAN_Tx][$FS])
    + (5 * $demand[$LAN_Tx][$GW]) + (5 * $demand[$LAN_Tx][$FS]));
pdq::SetDemand("LAN", $dumCD,
      (1 * $demand[$LAN_Tx][$PC]) + (1 * $demand[$LAN_Tx][$FS])
    + (5 * $demand[$LAN_Tx][$GW]) + (5 * $demand[$LAN_Tx][$FS]));


#----------------------------------------------------
# RemoteQuote request + reply chain ...
#----------------------------------------------------
pdq::SetDemand("PC", $txRQ,
    $demand[$RQ_Req][$PC] + (3 * $demand[$RQ_Rpy][$PC]));
pdq::SetDemand("AS", $txRQ,
    $demand[$Req_RQ][$FS] + (3 * $demand[$RQ_Msg][$FS]));
```

```
pdq::SetDemand("AS", $dumRQ,
    $demand[$Req_RQ][$FS] + (3 * $demand[$RQ_Msg][$FS]));
for ($i = 0; $i < $WEB_SERVS; $i++) {
   pdq::SetDemand($FDarray[$i]->{label}, $txRQ,
         $demand[$Req_RQ][$FDarray[$i]->{id}] +
     (3 * $demand[$RQ_Msg][$FDarray[$i]->{id}]));
   pdq::SetDemand($FDarray[$i]->{label}, $dumRQ,
         $demand[$Req_RQ][$FDarray[$i]->{id}] +
     (3 * $demand[$RQ_Msg][$FDarray[$i]->{id}]));
}
pdq::SetDemand("LB", $txRQ, $demand[$GT_Snd][$GW] +
    (3 * $demand[$GT_Rcv][$GW]));
pdq::SetDemand("LB", $dumRQ, $demand[$GT_Snd][$GW] +
    (3 * $demand[$GT_Rcv][$GW]));
pdq::SetDemand("DB", $txRQ, $demand[$MF_RQ][$MF]);
pdq::SetDemand("DB", $dumRQ, $demand[$MF_RQ][$MF]);
for ($i = 0; $i < $DB_DISKS; $i++) {
   pdq::SetDemand($MDarray[$i]->{label}, $txRQ,
       $demand[$MF_RQ][$MDarray[$i]->{id}]);
   pdq::SetDemand($MDarray[$i]->{label}, $dumRQ,
       $demand[$MF_RQ][$MDarray[$i]->{id}]);
}
pdq::SetDemand("LAN", $txRQ,
     (1 * $demand[$LAN_Tx][$PC]) + (1 * $demand[$LAN_Tx][$FS])
   + (3 * $demand[$LAN_Tx][$GW]) + (3 * $demand[$LAN_Tx][$FS]));
pdq::SetDemand("LAN", $dumRQ,
     (1 * $demand[$LAN_Tx][$PC]) + (1 * $demand[$LAN_Tx][$FS])
   + (3 * $demand[$LAN_Tx][$GW]) + (3 * $demand[$LAN_Tx][$FS]));

#-----------------------------------------------------
# StatusUpdate request + reply chain  ...
#-----------------------------------------------------
pdq::SetDemand("PC", $txSU, $demand[$SU_Req][$PC] +
    $demand[$SU_Rpy][$PC]);
pdq::SetDemand("AS",  $txSU, $demand[$Req_SU][$FS] +
    $demand[$SU_Msg][$FS]);
pdq::SetDemand("AS",  $dumSU, $demand[$Req_SU][$FS] +
    $demand[$SU_Msg][$FS]);
for ($i = 0; $i < $WEB_SERVS; $i++) {
   pdq::SetDemand($FDarray[$i]->{label}, $txSU,
       $demand[$Req_SU][$FDarray[$i]->{id}] +
                      $demand[$SU_Msg][$FDarray[$i]->{id}]);
   pdq::SetDemand($FDarray[$i]->{label}, $dumSU,
       $demand[$Req_SU][$FDarray[$i]->{id}] +
                      $demand[$SU_Msg][$FDarray[$i]->{id}]);
}
pdq::SetDemand("LB", $txSU, $demand[$GT_Snd][$GW] +
    $demand[$GT_Rcv][$GW]);
pdq::SetDemand("LB", $dumSU, $demand[$GT_Snd][$GW] +
```

```
    $demand[$GT_Rcv][$GW]);
pdq::SetDemand("DB", $txSU, $demand[$MF_SU][$MF]);
pdq::SetDemand("DB", $dumSU, $demand[$MF_SU][$MF]);
for ($i = 0; $i < $DB_DISKS; $i++) {
   pdq::SetDemand($MDarray[$i]->{label}, $txSU,
       $demand[$MF_SU][$MDarray[$i]->{id}]);
   pdq::SetDemand($MDarray[$i]->{label}, $dumSU,
       $demand[$MF_SU][$MDarray[$i]->{id}]);
}
pdq::SetDemand("LAN", $txSU,
      (1 * $demand[$LAN_Tx][$PC]) + (1 * $demand[$LAN_Tx][$FS])
    + (1 * $demand[$LAN_Tx][$GW]) + (1 * $demand[$LAN_Tx][$FS]));
pdq::SetDemand("LAN", $dumSU,
      (1 * $demand[$LAN_Tx][$PC]) + (1 * $demand[$LAN_Tx][$FS])
    + (1 * $demand[$LAN_Tx][$GW]) + (1 * $demand[$LAN_Tx][$FS]));
pdq::SetWUnit("Trans");

pdq::Solve($pdq::CANON);
pdq::Report();
```

A key point is the use of three PDQ streams to represent the three workloads of interest, as well as three *dummy* streams to represent the other workloads as background resource consumption.

The complete standard PDQ report produced by `baseline.pl` is extremely long (about 8 pages) and is not reproduced here. The reader can find it in the PDQ code distribution available from `www.perfdynamics.com`. A more compact approach to generating the full standard PDQ report is to make use of PDQ functions like `PDQ::GetResponse()` (Sect. 6.6.9) and `PDQ::GetUtilization()` (Sect. 6.6.12) to report individually the most important transaction response times and the node utilizations. An example follows.

```
*** Resource Breakout "Client/Server Baseline" (100 clients) ***

Transaction Rmean  R80th  R90th  R95th
----------- -----  -----  -----  -----
CatDsply    0.0431 0.0718 0.1005 0.1292
RemQuote    0.0393 0.0655 0.0917 0.1180
StatusUp    0.0152 0.0253 0.0354 0.0455
CDbkgnd     0.0416 0.0694 0.0971 0.1248
RQbkgnd     0.0378 0.0630 0.0882 0.1133
SUbkgnd     0.0139 0.0232 0.0325 0.0418


PDQ Node       % Busy
--------       -------
100Base-T LAN   1.5838
PC Driver       0.0003
Appln Server    5.0532
```

```
Web Server10      7.5729
Web Server11      7.5729
Balancer CPU     12.2812
Database CPU     12.1141
SCSI Array20      6.8333
SCSI Array21      6.8333
SCSI Array22      6.8333
SCSI Array23      6.8333
```

This breakout of PDQ performance metrics has also made use of the rules of thumb for the 80th, 90th and 95th percentiles discussed in Sect. 1.5.2 of Chap. 1:

1. 80th percentile is `R80th = 5 * PDQ::GetResponse() / 3;`
2. 90th percentile is `R90th = 7 * PDQ::GetResponse() / 3;`
3. 95th percentile is `R95th = 9 * PDQ::GetResponse() / 3;`

As expected, the *mean* response times `Rmean` are identical to those previously reported in the `SYSTEM Performance` section of the standard PDQ report. It can also be verified that they are the respective sums of the residence times listed in the `RESOURCE Performance` section of the PDQ report. Figure 9.7 shows that each of the baseline transaction response times are well within the SLA requirements.

The consumption of hardware resources by the aggregate of the three transactions follows the response time statistics in the breakout report, but these numbers are *total* utilizations that are useful for bottleneck ranking. Alternatively, we can identify which transaction is consuming the most resources at any PDQ node by referring to the `RESOURCE Performance` section of the standard PDQ report. This information will be useful in the subsequent sections as we apply more client load to the PDQ model. The PDQ baseline model should be validated against measurements on the actual benchmark platform with end-to-end response time statistics compared. The next step is to scale up the client load to 1,000 users.

9.4.2 Client Scaleup

To assess the impact of scaling up the number of user to 1,000 clients in PDQ is simply a matter of changing the `$USERS` parameter (line 16) in the `cs_baseline.pl` model. However, it is better practice to copy the original `cs_baseline.pl` file to another file, e.g., `cs_scaleup.pl` and make the edits to that version.

> If you persist in making a succession of edits to the same PDQ model file, there will inevitably come a point where you can no longer recall what the succession of changes mean or what motivated them in the first place. The best practice is to keep separate PDQ model files for each set of scenario parameters.

A result of scaling the client load to 1,000 in `cs_scaleup.pl` and running that scenario is the following PDQ error message:

```
ERROR in model:" 122.81% (>100%)" at canonical():
Total utilization of node LB is 122.81% (>100%)
```

which tells us that the PDQ node `LB` representing the *load balancer* in Fig. 9.6 is oversaturated ($\rho > 1$). This would make the denominator in the response time formula (2.35) negative, as well as render other calculations meaningless. Therefore, PDQ does not attempt solve the model.

9.4.3 Load Balancer Bottleneck

The SPEC CPU2000 rating of the load balancer is 499 in Table 9.1. We consider an upgrade scenario (line 21 in the PDQ Perlcode) where the load balancer is replaced by a model that has a rating of 792 SPECint2000. The parameter change is made in the file called `cs_upgrade1.pl` but causes the following PDQ error report when run:

```
ERROR in model:" 121.14% (>100%)" at canonical():
Total utilization of node DB is 121.14% (>100%)
```

which tells is that the PDQ node (`DB`) representing the *database server* in Fig. 9.6 is over-saturated.

9.4.4 Database Server Bottleneck

The SPEC CPU2000 rating of the database server is 479 in Table 9.1. We consider an upgrade scenario (line 22 in the PDQ Perlcode) where the database server is replaced by a model which has a CPU rating of 792 SPECint2000. The parameter change is made in the file called `cs_upgrade2.pl`, which when run produces the following performance report:

```
*** Resource Breakout "Client/Server Upgrade2" (1000 clients) ***

Transaction  Rmean   R80th   R90th   R95th
-----------  -----   -----   -----   -----
CatDsply     0.0986  0.1643  0.2300  0.2958
RemQuote     0.1022  0.1704  0.2386  0.3067
StatusUp     0.0319  0.0532  0.0745  0.0958
CDbkgnd      0.0971  0.1619  0.2267  0.2914
RQbkgnd      0.1007  0.1678  0.2350  0.3021
SUbkgnd      0.0307  0.0512  0.0716  0.0921
```

```
PDQ Node          % Busy
--------          -------
100Base-T LAN     15.8379
PC Driver          0.0000
Appln Server      50.5320
Web Server10      75.7292
Web Server11      75.7292
Balancer CPU      62.1776
Database CPU      72.8978
SCSI Array20      68.3333
SCSI Array21      68.3333
SCSI Array22      68.3333
SCSI Array23      68.3333
```

We see that at 1,000 users, the mean and the 95th percentile response times still do not exceed the 0.5000 s SLA requirement. The *Web server*, however, is likely to become a bottleneck at production-level loads.

9.4.5 Production Client Load

We increment the client load to 1,500 and make some additional parameter changes (for reasons that lie outside the scope of this discussion) in the PDQ file called `cs_upgrade3.pl`:

```
#!/usr/bin/perl
#
##  cs_upgrade3.pl

use pdq;

#########################################################################
# PDQ model parameters
#########################################################################
$scenario              = "Client/Server Upgrade3";

#  Useful multipliers ...
$K                     =  1024;
$MIPS                  =   1E6;

$USERS                 = 1500;
$WEB_SERVS             = (2 + 4);
$DB_DISKS              = (4 + 1);
$PC_MIPS               = (499 * MIPS);
$AS_MIPS               = (792 * MIPS);
$LB_MIPS               = (1056 * MIPS);
$DB_MIPS               = (1244 * MIPS);
$LAN_RATE              = (100 * Mbps);
```

```
$LAN_INST           = 4;   # scale factor
$WS_OPS             = 400;    # Web server SPEC Web99 ops/sec
$MS_DKIOS           = 250;    # RDBMS SCSI IOs
```

The following performance report is produced:

```
*** Resource Breakout "Client/Server Upgrade3" (1500 clients) ***

Transaction        Rmean   R80th   R90th   R95th
-----------        -----   -----   -----   -----
CatDsply           0.0948  0.1579  0.2211  0.2843
RemQuote           0.1233  0.2056  0.2878  0.3700
StatusUp           0.0364  0.0607  0.0850  0.1093
CDbkgnd            0.0933  0.1555  0.2178  0.2800
RQbkgnd            0.1218  0.2030  0.2842  0.3654
SUbkgnd            0.0352  0.0587  0.0822  0.1056


PDQ Node          % Busy
--------          -------
100Base-T LAN     23.7568
PC Driver          0.0000
Appln Server      75.7980
Web Server10      37.8646
Web Server11      37.8646
Web Server12      37.8646
Web Server13      37.8646
Web Server14      37.8646
Web Server15      37.8646
Balancer CPU      70.3030
Database CPU      69.9678
SCSI Array20      82.0000
SCSI Array21      82.0000
SCSI Array22      82.0000
SCSI Array23      82.0000
SCSI Array24      82.0000
```

The impact of these upgrades on each of the response time metrics compared to the baseline benchmark system is summarized in Fig. 9.7.

We see the SCSI disk array becoming the next bottleneck. With that in mind, we consider the last of the scenario objectives in Sect. 9.3.1.

9.4.6 Saturation Client Load

Maintaining the same system parameters as those in Sect. 9.4.5, we adjust the `$USERS` parameter to find where the PDQ model reaches saturation.

```
*** Resource Breakout "Client/Server Upgrade4" (1800 clients) ***
```

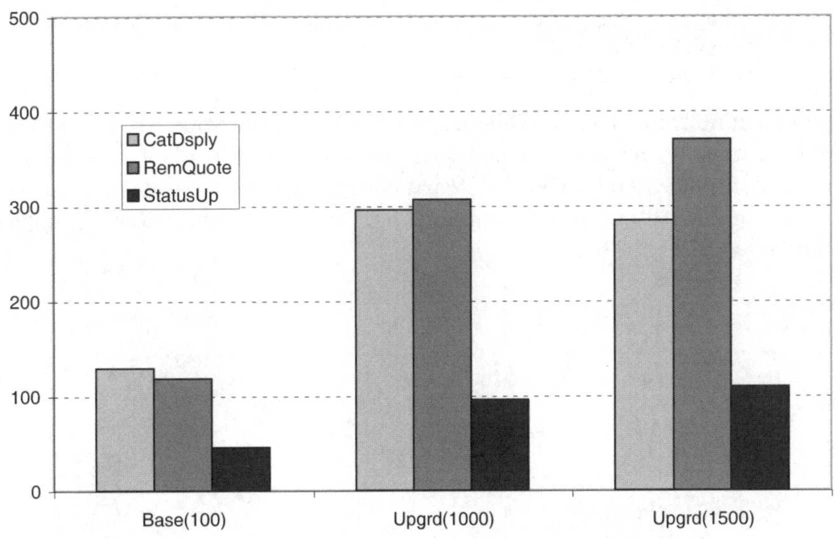

Fig. 9.7. Summary of the response time (ms) statistics for baseline client/server performance together with two of the possible upgrade scenarios presented in Sect. 9.4

```
Transaction  Rmean   R80th   R90th   R95th
-----------  -----   -----   -----   -----
CatDsply     0.5930  0.9883  1.3837  1.7790
RemQuote     1.0613  1.7689  2.4764  3.1840
StatusUp     0.2762  0.4603  0.6445  0.8286
CDbkgnd      0.5916  0.9859  1.3803  1.7747
RQbkgnd      1.0598  1.7663  2.4728  3.1794
SUbkgnd      0.2750  0.4583  0.6416  0.8249


PDQ Node         % Busy
--------         -------
100Base-T LAN    28.5082
PC Driver         0.0000
Appln Server     90.9576
Web Server10     45.4375
Web Server11     45.4375
Web Server12     45.4375
Web Server13     45.4375
Web Server14     45.4375
Web Server15     45.4375
Balancer CPU     84.3636
Database CPU     83.9614
SCSI Array20     98.4000
```

```
SCSI Array21    98.4000
SCSI Array22    98.4000
SCSI Array23    98.4000
SCSI Array24    98.4000
```

We determine that around 1,800 users both the application servers and the database disk arrays are nearing saturation, even with all of the previous upgrades in place. And naturally, nearly every response time statistic grossly exceeds the SLA objective. A comparison of all the response times (in ms) is summarized in Fig. 9.8.

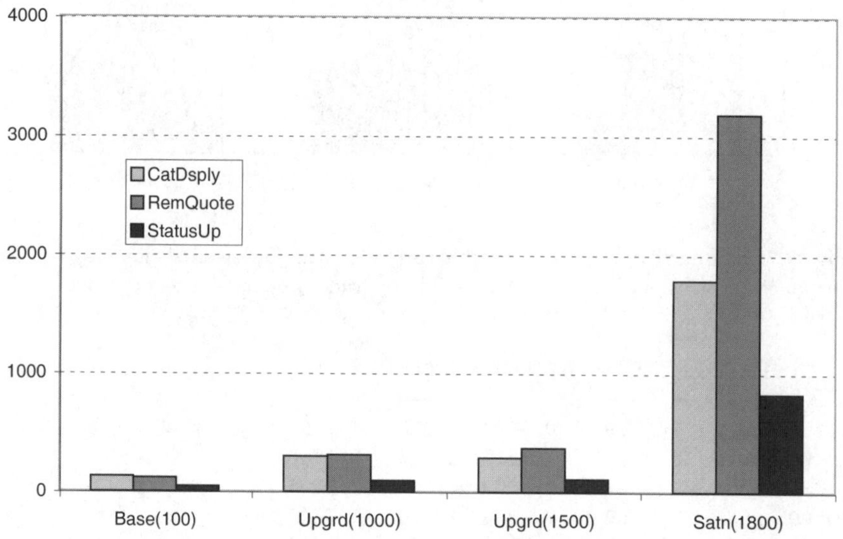

Fig. 9.8. Response times (ms) including those predicted when the system reaches saturation with 1,800 users

9.4.7 Per-Process Analysis

An analysis of the transaction times can also be carried out at the per-process level by further inspection of the PDQ report. For example, the time taken by the `$CD_Msg` process can be assessed as follows.

Using any of the PDQ model files, a global search for the string CD_Msg reveals that it runs on both the *application servers* (AS) and the *Web servers* (WS). That is also consistent with the process flows shown in Fig. 9.5. Without loss of generality, we focus on the `$CD_Msg` process executing on the application server in the *baseline* configuration. Specifically, line 20 of `baseline.rpt` states:

```
20 CEN   FCFS  AS           CatDsply   TRANS      0.0029
```

which corresponds to a service demand of 2.9 ms for the $CD_Msg process running the application server. In the presence of contention from other work, however, the residence time at the application server has become 3.1 ms for the $CD_Msg process, as indicated at line 196 of the PDQ report:

```
196 Residence Time   AS   CatDsply      0.0031      Sec
```

By the time we get to the production loads of Sect. 9.4.5 with 1500 users, this time has grown to 12 ms:

```
205 Residence Time   AS   CatDsply      0.0120      Sec
```

In other words, the effective $CD_Msg process *stretch factor* is 4 times the baseline service demand due to increased queueing contention (waiting time). The complete PDQ report for this scenario is not shown here but is available for download from www.perfdynamics.com.

9.5 Review

In this chapter, we have seen how to apply PDQ to the performance analysis of a multitier B2C client/server environment. A key point to note is that PDQ can be used to predict the scalability of distributed *software* applications, not just hardware as in Chap. 7. This is achieved by using the workflow analysis of Sect. 9.3.3.

Another merit of the techniques presented in this chapter pertains to more cost-effective benchmarking and load testing. The performance of many large-scale benchmark configurations can be predicted using PDQ, and those results only need be verified against a relatively sparse set of selected platform configurations. PDQ offers another way to keep the cost of load testing and benchmarking down.

Exercises

9.1. How do the predicted performance metrics change in the PDQ model cs_baseline.pl if there is just a single workload, rather than the two-class workload discussed in this chapter?

9.2. How does the predicted performance outcome change in the PDQ model cs_upgrade4.pl if the ordering of the hardware components is reversed in the Perlcode?

10

Web Application Analysis with PDQ

10.1 Introduction

In this chapter we examine the performance characteristics of the latest innovation in client/server technology—Web technology. Unlike the traditional client/server systems discussed in Chap. 9, each Web client typically makes high-frequency, short-term accesses to a relatively small number of servers.

First, we examine some elementary mistakes made in the course of taking Hypertext Transfer Protocol (HTTP) server performance measurements. Based on the queueing theory of Chaps. 2 and 3 and PDQ, we uncover the cause of these mistakes. Next, we analyze the performance a Web-based middleware architecture, which will require the introduction of two novel techniques to calibrate PDQ against the available performance data:

1. the introduction of "dummy" PDQ nodes to account for unmeasured latencies
2. a load-dependent PDQ node to account for the overdriven roll-off observed in the throughput data

These two techniques are extemely important for constructing realistic PDQ performance models. The reader might like to review the concept of load-dependent servers presented in Chaps. 2 and 6.

10.2 HTTP Protocol

The HTTP is a Web protocol that uses the TCP/IP Internet transport protocol. The files are usually resident on remote file servers distributed across the internet. The protocol model is very simple. A client machine establishes a connection to the remote server machine, then issues a request. The server processes that request, returns a response with the requested data, and generally closes the connection.

The request format in HTTP GET is straightforward, as the following example Perlcode, which uses the powerful *LWP* (Library for WWW access in Perl) module, demonstrates:

```
 1 #! /usr/bin/perl
 2 #
 3 # getHTML.pl - fetch HTML from a URL
 4
 5 use HTTP::Request::Common qw(GET);
 6 use LWP::UserAgent;
 7 use POSIX;
 8
 9 $url = "http://www.neilgunther.com/";
10
11 # Set up and issue the GET ...
12 my $ua = new LWP::UserAgent;
13 my $request = new HTTP::Request('GET',$url);
14 $request->content_type('application/x-www-form-urlencoded');
15 printf("%s\n", $request->as_string);
16
17 # Print the result ...
18 my $result = $ua->request($request);
19 if (!$result->is_success) { print $result->error_as_HTML; }
20 printf("%s\n", $result->as_string);
```

Issuing the HTTP GET (from line 11 to line 15 in the above) produces a result like this:

```
1 GET http://www.neilgunther.com/
2 Content-Type: application/x-www-form-urlencoded
```

The first line in the result specifies an object (an HTML file in this case), together with the name of an object to apply the method to. The most commonly used method is GET, which asks the server to send a copy of the object to the client. The client can also send a series of optional headers in RFC-822 format. The most common headers are Accept, which informs the server of object types that the client can accommodate, and User-Agent, which reveals the implementation name of the client. The response from the remote server starts at line 3 as follows:

```
 3 HTTP/1.1 200 OK
 4 Connection: close
 5 Date: Thu, 29 Jan 2004 18:08:45 GMT
 6 Accept-Ranges: bytes
 7 ETag: "2ef26b7a1addc31:11a2b"
 8 Server: Microsoft-IIS/5.0
 9 Content-Length: 2419
10 Content-Location: http://www.neilgunther.com/index.html
11 Content-Type: text/html
```

```
12 Content-Type: text/html;CHARSET=iso-8859-1
13 Last-Modified: Sat, 17 Jan 2004 16:53:48 GMT
14 Client-Date: Thu, 29 Jan 2004 18:07:40 GMT
15 Client-Response-Num: 1
16 Title: www.neilgunther.com
17 X-Meta-GENERATOR: Symantec Visual Page 1.0
18
19 <!DOCTYPE HTML PUBLIC "-//W3C//DTD HTML 3.2//EN">
20 <HTML>
21
22 <HEAD>
23  <META NAME="GENERATOR" Content="Symantec Visual Page 1.0">
24  <META HTTP-EQUIV="Content-Type" CONTENT="text/html;CHARSET=iso-8859-1">
25  <TITLE>www.neilgunther.com</TITLE>
26 </HEAD>
27
28 <BODY BACKGROUND="imacs.jpg" BGCOLOR="#FFFFFF">
```

The HTML belonging to the actual Web page starts at line 20 in the above output. The rest of the response, down to `</HTML>`, has been elided for brevity.

Responses start with a status line indicating which version of HTTP is running on the server together with a result code and an optional message. This is followed by a series of optional object headers; the most important of these are Content-Type, which describes the type of the object being returned, and Content-Length, which indicates the length. The headers are terminated with a blank line. The server sends any requested data, and drops the connection. HTTP transfers exhibit a common access pattern. A client requests a hypertext page, then issues a sequence of requests to retrieve any icons (connected by Web hyperlinks) referenced on the first HTML page. Once the client has retrieved the icons, the user will typically select a hypertext link to follow. Most often the referenced page is on the same server as the original HTML page.

More detailed performance data reveal a timing chain for a typical HTTP client/server request/response sequence. The Web request is to fetch an HTML page comprising 1,668 B that include 42 lines of response headers totaling about 1,130 B. Phase 1 involves setting up a three-way handshake between client and server. The connect request is sent to the server's HTTP port. When TCP transfers a stream of data, it breaks the stream up into smaller packets or segments. The size of each segment may vary up to a *maximum segement size* (MSS). The default MSS is 536 B. The remainder of the transaction, together with timings, is summarized in Table 10.1.

Rather than having to wait for each packet to be acknowledged, TCP allows a sender to issue new segments even though it may not have received acknowledgments for the previous ones. To prevent the sender from overflowing the receiving buffers, the receiver tells the sender how much data it is prepared to accept without acknowledgments. This amount of data determines what is known as the *window size.*

Table 10.1. Timing sequence for an HTML Web retrieval

Phase	Client action		Server action	Data (B/pkt)	Elapsed time (ms)	Delta time (ms)
1	SYN pkt	⇒		0	0.00	0.00
2			⇐ SYN-ACK		77.69	77.69
	ACK+ reqdata1	⇒		536	79.89	2.20
3			⇐ ACK(1)		350.79	270.90
	reqdata2	⇒		536	350.92	0.13
	reqdata3			74	351.04	0.12
4			⇐ ACK(2,3)+data1	512	451.16	100.12
			⇐ data2	512	454.73	3.57
	ACK data	⇒		1	454.92	0.19
			⇐ data3	512	525.21	70.29
			⇐ data4+close	316	527.46	2.25
	ACK data	⇒		1	527.55	0.09
5	close				528.76	1.21
			⇐ ACK close		599.04	70.28

Although the window size informs the sender of the maximum amount of unacknowledged data the receiver is prepared to let it have outstanding, the receiver cannot know how much data the connecting networks are prepared to carry. If the network is quite congested, sending a full window of data will only aggravate congestion. The ideal transmission rate is one in which acknowledgments and outgoing packets enter the network at the same rate. TCP determines the best rate to use through a process called *Slow Start.* Under Slow Start the sender calculates a second window of unacknowledged segments known as the *congestion window.*

When a connection commences, a sender is only permitted to have a single unacknowledged segment outstanding. For every segment that is acknowledged without loss, the congestion window is incremented by 1. Conversely, the window is decremented by 1 for every segment that is lost and times out. The lifetimes of typical network connections are usually longer than the time required to open up the congestion window under Slow Start. But HTTP uses very short-lived connections and so the effect of Slow Start can have a significant performance impact on both the client and the server.

Because the HTTP headers are longer than the MSS, the client TCP must use two segments in phase 2. With the congestion window initialized to 1 packet, there is a delay for the first segment to be acknowledged before the second and third segments can be sent in phase 3. This adds an extra round-trip delay (RTD) to the minimum transaction time. One the server side, when it is ready to send the response it starts with a congestion window of 2 packets because the acknowledgement (ACK) it sent in phase 3 was counted as a successful transmission so the window was incremented by 1. Although its window is slightly open, it is still insufficient to send the entire response without pausing. In phase 4, the server sends two segments for a combined payload of 1,024 B, but then waits to receive another ACK from the client before it sends the final two segments in phase 5.

Since most Web pages are larger than 1,024 B, Slow Start in the server typically adds at least one RTD to the total transaction time. Under HTTP 1.0, larger HTML files experienced several Slow Start-induced delays, until the congestion window became as big as the receiver's window. This antagonism between Slow Start and HTTP GETs has been with more persistent connections under HTML 1.2.

From the performance data Table 10.1, we can calculate the average RTD and network bandwidth. Using the timing information in phases 1 and 5, the connection request and grant takes 77.69 ms and the closing sequence in Phase 5 takes 70.28 ms. The average of these two RTDs is about 74 ms.

$$\text{RTD} = 77.69 + 70.282 = 73.99 \text{ ms} . \tag{10.1}$$

The network bandwidth BW can be determined from Phase 4 where data2 returns 512 B in 3.57 ms. This gives:

$$BW = \frac{512}{3.57} = 143,420 \text{ B/s} , \tag{10.2}$$

which is a minimum throughput of about 1.15 Mb/s (cf. T1 line speed of 1.544 Mb/s).

The most significant latencies occur in phases 3 and 4, which are both due to processing time on the server. There is no direct measure of the server processing time, but it can be estimated from the delay between issuing the request (end phase 3) and the return of data (start of phase 4). This is about 100 ms, minus the RTD of 73.99 ms from (10.1). The calculated value is:

$$T_{\text{serv}} = 100.12 - 73.99 = 26.13 \text{ ms} . \tag{10.3}$$

We can now use this estimate of the server processing time to calculate the improved response time that would attend the use of a persistent TCP connection. The total transaction time of nearly 530 ms includes the time for opening a new connection for each request. By reusing an existing connection the transaction time can be calculated as the sum of the following times:

1. the time to send the request: $(536 \times 2 + 74)/143.75 = 7.97$ ms
2. from (10.1), the round trip time: 73.99 ms
3. from (10.3), server processing time: 26.13 ms
4. time to send the response: $(512 \times 3) + 316 + 1 + 1143.75 = 10.91$ ms

for a total response time of 119.0 ms, or a 77% performance improvement.

The single request per connection can also cause problems for server scalability because of the `TIME_WAIT` state in TCP. When a server closes a TCP connection it is required to keep information about that connection for some time afterward, in case a delayed packet finally shows up and sabotages a new incarnation of the connection. The recommended time to keep this information is 240 s. Because of this persistence period, a server must leave some amount of resources allocated for every connection closed in the past 4 min. For a server under heavy load, thousands of control blocks can end up being accumulated.

10.2.1 HTTP Performance

A major problem faced by Web site administrators is host configuration. Configuring demons, file systems, memory, disk storage, and so on, to meet the increasing demand imposed by a growing client community is ultimately a decision that must be based on price and performance. That metric can only be assessed accurately if appropriate performance measurement tools are available. Key performance issues include:

- file caching
- file system activity
- forking slaves
- memory consumption
- process activity
- network activity
- response time characteristics
- scalability of server/host
- throughput characteristics
- server configuration
- proxy/gateway capacity

Even though a client may receive the message: "`ERROR: server not responding ...`", the Web host performance can still appear to be acceptable to the analyst. There is no way to report connections that are not established.

High rates of opening and closing TCP/IP connections for long periods are known to cause instabilities in the UNIX operating system. The available HTTP demons track each connection to the server and keep varying amounts of *footprint* information while a connection is being serviced. These time-stamped data are kept in log files on the host system. Other tools can scan these logs and pretty-print the data.

By examining these logs, the analyst can estimate the throughput in terms of metrics such as *connections per second* (cps). But there is no way to synchronously associate such Web-based metrics with resource consumption in the host operating system. The classic approach to invoking service when a client request arrives is to fork a copy of the service process for each request.

The alternative is to prefork a finite of server processes ahead of time, usually at bootup. In the following, we shall make a comparative analysis of preforking and fork-on-demand. A key issue is: what is the optimal number of servers to prefork?

10.2.2 HTTP Analysis Using PDQ

Network latency is taken to be small and not load-dependent, so that it is simply included in service time at the demon. In a load-test environment, this is a reasonable assumption. Figure 10.1 shows the PDQ model used to represent the prefork configuration with the master demon modeled as a single queueing center and the slave processes modeled as a multiserver queue (see Chap. 2).

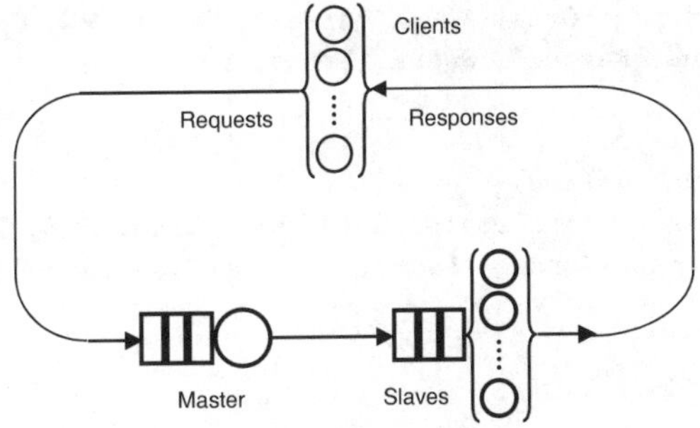

Fig. 10.1. HTTP master and preforked slaves

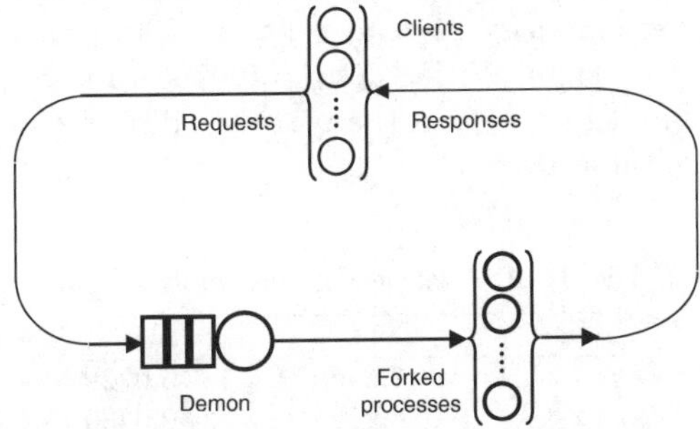

Fig. 10.2. A fork-on-demand HTTP server

The fork-on-demand processes in Fig. 10.2 are modeled as a PDQ delay center (`$ISRV`) defined in Chap. 2.

```
#!/usr/bin/perl
# httpd.pl

use pdq;

$clients = 5;
$smaster = 0.0109; #seconds
```

```
$sdemon = 0.0044; #seconds
$work = "homepage";
@slave = ("slave1", "slave2", "slave3", "slave4", "slave5",
"slave6", "slave7", "slave8", "slave9", "slave10",
"slave11", "slave12", "slave13", "slave14", "slave15",
"slave16");

pdq::Init("HTTPd Prefork");

$pdq::streams = pdq::CreateClosed($work, $pdq::TERM, $clients, 0.0);
$pdq::nodes = pdq::CreateNode("master", $pdq::CEN, $pdq::FCFS);
pdq::SetDemand("master", $work, $smaster);

$nslaves = @slave;
foreach $sname (@slave) {
   $pdq::nodes = pdq::CreateNode($sname, $pdq::CEN, $pdq::FCFS);
   pdq::SetDemand($sname, $work, $sdemon / $nslaves);
}

pdq::Solve($pdq::EXACT);
pdq::Report();
```

10.2.3 Fork-on-Demand Analysis

In the fork-on-demand case (Fig. 10.2), a single demon process (queue) feeds requests to the servers modeled as delay centers because there can be as many servers as requests in system. With $S_{\text{demon}} = 0.0165$ s and $S_{\text{slave}} = 0.0044$ s the throughput (measured in cps) and the corresponding response times (RTD) are summarized in Table 10.2.

Table 10.2. Fork-on-demand model results

Clients	Conn/s	RTD (s)
1	47.8469	0.0209
2	58.9513	0.0339
3	60.4593	0.0496
4	60.5963	0.0660
5	60.6055	0.0825
6	60.6060	0.0990
7	60.6061	0.1155
8	60.6061	0.1320
9	60.6061	0.1485
10	60.6061	0.1650

These throughput data match the throughput measurements reported by McGrath and Yeager [1996] for their National Center for Supercomputing Applications (NCSA) stress tests. The performance of Windows IIS Web server is discussed in Friedman and Pentakalos [2002].

10.2.4 Prefork Analysis

In the pre-fork case, there is a single master process (queue) and up to $m = 16$ slaves (Fig. 10.1). If $S_{\text{master}} > S_{\text{slave}}$ then $m > 1$ slave is ineffective, since the master is the bottleneck center. If instead we assume that $S_{\text{master}} < S_{\text{slave}}$ there is no runtime overhead to fork processes.

The PDQ script `httpd.pl` with 5 clients and 16 forked processes with $S_{\text{master}} = 0.0109$ s and $S_{\text{slave}} = 0.0044/16$ s produces the following output:

```
        ***************************************
        ****** Pretty Damn Quick REPORT *******
        ***************************************
        ***  of : Tue Jul 20 20:30:02 2004  ***
        ***  for: HTTPd Prefork             ***
        ***  Ver: PDQ Analyzer v2.8 120803  ***
        ***************************************
        ***************************************

Queueing Circuit Totals:

    Clients:     5.00
    Streams:        1
    Nodes:         17

WORKLOAD Parameters

Client         Number        Demand   Thinktime
----           ------        ------   ---------
homepage         5.00        0.0153       0.00

         ***************************************
         ******    PDQ Model OUTPUTS      *******
         ***************************************

Solution Method: EXACT

         ******    SYSTEM Performance     *******

Metric                              Value   Unit
-----------------                   -----   ----
Workload: "homepage"
Mean Throughput               91.7335       Job/Sec
Response Time                  0.0545       Sec
Mean Concurrency               5.0000       Job
Stretch Factor                 3.5625
```

```
38 Bounds Analysis:
39 Max Throughput         91.7431      Job/Sec
40 Min Response            0.0153      Sec
41 Max Demand              0.0109      Sec
42 Tot Demand              0.0153      Sec
43 Think time              0.0000      Sec
44 Optimal Clients         1.4037      Clients
```

The system throughput and response time appear on lines 33 and 34 respectively. Note that the predicted optimal client load on line 44 is $N_{\mathrm{opt}} = 2$ clients (rounded up). A complete set of results for up to 10 clients is summarized in Table 10.3.

Table 10.3. Preforking model results

Clients	Conn/s	RTD (s)
1	65.3595	0.0153
2	86.4138	0.0231
3	90.9434	0.0330
4	91.6474	0.0436
5	91.7335	0.0545
6	91.7423	0.0654
7	91.7431	0.0763
8	91.7431	0.0872
9	91.7431	0.0981
10	91.7431	0.1090

Once again, these throughput data match the NCSA measurements but the NCSA measurements are likely flawed; this is a point we take up in more detail in Sect. 10.3. The two sets of throughput data for each type of HTTP server are shown together in Fig. 10.3. The corresponding response times are shown in Fig. 10.4. Under the conditions of the load-test, the HTTP demon (HTTPd) saturates beyond two client generators.

This performance model shows that throughput is bottlenecked by the HTTPd, not the slave processes. The better throughput performance of preforking is simply a consequence of the reduced overhead that ensues by not having to fork a process for HTTP request. It is neither limited nor enhanced by the number of preforked processes. Since the demon that is the bottleneck, preforking more than a single slave has no impact on throughput.

This conclusion is true only for the NCSA stress test workload. The file size is small, so the demon service time dominates. For larger files and files that are not cached, the service time of the slaves should be larger than that of the demon, in which case $m > 1$ slaves would contribute to further performance improvements of the HTTPd. The predicted delays in Fig. 10.4 show that the system is already above saturation, and climbing the linear "hockey-stick handle" discssed in Chap. 5.

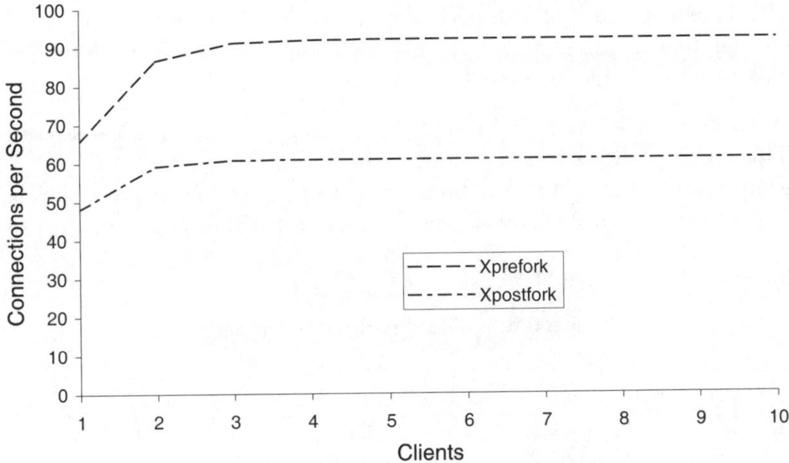

Fig. 10.3. Predicted HTTPd throughputs

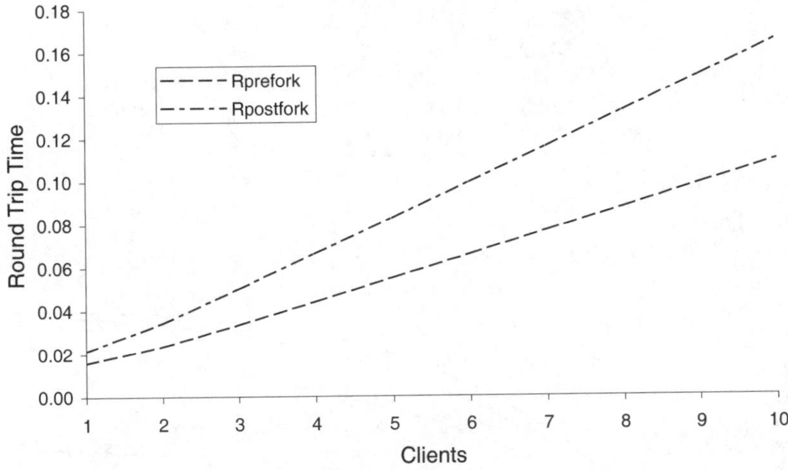

Fig. 10.4. Server response times corresponding to Fig. 10.3

Since the service demand at the demon is greater than the time to service the stress test workload (request a 100-B file), the demon or master process is the bottleneck process in *both* cases. Hence the throughput saturates immediately above two clients. The 50% improvement in throughput from preforking is merely a reflection of the lower overhead in the demon process. The time to pre-process the request is less with the preforking.

Preforking more than $m = 1$ slaves (Table 10.4) has no impact on throughput (Fig. 10.5). This is only true for the stress test workload. There, the service time to process the file descriptor is estimated at 4.5 ms. Requesting a typical

HTML page of about 1,000 B, does demonstrate the advantages of preforking a finite number of slaves.

The following PDQ results show that for this workload:

- With $m = 1$, the overall throughput is much less than for the stress test. This simply follows from the longer total processing time.
- More slaves improves throughput, even restores it to stress-test levels.
- More than $m = 8$ slaves is not very effective (in this simple model).

Table 10.4. HTTPd multislave throughput

	Slave processes				
Clients	$m = 1$	$m = 2$	$m = 4$	$m = 8$	$m = 16$
1	24.45	24.45	24.45	24.45	24.45
2	30.39	36.49	40.56	42.96	44.27
3	32.30	43.58	51.90	56.99	59.80
4	32.96	48.21	60.24	67.54	71.42
5	33.20	51.44	66.58	75.33	79.61
6	33.28	53.80	71.50	80.95	84.98
7	33.32	55.58	75.39	84.87	88.23
8	33.33	56.98	78.50	87.52	90.04
9	33.33	58.09	81.02	89.23	90.97
10	33.33	58.99	83.06	90.30	91.41

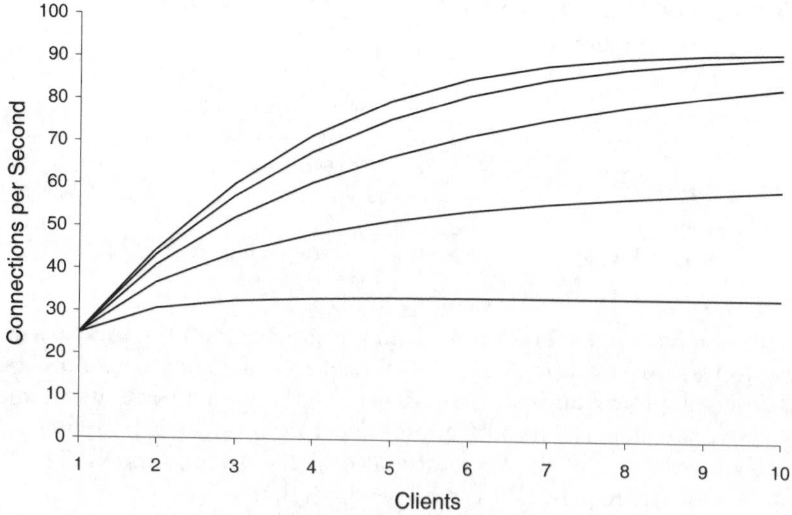

Fig. 10.5. HTTP server throughput

The response times predicted by PDQ are shown in Table 10.5 and Fig. 10.6.

Table 10.5. HTTPd multislave delay

Clients	Slave processes $m = 1$	$m = 2$	$m = 4$	$m = 8$	$m = 16$
1	0.0409	0.0409	0.0409	0.0409	0.0409
2	0.0658	0.0548	0.0493	0.0466	0.0452
3	0.0929	0.0688	0.0578	0.0526	0.0502
4	0.1214	0.0830	0.0664	0.0592	0.0560
5	0.1506	0.0972	0.0751	0.0664	0.0628
6	0.1803	0.1115	0.0839	0.0741	0.0706
7	0.2101	0.1259	0.0928	0.0825	0.0793
8	0.2400	0.1404	0.1019	0.0914	0.0889
9	0.2700	0.1549	0.1111	0.1009	0.0989
10	0.3000	0.1695	0.1204	0.1107	0.1094

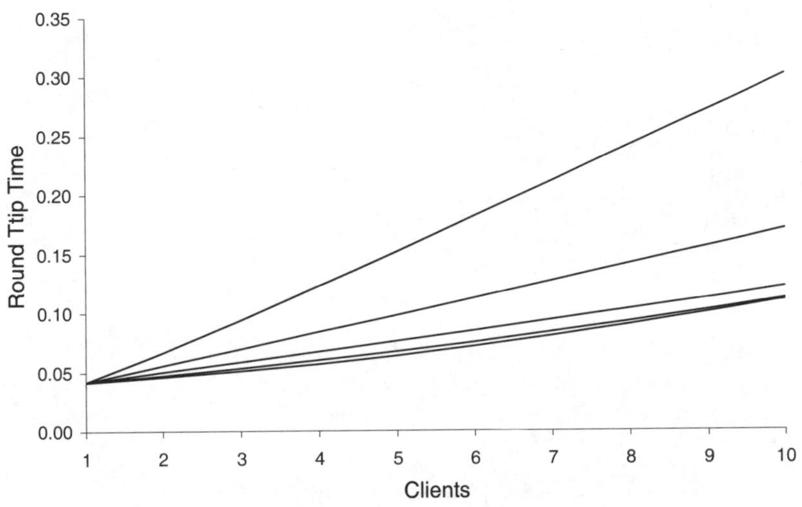

Fig. 10.6. Corresponding HTTP server response times

By way of contrast, the fork-on-demand model also shows improved throughput performance under the heavier home page workload, but has lower single-client performance due to the cost of a fork. Performance becomes throttled at 60 cps above six clients in Fig. 10.7, whereas it was throttled at two clients under the stress test. The corresponding round-trip delay times are also plotted in Fig. 10.8.

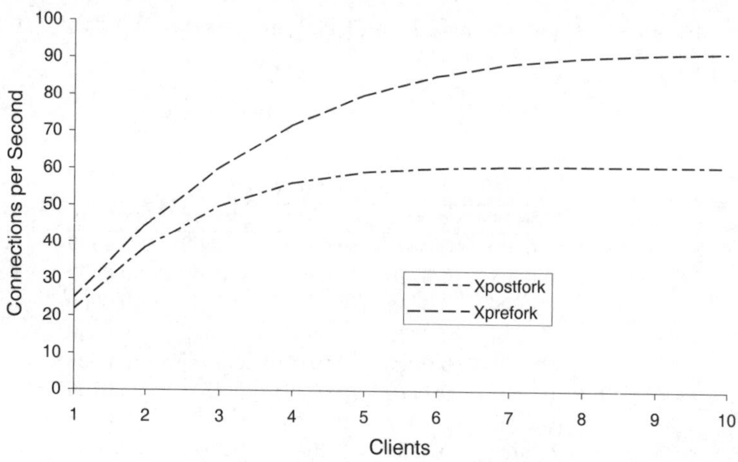

Fig. 10.7. Throughput comparisons

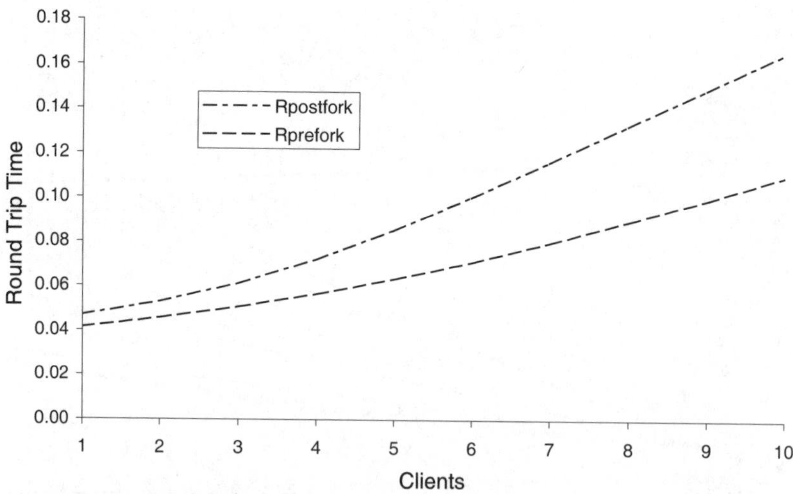

Fig. 10.8. Round trip delay

Finally, it is worth noting some new tools that are available for assisting in the performance analysis of Web servers. (Appendix D). In addition, a number of Web server benchmarks are available. Among them are the SPEC Web99 benchmark (`www.spec.org/Web99/`) and TPC-W (`www.tpc.org/information/benchmarks.asp`). The SPECWeb99 benchmark is modeled after the SPEC SFS client/server benchmark but has stricter rules of engagement and a well-defined workload mix.

As with all benchmarks, you need to be cautious about the representativeness of the workload. A server that stores a large number of MPEG files will have different access characteristics than one that stores smaller text files. The file size and distribution can also skew benchmark results and performance in general. Moreover, the performance metrics used may be misleading. In some cases the throughput is measured as the number of TCP connections per second. There can be a large variance (e.g., whether access requests are issued by a human or a software robot). A better metric might be the average number of successfully completed HTTP operations per second or the average number of bytes transferred, combined with the average response time (a throughput delay metric).

10.3 Two-Tier PDQ Model

The examples presented in the next three sections are intended to demonstrate how real this effect can be in the context of performance analysis.

10.3.1 Data and Information Are Not the Same

The following examples are intended to demonstrate what can go wrong with load test measurements if the tester has no conceptual framework of the type discussed in Chap. 5. In the vernacular, "Data is not information." A conceptual framework acts like a tool for sifting through the generated data. Informational *nuggets* are embedded in the data, and tools like PDQ offer a way to pan for informational *gold*.

10.3.2 HTTPd Performance Measurements

Compare the following load test measurements made on a variety of HTTP demons [McGrath and Yeager 1996]. Figure 10.9 shows the measured throughput data. They exhibit the generally expected throughput characteristic for a system with a finite number of requests as discussed in Sect. 2.8.1 of Chap. 2.

The slightly odd feature in this case is the fact that the HTTP servers appear to saturate rapidly for loads between two and four clients. Turning next to Fig. 10.10, we see somewhat similar features in many of the curves. Except for the bottom curve, the top three curves appear to *saturate* at $N = 2$ client generators, while the other one has a knee at four clients. Beyond the knee it exhibits *retrograde* behavior; this is something we shall examine more closely in Sect. 10.4.6.

But these are *response time* curves, not throughput curves, and this should never happen! These data defy the queueing theory presented in Sect. 2.8.1 of Chap. 2. Above saturation, the response time curves should start to climb up a *hockey stick* handle with a slope determined by the bottleneck stage with service demand $D_{\max}$.

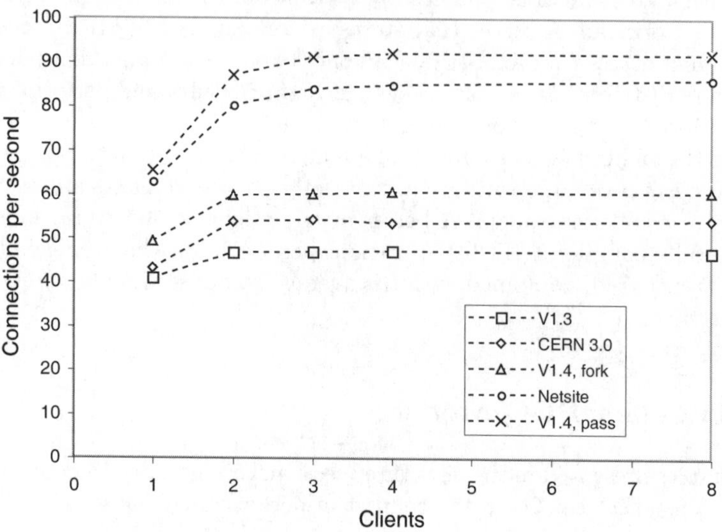

Fig. 10.9. Measured throughput for a suite of HTTPd servers

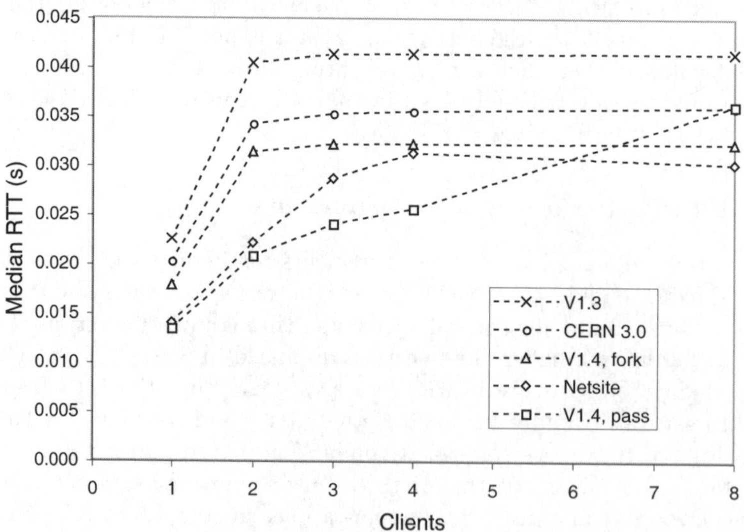

Fig. 10.10. Measured response times of the same HTTPd servers in Fig. 10.9

10.3.3 Java Performance Measurements

In their book on Java®performance analysis, Wilson and Kesselman [2000, pp. 6–7] refer to the classic convex response time characteristic of (Fig. 2.20) in Chap. 2 as being undesirable for good scalability.

> "(The equivalent of Fig. 2.20) isn't scaling well because response time is increasing exponentially with increasing user load."

They define scalability rather narrowly as "the study of how systems perform under heavy loads." As we discussed in Chap. 8, this is not necessarily so. As we have just seen in Sect. 10.3.2, saturation may set in with just a few active users. Their conclusion is apparently keyed off the incorrect statement that the response time is increasing "exponentially" with increasing user load. No other evidence is provided to support this claim.

Not only is the response time not rising exponentially, the application may be scaling as well as it can on that platform. We know from Chap. 5 that saturation is to be expected and from (5.14) that the growth above saturation is *linear*, not exponential. Moreover, such behavior does not by itself imply poor scalability. Indeed, we saw in Fig. 5.12 of Chap. 5 that the response time curve may rise *superlinearly* in the presence of thrashing effects, but this special case is not discussed either.

These authors then go on to claim that a (strange) response time characteristic like that shown in Fig. 10.10 is more desirable.

> "(The equivalent of Fig. 10.10) scales in a more desirable manner because response time degradation is more gradual with increasing user load."

Assuming the authors did not mislabel their own plots (and their text indicates that they did not), they have failed to comprehend that the flattening effect is most likely caused by throttling due to a limit on the number of threads that the client can execute (as we discuss in the next section) or the inability of the server to keep up with requests or related behavior. Whatever the precise cause, any constancy or sublinearity in the response time characteristic above saturation is a signal that the measurement system has a flaw. It can never mean that the application is exhibiting a desirable scalability characteristic. It may be desirable but it is not realistic.

10.4 Middleware Analysis Using PDQ

The right approach to analyzing sublinear response times is presented by Buch and Pentkovski [2001] while using the Web Application Stress (WAS) tool, which can be downloaded from Microsoft's Web site `www.microsoft.com`. The context for their measurements is a three-tier (cf. Chap. 9) e-business application comprising:

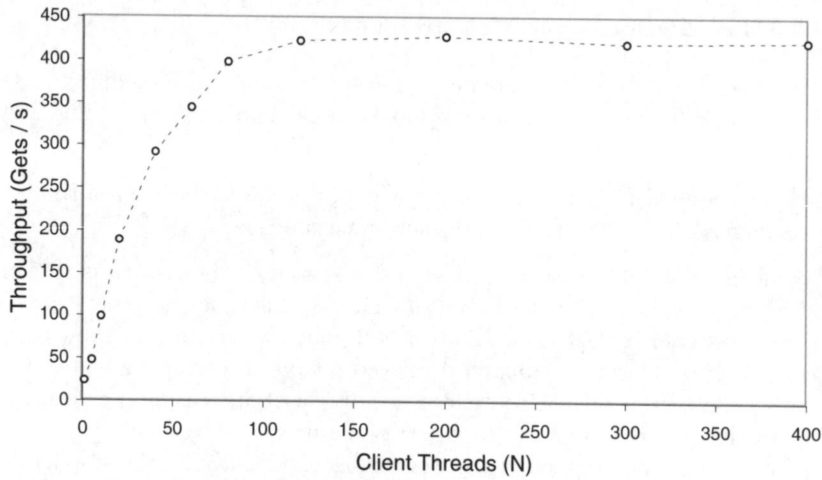

Fig. 10.11. Measured middleware throughput

1. Web services
2. application services
3. database backend

In the subsequent sections we use the reported measurements to construct a PDQ model of this e-business application. The measured throughput in

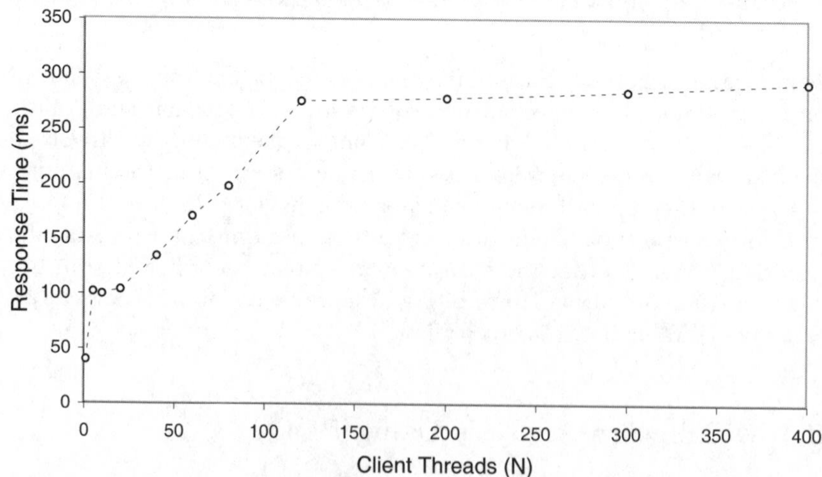

Fig. 10.12. Measured middleware response time

Fig. 10.11 exhibits saturation in the range $100 < N_{\text{was}} < 150$ clients. The corresponding response time data in Fig. 10.12 exhibit sublinear behavior of the type discussed in Sects. 10.3.2 and 10.3.3.

10.4.1 Active Client Threads

In Table 10.6 N_{was} is the number of client threads that are assumed to be running. The number of threads that are actually executing can be determined from the WAS data using Little's law given by (2.14) in the form $N_{\text{run}} = X_{\text{was}} \times R_{\text{was}}$. We see immediately in the fourth column of Table 10.6 that no

Table 10.6. The number of running and idle client threads

Client threads N_{was}	System throughput X_{was}	Response time R_{was}	Running threads N_{run}	Idle threads N_{idle}
1	24	40	0.96	0.04
5	48	102	4.90	0.10
10	99	100	9.90	0.10
20	189	104	19.66	0.34
40	292	135	39.42	0.58
60	344	171	58.82	1.18
80	398	198	78.80	1.20
120	423	276	116.75	3.25
200	428	279	**119.41**	80.59
300	420	285	**119.70**	180.30
400	423	293	**123.94**	276.06

more than 120 threads (shown in bold) are ever actually running (Fig. 10.13) on the client CPU even though up to 400 client processes have been requested. In fact there are $N_{\text{idle}} = N_{\text{was}} - N_{\text{run}}$ threads that remain idle in the pool. This throttling by the client thread pool shows up in the response data of Fig. 10.12 and also accounts for the sublinearity discussed in Sects. 10.3.2 and 10.3.3.

10.4.2 Load Test Results

The key load test measurements in Buch and Pentkovski [2001] are summarized in Table 10.7. Unfortunately, the data are not presented in equal user-load increments, which is less than ideal for proper performance analysis. Both X_{was} and R_{was} are system metrics reported from the client-side. The utilizations was obtained separately from performance monitors on each of the local servers. The average think-time in the WAS tool was set to $Z = 0$. The Microsoft IIS Web server was also known to be a serious bottleneck.

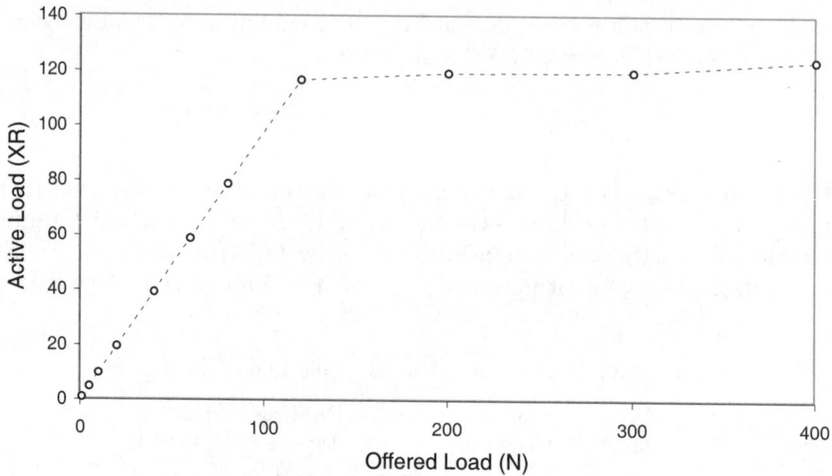

Fig. 10.13. Plot of N_{run} determined by applying Little's law to the data in Table 10.6

Table 10.7. Measured performance data for the middleware application

N	X_{was} (GPS)	R_{was} (ms)	U_{ws} (%)	U_{as} (%)	U_{db} (%)
1	24	39	21	8	4
2	48	39	41	13	5
4	85	44	74	20	5
7	100	67	95	23	5
10	99	99	96	22	6
20	94	210	97	22	6

10.4.3 Derived Service Demands

The measured utilizations and throughputs can be used together with the microscopic version of Little's law given by (2.15) to calculate the service demands for each application service in Table 10.8.

The average of the derived values (the last row in Table 10.8) can be used to parameterize the PDQ model.

10.4.4 Naive PDQ Model

As a first attempt to model the performance characteristics of the e-business application in PDQ (see Fig. 10.14), we simply represent each application service as a separate PDQ node with the respective service demand determined from Table 10.8 as shown in the following PDQ code fragment:

```
PDQ::Init(model);
$pdq::streams = PDQ::CreateClosed($work, $pdq::TERM, $users, $think);
```

Table 10.8. Derived service demands for the middleware application for each client load. The *last row* shows the average service demand for each middleware PDQ queueing center in Fig. 10.14

N	D_{ws}	D_{as}	D_{db}
1	0.0088	0.0021	0.0019
2	0.0085	0.0033	0.0012
4	0.0087	0.0045	0.0007
7	0.0095	0.0034	0.0005
10	0.0097	0.0022	0.0006
20	0.0103	0.0010	0.0006
	0.0093	0.0028	0.0009

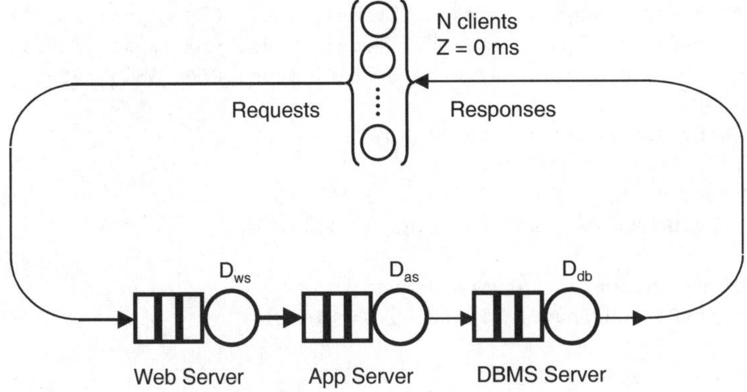

Fig. 10.14. Naive PDQ model

```
...
# Create a queue for each of the three tiers
$pdq::nodes = PDQ::CreateNode($node1, $pdq::CEN, $pdq::FCFS);
$pdq::nodes = PDQ::CreateNode($node2, $pdq::CEN, $pdq::FCFS);
$pdq::nodes = PDQ::CreateNode($node3, $pdq::CEN, $pdq::FCFS);
...
# Set service demands (in seconds)
PDQ::SetDemand($node1, $work, 0.0093);
PDQ::SetDemand($node2, $work, 0.0028);
PDQ::SetDemand($node3, $work, 0.0009);
```

The Perlcode for the complete model follows:

```
#!/usr/bin/perl
# ebiz.pl
use pdq;

$model    = "Middleware";
$work     = "eBiz-tx";
$node1    = "WebServer";
```

```
$node2     = "AppServer";
$node3     = "DBMServer";
$think     = 0.0 * 1e-3;  # treat as free param

#  Add dummy node names here
$node4 = "DummySvr";

$users = 10;
pdq::Init($model);

$pdq::streams = pdq::CreateClosed($work, $pdq::TERM, $users, $think);

$pdq::nodes = pdq::CreateNode($node1, $pdq::CEN, $pdq::FCFS);
$pdq::nodes = pdq::CreateNode($node2, $pdq::CEN, $pdq::FCFS);
$pdq::nodes = pdq::CreateNode($node3, $pdq::CEN, $pdq::FCFS);
$pdq::nodes = pdq::CreateNode($node4, $pdq::CEN, $pdq::FCFS);

#  NOTE: timebase is seconds
pdq::SetDemand($node1, $work, 9.8 * 1e-3);
pdq::SetDemand($node2, $work, 2.5 * 1e-3);
pdq::SetDemand($node3, $work, 0.72 * 1e-3);

#  dummy (network) service demand
pdq::SetDemand($node4, $work, 9.8 * 1e-3);

pdq::Solve($pdq::EXACT);
pdq::Report();
```

As indicated in Fig. 10.15, this naive PDQ model has throughput that saturates too quickly when compared with the WAS data, and similarly for the response time in Fig. 10.16.

A simple method to offset this rapid saturation in the throughput is to introduce a nonzero value to the think-time $Z > 0$:

```
$think = 28.0 * 1e-3; # free parameter
...
PDQ::Init(model);
$streams = PDQ::CreateClosed($work, $pdq::TERM, $users, $think);
```

In other words, the think-time is treated as a *free parameter*. This disagrees with the measurements and settings in the actual load tests, but it can give some perspective on how far away we are from finding an improved PDQ model. As Fig. 10.17 shows, this nonzero think-time improves the throughput profile quite dramatically. Similarly, the response time in Fig. 10.18 indicates the development of a *foot* on the *hockey stick* handle.

This trick with the think time tells us that there are additional latencies not accounted for in the load test measurements. The effect of the nonzero think-time is to add latency and to make the round trip time of a request longer than anticipated. This also has the effect of reducing the throughput

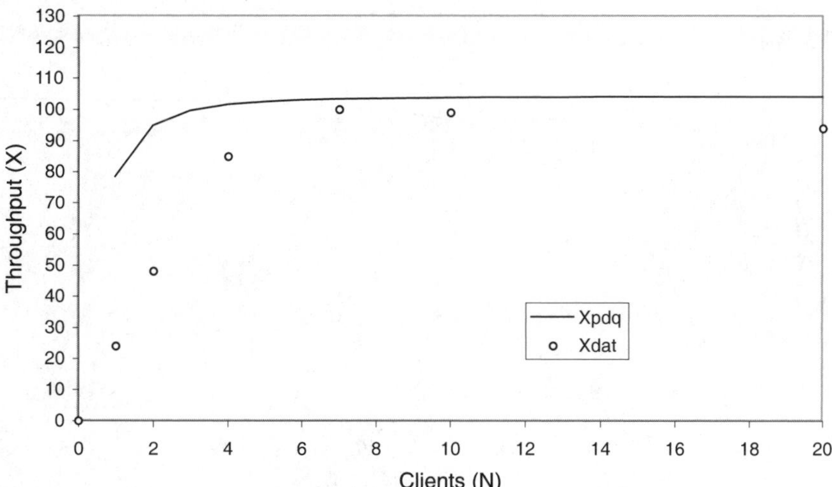

Fig. 10.15. Naive PDQ model of middleware application throughput

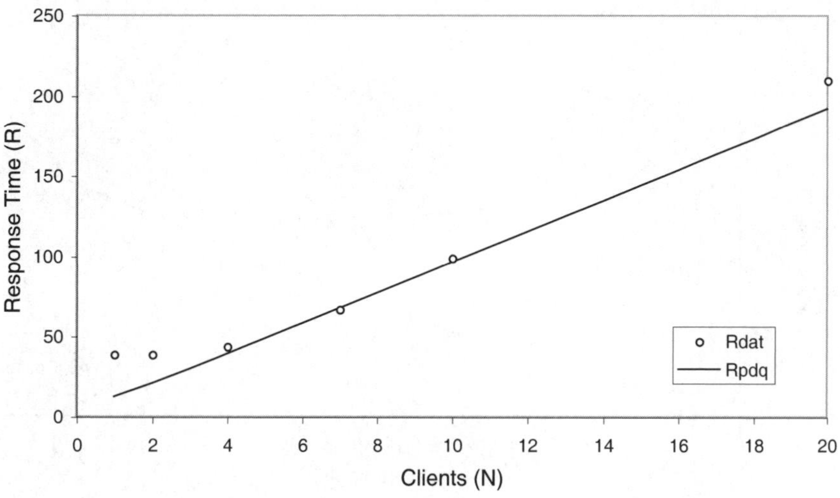

Fig. 10.16. Naive PDQ model of middleware application response time

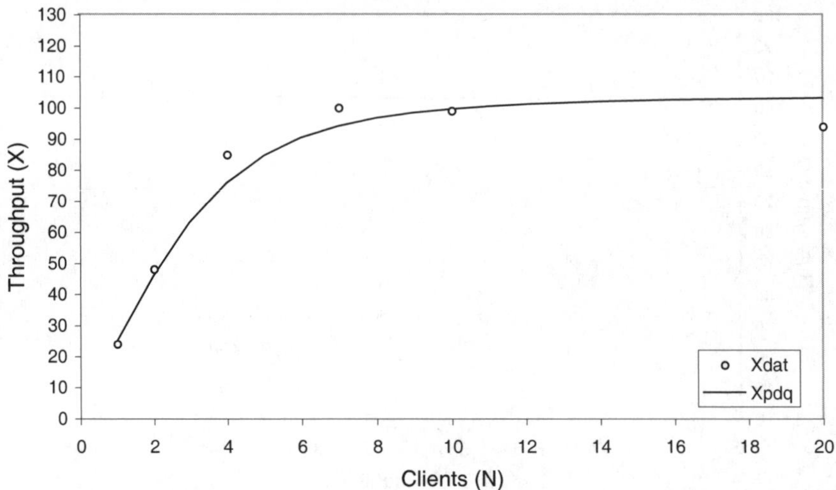

Fig. 10.17. PDQ model of throughput with nonzero think-time

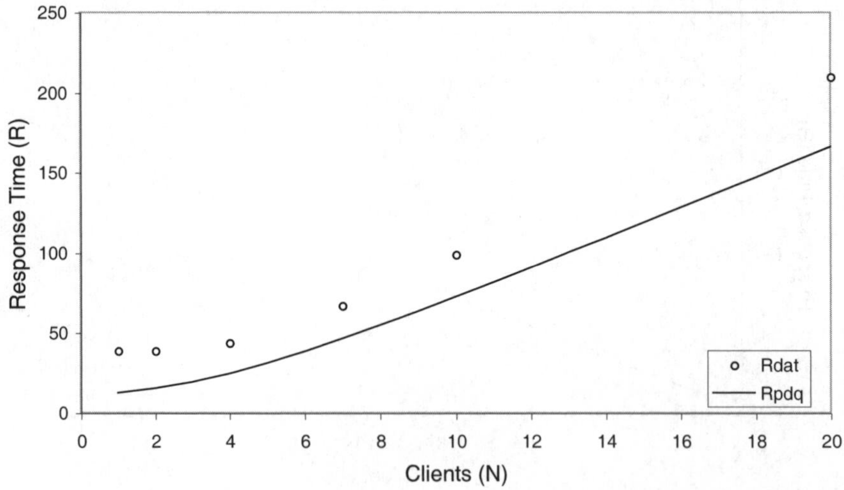

Fig. 10.18. PDQ model of response time with nonzero think-time

at low loads. But the think-time was set to zero in the actual measurements. How can this paradox be resolved?

10.4.5 Adding Hidden Latencies in PDQ

The next trick is to add *dummy nodes* to the PDQ model in Fig. 10.19. There are, however, constraints that must be satisfied by the service demands of these virtual nodes. The service demand of each dummy node must be chosen in such a way that it does not exceed the service demand of the bottleneck node. In addition, the number of dummy nodes must be chosen such that the

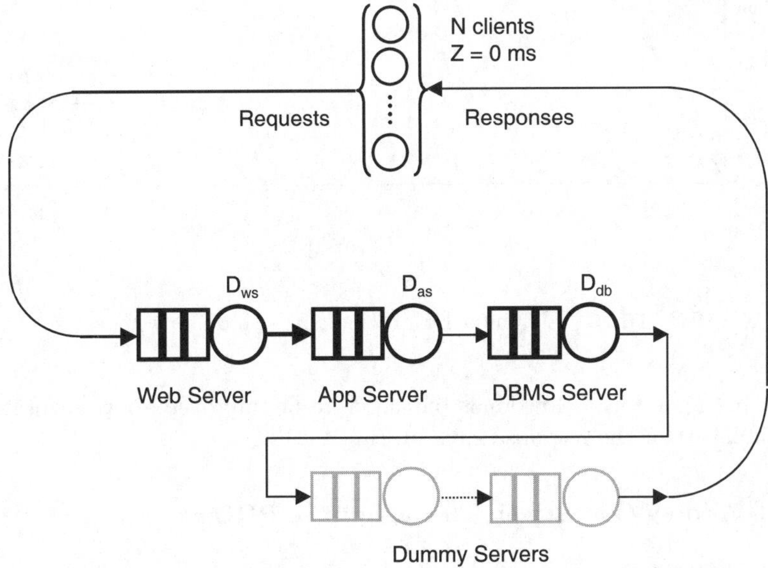

Fig. 10.19. Hidden latencies modeled in PDQ by additional dummy nodes

sum of their respective service demands does not exceed $R_{\min} = R(1)$ when there is no contention, i.e., for a single request. It turns out that we can satisfy all these constraints if we introduce 12 uniform dummy nodes, each with a service demand of 2.2 ms. The change to the relevant PDQ code fragment is:

```
constant $MAXDUMMIES = 12;
$ddemand = 2.2 * 1e-3; # dummy demand
$think = 0.0 * 1e-3;   # free parameter
# Create the dummy nodes
for ($i = 0; $i < MAXDUMMIES; $i++) {
    nodes = PDQ::CreateNode($dummy[i], CEN, FCFS);
    PDQ::SetDemand($dummy[i], $work, $ddemand);
}
```

Notice that the think-time is now set back to zero. The results of this change to the PDQ model are shown in Figs. 10.20 and 10.21. The throughput profile still

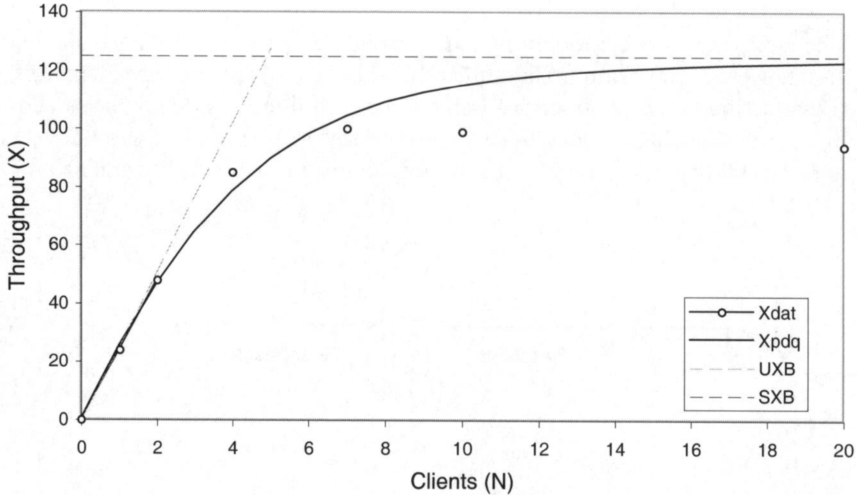

Fig. 10.20. PDQ model of throughput with dummy nodes

maintains a good fit at low loads but needs to be improved above saturation, and similarly for the response time in Fig. 10.21.

10.4.6 Adding Overdriven Throughput in PDQ

Certain aspects of the physical system were not measured, and this makes PDQ model validation difficult. So far, we have tried adjusting the workload intensity by setting the think-time to a nonzero value. That removed the rapid saturation, but the think-time was actually zero in the measurements. Introducing the dummy queueing nodes into the PDQ model improved the low-load model, but it does not accommodate the throughput *roll-off* observed in the data. For this, we replace the Web service node in Fig. 10.22 with a load-dependent node to represent the PDQ Web server node (WS). The general approach to load-dependent servers was presented in Chaps. 3 and 6. Here, we adopt a slightly simpler approach. The Web service demand (WS) in Table 10.8 indicates that it is not constant. We need a way to express this variability. If we plot the Web service demand in a spreadsheet such as Microsoft Excel, we can do a statistical regression fit like that shown in Fig. 10.23. The resulting power-law form is shown in (10.4).

$$D_{\text{ws}}(N) = 8.3437\, N^{0.0645} \,. \tag{10.4}$$

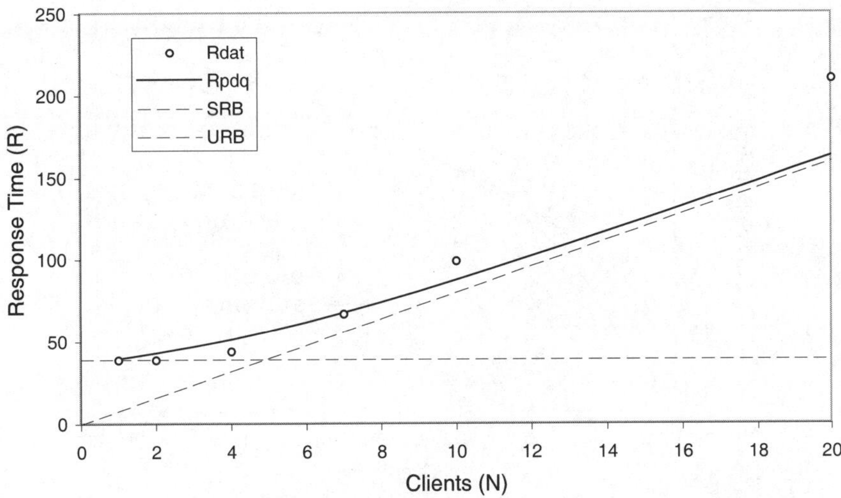

Fig. 10.21. PDQ model of response time with dummy nodes

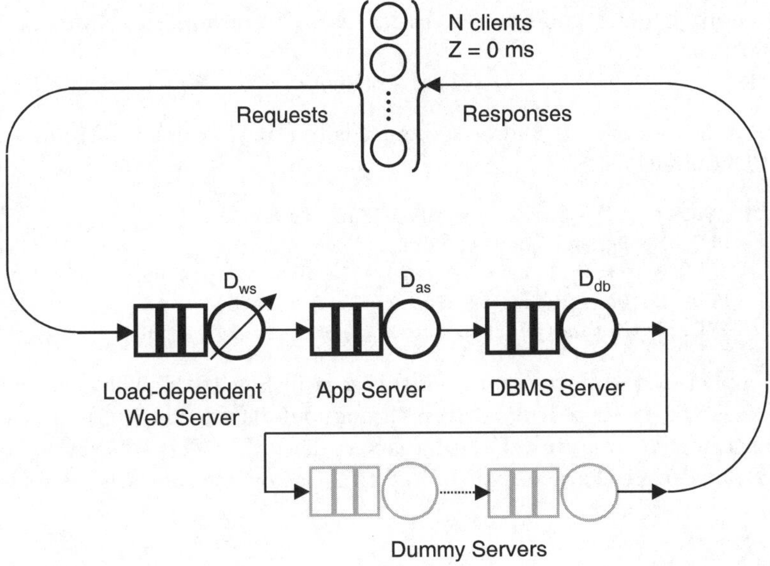

Fig. 10.22. Overdriven throughput modeled in PDQ by a load-dependent Web server node

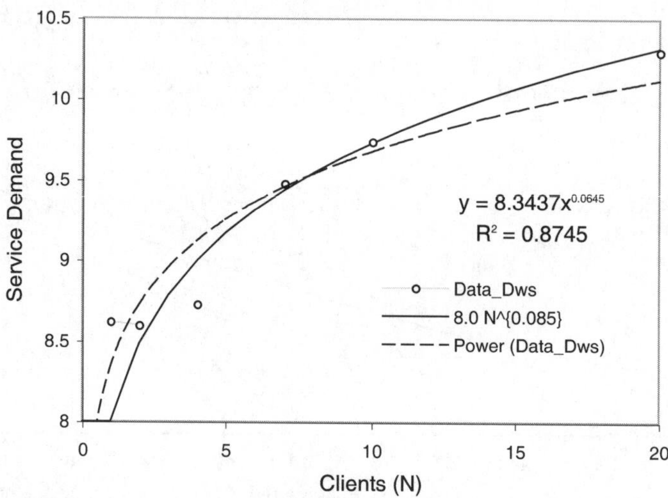

Fig. 10.23. Regression analysis of the load-dependent Web server demand

This result is quite good with a *coefficient of determination* value of $R^2 = 0.8745$.

$$D_{\mathrm{ws}}(N) = 8.0000\, N^{0.0850} . \tag{10.5}$$

Nonetheless, a little manual tweaking leads to (10.5), which is introduced into the PDQ model as:

```
for ($users = 1; $users <= $MAXUSERS; $users++) {
    PDQ::SetDemand($node1, work,
        8.0 * ($users ** 0.085) * 1e-3);        # WS
    PDQ::SetDemand($node2, $work, 3.12 * 1e-3); # AS
    PDQ::SetDemand($node3, $work, 1.56 * 1e-3); # DB
```

The impact on the throughput model is seen in Fig. 10.24. The curve labeled *Xpdq*2 is the predicted overdriven throughput based on (10.5). It fits well within the error margins of the measured data. The *hockey stick* handle in the response time characteristic of Fig. 10.25 is now appropriately *superlinear*.

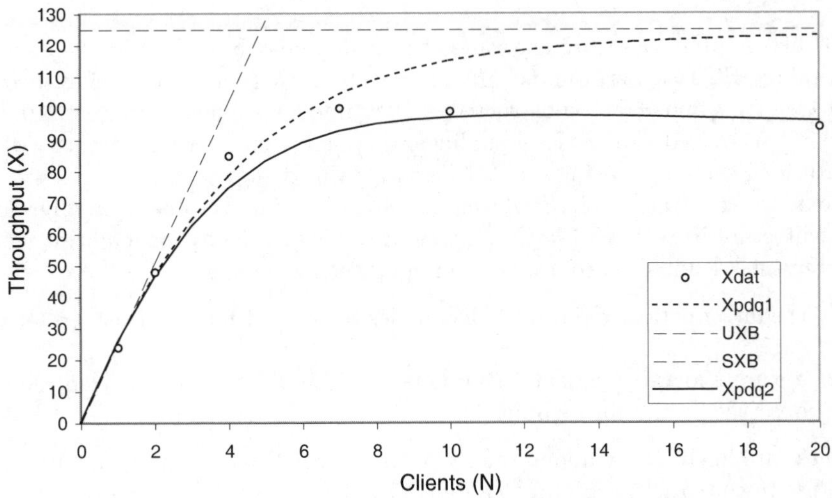

Fig. 10.24. PDQ model of overdriven throughput

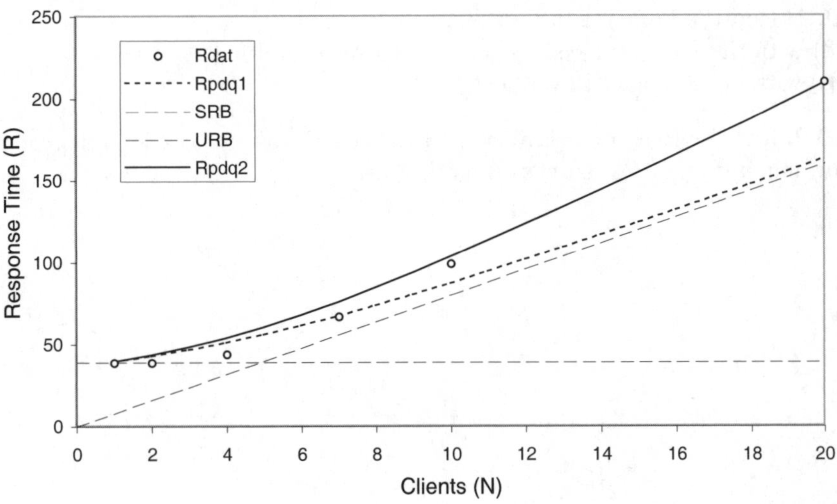

Fig. 10.25. PDQ model of overdriven response time

10.5 Review

In this chapter we examined some elementary mistakes made in the course of taking HTTPd performance measurements. Based on the queueing theory of Chaps. 2 and 3, we constructed a PDQ model `httpd.pl` in Sect. 10.2.2 which uncovered the cause of sublinear response characteristics in otherwise saturated servers as being due to client-side throttling.
Next, we constructed the PDQ model `ebiz.pl` of a Web-based middleware architecture in Sect. 10.4.4. Calibrating the PDQ model to the load test measurements required us to apply two important techniques:

1. the introduction of dummy PDQ nodes to account for un-measured latencies
2. a simple load-dependent PDQ node to account for the overdriven roll-off observed in the throughput data

These are likely to be among the most sophisticated techniques you will need to use in constructing useful PDQ models.

Exercises

10.1. Run the Perlcode in Sect.10.2
(**a**) with the URL replaced by one of your own choosing.
(**b**) with GET replaced by POST.

10.2. Run the PDQ model in Sect. 10.4.6 with the alternative load-dependent formula in Fig. 10.23. Discuss the differences.

Part III

Appendices

A

Glossary of Terms

In this chapter we collect a set of terms and acronyms that arise frequently in the context of performance analysis. Not all the terms are used in this book. Where they are used, a chapter reference is provided. In addition to the terms defined here, there are a number of free online dictionaries and encyclopedias that cover computing terminology. For example:

- *Acronym Server:* `www.ucc.ie/cgi-bin/acronym`
- *Dictionary of Algorithms:* `www.nist.gov/dads/`
- *FOLDOC:* `wombat.doc.ic.ac.uk/`
- *Google:* `www.google.com`
- *High-Tech Dictionary:* `www.computeruser.com/resources/dictionary/dictionary.html`
- *Vivisimo:* `vivisimo.com`
- *Webopedia:* `www.webopedia.com/Computer_Science/`
- *WhatIs:* `whatis.com`
- *Wikipedia:* `www.wikipedia.org/wiki/Computer_science`

ACID Acronym for atomicity, consistency, isolation and durability. A desirable requirement for database transactions:

1. Atomicity: A transaction is an indivisible unit of work where all the operations used to implement it either succeed or fail.
2. Consistency: A transaction must leave the system in a correct state upon completion.
3. Isolation: The operation of any transaction is not affected by the operation of any other.
4. Durability: The result of committing a transaction should be permanent; up to and including system failures; also known as a *persistent* transaction.

ANSI American National Standards Institute. US member body of OSI.

Analytic model A model is analytic if it can be expressed either as a mathematical equation or an algorithm, e.g., in Perl or Mathematica. The PDQ models in this book are classed as analytic models.

ANOVA Acronym for analysis of variance (sometimes ANOVAR). A formal test of the hypothesis that the means of multiple sample distributions are equal. Commonly applied to factorial experiments, where multiple factors in a computer system are varied. Spreadsheet programs, like Microsoft Excel, can do this for up to 2-factor experiments.

APPLMIB Extensions to the SNMP and MIB network protocol standards to include application metrics.

AQRM Application Quality Resource Management, also known as *Aquarium*. Emerging Open Group standard online at `www.opengroup.org/aquarium`.

ARIMA Auto-regression integrated moving average.

ARM Application Response Measurement. Open Group standard available online at `www.opengroup.org/management/arm.htm`

Availability The percentage of uptime during an observation period. Back-of-the-Envelope Models Pencil and paper calculations based on guesses and other rough estimates. Often a very powerful way to test results derived from more sophisticated methods and tools such as simulations and benchmarks.

B2B See Business-to-business.

B2C See Business-to-consumer.

Bandwidth The maximum possible or peak throughput of a resource. See also Latency.

Batch means Used in simulation experiments. A more efficient method for establishing confidence intervals than replication and run means. Efficiency is achieved through eliminating the warm-up period by dividing a single long run into a set of subruns or batches. The sample means from these batches are then used to calculate a grand mean and the confidence interval.

BCMP A set of rules that determine the applicability of the MVA technique for solving queueing systems (see Chap. 3). The rules ensure the queueing system is separable and has a product-form solution (see Chap. 2). An acronym based on the names of the authors who developed the rules: F. Baskett, K. Chandy, R. Muntz, and F. Palacios.

Benchmarks Stones: Dhrystones, Whetstones, etc. Can be optimized into oblivion by clever compiler optimization techniques and are therefore rendered less useful for commercial workload assessment.

Standard: Industry standard benchmarks like those developed by BAPCo, SPEC, and TPC. Publicly defined workloads and requirements for the presentation of benchmark results. These benchmarks are representative of certain classes relatively simple workloads. See Chap. 8.

Custom: Usually requires building a representative architecture and running code that represents a specific customer workloads.

BEP Back-end processor. See Chap. 7.

BPR Business process re-engineering. Any significant change in the way an organization performs its business activities, often impacting software applications.

Browser A GUI-based application capable of rendering HTML and other Web-based technologies, e.g., Macromedia Flash and Java.

BSS Block started by symbol. Memory allocated for uninitialized variables. Appears in the output of some performance monitoring tools.

Business-to-business (B2B) Similar to be B2C, where the consumer is another company or supplier. The transactions are generally more complex and involve higher levels of security than B2C.

Business-to-consumer (B2C) Any retail business or organization that sells its products or services to consumers over the Internet for their own use. A well-known example is `www.amazon.com`. Today, online banking, health and travel services, online auctions, and real estate sites are often considered to be B2C. See also `www.b2cbenchmarking.com`.

BWU Business work unit. A high-level measure used in capacity planning. A unit usually appropriate to both financial analysis and a coarse type of performance analysis. For example, the number of claims processed per day at an insurance carrier might involve several different database transactions. The former is a BWU, while the latter are likely to be more meaningful for performance analysis. Clearly, the BWU is also a measure of throughput. See Chap. 9.

C2C See Consumer-to-consumer.

Capacity planning In the context of computer performance analysis it refers to the planning of computer resources to insure that workload service-level objectives (SLO) will be met. Tends to favor the use of analytic and simulation models. Once calibrated, capacity planning models should be tracked against future revisions of system software and hardware.

Capture ratio The ratio of the total CPU-seconds accumulated by all processes running on the CPU to the total CPU-seconds monitored by the system during a particular sample interval. Ideally, the ratio should be 1, but sampling is always susceptible to missing some short-lived processes. See Appendix D.

Central Server Model The classic closed queue representation of a time-share computer system in which all requests flow through a queueing center representating the processor and then visit other queueing centers (e.g., disks) returning either to the processor or delay centers representing the users.

CERN An acronym for *Conseil Europeen pour la Recherche Nucleaire*, which loosely translates as the European Agency for Nuclear Research. Based in Geneva, Switzerland, CERN `www.cern.ch` is one of the major institutes for high-energy particle physics research in Europe and the birthplace of the Web.

CGI Common gateway interface. The a program (often written in Perl) that enables access to an information repository and return the results as HTML format.

CICS Customer information control system. IBM/MVA term. Essentially, a transaction monitor.

CMG Computer Measurement Group (`www.cmg.org`). An organization for professional performance analysts and capacity planners. The international conference is held every December in the USA.

CMOS Complementary metal-oxide semiconductor. Refers to the dual p-type/n-type implanting used to form the transistor switch. Compare with NMOS.

COMA Cache only memory architecture. See also NUMA and Chap. 7.

Consumer-to-Consumer Person-to-person transactions such as those supported by Web-based auctions, e.g., `www.ebay.com` and some forms of peer-to-peer transactions.

COW Copy on write. Cache update protocol. See Chap. 7.

CPAN Comprehensive Perl archive network. Online at `www.cpan.org`. A large collection of Perlsoftware and documentation. Particularly relevant for Chap. 6.

CRM Customer relationship management. Web-based software applications that enable companies to manage every aspect of their relationship with a customer.

DCE Distributed Computing Environment. Originated by Digital Equipment Corporation, acquired by Hewlett-Packard, and now maintained by Entegrity Solutions `www.entegrity.com/products/dce/dce.shtml`.

DNS Domain name service.

DSS Decision support system. Query intensive and often amenable to higher degrees of parallelism than OLTP workloads. See Chap. 7.

DTS Digital time service. A network timing protocol developed by Digital Equipment Corporation (now part of Hewlett-Packard).

Exa SI unit prefix for 10^{18}. Approximately the number of memory bytes that can be reached by 64-bit addressing = 1 million terabytes. See also tera and peta.

False sharing Occurs when adjacent words in a cache line are modified by different processors. The first occurrence of a write moves the line to that processor's cache and the next occurrence from another processor moves the line to that processor's cache. See Chap. 7.

FCFS First-come-first-served scheduling discipline at a queueing server. Equivalent to FIFO. See Chap. 2.

FDDI Fiber distributed data interface.

FEP Front-end processor. See also BEP. See Chap. 7.

FTP File transfer protocol. See Chap. 10.

Gateway Multiple definitions:

- A network protocol converter.

- A networking term that was previously used for a router or other kind of inter-networking device but this use is now deprecated. By this definition, a router is a layer 3 (network layer) gateway, and a mail gateway is a layer 7 (application layer) gateway.
- An interface between some external source of information and a World-Wide Web server. Common Gateway Interface is a standard for such interfaces. See Chap. 10.

GIF Graphic Interchange Format. Is it pronounced *jiff* or *giff*? See `www.olsenhome.com/gif/` if you have nothing better to do. When you have sorted that out, is it *queueing* or *queuing*?

GUI Graphical user interface. See Chap. 5.

HTML Hypertext Markup Language. The most common way to create Web pages. See Chap. 10.

HTTP Hypertext Transfer Protocol. The protocol used to transfer files on the Web. See Chap. 10.

HTTPd The demon that understands the HTTP protocol and provides the corresponding services. See Chap. 10.

ICMP Internet Control Message Protocol. RFC 792. See Chap. 10.

IETF Internet Engineering Task Force. Oversight body for the development of Internet protocols. See Chap. 10.

Internet Descendent of ARPANET comprising globally interconnected networks. See Chap. 10.

Intranet Private network that supports many of the same protocols as the Internet. See Chap. 10.

IP Internet Protocol. RFC 781. See Chap. 10.

IPC Interprocess communication. See Chap. 9.

ISP Internet service provider. Usually a commercial operation that enables individuals, organizations and companies to access the Internet. See Chap. 10.

ISO International Organization for Standardization. Established in 1946.

J2EE Java 2 Platform, Enterprise Edition. Standard for developing component-based multitier enterprise applications, including Web services support and development tools.

Java A C^{++}-like language that is supported by an interpreter (JVM) and automatic garbage collection. Client-side Java applets can be executed in a web browser.

Java applet A portable Java program that can be executed in a Java-enabled Web browser.

Java bean A reusable software component in Java that supports all the attributes of object-oriented programming as well as introspection, customization, persistence, and interbean communication.

Java servlet A server-side Java applet.

JMX Java Management Extensions. A java-basd technology for building distributed instrumentation for managing and monitoring devices and applications.

JPEG Joint Photographic Experts Group. The name of the committee that designed the standard image compression algorithm. JPEG is most appropriate for compressing real-world scenes. It does not work so well on nonrealistic images, and does not handle compression of black-and-white (1-bit-per-pixel) images or moving pictures. Standards for compressing those images include JBIG and MPEG.

JVM Java Virtual Machine.

LAN Local area network.

Latch A method for serializing database buffer accesses. Usually held for only a short time of order of milliseconds.

LCFS Last-come-first-served scheduling discipline at a queueing server. Equivalent to LIFO. The logical equivalent of a stack of plates in a cafeteria. See Chap. 2.

LCFS-PR Last-come-first-served-preempt-resume scheduling at a queueing server. Variation on LCFS where incoming request preempts the current request in service but the preempted request resumes service immediately afterwards. One of the permitted service disciplines in BCMP rules. See Chap. 2.

LIFO Last-in-first-out scheduling discipline at a queueing center. Equivalent to LCFS. See Chap. 2.

Load-dependent server A queueing center where the service rate is not constant but is a function of the demand for services; usually characterized by the queue length. See Chaps. 6 and 10.

MAC Media access control. Low level OSI data link interface to the physical network layer.

Mathematica A powerful commercial symbolic computation system for doing mathematics and mathematical modeling. See Chap. 2 and `www.wolfram.com` for examples.

MIMD Multiple instruction multiple data. A form of parallel computation. See Chap. 7, SIMD and SPMD.

MIPS Mega (10^6) instructions per second. A nominal measure of processor throughput. Since the type of workload or instruction sequence is not explicitly stated, more cynical interpretations abound. See also ETR and ITR.

Mirror Multiple definitions:

1. Hardware. Writing duplicate data to more than one device (usually a disk), in order to protect against loss of data in the event of device failure. This technique may be implemented in either hardware (sharing a disk controller and cables) or in software. Some operating systems support software disk mirroring. See also RAID.
2. Networking. An archive site which keeps a copy of some or all files at another site so as to make them more quickly available to local users and to reduce the load on the source site. Commonly used by Web sites to minimize the performance impact on the Internet.

Model A noun, a verb and an adjective. One of the most over-worked words in the English language:
- Fashion supermodel, e.g., Cindy Crawford.
- Financial spreadsheet.
- A mathematical equation.
- Classification of an automobile, e.g., GTO.
- Scaled mock-up with lots of working detail, e.g., a model railway.
- An explanation in physics or chemistry.
- Simple rules mimicking more complex system, e.g., the Game of Life screen-saver.
- Computer model. See Analytic, Simulation, Back of the Envelope, and Rule of Thumb definitions. There are many examples throughout this book.

Moore's Law VLSI transistor density doubles approximately every 18 months or about 70% per annum.

MPEG Moving Picture Experts Group. An ISO committee that generates standards for digital video compression and audio. Also the name of their algorithm. MPEG-1 is optimized for CD-ROM. Variants under development in Nov. 1994 are MPEG-2 for broadcast quality video and MPEG-4 for low bandwidth video telephony.

MPP Massively parallel processor.

MRTG Multirouter Traffic Grapher. See Appendix D.

Mutex Mutual exclusion lock. An operating system construct that allows multiple threads to synchronise access to a shared resource. A mutex has two states: locked and unlocked. Chaps. 6 and 7.

MUX Abbreviation for *multiplexer*. Combine several inputs into a single output. Usually a hardware component.

MVS Multiple Virtual Storage. IBM mainframe operating system since renamed z/OS.

NCSA National Center for Supercomputing Applications. Birthplace of the *Mosaic* Web browser. See Chap. 10.

NFS Network file system. RFC 1094. A facility for mounting files across a network of clients. See Chap. 5.

NTP Network Time Protocol. RFC 1305. See Chap. 1.

NUMA Nonuniform memory architecture. A method for improving multiprocessor scalability by partitioning memory across processing nodes rather than have multiple processors access the same memory module. Protocols like DASH, COMA and SCI are used to maintain coherency between memories. IBM/Sequent and SGI are based on variants of a NUMA architecture. See Chap. 7.

OLTP Online transaction processing. Database accesses that involve updates as well as queries. For a given response time criterion, throughput is the key metric. Refers to the operational side of database usage. Compare with DSS, and OLAP.

Open Group An international consortium of vendors whose purpose is to define the to provide open systems applications portability. They also own POSIX and the UMA performance measurement standards, among others. Online at `www.opengroup.org`.

OSF Open Software Foundation. OSF owns Motif, DCE, and DME.

OSI Multiple definitions:

1. Open Systems Interconnection. Begat by ISO standards body.
2. Open Systems Initiative. Online at `www.opensource.org`.

P2P Refer to peer-to-peer.

PCMCIA Personal Computer Memory Card International Association. An international trade association that has developed standards for devices, such as modems and external hard disk drives, that can be plugged into laptop computers. Online at `www.pcmcia.org`.

PDA Personal digital assistant. A small hand-held computer typically providing calendar, contacts, note-taking applications, and in some cases a web browser. User input is provided by pens or small keyboards. More and more of these devices are Internet ready. There is an ongoing convergence between PDAs and cell phone functionality.

PDQ Pretty Damn Quick. The queueing circuit analyzer described in Chap. 6. Download the PDQ source code from `www.perfdynamics.com`.

Peer-to-peer Network-connected architecture (commonly the Internet) where clients and servers are indistinguishable or identical peers. Examples include the infamous music download services like `www.napster.com` and `www.kazaa.com`.

Performance By Design The notion of doing performance analysis during the design phase of a new product or architecture. Originally coined as the subtitle for my first book [Gunther 2000a] Compare performance-by-design with *performance evaluation*, or *performance engineering*, where the performance analysis is done just prior to general availability (usually too late).

Performance model For a computer system, the model is specifically built to provide estimates of certain performance metrics such as throughput, delay, and so on. See Model.

Perl Practical Extraction and Report Language. The language of PDQ used to construct the performance models presented in this book. See Chap. 6 and `www.perl.org`. Related Perltools and source can be found on CPAN at `www.cpan.org`.

Peta SI unit prefix for 10^{15}. See also tera and exa.

Petri nets An extension to the idea of queueing systems that includes the possibility of synchronization mechanisms which classical queueing theory does not accommodate easily.

PHP Hypertext Preprocessor. A server-side, cross-platform, HTML-embedded scripting language used to create dynamic web pages.

POSIX Portable Operating System Interface Exchange. A set of IEEE standards owned by the Open Group. Designed to provide application portability. IEEE-1003.1 defines a Unix-like operating system interface, 1003.2 the shell and utilities, and 1003.4 real-time extensions.

Power Processing *power* is defined for a queueing system by $Power = \rho S/R$ where, ρ is the utilization, S is the mean service time in a p-processor system, and R is the mean response time (Chap. 2). This metric is often used when discussing parallel processing efficiency (see Chap. 7). The power metric combines two otherwise competing performance measures: the utilization and the response time. Processor utilization can be increased by reducing the number of physical processors (but at the cost of increased response time). Conversely, R can be lowered at the expense of processor efficiency. The power increases in either case.

Python An interpreted, interactive, object-oriented programming language with many similarities to Perl and to Java. Online at `www.python.org`. PDQ is also available in Python from `www.perfdynamics.com/Tools/PDQpython.html`.

QNM Queueing network model. Not to be confused with a queueing model of a data network. Called a queueing circuit in this book. A model that contains more than one queueing center. In this collection of queueing centers, work is serviced at one center and then proceeds to another center before either returning to a delay center or leaving the system altogether.

QOS Quality of service. CCITTT Recommendation I.350 defines it as:

> The collective effect of service performances which determine the degree of satisfaction of a user of the specific service.

QOS metrics of interest include end-to-end delays and error rates.

RAID Redundant array of inexpensive disks. A cheaper form of high-availability disk storage than mirroring. See Chap. 1.

RDBMS Relational Database Management System.

Reliability A measure of the occurrence of system failures. Formally defined as the conditional probability that the system is up at time t, given that it was already up at time $t = 0$. See Chap. 1 for more details.

RMF Resource measurement facility in the IBM/MVS operating system.

RPC Remote procedure call.

RPS Rotational position sensing. Disk terminology. Permits the use of the SCSI bus or other transfer path to be utilized by other disks during the rotational latency and seek time of the responding disk.

RSS Resident set size. Appears in some performance monitoring tools e.g., the UNIXtool called `top`.

RTD Round trip delay. The elapsed time measured from the time a request is issued until the response (often in the form of data) is completed. Whether the RTD refers to the time to complete sub-requests or the entire transaction (usually the response time) depends on the context. See also RTT. See Chap. 10.

RTE Remote terminal emulator. Used to simulate actual users in workload characterization studies and benchmarks.

RTT Round trip time. See RTD. See Chaps. 5 and 10.

Rule of thumb Configuration and sizing guidelines that have passed into folklore. No one remembers why the rules work. Useful for estimating performance limits but they are also subject to decay over time (rot?). At some point they may not work because an undocumented assumption (not captured in the rule) has changed. Examples:
- 50% of the I/Os go to 20% of the disks.
- CPU busy should never exceed 75%.

SAN Storage Area Networks.

SAR System Activity Reporter. A standard performance collection tool on System V UNIXsystems.

SCI Scalable coherent interface. A type of bus architecture. IEEE standard. Analogous to a directory-based token ring. See also NUMA.

SCSI Small computer systems interface. A highly ubiquitous disk interface.

SIMD Single instruction multiple data. A form of fine-grain parallelism. See Chap. 7.

SLA Service level agreement. Customer-specified values of certain performance metrics, such as throughput or response time, that must be met by a platform vendor.

SLO Service level objective. Target performance level often specified in an SLA.

SMP Symmetric multiprocessor. General purpose multiprocessor architecture in which any of the CPUs can execute the workload concurrently.

SMF System management facility available under the IBM/MVS operating system.

SMTP Simple Mail Transfer Protocol.

SNMP Simple Network Management Protocol. Used by all network management tools and a growing number of general performance management tools. See Chap. 1.

Snooping Bus-based cache consistency protocol. Any number of caches can simultaneously read a block of memory, but only one cache at a time is permitted to write to that block. To determine their state with respect to a write that may have occurred, each cache controller *listens* or *snoops* on bus transactions and determines the appropriate coherency action.

SPEC System Performance Evaluation Corporation. Online at `www.spec.org`. See Chap. 8.

SPMD Single program multiple data. A form of data-flow parallelism. See also MIMD and SIMD.

Steady state The equilibrium state reached by a system after sufficient time has allowed transient effects to dissipate.

Stretch Factor In PDQ, it is reported as the ratio of the system response time under load to the system response time when it is uncontended (i.e., no queueing). At a single queueing center, the stretch factor is the ratio R/S of the residence time R to the service time S.

SUT System under test.

TCP Transmission Control Protocol defined in RFC 793. A connection-based packet protocol. Compare with UDP. See Chap. 10.

Test-and-set An atomic operation used to implement synchronization on multiprocessors. A well-known performance problem relates to contending processors passing the lock between their respective caches thereby increasing bus utilization. One way around this is to test the lock state before applying the *test-and-set* primitive. Also known as *test-and-test-and-set*.

Tera SI unit prefix for 10^{12}. A single disk with a quarter terabyte capacity can now be purchased for a few hundred dollars, so it is rapidly becoming a commonplace form of personal storage for photos and home movies. See exa and peta.

TPC Transaction Processing (Performance) Council. Responsible for the development and oversight of industry standard database benchmarks. See `www.tpc.org`. See Chap. 10.

TSP Time stamp protocol. See NTP and Chap. 1.

UDP User datagram protocol. Connectionless packet protocol defined in RFC 768. Compare with TPC. See Chap. 9.

UI User interface. See also GUI and Appendix D.

UMA Universal Measurement Architecture. Open Group architectural specification for distributed performance data collection and monitoring. Download from `www.opengroup.org/products/publications/catalog/c427.htm`

UNIX Highly portable operating system developed at AT&T Bell Laboratories. The name comes from a whimsical reference to its predecessor, the Multics operating system. See Appendix B.

URC Uniform resource citation. Web term. A data structure of attribute–value pairs used to describe a Web files.

URI Uniform resource identifier. Web term. There are two types: URL (transient) and URN (persistent).

URL Uniform resource locator. A transient hyperlink to a Web file.

URN Uniform resource name. A persistent hyperlink to a Web file.

VM Virtual memory.

WAN Wide area network.

Write-back Cache coherency protocol. Also called a *copy-back* policy. A copy is written back to main memory only if the cache line has to be replaced or is marked *dirty*. Generally, has better performance and multiprocessor scalability than the *write-through* protocol.

Write-through Cache coherency protocol. Each time a cache line is modified it is also written to main memory. Generally, has poorer performance than *write-back*.

XML Extensible markup language. Compare to HTML.

z/OS IBM mainframe operating system. See z/OS.

B

A Short History of Buffers

A *buffer* is a familiar form of temporary storage area in computer systems. It was also pointed out in Chap. 2 that a buffer is an example of a *queue*—either constrained or unconstrained. The UNIX *history buffer* is a familiar queue for storing recently used shell commands. What is likely less familiar to many readers is the history of queues.

With apologies to Stephen Hawking [1988] the following time line offers a potted history of the development of queueing theory as it pertains to computer performance analysis. It reflects the author's personal bias by highlighting those events that are discussed in the main text. No attempt has been made to be all inclusive.

1917 To paraphrase Pope's couplet on Newton:

Queueing and queueing laws lay hid in wait;
God said, "Let Erlang be!" and all was great.

Agner Erlang [1917] publishes his seminal work where he develops the first queueing models (see Sects. 2.7.1 and 2.7.3) to analyze the performance of the Internet of his day—the telephone system.

Start of the 50-Year Gap

The *Gap* refers to the apparent fifty year hiatus between Erlang's development of queueing models in the context of analyzing teletraffic performance in 1917 and the application of queueing theory to computer performance analysis by Allan Scherr in 1967.

1930 Felix Pollaczek contributes to the PK formula for the M/G/1 queue (2.118).

1932 Alexi Khintchine derives (2.118) for the M/G/1 queue. See Chap. 2.

1942 The first digital electronic computers begin to appear. John Atanasoff and Clifford Berry test a full-scale prototype of the *ABC* computer at Iowa State University. See www.cs.iastate.edu/jva/jva-archive.shtml.

1943 Alan Turing and colleagues build the *Colossus* to crack the German *enigma* codes during World War II. Arguably, Colossus is not usually considered to be a complete general-purpose computer.

1945 Presper Eckert, John Mauchly, and John von Neumann build the *ENIAC* thermionic-tube digital computer at the University of Pennsylvania during World War II. In part, the motivation was antiaircraft ballistics, which took into account the motion of the aircraft during the time it took the shell to reach it; this was a form of *operations research.*

1951 David Kendall invents his notation for queues. See Chap. 2.

1953 UNIVAC, the first electronic computer built for commercial applications.

The IBM 701 was designed exclusively for business data processing. It was a vacuum tube computer programmed with punch cards. It would still be another 15 years before anyone would apply queueing theory to analyzing the performance of these new electronic beasts.

1955 Dennis Cox generalizes one of Erlang's queueing concepts to the case of heterogeneous service times and exit probabilities. See Sect. 2.11.8.

Circa 1955 Toyota Motor Corporation in Japan develops the *Kanban* process for efficient inventory control of manufacturing systems. Today, this concept is more familiar as *just in time* or JIT processing.

1957 Jim Jackson's paper is a significant development in queueing theory because it was the first solvable instance of a circuit of queues, not just a single queue. See Sect. 3.4.4.

1961 John Little proves the theorem that now bares his name in the full context of stochastic queueing theory. See Sect. 2.5.

End of the 50-Year Gap

1967 Fifty years after Erlang's teletraffic models, Allan Scherr [1967] presents a closed queueing model of the CTSS and Multics [Saltzer and Gintell 1970] time-share computer system in his Ph.D. thesis. See Chap. 2 and Sect. 3.9.1.

1967 Bill Gordon and Gordon Newell extended Jackson's theorem to *closed* queueing circuits.

1973 Jeff Buzen introduces the *convolution* algorithm for solving closed circuits of queues.

1975 Forrest Baskett and colleagues write down the BCMP rules for applying queueing theory to computer systems. See Sect. 3.8.2.

1976 Jeff Buzen introduces *operational* equations for Markovian queues. See Chap. 2, Sect. 2.4.

1977 Pierre-Jacques Courtois introduces formal concepts of hierarchical decomposition and aggregation for queueing models [Courtois 1985], [Bloch et al. 1998, Chap. 4]. See Sect. 1.8.4 in Chap. 1 and 3.8 in Chap. 3.

1977 Ken Sevcik introduces the *shadow server* concept for analyzing non-FIFO scheduling within the context of the MVA algorithm. See 3.9.3 in Chap. 3 and Chap. 6.

1978 Peter Denning and Jeff Buzen extend their *operational* approach. One result, the *utilization law*, is a special case of Little's law. See Chap. 2.

1979 Paul Schweitzer introduces a fast, approximate algorithm for solving closed queueing circuits with large N. See Sect. 3.5.3.

1980 Steve Lavenburg and Marty Reiser introduce the MVA algorithm for solving multiclass closed circuits of queues.

1981 Ken Sevcik and Isi Mitrani introduce the *Arrival Theorem*, which enables the MVA to be solved as an iterative algorithm. See Sect. 3.5.1 in Chap. 3.

1982 Jeff Buzen's company, BGS Inc., introduces their proprietary queueing analyzer called *BEST/1* aimed at IBM mainframes.

1982 Mani Chandy and Doug Neuse develop the *Linearizer* algorithm.

1982 Ed Lazowska, Ken Sevcik, and colleagues develop *MAP* (Mean value Analysis Package), a semicommercial MVA solver written in FORTRAN.

1983 IBM Corporation introduces the proprietary queueing circuit solver called *RESQ* (RESearch Queueing).

1984 Sperry introduces the Mean Value Approximation Package (MVAP), a queuing network solver for Sperry 1100 Systems.

1986 Alan Weiss applies the mathematics of *large deviations theory* to the problem of transients effects in network performance analysis. See [Schwartz and Weiss 1995].

1987 Randy Nelson applies the mathematics of *catastrophe theory* to the problem of bistable queueing in virtual memory computer systems and the ALOHA packet networks. See Sect. 1.8.4 for more details.

1988 The author reads Courtois [1985] and develops the *Instanton* method (borrowed from quantum mechanics) to solve the same transient performance problems as Randy Nelson and Alan Weiss. See Sect. 1.8.4, and Gunther [1989, 2000a] for further details.

1989 The author studies *phase transition effects* in queueing models of circuit-switched networks with dynamic routing [Gunther 1990].

1992 TeamQuest Corporation (a subsudiary of Sperry/Unisys) introduces *CMF.Models*, a queueing network solver for Unisys 2200 mainframes.

1992 While at Pyramid Technology, the author develops the proprietary queueing analyzer called *ENQUIAR* (ENterprise QUeueIng AnalyzeR). Later, this would form the basis for PDQ.

1993 A group of researchers at Bellcore, looking into the possible impact of ISDN on teletraffic, examine a multitude of IP packet traces captured over a five-year period. They discover that some IP packet arrivals can be autocorrelated over many decades of time (from milliseconds to hours). These long-lived correlations are best described using power laws [Park and Willinger 2000] rather than usual Poisson assumptions. This is one of the most significant performance analysis results in the past decade.

1994 Ilkka Norros generalizes the $M/M/1$ queue length formula to accommodate non-Poisson power law effects:

$$Q = \frac{\rho^{\frac{1}{2(1-H)}}}{(1-\rho)^{\frac{H}{1-H}}} ,$$

where the Hurst parameter $0 < H < 1$. The standard $M/M/1$ result given in (2.36) corresponds to $H = 0.5$ while $H = 0.9$ is a better fit to the Bellcore data [Park and Willinger 2000, Chap. 4].

1995 Ken Sevcik and Jerry Rolia develop the *method of layers*.

1997 Sun Microsystems introduces the *HotSpot* JIT byte-code compiler for Java. (cf. Toyota's *Kanban* approach to manufacturing in the 1950s).

1997 TeamQuest Corporation introduces TeamQuest Model for UNIX Systems, with proprietary iterative MVA approximation and simulation queuing network solvers.

1998 The author releases the PDQ queueing analyzer as an open-source library written in C with the first edition of *The Practical Performance Analyst* [Gunther 2000a].

2002 The author proves that Amdahl's law is equivalent to synchronous queueing in the repairman model. See Gunther [2002a] and Chap. 8.

2003 In an attempt to make PDQ more widely accessible to UNIX and Linux system administrators (who are often tasked with doing impromptu performance analysis), the author and Peter Harding release an open-source version of PDQ in Perland Python.

2003 Julie Stuart develops a new scheduling policy to increase the performance of electronics recycling operations (see `news.uns.purdue.edu/UNS/html4ever/031013.Stuart.recycle.html`). Similar to the *Kanban* concept developed by Toyota in the 1950s (see above), the largest objects that can be disassembled quickly are moved from the staging area first because it significantly reduces the amount of storage space needed. Like JIT, will this algorithm also find its way into improved computer performance?

As this chronology indicates, subsequent to Erlang [1917] the development of queueing theory was not dormant but continued primarily within the context of manufacturing systems and formal probability theory, rather than computer and communication systems.

Today, the mathematical theory of queues is regarded as a subset of the broader disciplines of *operations research* (a subject that had its origins in the same wartime logistics that led to the development of the first electronic computers) and applied probability theory. This synergy between the development of queueing theory and the development of computer systems has led to what we now refer to as *computer performance analysis*—the subject of this book.

C

Thanks for No Memories

Throughout this book we use the Kendall queue notation introduced in Chap. 2. In that notation the 'M' in $M/M/1$ stands for either *Markovian* (after the mathematician Andrei Andreevich Markov (1856–1922)) or *memoryless*, and refers respectively to the probability distribution of the interarrival and service periods. The terms Markovian and memoryless are used interchangeably. As we demonstrate in Sect. C.2, the only continuous probability distribution that satisfies this *memoryless* property is the *exponential* distribution discussed in Chap. 1. Here, we present a deeper explanation of this important but counterintuitive statistical property in the context of queueing theory.

C.1 Life in the Markov Lane

The memoryless property means that the past is no predictor of the future. Like flipping a coin for a head, the fact that you have not produced a head in the last five tosses does not increase or decrease your chances of producing a head in the next toss. Coin tosses are statistically *independent*, and therefore the past number of tails is no predictor of getting a head in the future. Coin tossing is a memoryless process described by a *geometric* distribution—the discrete counterpart of the *exponential* distribution. The appearance of a head in coin tossing is analogous to the arrival of a customer at the grocery checkout.

Bumping into a doorway with your hip is another memoryless process. Whether you bumped into a door last week or last year has no bearing on your next door collision. The (continuous time) period between such bumps could therefore be modeled accurately by an exponential distribution (See Sect. C.2). On the other hand, having your hip surgically replaced is not a memoryless process because the likelihood of developing arthritis in your hip joint is strongly correlated with your age (but completely uncorrelated with the number of door collisions). Statistically speaking, the longer you live the more likely you are to need your hip replaced. Therefore, these periods would *not* be accurately modeled by an exponential distribution. This seems intuitively reasonable.

Now, let us apply this notion to queues. Suppose you have been watching a checkout lane at the grocery store (Sect. 2.3) for 30 s and there have been no arrivals. Should you join it? Put more formally, is the likelihood of an arrival in the next second greater or less than the likelihood during the past 30 s? If the arrivals are Markovian, the likelihood remains the same. This does not seem quite so intuitive. If you have already been watching the queue for 30 s and there were no arrivals, surely the likelihood of a new arrival must now be greater? Not so in the Markovian lane.

Let us turn to the service process. You decide to join that checkout lane. How long will it take before you are served? From the Arrival theorem (Sect. 3.5.1), your expected waiting time is determined by the number of people waiting in line ahead of you plus the time for the customer already being served. If the expected customer service time is 2 min and the customer being served was already 1 min into their service time when you joined the queue, will that not shorten your expected waiting time? Not in the Markovian lane.

Although it seems counterintuitive, the remaining time before the next arrival, and the residual time before the customer in service departs, are both uncorrelated with your joining the queue. In the Markovian checkout lane or $M/M/1$ queue, those remaining periods behave like the time to the next hip bump (*ageless*) rather than the time to hip surgery (*age-dependent*). In a real checkout lane, of course, your Markovian mileage may vary. See Sect. 2.11.10 for discussion about including the residual service time $\frac{1}{2}S(1 + C_S^2)$ in an $M/G/1$ queue.

C.2 Exponential Invariance

We now examine this memoryless property more formally. The intense interest in the memoryless property stems from its making the mathematics of queues soluble rather than realistic. The Markov checkout lane in Sect. C.1 seems counterintuitive because it does not agree with your perceptions of a real grocery store and most real systems *are* correlated in time to some degree. What is surprising, therefore, is that many real systems can be approximated by a Markov process quite well; well enough to make queueing theory and PDQ useful—otherwise, Erlang would have remained just be another telephone engineer (Appendix B). How well the memoryless assumption applies to your performance measurements must be determined experimentally (Appendix D).

The remainder of this Appendix assumes that you are familiar with integral calculus and probability theory. To demonstrate that the *exponential* distribution is the only probability distribution that satisfies the memoryless property, we first note that the time periods can be regarded as random variables. The conditional probability for two events A and B is defined as:

$$\Pr(A \mid B) = \frac{\Pr(A \cap B)}{\Pr(B)} , \tag{C.1}$$

Let the probability density function of X be (Sect. 1.5.2):

$$f(x) = \lambda \mathrm{e}^{-\lambda x} , \tag{C.2}$$

with corresponding probability distribution (CDF):

$$F(x) = 1 - \mathrm{e}^{-\lambda x}, \; 0 \leq x < \infty . \tag{C.3}$$

The probability that a random variable X exceeds some value x is given by

$$\Pr(X \geq x) = \int_x^\infty f(x) \, \mathrm{d}x = \mathrm{e}^{-\lambda x} , \tag{C.4}$$

and

$$\Pr(a \leq X \leq b) = F(b) - F(a) = \mathrm{e}^{-\lambda a} - \mathrm{e}^{-\lambda b} , \tag{C.5}$$

Suppose we have been observing a system and we know that an exponential random variable X exceeds an age $t = a$ in Fig. C.1 then $X > a$. We are interested in the distribution of the remaining time which we associate with another random variable $Y = X - a$.

The probability $F(y \mid a)$ that $Y \leq y$ given $X > a$ can be expressed in terms of a conditional probability as:

$$\begin{aligned} F(y \mid a) &= \Pr(Y \leq y \mid X > a) \\ &= \Pr((X - a) \leq y \mid X > a) \\ &= \Pr(X \leq (y + a) \mid X > a) \\ &= \frac{\Pr(X \leq (y + a) \; \cap \; X > a)}{\Pr(X > a)} && \text{(from Eqn. C.1)} \\ &= \frac{\Pr(a < X \leq (y + a))}{\Pr(X > a)} . && \text{(from Fig. C.1)} \end{aligned}$$

We can now calculate these probabilities as definite integrals between the corresponding limits. Thus,

$$\begin{aligned} F(y \mid a) &= \frac{\int_a^{y+a} f(x) \, \mathrm{d}x}{\int_a^\infty f(x) \, \mathrm{d}x} && \text{(from Eqn. C.4)} \\ &= \frac{\mathrm{e}^{-\lambda a} \; (1 - \mathrm{e}^{-\lambda y})}{\mathrm{e}^{-\lambda a}} && \text{(from Eqn. C.2)} \\ &= 1 - \mathrm{e}^{-\lambda y} . \end{aligned}$$

Differentiating $F(y \mid a)$ produces the conditional probability density:

$$f(y \mid a) = \lambda \mathrm{e}^{-\lambda y} \equiv \lambda \mathrm{e}^{-\lambda (x - a)} , \tag{C.6}$$

which is identical in form to (C.2), the distribution of the random variable X.

C.3 Shape Preservation

The density function $f(y \mid a)$ appears as the dashed curve in Fig. C.1 where, without loss of generality, we have chosen $a = 2$. This is the same value as the mean $1/\lambda$ in $f(x)$. This function has a value of $\frac{1}{2}$ at the origin, and that corresponds identically to the value of $f(y \mid a)$ at $x = 2$.

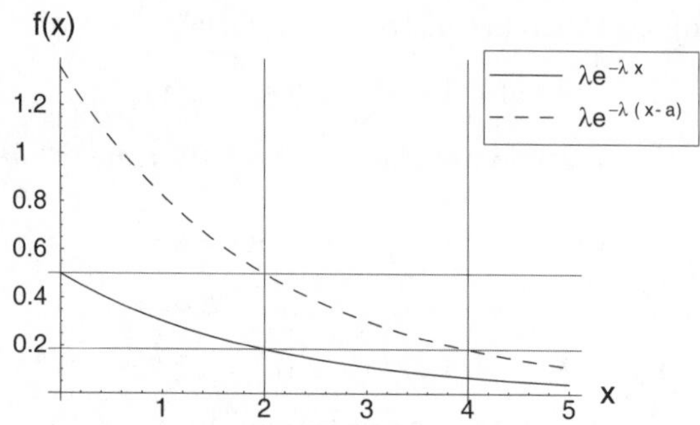

Fig. C.1. Exponential density function $f(x) = \lambda e^{-\lambda x}$ and the conditional density function $f(y \mid a) = \lambda e^{-\lambda(x-a)}$ with $a = 2$

Moreover, if attention is confined to the area below the horizontal line $f = \frac{1}{2}$, we see that the dashed curve $f(y \mid a)$ replicates the original density function $f(x)$ but is shifted to the right along the x-axis by an amount a. The mean is preserved in this right shift of the distribution since $f(2) = f(4 \mid 2) = 1.35914$. This *shape preservation* under arbitrary translations along the x-axis is responsible for the memoryless property of the exponential distribution.

C.4 A Counterexample

If we try this procedure on any other distribution, the shape-preserving property is lost. Consider, for example, the standard normal distribution (i.e., $\mu = 0$ and $\sigma^2 = 1$):

$$f(x) = (2\pi)^{-\frac{1}{2}} e^{-\frac{1}{2}x^2} . \tag{C.7}$$

The conditional probability distribution is given by:

$$F(y \mid a) = \frac{\text{erf}[a/\sqrt{2}] - \text{erf}[(a+b)/\sqrt{2}]}{\text{erf}[a/\sqrt{2}] - 1} , \tag{C.8}$$

where $\text{erf}[z] = 2\pi^{-\frac{1}{2}} \int_0^z e^{-t^2} dt$ is the error function. As before, differentiating $F(y \mid a)$ produces the conditional probability density:

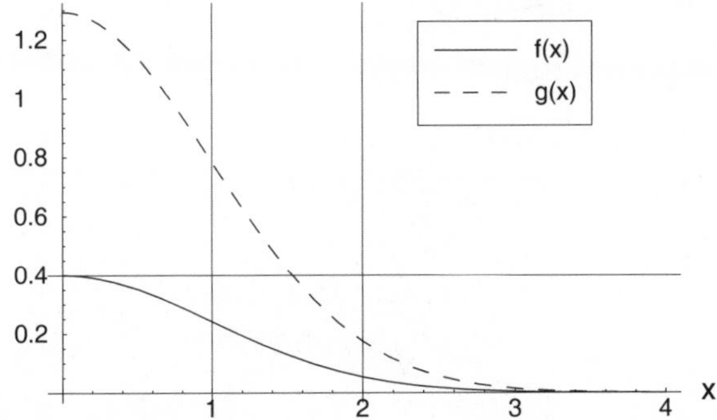

Fig. C.2. Normal density function $f(x) = (2\pi)^{-\frac{1}{2}} e^{-\frac{1}{2}x^2}$ and the conditional density function $f(y \mid a)$ with $a = \frac{1}{2}$

$$f(y|a) = \frac{e^{-\frac{1}{2}x^2} \sqrt{2/\pi}}{\text{erf}[a/\sqrt{2}] - 1} \,. \tag{C.9}$$

Both $f(x)$ and $f(y \mid a)$ are plotted in Fig. C.2, but we see immediately that, unlike the exponential distribution in Fig. C.1, the shape of the original standard normal distribution is not preserved under x-translations.

D

Performance Measurements and Tools

This Appendix briefly summarizes some of the available measurement interfaces for collecting performance data as well as its presentation, storage, and standardization.

D.1 Performance Counters and Objects

Performance data is sampled and typically stored temporarily into respective *counter* locations. These locations are updated at the end of each sample period. The counters may be kernel memory locations or more sophisticated entities such as the performance object registry in the Microsoft Windows® operating system [Friedman and Pentakalos 2002].

The content of these counters may be retrieved in various ways, such as direct memory addressing, via an appropriate network MIBS schema, or by traversing a data structure. Direct memory addressing is a brittle operation since the locations will likely change across different releases of the kernel. This problem can be ameliorated by interposing a data structure that references the counters through pointer references. In UNIX systems a variety of such performance data structures are available.

The Solaris® interface to performance statistics in the kernel is called `kstat` [Cockcroft and Pettit 1998, Musumeci and Loukides 2002]. The associated Perl module can be found at `search.cpan.org/~aburlison/Solaris-0.05a/Kstat/Kstat.pm`. Similarly, AIX® interface is called `rstat` (remote kernels statistics). See `publibn.boulder.ibm.com/doc_link/en_US/a_doc_lib/libs/basetrf2/rstat.htm`.

D.2 Java Bytecode Instrumentation

Because Java runs on a virtual machine, performance data can be collected from Java applications on the server side (e.g., J2EE) in a way that is different from typical compiled applications.

Instrumentation of the Java bytecode [See e.g., Cohen and Chase 2001] can be achieved by inserting special, short sequences of bytecode at designated points in the Java classes of an application. This facilitates runtime analysis of instrumented classes, for profiling, and performance monitoring. Static instrumentation of code can occur either during or after compilation. Dynamic instrumentation, however, can only take place at runtime. A typical way to perform runtime class instrumentation is through the preprocessing mechanism in which profiling and monitoring tools use a class preprocessor to insert instrumentation code at the required places in the Java classes just prior to being loaded by the JVM.

Java Management Extensions (JMX) is a java-based technology for building distributed instrumentation for managing and monitoring devices and applications. In addition, a number of other projects like:

- JikesBT at IBM `www.alphaworks.ibm.com/tech/jikesbt`
- BCEL - Open Source project `jakarta.apache.org/bcel`
- JBoss `www.jboss.org`

have evolved to enable Java bytecode instrumentation.

D.3 Generic Performance Tools

Generic performance analysis tools are resident on all the major computer operating systems. For example, some variants of the UNIX operating system have SAR (System Activity Reporter) [Peek et al. 1997, Musumeci and Loukides 2002]. Most UNIX variants have `vmstat` (see sample output in Figs. 2.7 and 5.13) while the Linux operating system also has the `procinfo` command (Fig. D.1).

These tools display in ASCII characters and the format can vary across different UNIX platforms. Microsoft Windows 2000® and XP® both have a graphically-based *System Monitor* [see e.g., Friedman and Pentakalos 2002].

A common limitation of most generic performance tools is that the metrics are not *time-stamped*. SAR is one exception among these older generic tools. Most modern commercial performance management tools now do time-stamping automatically. They support the *performance monitoring* phase discussed in Chap. 1 (see Fig. 1.1).

Mainframes, such as IBM platforms running z/OS®, possess generic performance monitoring facilities like RMF (Resource measurement facility) and SMF (System management facility). The UMA standard mentioned in Sect. 1 was developed as the logical equivalent of RMF for UNIX systems.

D.4 Displaying Performance Metrics

The generic UNIX performance monitoring tools mentioned in Sect. D.3 present performance statistics in formatted ASCII characters. Modern performance

```
Linux 2.4.22-1.2149.nptl (bhcompile@daffy) (gcc 3.2.3 20030422 ) #1 1CPU [pax]

Memory:       Total       Used       Free      Shared     Buffers     Cached
Mem:         514672     501928      12744           0      189932      83804
Swap:        594396      47704     546692

Bootup: Mon Jan 26 10:47:13 2004    Load average: 0.10 0.05 0.01 1/93 21142

user  :    1d  1:40:40.16   6.4%  page in :  2185526  disk 1:       45r        1w
nice  :        0:01:56.80   0.0%  page out: 17943250  disk 2:  287031r  2014488w
system:       16:19:44.16   4.0%  swap in :    14061  disk 3:    17512r   131673w
idle  :  15d  1:55:06.23  89.6%  swap out:    32127  disk 4:      593r      523w
uptime:  16d 19:57:27.35          context :431330839

irq  0: 145424735 timer              irq  8:          1 rtc
irq  1:    156715 keyboard           irq  9:   19757050 eth0, eth1
irq  2:         0 cascade [4]        irq 10:      12236 usb-uhci
irq  3:  14023393 serial             irq 11:       5658 es1371
irq  4:  21183769 serial             irq 12:  143313718 PS/2 Mouse
irq  6:       161                    irq 14:    2437954 ide0
irq  7:   4818744 serial             irq 15:    6405449 ide1
```

Fig. D.1. Output of the Linux `procinfo` command

monitoring tools have a graphical user interface (GUI), so the most common visual presentation format is the *strip chart* (Fig. D.2).

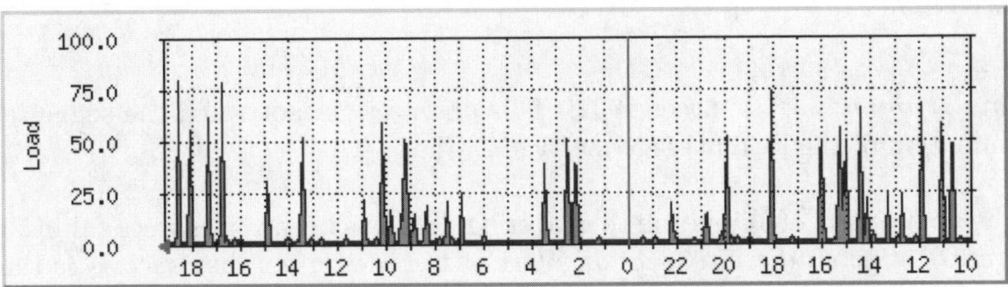

Fig. D.2. Screenshot of an MRTG strip chart showing load average as a time series. The intervals on the time axis are the reverse of normal convention (cf. Figs. 1.1 and D.3)

The astute reader will note that the multirouter traffic grapher (MRTG) plot in Fig. D.2 has the time axis reversed with intervals *decreasing* from left to right. Not only does this defy convention, but it is very likely to lead to incorrect performance analysis. Remarkably, there are several examples of this undesirable miscue on the MRTG Web page `people.ee.ethz.ch/~oetiker/webtools/mrtg/users.html`.

Professional commercial performance management tools, e.g., TeamQuest View®, follow well established conventions regarding the time axis (Fig. D.3). A more powerful visual alternative for displaying the time development of

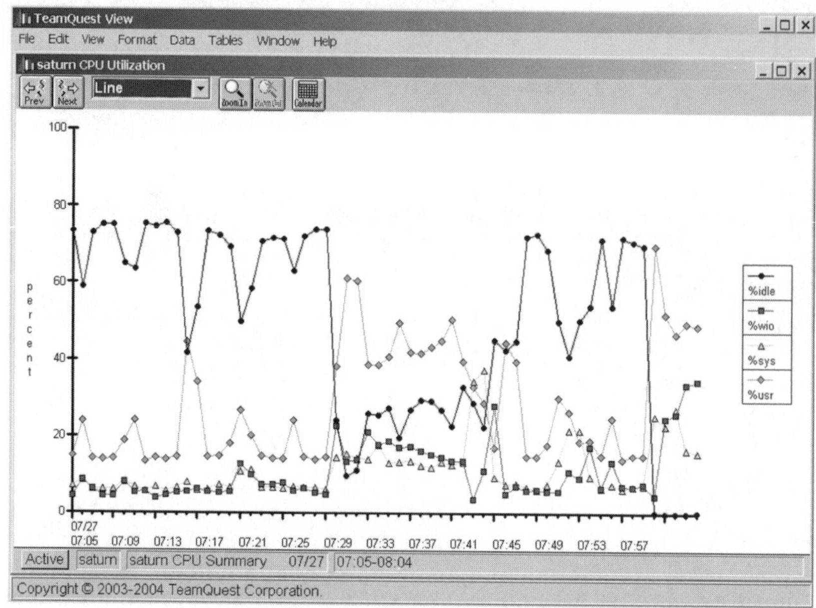

Fig. D.3. Screenshot of CPU utilization components showing how the intervals on the time axis increase correctly from left to right in TeamQuest View (Used with permission)

data is *animation* [Gunther 1992]. This observation motivated the suggested animation of the load average metrics in Chap. 4.

The application of animation to analyzing data has been very successful in the context of *scientific visualization*. Part of the reason for that success is that physical data inherently belongs to $(3 + 1)$-dimensions: three spatial and one temporal. Performance data, on the other hand, is inherently N-dimensional. Consider the 300 or so performance metrics available in most UNIX and Windows systems. To achieve *performance visualization* we need to find ways to display a subset of that N-dimensional data on a 2-dimensional screen.

This is a hard problem and little is currently available to assist the performance analyst along these lines. The central problem is to find the best impedence match between the data being monitored on the *digital* computer and its interpretation by the *cognitive* computer (primarily the visual cortex) of the performance analyst. A lot is known about the former but a lot less is known about the latter.

D.5 Storing Performance Metrics

Having retrieved performance metrics from the respective counters or data structures, the next issue is to store them for later review. This is the only sensible way to search for *patterns* in the data that can aid the performance analysis process. There are good ways and bad ways to do this.

Historically, SAR is stored in a binary format. This presents problems if trying to display on a platform that is different from that where the data was collected.

RRDtool (`people.ee.ethz.ch/~oetiker/webtools/rrdtool`) offers a partial solution. RRD uses a round-robin database on top of MRTG (see Sect. D.4 about time ordering) to store and display simple data as a time-series. It can display this data in graphical form. It can be used with simple wrapper scripts (e.g., UNIX shell or Perl scripts) or via front-ends that poll network devices. RRDtool is also the basis of the ORCA tool mentioned in Chap. 4. These tools support the *performance analysis* phase in Fig. 1.1 of Chap. 1.

Commerical products such as, BMC Patrol 2000® (`www.bmc.com`), and TeamQuest Performance Software® (`www.teamquest.com`), store collected monitored statistics in a sophisticated performance database, that can then be queried to display selected subsets of relevant performance data in a time range of interest.

D.6 Performance Prediction Tools

Having collected performance metrics on a scheduled (time-stamped) basis and stored them in a performance database, those data can be used to construct *derived metrics* of the type discussed in Chap. 2. Derived metrics can be used to parameterize predictive tools, e.g., spreadsheets and queueing analyzers like PDQ.

Table D.1. Partial list of vendors who offer commercial performance prediction tools

Vendor	Web site
Altaworks	`www.altaworks.com`
BMC Software	`www.bmc.com`
RadView	`www.radview.com`
TeamQuest	`www.teamquest.com`

This supports the *performance prediction* phase of the performance management process in Fig. 1.1 of Chap. 1. There are also large number of commercial performance management tools available for doing performance prediction (see Table D.1). One significant advantage that commercial analysis and prediction tools offer over PDQ is, they collect workload service times (Chap. 2) and build the queueing models automatically.

D.7 How Accurate are Your Data?

In the rush to judge the accuracy of predictions made by performance tools like PDQ, the question, How accurate is the measurement data? usually remains unasked. All performance measurement comes with errors. Do you know how big those errors are? There are many well-known statistical techniques for determining measurement errors in performance data [see e.g., Lilja 2000], but few people take the time to carry out the analysis.

A good example is aliasing errors in the measurement of CPU utilization which can be as high as 80% [McCanne and Torek 1993]. This happens when a task becomes synchronized by being sampled on the system clock boundary (Chap. 1). For example, a task might execute in phase with the system clock such that it relinquishes the CPU before the next clock interrupt occurs. In this way, no CPU busy time is accumulated, giving rise to significant errors at relatively low loads. Some platforms offer higher resolution clocking to ameliorate this problem [see e.g., Cockcroft and Pettit 1998].

D.8 Are Your Data Poissonian?

One of the assumptions embedded in PDQ is that both interarrival and service periods are distributed exponentially (Chaps. 1, 2 and 6). Only Poisson processes can produce exponentially distributed periods. The question naturally arises, how can you determine if your data are Poisson or not?

Erlang [1909] was the first to note that incoming telephone calls are exponentially distributed and this led to the development of Markovian queues like $M/M/m$ discussed in Chap. 2. A commonly used statisitcal test for how well data fits a particular distribution is the Chi-square *goodness of fit* test [Lilja 2000]. One drawback of this technique is that it is not very robust unless the distribution you are fitting is *discrete* and you have a large number of sample measurements.

A better test for fit to an exponential distribution is the Kolmogorov–Smirnov (or K-S) test (NIST `www.itl.nist.gov/div898/handbook/eda/section3/eda35g.htm`). It is particularly well suited to fitting a small number of sample measurements to a *continuous* distribution, like the exponential distribution.

The comparison is made between the measured cumulative frequency F_n and the cumulative distribution function F_o of the exponential distribution. Both the positive and negative differences:

$$D_+ = F_n - F_o \tag{D.1}$$

$$D_- = F_o - F_{n-1} \tag{D.2}$$

are calculated. The key statistic is the quantity:

$$K = D_{\max}\sqrt{N} \tag{D.3}$$

where $D_{\max}$ is the largest of D_+ and D_-.

Table D.2. K–S parameters for exponential fit of ranked data

n	Data	F_o	F_n	F_{n-1}	D_+	D_-
1	1.43	0.1797	0.12	0.0000	-0.0577	0.1797
2	4.12	0.4348	0.35	0.1220	-0.0833	0.3128
3	7.58	0.6500	0.65	0.3515	-0.0033	0.2985
4	8.02	0.6707	0.68	0.6468	0.0136	0.0239
5	10.43	0.7642	0.89	0.6843	0.1258	0.0799
6	11.72	0.8027	1.00	0.8899	0.1973	-0.0872

Example D.1. Consider the following set of $N = 6$ service periods measurements: 11.72, 10.43, 8.02, 7.58, 1.43, 4.12. The steps required to determine if these data are exponentially distributed can be summarized as:

- Estimate the sample mean ($\mu = 7.22$).
- Rank the data in ascending order.
- Calculate the exponential CDF F_o with mean μ.
- Calculate the empirical cumulative frequencies F_n and F_{n-1}.
- Calculate D_+ using (D.1), D_- using (D.2), and $D_{\max} = 0.3128$.
- Calculate the K–S statistic $K = 0.7663$ and compare it with tabulated values.

These steps are summarized in Table D.2. Fig. D.4 provides a visual comparison between the measurements and the theoretical distribution. From Table D.3 we conclude that for these 6 data samples the probability $K_{\text{data}} \leq K_{\text{crit}}$ is 75%, and therefore these data are exponentially distributed (the *Null Hypothesis*) at this level of signficance ($\alpha = 0.25$). □

Table D.3. Critical K–S statistics for exponential fit

Statistic	Value
N	6
$D_{\max}$	0.3128
K_{data}	0.7663
K_{crit}	0.7703
p-value	0.75
α	0.25

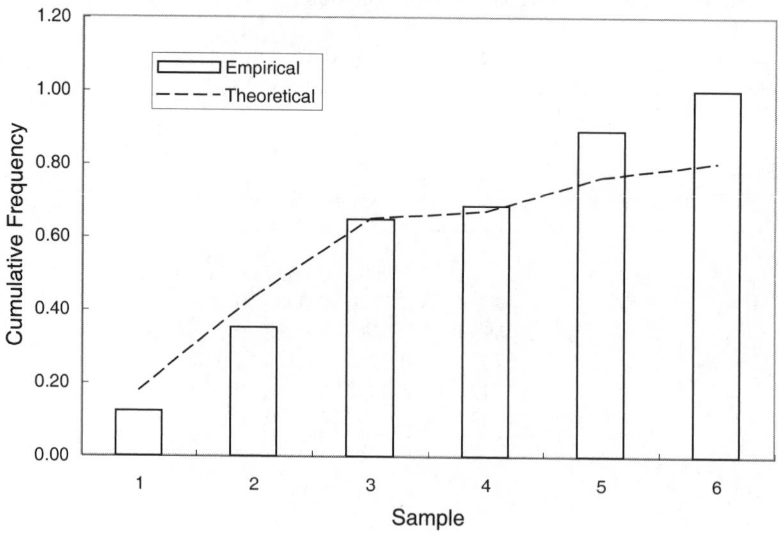

Fig. D.4. Exponential fit to cumulative frequency data

Looking up the relevant K–S statistics in tables can be extremely inconvenient. The following Perlscript `kstest.pl` sorts the measured data and computes the coresponding K–S p-value:

```
#! /usr/bin/perl
# kstest.pl

@data = (11.72, 10.43, 8.02, 7.58, 1.43, 4.12);
@sorted = sort { $a <=> $b } @data;
$num= @sorted; # number of observations

$smean = 0.0;
foreach $ds (@sorted ) { $smean += $ds; }
$smean /= $num;

# Compute Exp CDF
foreach $ds (@sorted) {
    push(@expCDF, 1 - exp(-$ds / $smean));
}

# Compare data against Exp CDF
$D = 0.0;
for ($j = 1; $j <= $num; $j++) {
    $fn = $j / $num;
    $ff = $expCDF[$j-1];
    $Dt = max(abs($fo - $ff), abs($fn - $ff));
```

```
    if ($Dt > $D) { $D = $Dt };
    $fo = $fn;
}
$K = sqrt($num) * $D;
$pvalue = 1 - exp(-2 * $K**2) * ( 1 - 2 * $K / (3 * sqrt($num)));

## Print the results
print "Data   : "; printdata(@data);
print "Ranked: "; printdata(@sorted);
print "ExpCDF: "; printdata(@expCDF);
print "\n" . "K-S Statistics\n" . "--------------\n";
printf("Observations: %2.0f\n", $num);
printf("Sample mean : %7.4f\n", $smean);
printf("D statistic : %7.4f\n", $D);
printf("K statistic : %7.4f\n", $K);
printf("Probability : %7.4f\n", $pvalue);

#---- Subroutines ----#
sub printdata {
    my $datum;
    foreach $datum (@_ ) {
        printf("%7.4f ", $datum);
    }
    print "\n";
}

sub max {
    my $max = shift(@_);
    foreach $next (@_) {
        $max = $next if $max < $next;
    }
    return $max;
}
```

The following output was generated by the `kstest.pl` script using the same data set as Example D.1:

```
Data   : 11.7200 10.4300  8.0200  7.5800  1.4300  4.1200

Ranked:  1.4300  4.1200  7.5800  8.0200 10.4300 11.7200
ExpCDF:  0.1798  0.4350  0.6502  0.6709  0.7643  0.8029

K-S Statistics
--------------
Observations:  6
Sample mean :  7.2167
D statistic :  0.3169
K statistic :  0.7761
Probability :  0.7635
```

The computed p-value (the probability that the data are exponentially distributed) differs from that in Table D.3 because it is calculated directly from the value of K_{data}.

Exponentially distributed values can be used to test programs like `kstest.pl`. The following Perlscript `genexp.pl` generates exponential variates using a robust pseudo-random number generator.

```
#! /usr/bin/perl
# genexp.pl

$x = 1; # Seed the RNG

# Generate 20 EXP variates with mean = 5
for ($i = 1; $i <= 20; $i++) {
    printf("%2d\t%6.4f\n", $i, exp_variate(5.0));
}

sub exp_variate {
# Return an exponential variate.
# log == Ln in Perl.
    my ($mean) = @_;
    return(-log(rand_num() / $mean));
}

sub rand_num {
# Portable RNG
# Return a (pseudo) random number between 0.0 and 1.0
    use integer;
    use constant ac =>      16807;  # Multiplier
    use constant mc => 2147483647;  # Modulus
    use constant qc =>     127773;  # m div a
    use constant rc =>       2836;  # m mod a
    my $x_div_q;                    # x divided by q
    my $x_mod_q;                    # x modulo q
    my $x_new;                      # New x value
    $x_div_q = $x / qc;
    $x_mod_q = $x % qc;
    $x_new = (ac * $x_mod_q) - (rc * $x_div_q);
    if ($x_new > 0) { $x = $x_new; }
    else { $x = $x_new + mc; }
    no integer;
    return($x / mc);
}
```

D.9 Performance Measurement Standards

A number of performance management standards that try to encompass many of the above requirements are either available or in development. Some of the better-known standards are listed here:

APPLMIB Application Management Infomation Base. Extensions to the SNMP and MIB internet protocols intended to include application-level performance statistics.
`www.ietf.org/html.charters/OLD/applmib-charter.html`

AQRM Application Quality Resource Management. Emerging Open Group standard. `www.opengroup.org/aquarium`

ARM Application Response Measurement. `www.opengroup.org/management/arm.htm`

SNMP Simple Network Management Protocol. Used by all network management tools as well as a growing number of general performance management tools. `www.ietf.org/html.charters/ snmpv3-charter.html`.

UMA Universal Measurement Architecture. Architectural specification `www.opengroup.org/products/ publications/catalog/c427.htm` for distributed performance data collection and monitoring.

Other than SNMP and APPLMIB, all these standards are now belong to the *Open Group*. For a more extended discussion about the role of performance management standards [see Gunther 2000a, Chap. 4].

E

Compendium of Queueing Equations

This compendium collects in one place the formulæ that are likely to be most useful for system performance analysis. Table E.1 summarizes the basic definitions and metrics used to characterize queues. Table E.2 summarizes the queueing delays presented in Chaps. 2 and 3.

E.1 Fundamental Metrics

The rightmost column contains a reference to the location where each formula can be found in the text.

Table E.1. Fundamental metric relationships

Definition	Formula	Reference
Total arrival count	A_k	Table 2.1
Total completion count	C_k	Table 2.1
Measurement period	T	Table 2.1
Busy time	B_k	Table 2.1
Visit count at server	V_k	Table 2.1
Think time (IS)	Z	Sect. 2.11.1
Number of servers	m	
Arrival rate	$\lambda_k = A_k/T$	(2.1)
System throughput	$X = C/T$	(2.3)
Service time at server	$S = B/C$	(2.8)
Demand at server	$D_k = V_k S_k$	(2.9)
Utilization	$\rho_k = B_k/T$	(2.10)
Residence time	$R_k = W_k + S_k$	(2.12)
Little's (macro) law	$Q = \lambda R = XR$	(2.14)
Little's (micro) law	$\rho_k = \lambda_k S_k = X_k S_k$	(2.15)

E.2 Queueing Delays

The equations in Table E.2 are expressed in terms of the more general service demand D defined by (2.9) in Chap. 2, rather than the service time S. For further clarification, the subscript k has been dropped. The service time defined in Table E.1 is equivalent to the service demand when the visit count $V = 1$.

Table E.2. Response time formulae

Queue	Delay	Equation
$M/M/1$	$R = D/(1 - \rho)$	(2.35)
Parallel	$R = D/(1 - \rho)$	(2.44)
$M/M/m$	$R \simeq D/(1 - \rho^m)$	(2.63)
$M/M/1//N$	$R(N) = (N/X) - Z$	(2.90)
$M/G/1$	$R_{\mathrm{PK}} = S + S(1 + C_s^2)\rho/2(1 - \rho)$	(2.118)
$M/D/1$	$R_{\mathrm{PK}} = S + S\rho/2(1 - \rho)$	(2.102)
$M/M/1$	$R_{\mathrm{PK}} = D + D\rho/(1 - \rho)$	(2.35)

F

Installing PDQ and PerlPrograms

F.1 Perl Scripts

Table F.1 contains the location and description of non-PDQ Perlscripts. For readers unfamiliar with writing Perlcode, several simple examples are denoted with bold page numbers.

Table F.1. Alphabetical list and page location of (non-PDQ) Perlscripts

Program	Page	Description
`arrivals.pl`	**54**	Calculates arrival rate from data set using Perl
`bench1.pl`	18	Example use of the PerlBenchmark timing module
`bench2.pl`	18	Example use of the PerlBenchmark CPU times
`erlang.pl`	84	Iterative algorithms for Erlang B and C functions
`genexp.pl`	406	Generates exponentially distributed variates
`getHTML.pl`	342	Using Perl`LWP::UserAgent` to fetch some HTML
`getload.pl`	170	Collect the load average using the UNIX`uptime` command
`kstest.pl`	404	Kolmogorov–Smirnov test for exponentially distributed data
`mvaapproxsub.pl`	139	Subroutine representation of the approximate MVA solution
`mvasub.pl`	138	Subroutine representation of the exact MVA solution
`passcalc.pl`	133	Manual calculation of performance metrics for `passport.pl`
`repair.pl`	90	Algorithm to solve the classic Repairman queueing model
`residence.pl`	**71**	Calculates residence time from data set using Perl
`servtime.pl`	**57**	Calculates service time from data set using Perl
`thruput1.pl`	**55**	Calculates throughput from data set using Perl
`timely.pl`	16	Format `Time::Local` in UNIX`tm` data structure
`timeshare.pl`	186	Calculates $M/M/m//N$ performance metrics
`timetz.pl`	20	Find equivalent time in a specified timezone
`timrez.pl`	17	Uses the Perl`Time::HiRes` high-resolution timer
`utiliz1.pl`	**58**	Elementary calculation of utilization using Perl

F.2 PDQ Scripts

Table F.2 contains the location and description of PerlPDQ scripts. The more didactic examples are denoted with bold page numbers.

Table F.2. Alphabetical list and page location of PerlPDQ scripts

Program	Page	Description
abcache.pl	280	SMP cache model with write-back and write-through protocols
cluster.pl	291	Query times for three-tier parallel cluster model
cs_baseline.pl	326	Client/server baseline model with three-class workload
ebiz.pl	361	Web application with load-dependent server and dummy queues
elephant.pl	**309**	SPEC multiuser benchmark model
feedback.pl	242	Single queue with feedback
feedforward.pl	240	Tandem queue circuit
fesc.pl	259	Load-dependent (flow-equivalent) server model
florida.pl	263	Florida benchmark performance bounds
httpd.pl	**347**	HTTP demon benchmark analysis
mm1.pl	**220**	$M/M/1$ uniserver queueing model
mm1n.pl	**239**	Closed-circuit uniserver with N finite requests
multibus.pl	276	SMP performance with multiple memory buses
mwl.pl	246	Multiclass workload model
passport.pl	244	Open series-parallel circuit with cross-coupled flows
shadowcpu.pl	252	Closed circuit with priority scheduling

F.3 Installing the PDQ Module

The Perlversion of *Pretty Damn Quick (PDQ)* can be downloaded from `www.perfdynamics.com`. The Perlinterpreter, needed to run PDQ, is inherently available on a wide variety of platforms. In general, it is already installed on UNIXor Linuxplatforms, so the following sequence of commands can be used to install the PDQ Perlmodule:

1. Unzip it: `gunzip pdq.tar.gz` will produce `pdq.tar`
2. Untar it: `tar -xvf pdq.tar` will produce the directory `pdq/`
3. Change to that directory: `cd pdq` and locate the directory `perl5/`
4. Change to that directory: `cd perl5`
5. Run the setup script: `./setup.sh`
6. Go back to the PDQ directory: `cd ..`

More explicit instructions can be found at the web site `www.perfdynamics.com`. You should also check that web site for any changes regarding future releases of PDQ. You are now ready to execute any of the Perlscripts listed in Tables F.1 and F.2. A similar procedure can be applied to the installation of almost any Perlmodule, including those from CPAN (`www.cpan.org`).

For other Perlenvironments, such as MacPerl (MacOS), ModPerl (Apache), Active Perl (Microsoft Windows), the reader should consult the appropriate documentation for the correct installation procedure.

G

Units and Abbreviations

G.1 SI Prefixes

Throughout this book, we use the conventions of the basic International System of Units (SI) for physical quantities summarized in Table G.1.

Table G.1. Prefixes for general SI units

Greater than 1			Less than 1		
Symbol	Name	Factor	Symbol	Name	Factor
Y	yotta	10^{+24}	m	milli	10^{-3}
E	exa	10^{+18}	µ	micro	10^{-6}
P	peta	10^{+15}	n	nano	10^{-9}
T	tera	10^{+12}	p	pico	10^{-12}
G	giga	10^{+9}	f	femto	10^{-15}
M	mega	10^{+6}	a	atto	10^{-18}
k	kilo	10^{+3}	y	yocto	10^{-24}

G.2 Time Suffixes

Table G.2 summarizes the conventions for units of time used throughout this book. The units in the lower half of Table G.2 are not officially a part of the SI unit system but occur frequently enough to be accepted implicitly.

G.3 Capacity Suffixes

Units of digital computer capacity, however, present some ambiguities. Although physical quantities like cycles per second (Hz) are measured in base-10

Table G.2. Units of time

Symbol	Name	SI unit
s	second	10^0 s
ms	millisecond	10^{-3} s
μs	microsecond	10^{-6} s
ns	nanosecond	10^{-9} s
min	minute	60 s
h	hour	60 m = 3,600 s
d	day	24 h = 86,400 s

(decimal) units, digital quantities involving bits (binary digits) are measured in base-2 (binary) units. The International Electrotechnical Commission (IEC) published unambiguous computing technology units in 1998. Further details are available at the NIST web site (`http://physics.nist.gov/cuu/Units/index.html`). This proposed convention has not yet been widely adopted in the industry, so we do not use it either. For completeness, we summarize the usual computer industry units that we do use, together with the IEC units in Table G.3. A kilobyte refers not to 1,000 bytes but the *power of two* clos-

Table G.3. Units of computer capacity

Symbol	Name	IEC-Symbol	IEC-Name	Decimal unit	Power of 2
b	bit	b	bit	8 b	2^0 b
B	byte	B	byte	8 b	2^3 b
KB	kilobyte	KiB	kibibyte	1,024 B	2^{10} B
MB	megabyte	MiB	mebibyte	1,048,576 B	2^{20} B
GB	gigabyte	GiB	gibibyte	1,073 741,824 B	2^{30} B
TB	terabyte	TiB	tebibyte	$1.099,511,6 \times 10^{12}$ B	2^{40} B

est to that number viz. 1,024 bytes = 2^{10} B; similarly for the other prefixes shown in Table G.3. Therefore, one has to know the context to know which interpretation of *kilo* applies. The strict SI convention introduces a new set of prefixes to remove this ambiguity. For example, 1,024 B would be referred to as a *kibibyte* (meaning, a kilobinary byte) and denoted 1 KiB.

H

Solutions to Selected Exercises

Solutions for Chap. 1

1.1 Same as GMT or UTC

1.2 A table of subsystem throughputs, expressed in equivalent TPS units, can be constructed as follows:

Subsystem	TPS	Pkt/s	IO/s
Client CPU	500.00	–	–
NIC card	120.00	2400	–
LAN network	52.50	1050	–
Router	350.00	7000	–
WAN network	40.00	800	–
Server CPU	120.00	–	–
Server disk	52.25	–	52.25

Therefore, the LAN is expected to be the primary system bottleneck, with the server disk the secondary bottleneck.

1.4
(**a**) 99.6%
(**b**) 34.94 h

Solutions for Chap. 2

2.1
(**a**) 60 customers
(**b**) $\frac{1}{2}$
(**c**) By the flow balance assumption $X \equiv \lambda = \frac{1}{2}$
(**d**) $S = \frac{B}{C} = 1.5$
(**e**) minutes

2.2
(a) 1.75 min
(b) 3.43 min

2.3
(a) 186.01%
(b) $R \simeq \frac{S}{1-\rho^2} = 7.41$ mins $W = R - S = 6.41$ min
(c) 4 servers

2.4 No. A useful mnemonic is:

Erlang B stands for *bounced call* because the call has to be retried whereas, Erlang C stands for *call waiting* because the call is enqueued.

2.7 $Z = 38.5$ s

2.8 $R = 5$ s

2.9 $Q = 5.6$

2.10 $R = \frac{6}{18}$ h

Solutions for Chap. 3

3.1 $p = V_{\text{dkA}}/V_{\text{cpu}}$ and $q = V/V_{\text{cpu}}$

3.2
(a) The branching equations are:

$$
\begin{aligned}
X_{\text{cpu}} &= X + (1-p)X_{\text{cpu}} \\
X_{\text{dkA}} &= q(1-p)X_{\text{cpu}} \\
X_{\text{dkB}} &= (1-q)(1-p)X_{\text{cpu}}
\end{aligned}
$$

Solving for X_{cpu} we find $X_{\text{cpu}} = X + X_{\text{dkA}} + X_{\text{dkB}}$. Dividing both sides by X produces the desired result.
(b) The visit ratios are:

$$
\begin{aligned}
V_{\text{cpu}} &= \frac{1}{p} \\
V_{\text{dkA}} &= \frac{X_{\text{dkA}}}{X} \\
V_{\text{dkB}} &= \frac{X_{\text{dkB}}}{X}
\end{aligned}
$$

Inverting the first of these gives p.
(c) $q = p\,V_{\text{dkA}}/(1-p)$
(d) $p = 0.006$, and $q = 0.444$

3.3 Selected circuit outputs:

$$\begin{aligned} X^{\mathrm{A}}_{\mathrm{cpu}} &= \lambda^{\mathrm{A}} V^{\mathrm{A}}_{\mathrm{cpu}} = 1.580 \text{ TPS} \\ U^{\mathrm{A}}_{\mathrm{cpu}} &= \lambda^{\mathrm{A}} D^{\mathrm{A}}_{\mathrm{cpu}} = 0.158 \\ R^{\mathrm{A}}_{\mathrm{cpu}} &= 1.58 \text{ s} \\ Q^{\mathrm{A}}_{\mathrm{cpu}} &= 0.25 \text{ transactions} \\ R^{\mathrm{A}} &= R^{\mathrm{A}}_{\mathrm{cpu}} + R^{\mathrm{A}}_{\mathrm{dsk}} = 30.08 \text{ s} \end{aligned}$$

3.4 Networked Storage
82% (not 75%)

Solutions for Chap. 4

4.2 Exponential smoothing

4.3 Using fixed-point 1.2 format
(**a**) 2.24
(**b**) 0.01
(**c**) 0.00

Solutions for Chap. 5

5.1 3 ms

5.2 499.60 TPS

Solutions for Chap. 7

7.1
(a) Use $W\mathfrak{P}/Z$
(b) Use $Z(R - W)/\mathfrak{P}$

7.2 Applying (7.12) produces:

$$X = \frac{1.25 \times 10^9}{(0.71)(965 \times 10^3)} = 1,824.42 \text{ TPS}$$

7.3 26 nodes

Solutions for Chap. 8

8.2 Steve Gaede

8.3 Let $T(1) = T$ be the execution time on a uniprocessor. With α the serial fraction of the execution time and $(1 - \alpha)$ the fraction that can be executed in parallel, the total execution time $T(p)$ on p processors is given by:

$$T(p) = \alpha T + \left(\frac{1-\alpha}{p}\right) T \,. \tag{H.1}$$

The *speed-up* is defined as:

$$S(p) = \frac{T(1)}{T(p)} = \frac{T}{\alpha T + \left(\frac{1-\alpha}{p}\right) T} \,, \tag{H.2}$$

which, on simplification, produces (8.1).

Bibliography

Ajmone-Marsan, M., Balbo, G., and Conte, G. (1990). *Performance Models of Multiprocessor Systems.* MIT, Boston, MA.

Albert, R. and Barabasi, A. (2002). Statistical mechanics of complex networks. *Rev. Mod. Phys.*, 74:47.

Allen, A. O. (1990). *Probability, Statistics, and Queueing Theory with Computer Science Applications.* Academic, San Diego, CA, 2nd edition.

Amdahl, G. (1967). Validity of the single processor approach to achieving large scale computing capabilities. *Proc. AFIPS Conf.*, 30:483–485.

Baskett, F., Chandy, K. M., Muntz, R. R., and Palacios, F. G. (1975). Open, closed and mixed networks of queues with different classes of customers. *J. ACM*, 22(2):248.

Bloch, G., Greiner, S., der Meer, H., and Trivedi, K. S. (1998). *Queueing Networks and Markov Chains.* Wiley, New York, NY.

Bovet, D. P. and Cesati, M. (2001). *Understanding the Linux Kernel.* O'Reilly, Sebastopol, CA.

Brownlee, N. and Ziedins, I. (2002). Response time distributions for global name servers. Passive and Active Measurement (PAM) Workshop. `www.labs.agilent.com/pam2002/proceedings/index.htm`. Cited Jul 3, 2004.

Buch, D. K. and Pentkovski, V. M. (2001). Experience in characterization of typical multi-tier e-Business systems using operational analysis. In *Proc. CMG Conference*, pages 671–681, Anaheim, CA.

Buyya, R., editor (1999). *High Performance Cluster Computing: Architectures and Systems*, volume 1. Prentice-Hall, Upper Saddle River, NJ.

Buzen, J. (1973). Computational algorithms for closed queueing networks with exponential servers. *Comm. ACM*, 16(9):527–531.

Buzen, J. P. (1971). *Queueing Network Models of Multiprogramming.* Ph.D. thesis, Harvard University, Cambridge, MA.

Cockcroft, A. and Pettit, R. (1998). *Sun Performance and Tuning.* SunSoft, Mountain View, CA, 2nd edition.

Cohen, G. A. and Chase, J. S. (2001). An architecture for safe bytecode insertion. *Softw. Pract. Exper.*, 34:1–12.

Courtois, P. J. (1985). On time and space decomposition of complex structures. *Comm. ACM*, 28(6):590–603.

Denning, P. J. and Buzen, J. P. (1978). The operational analysis of queueing network models. *Computing Surveys*, 10(3):225–261.

DeVany, A. S. and Walls, D. (1996). Bose-Einstein dynamics and adaptive contracting in the motion picture industry. *The Economic Journal*, pages 1493–1514.

Diao, Y., Gandhi, N., Hellerstein, J. L., Parekh, S., and Tilbury, D. M. (2002). MIMO control of an apache web server: Modeling and controller design. In *American Control Conference*, pages 11–12, Anchorage, AK.

Dietz, M., Ellis, C. S., and Starmer, C. F. (1995). Clock instability and its effect on time intervals in performance studies". In *Proc. CMG Conference*, pages 439–448, Nashville, TN.

Dinda, P. and O'Hallaron, D. (1999). An extensible toolkit for resource prediction in distributed systems. Technical Report CMU-CS-99-138, School of Computer Science, Carnegie Mellon University, Pittsburgh, PA.

Erlang, A. (1909). The theory of probabilities and telephone conversations. *Nyt Tidsskrift for Matematik B*, 20:33–40.

Erlang, A. (1917). Solution of some problems in the theory of probabilities of significance in automatic telephone exchanges. *The Post Office Electrical Engineer's Journal*, 10:189–197.

Flynn, M. J. (1995). *Computer Architecture: Pipelined and Parallel Processor Design.* Jones and Bartlett, London, UK.

Franklin, G. F., Powell, J. D., and Emami-Naeini, A. (1994). *Feedback Control of Dynamic Systems.* Addison-Wesley, Reading, MA, 3rd edition.

Friedman, M. and Pentakalos, O. (2002). *Windows 2000 Performance Guide.* O'Reilly, Sebastopol, CA.

Gennaro, C. and King, P. J. B. (1999). Parallelising the mean value analysis algorithm. *Transactions of The Society for Computer Simulation International*, 16(1):16–22.

Gold, T., editor (1967). *The Nature of Time.* Cornell University, Ithaca, NY.

Gordon, W. J. and Newell, G. F. (1967). Closed queueing networks with exponential servers. *Operations Research*, 15:244–265.

Gunther, N. J. (1989). Path integral methods for computer performance analysis. *Information Processing Letters*, 32(1):7–13.

Gunther, N. J. (1990). Bilinear model of blocking transients in large circuit-switching networks. In King, P. J. B., Mitriani, I., and Pooley, R. J., editors, *PERFORMANCE '90*, volume Proc. 14th IFIP WG 7.3 International Symposium on Computer Performance Modelling, Measurement and Evaluation, pages 175–189. North-Holland, Amsterdam.

Gunther, N. J. (1992). On the application of barycentric coordinates to the prompt and visually efficient display of multiprocessor performance data. In Pooley, R. and Hillston, J., editors, *Performance TOOLS 1992 — Proceedings of Sixth International Conference on Modelling Techniques and Tools for Computer Performance Evaluation*, pages 67–80. Antony Rowe, Wiltshire, UK.

Gunther, N. J. (1996). Understanding the MP effect: Multiprocessing in pictures. In *Proc. CMG Conference*, pages 957–968, San Diego, CA.

Gunther, N. J. (1999). Capacity planning for Solaris SRM: All I ever wanted was my unfair advantage (And why you can't get it!). In *Proc. CMG Conference*, pages 194–205, Reno, NV.

Gunther, N. J. (2000a). *The Practical Performance Analyst: Performance-by-Design Techniques for Distributed Systems.* iUniverse, Lincoln, NE, Reprint edition. Originally published by McGraw-Hill, New York, NY (1998).

Gunther, N. J. (2000b). The dynamics of performance collapse in large-scale networks and computers. *International Journal of High Performance Computing Applications*, 14(4):367–372.

Gunther, N. J. (2002a). A new interpretation of Amdahl's law and Geometric scalability. LANL e-print `xxx.lanl.gov/abs/cs.DC/0210017`. Cited Jun 12, 2004.

Gunther, N. J. (2002b). Hit-and-run tactics enable guerrilla capacity planning. *IEEE IT Professional*, July–August:40–46.

Gunther, N. J. (2004). On the connection between scaling laws in parallel computers and manufacturing systems. In Erkut, E., Laporte, G., Gendreau, M., Verter, V., and Castillo, I., editors, *CORS/INFORMS International Meeting*, pages 27–28, Banff, Alberta, Canada. Institute for Operations Research and the Management Sciences.

Gunther, N. J., Christensen, K. J., and Yoshigoe, K. (2003). "Characterization of the burst stabilization protocol for the RR/CICQ switch. In *IEEE Conference on Local Computer Networks*, Bonn, Germany.

Gunther, N. J. and Shaw, J. (1990). Path integral evaluation of ALOHA network transients. *Information Processing Letters*, 33(6):289–295.

Hawking, S. (1988). *A Brief History of Time*. Bantam Books, New York, NY.

Hellerstein, J. L., Gandhi, N., and Parekh, S. (2001). Managing the performance of Lotus Notes: A control theoretic approach. In *Proc. CMG Conference*, pages 397–408, Anaheim, CA.

Jackson, J. R. (1957). Networks of waiting lines. *Operations Research*, 5:518–521.

Jagerman, D. L. (1974). Some properties of the Erlang loss function. *Bell Systems Technical Journal*, 55:525.

Jain, R. (1990). *The Art of Computer Systems Performance Analysis*. Wiley, New York, NY.

Joines, S., Willenborg, R., and Hygh, K. (2002). *Performance Analysis for Java^{TM} Web Sites*. Addison-Wesley, Boston, MA.

Kendall, D. G. (1951). Some problems in the theory of queues. *Journal of Royal Statistical Society*, Series B13:151–185.

Keshav, S. (1998). *An Engineering Approach to Computer Networking*. Addison-Wesley, Reading, MA, 3rd edition.

Kleeman, L. and Cantoni, A. (1987). On the unavoidability of metastable behavior in digital systems. *IEEE Trans. Computers*, C-36(1):109–112.

Kleinrock, L. (1976). *Queueing Systems, I: Theory*. Wiley, New York, NY.

Lamport, L. (1978). Time, clocks, and the ordering of events in a distributed system. *Comm. ACM*, 21(7):558–565.

Lazowska, E. D., Zahorjan, J., Graham, G. S., and Sevcik, K. C. (1984). *Quantitative System Performance: Computer System Analysis Using Queueing Network Models*. Prentice-Hall, Engelwood Cliffs, NJ. Out of print but available online at `http://www.cs.washington.edu/homes/lazowska/qsp/`. Cited Jun 12, 2004.

Lilja, D. J. (2000). *Measuring Computer Performance: A Practitioner's Guide*. Cambridge Univ. Press, Cambridge, UK.

Little, J. D. C. (1961). A proof of the queueing formula $L = \lambda W$. *Operations Research*, 9:383–387.

McCanne, S. and Torek, C. (1993). A randomized sampling clock for CPU utilization estimation and code profiling. In *Winter USENIX Conference*, pages 387–394, San Diego, CA.

McGrath, R. E. and Yeager, N. J. (1996). *Web Server Technology: The Advanced Guide for World-Wide Web Information Providers*. Morgan Kaufmann, San Francisco, CA.

Mills, D. L. (1992). Network Time Protocol (version 3): Specification, implementation, and analysis. IETF Network Working Group RFC 1305. www.ietf.org/rfc/rfc1305.txt. Cited Jun 12, 2004.

Moore, C. G. (1971). Network models for large-scale time-sharing systems. Technical Report 71-1, Dept. Industrial Engineering, Univ. Michigan, Ann Arbor, MI.

Musumeci, G. P. D. and Loukides, M. (2002). *System Performance Tuning.* O'Reilly, Sebastopol, CA, 2nd edition.

Nelson, B. and Cheng, Y. P. (1991). The anatomy of an NFS I/O operation: How and why SCSI is better than IPI-2 for NFS. Technical Report No. 6, Auspex Systems Inc., Santa Clara, CA.

Nelson, R. (1984). Stochastic catastrophe theory in computer performance modeling. *Comm. ACM*, 34:661.

Oppenheim, A., Willsky, A., and Young, I. (1983). *Signals and Systems.* Prentice-Hall, Englewood Cliffs, NJ.

Orwant, J., Heitaniemi, J., and MacDonald, J. (1999). *Mastering Algorithms with Perl.* O'Reilly, Sebastopol, CA.

Park, K. and Willinger, W., editors (2000). *Self-Similar Network Traffic and Performance Evaluation.* Wiley, New York, NY.

Peek, J., O'Reilly, T., and Loukides, M. (1997). *UNIX Power Tools.* O'Reilly, Sebastopol, CA, 2nd edition.

Plale, B., Dinda, P., and von Laszewski, G. (2002). Key concepts and services of a GRID information service. In *Proceedings of the 15th International Conference on Parallel and Distributed Computing Systems (PDCS 2002)*, pages 437–442, Louisville, KY.

Raynal, M. and Singhal, M. (1996). Logical time: Capturing causality in distributed systems. *IEEE Computer*, 29(2):49–56.

Reiser, M. and Lavenberg, S. (1980). Mean-value analysis of closed multi-chain queueing networks. *J. ACM*, 27(2):313–322.

Saltzer, J. and Gintell, J. (1970). The instrumentation of Multics. *Comm. ACM*, 13(8):495–500.

Samson, S. L. (1997). *MVS Performance Management: OS/390 Edition.* McGraw-Hill, New York, NY.

Scherr, A. L. (1967). *An Analysis of Time-Shared Computer Systems.* MIT, Cambridge MA.

Schwartz, A. and Weiss, A. (1995). *Large Deviations for Performance Analysis: Queues, Communications, and Computing.* Chapman & Hall, London, UK.

Schwartz, R. L. and Phoenix, T. (2001). *Learning Perl.* O'Reilly, Sebastopol, CA, 3rd edition.

Sevcik, K. and Mitrani, I. (1981). The distribution of queueing network states at input and output instants. *J. ACM*, 28(2):358–371.

Smith, C. U. and Williams, L. G. (2001). *Performance Solutions: A Practical Guide to Creating Responsive, Scalable Software.* Pearson Education, Indianapolis, IN.

Sornette, D. (2002). *Why Stock Markets Crash? Critical Events in Complex Financial Systems.* Princeton Univ. Press, Princeton, NJ.

Splaine, S. and Jaskiel, S. P. (2001). *The Web Testing Handbook.* STQE, Orange Park, FL.

Trivedi, K. S. (2000). *Probability and Statistics with Reliability, Queueing, and Computer Science Applications.* Wiley, New York, NY, 2nd edition.

Tsuei, T. F. and Vernon, M. K. (1992). A multiprocessor bus design model validated by system measurement. *IEEE Trans. Parallel and Distributed Systems*, 3(6):712–727.

Vahalia, U. (1996). *UNIX Internals: The New Frontier.* Prentice-Hall, Upper Saddle River, NJ.

Verma, V. (1992). A meaningful measure of response time for SLA. In *Proc. CMG Conference*, pages 1–7, Reno, NV.

Wall, L., Christiansen, T., and Orwant, J. (2003). *Programming Perl.* O'Reilly, Sebastopol, CA, 3rd edition.

Walrand, J. and Varaiya, P. (1996). *High Performance Communication Networks.* Morgan Kaufmann, San Francisco, CA.

Westall, J. and Geist, R. (1997). A hybrid tool for the performance evaluation of NUMA architectures. In *Winter Simulation Conference*, pages 1029–1036, Atlanta, GA.

Wilson, S. and Kesselman, J. (2000). *Java™ Platform Performance: Strategies and Tactics.* Pearson Education, Indianapolis, IN.

Wolski, R., Spring, N., and Hayes, J. (2000). Predicting the CPU availability of time-shared UNIX systems on the computational grid. *Cluster Computing*, 3(4):293–301.

Xie, M. (1991). *Software Reliability Modeling.* World Scientific, Singapore.

Index